OPPOSITION
IN THE
U. S. S. R.
1917–1967

OPPOSITION IN THE U.S.S.R.

1917-1967

BY ROLAND GAUCHER
TRANSLATED BY
CHARLES LAM MARKMANN

FUNK & WAGNALLS
NEW YORK

CONTENTS

PART ONE

PART TWO

PART

ONE

(1)

THE BOLSHEVIKS
SEIZE POWER

T HE WINTER PALACE fell at two o'clock in the morning of October 26, 1917.

During that night, after the capture of the palace, Lieutenant Danilevich, who with other junkers had taken part in the defense of the provisional government, succeeded once more in establishing telegraphic communication with General Baranovsky, Chief of Staff of the northern front, in Pskov. The texts of their messages, recorded on paper tape by the Hughes machine then in use in the Russian army, recreates for us the breathless drama of the fall of the provisional government: the disorder of the defenders; the penetrations of small groups of attackers through unguarded passages, hurling grenades, allowing themselves to be disarmed, yet always surging up again in even greater numbers, while the room in which the provisional government was working was by now defended only by a force of fifteen junkers.

"At two o'clock in the morning," Danilevich related, "we were informed that four hundred insurgents were already in the corridor and were coming up to where we were. The provisional government decided not to resort to armed force, and two hundred of the insurgents entered and announced that

the provisional government had been placed under arrest. . . .
As you can see [Danilevich, being a relative of General Baranovsky, addressed him in the familiar second person], all this
took place with amazing simplicity and can be explained only
by a disgraceful negligence and the total lack of any resistance. . . ."

"Are you alone?" General Baranovsky wired back.

"I am alone with the telegrapher."

"I can tell you that Kerensky is marching on Petrograd with
the cavalry corps. . . . Alexander Fyodorovich [Kerensky]
spent the night with me waiting for the arrival of General
Krasnov, with whom he left for Ostrov."

Baranovsky added that he was convinced that the rule established by the Bolsheviks would quickly crumble. Danilevich was of the same opinion: "The Bolsheviks are isolated,"
he said. "No one backs them except their partisans. Three-
quarters of them are thieves."

*You are isolated. No one supports you. No government will
recognize you.* That was the message the newspapers too repeated in the days that immediately followed the armed attack. On October 30 an editorial in the Socialist paper, *Dyelo
Naroda,* began with this categorical declaration: "To every
unbiased man it is clear that the Bolsheviks' adventure has ir-
reparably failed."

No party was willing to share the responsibility of power
with the Bolsheviks. The municipal Duma declared its opposition to the usurpers. The executive committee of the railway
workers' union, the *Vikzhel,* threatened to call a general strike.
Government employes were already on strike. The ministries
were deserted. The banks had closed their doors. The Committee of Patriotic Safety, created as soon as the provisional
government had fallen, was calling for resistance. In Moscow
the junkers and the White Guards, recruited among prepara-
tory-school and university students, had seized the Kremlin.

And Kerensky, the head of the provisional government, was
at the gates of Petrograd. He had left the city early in the

morning of October 25 to meet the troops he had called in as reinforcements. He had taken Gatchina and occupied the former imperial residence of Tsarskoye-Selo, his artillery easily overcoming the resistance offered by the garrison. Between his troops and Petrograd there were now only a few dozen miles. . . .

But Kerensky's forces, made up essentially of *sotnias* (hundreds) of Cossacks, were no more than a thousand men equipped with artillery but lacking in infantry. During October 30–31, the date of the editorial in *Dyelo Naroda,* this detachment, commanded by General Krasnov, confronted fifteen thousand Bolsheviks hastily assembled by Trotsky. The sailors of Kronstadt, the Red Guards, and a few miscellaneous units entrenched on the heights of Pulkovo, the last natural barrier on the road to the capital, threw back the charging Cossacks, who were too few to pierce their lines. Bitter, discouraged, weary at the absence of the reinforcements that were constantly promised to them, the Cossacks evacuated Tsarskoye-Selo during the night. Immediately Trotsky published an announcement of victory: "The enemy is retreating. We are advancing."

Kerensky's attempt was to collapse after a defeat in a skirmish. In order to avoid being handed over to the Bolsheviks by the Cossacks he had to flee from Gatchina in the dress of a sailor. The day before the fighting at Pulkovo a revolt by the junkers had been arduously put down in Petrograd. In spite of their initial successes, those in Moscow, lacking artillery and reinforcements, had no choice but to surrender.

In order to back up Kerensky's offensive the core of the *Stavka* (General Staff), installed in Mogilev, had made a real effort to rally a body of troops. But almost everywhere their advance was blocked by the revolutionary committees. Furthermore, the northern front, which was the best situated for the speedy access of reinforcements, was under the command of General Cheremissov, who, in complete collaboration with the revolutionary committee, was sabotaging the operations.

For all that Kerensky was the Generalissimo, he could not prevail on General Dukhonin, his Chief of Staff, to remove Cheremissov.

Though it was true that the Bolsheviks were isolated, Kerensky was even more so. Within his detachment, the officers in command of the Cossacks hated him. They could not forgive him for having suppressed General Kornilov's attempted coup in September. Many other officers and members of patriotic organizations nursed the same rancor. "Let's leave this Kerensky to fall into his own pit. Afterward we will turn against the Bolsheviks and set up a military dictatorship, which is the only thing that can save the country." This was their appraisal, peremptory and rash.

The leaders of the Revolutionary Socialist party, the Mensheviks, the directors of the *Vikzhel* were unquestionably opposed to Lenin's act of force. But they also dreaded the arrival of the Cossacks, the spearhead of counterrevolution. In the Revolutionary Socialist camp there was much talk of and hope for a coalition government. With or without Bolshevik participation? No one could decide. In any event, certainly without Lenin and Trotsky. The problem was that these two men were in power and were resolved not to give it up.

For its part, the majority of the garrison of two hundred thousand men, was inclined to passivity. Lenin could count on the effective support of barely fifteen or twenty thousand men in its ranks. The others, who said that they were "too tired" to fight, were equally intent on not getting themselves killed for Kerensky's sake. As for the men at the front, they yearned after only one thing: peace—and quickly!

That was why, in the face of adversaries who were numerout but divided, and whose determination was shaky, the handful of Bolsheviks dominated by the tireless Lenin and Trotsky was able to impose its will. Two slogans, remarkably effective in their simplicity, were enough to bring down the last obstacles: the land decree, which neutralized the huge mass of the peasantry, and immediate peace. When Dukhonin refused to send plenipotentiaries to the Germans a few days after Kerensky's defeat, a speech by Lenin to the army, broadcast on the radio, was sufficient to isolate the *Stavka*. Several thousand sailors under the leadership of Ensign Krylenko, whom Lenin had immediately appointed Generalissimo, invested Mogilev. The generals found that they had neither men nor arms. And the wretched Dukhonin, abandoned to the fury of the soldiers, was impaled on their bayonets.

Thus all organized military resistance had disappeared by the middle of November.

There was still political opposition. The Revolutionary Socialists, the Mensheviks, and the Cadets (Constitutional Democrats) focused all their hopes now on the meeting of the Constituent Assembly. Elections to it had been held in mid-November at the height of the revolutionary chaos. As the results became public, they reflected the defeat of the Bolshevik party at the polls.

True, Bolshevik candidates had won 45 per cent of the votes in Petrograd. But in the country as a whole the party had obtained only 9 million votes (25 per cent of the total). This figure seemed large when compared with the 1.7 million votes (4 per cent) for the Mensheviks or the 4.6 million (12.5 per cent) for the Cadets. It was small in comparison with the triumph gained by the big victor, the Revolutionary Socialist party, which amassed 20.9 million votes (58 per cent), an absolute majority. The peasants in a mass had made this party their choice.

But the peasants were scattered. Lenin's backers were thickly concentrated at the crucial points: Moscow and Leningrad. Moreover, 50 per cent of the army and navy had voted for the Bolsheviks. The Bolsheviks could rely on the sailors of Kronstadt and the battalion of Latvian infantrymen to guard against any rising in the capital. It was too soon to oppose them with other forces. The only hope of the electoral majority lay in Lenin's good will. *If* he was willing to accept the verdict of universal suffrage—its first and until today its only appearance in Russia—hope was legitimate.

The verdict of universal suffrage did not even occur to Lenin. Unquestionably the Bolsheviks had waged a fierce campaign against Kerensky before they came to power, berating him in particular because he had indefinitely postponed the consultation of the electorate. On October 23 Stalin was still calling in *Pravda* for the convocation of the Constituent Assembly. But Lenin did not concern himself in the slightest with his enemies' accusations that he did not keep his promises. Of course he had pledged freedom of the press! Yet as soon as he had seized power his first step had been to prohibit the "bourgeois" newspapers. As far as Lenin was concerned, he would gladly have deferred the elections, in which he very rightly saw the seed of future difficulties.

"The elections should be postponed," he told Trotsky, "and the voting age should be lowered to eighteen; otherwise we shall be beaten by the Cadets and Kornilov's backers."

It was pointed out to him that this would be doing exactly what was being criticized in Kerensky. Lenin shrugged: "Don't talk nonsense! All that matters is the result. . . ."

If Lenin yielded to the insistence of those round him, it was in order to obtain the allegiance of the left-wing Revolutionary Socialists, who possessed a certain influence over the peasant masses. So he resigned himself to allowing elections to be held. But as soon as he had become convinced that the left Revolutionary Socialists would enter the Soviet of People's Commissars (in other words, the government), he postponed the meeting of the Constituent Assembly and concentrated his attention on means of reducing it to a nullity.

This naturally required a certain amount of police work. So did the constant fabrication of plots, the sabotage by officials, the nocturnal dominion of bandits over the city, the daily increasing hunger in Petrograd. On December 7, 1917, the Soviet of People's Commissars created an "extraordinary pan-Russian committee to combat counterrevolution, sabotage, and

speculation." The *Cheka*—more accurately, the fifth *Cheka*—
was born. Its director was a Pole, Dzerzhinsky.

He was a tall, very thin man, always booted and dressed in
a gray cloak or a military tunic. His light, glazed eyes stood
out in his long, thin-featured face. This nobleman's son had
joined the proletarians, but with his comrades he always maintained a distant, highly aristocratic reserve. He seldom spoke.
His taciturnity might have been the product of eleven years
spent in the tsar's prisons, where he had learned patience. At
times his rage broke out, so intense that it caused him to stam-
mer. He was utterly honest, fanatically devoted to the cause of
the revolution, and devoid of personal ambition. He sought
to be no more than the "watchdog" of the government. After
his years in prison cells, he closed himself off in another cell
in the Smolny Institute and, later, in the Lyubyanka Prison
in Moscow, where he worked late into the night under a harsh
electric light, studying the files and records of suspects.

In his prison diary he had recorded the recollection of an
execution: "See how nothing has changed here after so abominable a crime. The sunny days, the guards, the police, the
changes of guards, the walks. . . . Only the cells have become
more silent." There is no way of knowing whether, later, he
would remark that again nothing was changed when, on his
orders, truck engines were accelerated so that their roar would
drown the sounds of shots and cries.

The *Cheka* started out with meager facilities: a few dozen
men without even transport for the execution of their missions.
But it soon imposed inordinate power. In his autobiography
the left Revolutionary Socialist Steinberg, who was People's
Commissar for Justice, included a very significant incident in
this connection. Dzerzhinsky had learned during December
that a certain number of deputies to the Constituent Assembly
was meeting privately, and he wanted to have them all arrested. Steinberg attended this meeting, which was already invested by sailors and *Chekists*, and he saw that the warrant
of arrest included the names of Chernov, Gotz, and two or

three others; in his own handwriting Dzerzhinsky had added, "as well as all other persons present." Steinberg insisted on legal formalities. He pointed out that warrants of arrest were required to name individually all persons sought. Since none of those actually named in this warrant was present at the meeting, it was illegal to arrest the others. After protracted discussion the sailors and *Chekists* withdrew in great anger.

Dzerzhinsky's wrath erupted the next day when the People's Commissars convened. "Our *Chekists* have been treated like street brats!" he shouted. "How can I be expected to crush counterrevolution with legal niceties of this character?"

This incident may be regarded as an early conflict between "Socialist legality" and terror. Lenin was entirely on Dzerzhinsky's side, but, in order to avert Steinberg's resignation, he arranged a clever compromise: The *Cheka* would have the right to arrest important political figures but it would be obligated to report such arrests to the Commissar for Justice during or, rather, after their execution. This was already an initial victory for the police. Obviously it was more difficult to wrest a seized citizen out of its hands than to prevent his arrest. And it was anything but long before the Commissariat for Justice became a mere annex of the *Cheka*.

Here was a most ominous augury for the future of the deputies. Nonetheless the Revolutionary Socialists went very earnestly forward with their preparations for the great opening day of democracy, which was definitely scheduled for January 5.[1] They set up working committees, appointed group leaders, established agenda. Beyond doubt their parliamentary apparatus was complete by the appointed date.

On the other hand, the deputies were hardly ever observed at factory meetings, where the Bolsheviks were omnipresent, though at times quite coolly received.

The Revolutionary Socialists had decided to stage a large demonstration in the streets on the morning of January 5.

---

[1] According to the old-style calendar still in effect at this time. The date corresponds to January 18, Western style.

Some of the party members would have liked to structure it on armed contingents. The Revolutionary Socialists' military committee insisted that it could count on the Preobrazhensky and Semyonovsky regiments, supported by a few tanks. The central committee opposed the use of these troops. Chernov, the supreme leader of the party, asserted with much nobility: "Not a drop of Russian blood must be shed."

"Suppose the Bolsheviks fire on us?" he was asked.

"They dare not."

So it was decided that the soldiers would parade unarmed. This decision made them angry. "Do you think the Bolsheviks are children?" one soldier said. "Or do you want to see us scatter like rabbits?"

On the morning of January 5 the factory workers, the white-collar personnel, the students, and the unarmed soldiers were met with salvos by the Red Guards, who then charged with bayonets. There was no choice but to scatter.

This barrage of rifle fire, which killed or wounded about a hundred persons, was the overture to the first session of the Constituent Assembly, which convened at four o'clock in the afternoon in the Tauride Palace. The maintenance of order, under the direction of a Bolshevik, Uritzky, was in the hands of the Kronstadt sailors, with cartridge belts twining round their dazzling new uniforms. The crowded galleries were packed with backers of the Bolsheviks, ready to shout down their opponents. The terror was already weighing on this Assembly, in which the majority did not breathe a word about the morning's killing. Chernov was elected president of the Assembly with a comfortable majority; his opponent, supported by the Bolsheviks and the left Revolutionary Socialists, was the former terrorist Marya Spiridonova.

The majority was comfortable. The presidency was ephemeral.

Lenin was there, sitting below the speakers' stand, laughing loudly or pretending to read his newspaper by way of demonstrating his contempt for chatterboxes, while Chernov, whom he detested, droned on and on interminably. Then Lenin walked out, as if he had had enough of all this talk. After a savage attack by Bukharin, the entire Bolshevik delegation walked out in its turn.

Sometime after four o'clock the following morning, while the proceedings were dragging on in the gloomy light, a sailor named Zheleznyakov went up to the rostrum and whispered something to Chernov. Apparently not understanding, Chernov asked him to repeat what he had said.

The sailor spoke more loudly: "You must stop. I have been given orders. The guards are tired."

"What orders?" Chernov demanded in amazement. "Who gave them?"

"Comrade Dybenko. I request that you leave the assembly hall at once."

For the sake of form, Chernov put a few more decrees to the vote at an accelerated pace, then hastened to adjourn the session. It would be resumed, he said, in the afternoon of that day.

The time was four forty in the morning. When the deputies returned to the Tauride Palace about noon, they found the doors locked. Uritzky's men were on guard. Two cannon were pointed at the square in front of the palace.

There was never a second session. The Constituent Assembly, the democrats' supreme hope, had lasted twelve hours and forty minutes.

The deputies were now unemployed. A few men who were not deputies refused to accept unemployment. In the Don region Ataman Kaledin made a vain effort to raise his Cossacks in revolt. On January 1, when Lenin had gone to review the troops of the Petrograd garrison who were to leave for the front—for peace had not yet been signed—a shot was fired at his car. Officers were forming clandestine groups or trying to reach the south in the hope that it would become a Cossack

Vendée.[2] At the beginning of the year, Boris Savinkov, a former terrorist who had broken with the Revolutionary Socialist party in September 1917, established an underground organization called the Union for the Defense of the Fatherland and Freedom. It embraced a few hundred men recruited essentially among tsarist officers and former Revolutionary Socialists. The *Cheka* discovered the conspiracy. Savinkov managed to flee. . . . Through its secret tribunals, the *Cheka* began to impose the death sentence that had been officially abolished.[3]

✳ Savinkov, a man of high intelligence and energetic character, was undoubtedly the only individual capable of confronting a Lenin or a Trotsky. During the summer of 1917 he had attempted to effect a union between Kornilov and Kerensky in the belief that the one would provide the strength of the army and the other would contribute the guaranty of democracy. He failed to reconcile the old campaigner and the man of many words. And he was rejected by the Revolutionary Socialists. As for the monarchists, they could not forgive him his revolutionary past. Caught between the blindness of the reactionaries and the weakness of the democrats, Savinkov had thrown himself into the risky, marginal world of conspiracies and armed action.

✳ At the moment it was too late for democracy and too soon for civil war. The Bolshevik party's difficulties came from the left wing of the Revolutionary Socialists as well as from its own left wing, under the leadership of Bukharin, when Lenin at last resigned himself to accepting the very harsh peace terms laid down by the Germans. Large segments of the Bolshevik party, particularly the majorities in the Petrograd committee and the Moscow regional office, proclaimed their backing for a revolutionary war. In a referendum conducted in February among two hundred soviets, a bare majority of 105

---

[2] In 1793 the opponents of the French Revolution organized a resistance that held out in the swamps of the Department of the Vendée for almost two years.—Translator.

[3] It was to be reinstated in June 1918.

against 95 endorsed the resumption of hostilities against the Germans.[4]

The central executive committee of the soviets approved the peace terms by only 116 votes to 84—there were 26 abstentions—on February 10, 1918. But for Lenin this was sufficient. He was clever enough to turn delicate situations to his own advantage. And once again his opponents were incapable of establishing unity of action against him. The left Communists confined themselves to expressing their opposition within the party, which was not slow in diluting it. The left Revolutionary Socialists, in contrast, broke away after the ratification of the Treaty of Brest-Litovsk. Their representatives in the government resigned. And they believed that, with the support of the peasant masses, they could wage a guerrilla war against the Germans in the areas occupied by the enemy.

It was also at this time that the position of the leaders of the Revolutionary Socialist party shifted. Thus far they had opposed any clandestine activity. Brest-Litovsk produced their *non possumus*. In April their central committee adopted a resolution accusing the Soviet government of having "betrayed democracy, Russia, the Revolution, and the International." The resolution concluded with this sentence: "It [the government] must and shall be overthrown." This was a call to arms. But there was still the question of finding them.

As for the Mensheviks, they tolerated only legal or semi-legal opposition, for their newspapers had been virtually eliminated. They kept up a certain agitation among the labor unions and the working class, in which their stock quickly rose again. For the Bolshevik factory committees were plunging industry into chaos, and food supplies were worse than ever. In contrast to the Revolutionary Socialists, the Mensheviks did not advocate recourse to violence and they refused to countenance foreign intervention.

[4] The detailed results of this referendum were not published until eleven years later. In this connection cf. Schapiro, *Les Bolcheviks et l'opposition*, p. 96.

But violence there was. The imperialist war was over. The civil war was following in its footsteps. In the Kuban, General Denikin was rallying the first volunteers for his White Army. The most dangerous threat surged up suddenly from the Czech army corps. It had been recruited among the Czech and Slovak prisoners of war who at the start of hostilities had been conscripted into the Austro-Hungarian army. Toward the end of 1917 this legion, which had been placed under French command, totaled forty-five thousand men. Since the largest number of its troops was in Siberia, it sought to reach Vladivostok in order to be repatriated to France and from there to continue the war against Germany. The Communists ordered the corps to lay down its arms. The Czech legion refused, and, taking the offensive in May, it swiftly occupied Chelyabinsk, Omsk, and Samara on the Volga.

The Czech legion enjoyed the support of the local population; units of Russian volunteers enlisted in it. Hostile to Denikin, the monarchist, the Revolutionary Socialists gave their backing to the Slavic "democrats." And the Allies regarded this rising as their opportunity to step in.[5]

The civil war flared up almost everywhere; each blaze was restricted, but all spread rapidly. In the north Petrograd was imperiled by the Finns' counterrevolution. On the Lower Volga, Krasnov and his Cossacks were threatening Tsaritsyn. In the Kuban, Denikin was organizing his first volunteers. In the rural areas, groups of partisans of both camps were engaging in random violence. At the same time inflation was surging ahead with giant steps, and, in order to feed the cities, Communist forces were seizing the peasants' stocks at gun point. In April the Moscow Bolsheviks, frightened by the growing power of the anarchists, attacked their headquarters with artillery.

In June 1918 the "anti-Soviet parties" (Mensheviks and Revolutionary Socialists) were ousted from the soviets. The

[5] Some British troops had already gone ashore at Murmansk, and the Japanese had occupied Vladivostok.

left Revolutionary Socialists began preparing terrorist activities. The *Cheka* seized hostages.

Early in July a young left Revolutionary Socialist, Blumkin, who was also a member of the *Cheka*, killed German Ambassador von Mirbach with a revolver shot, hoping that this provocatory act would re-ignite the war. On the same day, during the Fifth Congress of Soviets, the left Revolutionary Socialists attempted armed action in Moscow (to which the government had removed at the beginning of March), bombarding the Kremlin, but the attempt was crushed by the Latvian infantrymen.

It was at this period that Savinkov and his supporters, in an audacious action, seized control of Yaroslav, 120 miles from Moscow, and held out there for a week against a vastly larger force of Soviet troops that poured artillery fire on them. The punishment was merciless: the defeated men were passed in review before a desk set up in an open field; behind the desk sat *Chekists* who selected those to be shot—approximately four hundred. Savinkov barely managed to escape.

But outside Tsaritsyn (later Stalingrad) the Red Army fell back under the charge of the Cossacks. The time had come for Trotsky to take command of the army.

In this month of July, when Russia was rocked by chaos, the fate of the imperial family was decided. Held first in Tsarskoye-Selo and then in Tobolsk, the tsar and his family had later been transferred to Ekaterinenburg. The Czechs were approaching. The city might fall within three days. What a triumph the rescue of Nicholas II would be for the monarchists, and perhaps, in this country with its back against the wall, what an upsurge of old ardors!

At about midnight on July 18, the Commander of the Red Guard, Yurovsky, awakened the tsar and his family and ordered them to gather in a downstairs room. All of them quite calm, Nicholas II, the tsarina, their children, and the servants dressed and went downstairs.

There were only three chairs in the room, and these were

taken by the tsar, the tsarina, and the young tsarevich, Alexis. The rest remained standing against the wall. Armed with rifles and revolvers, sailors and Latvian infantrymen entered in silence. But the imperial family was accustomed to seeing armed men about.

Yurovsky took one of his subordinates, a certain Medvedyev, aside and quietly asked him to leave the room, saying: "Tell me if you hear shots." Medvedyev went out, and almost immediately there was the sound of guns. He returned to inform Yurovsky. And he saw *them*, all motionless on the floor in great pools of blood. Alone of all these people, the frailest, Tsarevich Alexis, was still twitching and moaning. Yurovsky fired two or three revolver bullets into him, and that was the end of the heir of the Romanovs. Medvedyev went out again and vomited.

The news of the massacre reached the Soviet of People's Commissars during its session at which a draft public-health law was under discussion. Sverdlov entered the room and whispered to Lenin.

"Comrade Sverdlov has an announcement to make," Lenin said.

"I wish to inform you," Sverdlov declared, "that, in conformance with a decision by the soviet of Ekaterinenburg, Nicholas has been shot for having attempted to escape when the Czechoslovaks were nearing the city. The decision is approved by the Politburo of the Central Committee."

"Let us return to our agenda," Lenin said. And the public-health discussion was resumed.

Trotsky was on assignment at the front. He would have preferred that a great public trial of Nicholas II be mounted and that its proceedings be broadcast by radio. He himself would have liked to perform the function of the public prosecutor. Lenin had told him that it was certain that there was insufficient time to organize the spectacle.

After the capture of Ekaterinenburg Trotsky returned to

Moscow. During a conversation with Sverdlov he raised some questions. "Where is the tsar?" Trotsky wanted to know.

"Dead. He was shot."

"And where is his family?"

"Also dead."

"Everyone?"

"Everyone! . . . What else?"

"Who made the decision?"

"We made it here. Vladimir Ilyich thought that we should not leave a living banner for the Whites, especially in the present difficult circumstances."

Trotsky did not press the point. If it was Vladimir Ilyich's decision, then Vladimir Ilyich must be right. Much later Trotsky recalled this conversation—in 1935, when he was in exile and confinement in Isère, cut off from all political activity, and driven by idleness to keep a diary. In it he recorded this interchange with Sverdlov.[6]

Trotsky's daughter Zenaïda had committed suicide in Berlin. Except for his son Lev Sedov, all the rest of his family was in Stalin's hands. The murder of Kirov augured further shootings. And for the massacre of children Stalin in his turn would easily find some justification in historical necessity.

[6] See Trotsky, *Journal d'exil.*

(2)

DEFEAT OF THE
WHITE ARMIES

T HE CIVIL WAR spread. The ancient empire of the tsars was plunged into a horror-filled chaos that was to persist for two and a half years. The offensive of the Czechs and the frustrated efforts of Kaledin on the Don were only a prelude. Three large White armies—Kolchak's in the east, Denikin's in the south, Yudenich's in the north—were to move forward in an effort to overthrow the Soviets' fledgling power. All started from the periphery of the empire, and the objective of each was Moscow. In principle these forces should have been adequate to crush the Bolshevik troops not yet blooded by war.

But dissensions, disorders, and political errors would soon burgeon among the Whites.

In the east, in Samara, which the Czechs had occupied, a Revolutionary Socialist committee was formed. Another was created in Omsk. Much haggling was required before a Directorate of five members, under the presidency of Avksentyev, could be set up in Ufa on September 8, 1918.

Soldiers and politicians loathed each other. The officers despised the Socialists, nursing the memory of the defeat of Kornilov's *Putsch* as a result of Kerensky's change of front.

(19)

Their resentment against the democratic politicians was at least as bitter as their enmity to the Bolsheviks. In November the civilian Directorate was overthrown. Power was assumed by Admiral Kolchak. Now the soldiers were rid of the "jabberers."

The consequence of this was the formation of armed bands by the Revolutionary Socialists to harry Kolchak's rear; in addition, the Czechs, who represented the most disciplined contingent, refused to fight on this front any longer. They were assigned to guard the Trans-Siberian Railroad. Meanwhile the Bolsheviks had counterattacked, and in October they recaptured Samara.

In the south Denikin, the loyal champion of imperial Russia, had refused to recognize a Directorate that included Revolutionary Socialists. Initially everything went well for him. The villagers welcomed his troops with bread and salt. The church bells rang. The Cossacks, who hated the Bolsheviks, were ready to march. Petlyura, the leader of the Ukrainian nationalists, offered the collaboration of his army.[1] All the conditions were right for the launching of a campaign.

But the peasants wanted land. The Cossacks, jealous of their autonomy, wanted to form federated republics. The Ukrainian nationalists wanted independence. Denikin would have none of this. He wanted Russia to be eternally what she had been in the days of the tsars. As for the former owners of estates, who were following the advance of his armies, they wanted to recover possession of their lands at once.

In Denikin's staff, as in Kolchak's, there was an overabundance of officers. At this time the foremost among them were a number of young men, heroes like the junkers who had fought in Petrograd and Moscow but lacking any great military experience. The experienced officers devoted their efforts

[1] It is important to remember, however, that the Petlyura brothers were leaders of the notorious Black Hundreds and were responsible for some of the Ukraine's bloodiest pogroms until they were finally killed. —Translator.

to supply problems: by requisition, pillage, and profiteering. Most important, everything needed was lacking.

In the east Kolchak retaliated for the disorder at his rear by burning villages and shooting and hanging their inhabitants. In the south the peasants turned to the Bolsheviks, who were promising them land, or toward the guerrillas of Makhno, the anarchist, who was giving them land. The Cossacks did not stir. Petlyura fought his own war, sometimes against one side, sometimes against the other. A dangerous peasant revolt was brewing at Denikin's rear.

His adjutant, General Wrangel, was the only White general capable of thinking politically. He wrote:

Initially, having suffered so much from the Bolsheviks and desiring only to live in peace, the population welcomed our troops with raptures of enthusiasm when we arrived. Soon, however, it had to undergo once more the horrors of pillage, violence, and tyranny. Result: confusion at the front and rebellions at the rear.

When the Germans invaded the Soviet Union in 1941 and in many areas were at first cordially welcomed, they were guilty of the error of not rereading Wrangel and of ignoring his lessons.

Meanwhile the Allies had come to the rescue of the Whites. In April 1918 Japanese troops had landed at Vladivostok without taking part in military operations. In August an Allied detachment occupied Arkhangelsk. American troops went ashore in Siberia and French detachments occupied Sebastopol. None of these expeditionary corps amounted to more than a few tens of thousands of men. But that was enough to enable Bolshevik propaganda to shout at the top of its voice about imperialist conspiracy and denounce the White armies as mercenaries in the pay of foreigners, while Lenin was able to take the part of defender of his country against foreign invasion.

Kolchak, who had had to fall back under the pressure of Bolshevik troops, resumed the offensive in the beginning of

1919. He reoccupied Ufa and advanced within eighty-five miles of Kazan.

Denikin, for his part, struck out toward the north. His advance was lightning-like. He captured Kharkov and Tsaritsyn and threatened Saratov in July. But he was too late to effect a junction with Kolchak, who was thrown back everywhere and forced to withdraw behind the Urals. Denikin drove toward Moscow. He occupied Kursk, Tambov, Orel. In September he marched on Tula. Moscow was only 130 miles farther.

But Denikin's army totaled only one hundred and thirty thousand men spread over an extended front. It was a column, an armed expedition that had advanced far beyond its bases into hostile territory. His supply services, hobbled as much by the financial morals of his associates as by the length of his lines of communication, did not follow it. Makhno's guerrillas ravaged his positions and threatened his security. There was no organized base at the rear, nor was there a line on which to fall back. Besides, as soon as the front yielded, Reds and Whites alike made precipitate retreats in these encounters: This was the only way of avoiding carnage, for no quarter was given on either side. Hence the importance of cavalry in this war, which gave the horsemen their revenge for the immobility enforced on them during the First World War.

So, when Denikin was defeated at Orel, everything fell apart. The army fled southward in frightful disorder without any hope of returning. The summer of 1919 had brought victory to the southern armies; the autumn brought their rout.

Yudenich in the north, starting from the Estonian base at which he had assembled an army with the help of the British, occupied Tsarskoye-Selo and threatened Petrograd. In that city panic reigned. Lenin himself was thinking of evacuation. Trotsky hastened there with his armored train, renewed everyone's courage, put spirit into the city's resistance. After heavy fighting outside the city, Yudenich was halted and then forced to retreat in disorder. But headlines in *The New York Times* were already proclaiming victory:

October 18, 1919: ANTI-SOVIET FORCES IN PETROGRAD, STOCK-
HOLM REPORTS.

October 20, 1919: FALL OF PETROGRAD CONFIRMED; LINE TO
MOSCOW CUT.

It was too belated an offensive, which had been unable to
come to Denikin's assistance when he was advancing on Moscow and which afforded him no relief in his disastrous retreat.

Kolchak's campaign turned into catastrophe in Siberia,
which was encased in snow and ice. His ragged men, their
boots in shreds, died by the thousands along the roads, the
partisans on their heels. Nevertheless Kolchak succeeded in
reaching Irkutsk. There, however, the population revolted and
established a soviet. Admiral Kolchak was captured, tried by
a revolutionary tribunal, and shot on February 7, 1920.

One and a half months later, on March 20, Denikin, whose
army had disintegrated, embarked from the Black Sea port of
Novorossisk under the protection of HMS *Emperor of India*
and France's *Waldeck-Rousseau,* whose guns were shelling
the Red columns; Denikin was withdrawing into the Crimea.
For him the war was over. Wrangel was to be assigned to the
erection of a bridgehead in the Crimea from which it might
be possible to go back to the attack.

But it was too late. Wrangel in turn was to be swept out of
his positions and into the sea at the end of 1920. The Bolsheviks had won. Against them they had had the disadvantages
of inexperience, lack of trained personnel, untested troops, the
confusion created by the soldiers' committees, lack of discipline. Their advantages lay in internal lines that made it possible for them to move their reserves easily from place to place
and to bring up reinforcements quickly to critical areas. In
this conflict, as much political as military, they succeeded in
swinging the peasant masses over to their side by promising
them land that the Whites did not want to give them. And,
above all, they had found a man: Trotsky, the indefatigable
inspiration, traveling from one front to another aboard his famous armored train, little by little forging and disciplining

the Red Army, incorporating the new proletarian noncommissioned officers trained in battle with the former officers of the Imperial Army who had been induced more by force than by free choice to serve under the suspicious supervision of political commissars. As time went on, the Red Army became stronger, more cohesive, better disciplined. As far as atrocities were concerned, however, it equaled if it did not outstrip the Whites.

The battles were without quarter, and their toll was inflicted not so much by the fighting, which as a rule was brief enough, as by what followed. Massacres of prisoners, reprisal actions, raids by various guerrilla bands, burnings of villages, hangings and shootings of suspects, epidemics, famines . . . the combined toll of all these scourges amounted to seven million deaths.

(3)

KRONSTADT—THE
RED REBELS

T HE TENTH CONGRESS of the Bolshevik
party, which was held in Moscow in March
1921, opened in the midst of drama: Kronstadt
was in revolt.

Four months earlier the Russian civil war had ended. But
now, barely out of that tumult—in the early months of 1921
there were still twenty-eight roving bands operating in the
provinces of the Ukraine—the revolution was engaged in conflict with itself. At eight forty-five on the morning of March 7,
after an ultimatum issued by Trotsky had been left unanswered, the batteries of Sestroretz, Lissinios, and Krasnaya
Gorka, all situated on the Gulf of Finland, opened fire on the
fortress of Kronstadt and on the Baltic fleet, whose garrisons
and crews had mutinied. And the guns of Kronstadt fired back
without delay.

The Congress opened the next day to the echoes of this
cannonade. One hundred sixty delegates, instead of taking part
in the discussions, were dispatched to the scene of the fighting
on that same day. Everyone was needed—but above all everyone who was "safe"—to put strength into the others. For it was
by no means certain that the troops would agree to fire on

these sailors of the Baltic fleet who in October 1917 had marched in the front ranks of insurrection.

In 1905 the fleet had been the first to engage in armed combat. On June 27 of that year the crew of the *Potemkin* had mutinied in the Black Sea. In October it was the turn of the Kronstadt fleet, where there were further risings a year later, as well as in Helsingfors (now Helsinki) and Reval. In these crews, governed by a very harsh discipline and recruited in large part from specialized workers, it was not difficult for the agitators of the Revolutionary Socialist party, the Social Democratic party, and, later, the anarchists to feed resentments further heightened by a disastrous war. They exploded in 1917 with the February revolution and at once led men to extremes. The crews killed the commander of the fortress, Admiral Virren, and forty other officers. And they adopted a revolutionary principle: Henceforth they would choose their own superiors.

Thus Kronstadt became a kind of autonomous republic, a strong point protected by the sea and the fleet, keeping the February government under the threat of its guns, and at the same time a symbol: the revolutionary Mecca constantly visited by delegations from the front and the rear. *All power to the Soviets*—this slogan was born in Anchor Square, a huge public forum permanently occupied by noisy meetings in which workers and sailors rubbed elbows.

On July 4, 1917, the meeting went into the street. Sailors and workers of Kronstadt paraded through Petrograd in a long procession bristling with rifles and cadenced by shouts. Outside the Tauride Palace, the seat of the capital's soviet, they seized Chernov, the leader of the Revolutionary Socialist party and minister of agriculture, and were prepared to lynch him. Trotsky was alerted and hurried to the scene. At this time his popularity was immeasurable among the sailors, whom he had often addressed. But now it was in vain that he raised his voice, in vain that he cried: "Long life to Kronstadt the Red! Pride and glory of the Revolution!" The mob drowned out his words with its outcries. Was Chernov about to be butchered? Finally Trotsky played his last card, the dangerous card of a challenge: "Let those who want Chernov to die raise their hands!" Not one hand appeared.

Now Comrade Trotsky, People's Commissar for National Defense, had just called on Kronstadt to surrender unconditionally. "I order all those who have lifted their hands against the Socialist fatherland to surrender their arms at once! . . . Only those who surrender unconditionally may expect mercy from the Soviet Republic" (March 7). Two days earlier the Petrograd Defense Committee, headed by Zinoviev, had been even more brutal: "You are surrounded on all sides. In a few more hours you will be compelled to surrender. Kronstadt has neither bread nor fuel. *You will be shot like partridges. . . .*" And as early as March 2 the Moscow radio had sounded the call to arms in the struggle against the mutineers: ". . . Everyone! Everyone! Everyone! Into battle against the conspiracy of the White Guards! The mutiny of former General Koslovsky and the ship *Petropavlovsk* was organized by spies of the Allies. . . ."

To this the "glorious sailors," rechristened "spies and White Guards" for the occasion, retorted in flamboyantly phrased communiqués in which they labeled Zinoviev a "satrap" and compared Trotsky with Petrov, the former prefect of police. As in 1917, they demanded all power for the Soviets, which they opposed to dictatorship by a single party whose bureaucratic tyranny they denounced.

Bureaucracy was the key word that underlay the revolt— ✳ bureaucracy, whose two breasts are called requisition and repression. Partly as a result of the exigencies of the civil war, partly as a result of dogmatic rigidity, control by the state had been extended everywhere. This onerous tutelage was nothing more or less than the application of the utmost penuriousness. At the end of 1920 the coal mines were producing less than 10 per cent and the metallurgical industries less than 5 per cent of their prewar output. The production of consumer goods was not more than one-quarter of the normal figure, rolling stock had not been replaced since 1914, and for six years the peasants had been unable to replace their tools. In the whole of Russia only one enterprise was producing at an impressive rate of speed: the banknote industry. It was turning out a flood of paper money whose value was depreciating at a vertiginous pace. Therefore part of the workers' wages had to be paid in kind: food rations, shoes, clothing. . . .

The aberration of the leaders—Lenin first of all—was such that this bureaucracy of galloping misery was taken by them as the model of the society of the future. The country's reaction was quite different. Subjected to constant requisitions that were organized by party commandos in the rural areas, the peasant limited his efforts to what was required for his own subsistence. At once famine set in in the cities, which were abandoned by the workers. There were only two possible ways out of this appalling situation: relax the controls or intensify them. It was the second possibility that was initially chosen by the party. The peasants must be made to work for everyone. As for the workers, Trotsky suggested that they be brought under military discipline: They must be marshaled into an army of labor in order to work them back into the cycle of production. The orders of the day that he issued to the workers had all the flavor of military communiqués:

Deploy an untiring energy in your work, as if you were on the march or in battle. . . . The deserter of labor is as contemptible and as base as the soldier who deserts on the field of battle. Let both be sternly punished.

Appeals and threats had virtually no effect in a country that had been stupefied by war. A bitter winter further aggravated an already painful situation. In the cities life had become a hell. The heart of Moscow, the real center of its activity, was now the "Sukharevka," the citadel of the black market. A mass of many thousands of persons swarmed over it, proletarians and former aristocrats jostling one another in the struggle for survival. Here the most miserable object had a price. Here everything was barter: Butter was traded for silk handkerchiefs, six eggs for one jacket, a tool for slippers. Sometimes in this market one would stumble on an old woman offering two lumps of sugar on a saucer:—her total assets.

In Petrograd the situation was perhaps worse. The blockade prevented any supplies from arriving by sea. The condition of land transport facilities precluded any attempt to seek food supplies from the interior of Russia or the Ukrainian granary, which in any case had been devastated. In January 1921 the ration of black bread was 28.25 ounces for workers in three-shift factories and 15.18 ounces for various categories of shock workers; it fell as low as 5.06 ounces for holders of "B" cards (the unemployed). Even these rations were distributed in a highly irregular fashion, for the supply services were incapable of meeting the requirements of their tasks. Houses were unheated. Neither clothes nor shoes were available.

All who had been unable to flee the city scrounged desperately for some means of muddling through. In the depth of the winter the ice-covered freight trains moving into Petrograd were thronged with men in rags, gray of face, each with his bundle on his shoulder. They were coming back from the nearby villages where they had offered to trade salt, matches, sometimes a pair of mended boots or a few drops of oil in a bottle. In exchange they had got a few pounds of potatoes, often frozen, or a little flour. Sometimes the trains were halted for lack of fuel. The men had to climb down into the snow and cut dead branches to provide wood for the locomotive; and still they considered themselves lucky if they had not caught some contagious disease during their journey.

In Petrograd as in Moscow a few half-clandestine, half-tolerated markets existed for some time. Zinoviev, who headed the Petrograd soviet, regarded the survival of these vestiges of capitalism as intolerable: They were broken up. A few shops were still doing business: They were closed. Then barriers were set up at the entrances to the city and manned by the militia. The soldiers questioned travelers, opened their packages, confiscated their meager food supplies. Petrograd was locked in its isolation, its hunger, and its hatred, all of them mounting steadily.

For hatred was rising in the factories against those despised militiamen, against the absurdity of a bureaucracy that issued orders one day that buttons be distributed at the rate of one and a half per person, against anyone who enjoyed the most minuscule of privileges, and above all against Zinoviev himself, who, completely absorbed in the tasks of the nascent International in which he hoped one day to play a leading part, took no interest whatever in the fate of the city. An article published by *Izvestia* of Kronstadt during the revolt is illustrative of the rancorous atmosphere of men's minds:

All the best houses and apartments have been requisitioned for the head offices and branches of Communist institutions. Hence only the bureaucrats are accommodated in pleasant, comfortable, spacious fashion. . . . Since buildings are not maintained, they are deteriorating, the heating apparatus no longer functions, the roofs are leaking, and water is beginning to trickle through them. Half the pipes are burst, and their contents are invading the rooms. . . . In order to find a place to live one must have a good "pull" in the housing office. . . . For food it is even worse: irresponsible functionaries have allowed thousands of tons of goods to go to waste. Such potatoes as are distributed are always frozen. . . . It was that honest Soviet fish, the herring, that saved the situation for quite a long time, but now even herring is short. . . . What is most difficult of all is to find clothing and shoes. . . . Nevertheless . . . the people connected with the so-called "cooperatives" and the rulers have everything. They have their own restaurants and special rations. They also have available "coupon offices" that distribute ration cards according to the whims of the commissars.[1]

Bolshevik descriptions of this period tend rather to emphasize the spartan lives of the rulers. Rosmer, a French delegate

---

[1] Quoted by Volin in *La Révolution inconnue*, pp. 485–486.

to the International, recalled in his *Moscou sous Lénine* (*Moscow Under Lenin*) the frugal meals of Trotsky and the terrible smell of fish that pervaded the labor-union canteens, where the food was niggardly. But, when the populace is deprived of everything and the revolution is made under the banner of equality, even the most infinitesimal advantages—a heated room, a little more food, an extra tobacco ration, a coupon for some cheap cloth—are looked on as outrageous privileges. The Soviet bureaucrats were the boyars of misery.

The revolt of Kronstadt was grafted onto this impoverishment of Petrograd. Suddenly disorders began in the capital. In the factories there were spontaneous meetings that adopted motions hostile to the government. Proclamations were posted in shops and on the walls of houses. Certain slogans—perhaps inspired by Mensheviks—began to be repeated: free trade, Constituent Assembly. . . . On February 25 the large Trubochny factory was closed by a strike.

Zinoviev retaliated next day by calling for a review of the individual files of Trubochny workers with a view to a purge. The tension increased; other factories went out. A very noisy procession of two or three thousand workers took shape in the street. Zinoviev dispatched the *Kursanty* (student officers), who dispersed it. A number of meetings was prohibited.

The following day there were more strikes and more meetings—and more clashes with the police and the troops.

The troops—aside from the *Kursanty*—could not be counted on. The authorities sent outside the city for elite units. On February 26 Zinoviev set up a Defense Committee that placed the city under a state of siege.

Excitement in Petersburg had always raised an echo in Kronstadt. "St. Petersburg kept Kronstadt breathless and sometimes infected it with fever," Volin, the anarchist, wrote.[2] The tendency that had just manifested itself was in harmony with the revolt that was brewing within the garrison and the Baltic

[2] *Op. cit.*, p. 412.

fleet. In this irrepressible republic during the early months of the Revolution anarchist ideas had rapidly found quite a large audience. But the soviets of apartment houses, neighborhoods, districts, which had been spontaneously created in Kronstadt, had little by little been replaced by bureaucratic agencies subject to the control of the party. Then the sailors were called on to provide detachments of volunteers for the battle against the Whites, as well as propagandists for the rural areas.

In February 1918 the Baltic fleet was dissolved and replaced by a Red fleet that recruited only on the basis of individual enlistment. The *Cheka* established its men in the town, and a new, more tractable soviet was installed. All these measures showed that the central authority had no confidence in those men who in October had marched out to storm the Winter Palace. But the measures adopted were not enough to master the crews, which were now recruited chiefly among the peasants, themselves marked by the sufferings of the countryside. They came back from their furloughs with somber faces, telling how the last cow had been requisitioned from the farms, the last grain of wheat, even household possessions. Hence, as soon as they learned what was occurring in Petrograd, the sailors sent their delegates into the capital. Their reports convinced the sailors that the time for action had come.

On February 28 the crew of the *Petropavlovsk* adopted a resolution embodying fifteen points, which was soon endorsed by the General Assembly of Sailors, the corps of Red soldiers, and the population of Kronstadt. Like the proclamations of the Petrograd workers, it commingled economic demands with political slogans, but with a substantially broader scope: not only the abolition of militia posts and equal rations for all workers, but also the right of the peasants to dispose of their land and freedom for artisans and small shopkeepers—all of which must have made the Bolsheviks howl.

✳ In addition Kronstadt called for freedom of speech and the press for all the left Socialist parties, freedom of assembly for trade-union and peasant organizations, and the abolition of the

Communist militia. Subsequently the whole of these demands was to be summed up in one slogan: *The Soviets without the party!*

The Kronstadt soviet was in fact scheduled to be reelected on March 2. The day before, sixteen thousand persons assembled in the great Anchor Square. Vassiliev, a Bolshevik who headed the local soviet, shared the chair with Kalinin, chairman of the executive committee of the pan-Russian Congress of Soviets (and later president of the Republic), and Kusmin, one of the fleet's political commissars. They were received with military honors, which only briefly preceded hoots.

As soon as the *Petropavlovsk* crew's resolution had been presented to Kalinin, he began to speak, asserting that "Kronstadt does not represent the whole of Russia." The crowd reacted and there were vehement interruptions. "Shut your trap, Kalinin!" a bearded sailor shouted. "You've got a good warm spot! And I know, with all the jobs you've got, you get a ration card with each one." Kusmin was no more successful: "Have you forgotten that you ordered one man in every ten shot on the northern front? Get out!"

For the Bolshevik leaders there was something more serious than these hecklings. When the resolution was put to a vote, approximately half the party members (two thousand) approved it; the others abstained. And when the question was asked who opposed the resolution, only two hands were raised: Kalinin's and Vassiliev's.

＊The Communists dispersed. This was an unprecedented phenomenon for the party, a danger signal that was perhaps more disturbing than the revolt itself.

On the next day, when Kalinin and Kusmin opposed the regular reelection of the soviet, they were placed under arrest. Rumors circulated that the Communists were about to attack Kronstadt. The Assembly created a "provisional revolutionary committee" composed of fifteen workers and sailors under the leadership of Petrichenko, a ship's clerk aboard the *Petropavlovsk*.

An attempt at negotiation with the authorities in Petrograd soon collapsed. When Trotsky's ultimatum was left unanswered, it was obvious that the conflict between the community of Kronstadt and the Bolshevik party could now be resolved only by artillery fire.

The fortress of Kronstadt had been built two centuries before on the island of Kotlin, some fifteen miles west of St. Petersburg in the Gulf of Finland. Built to repel any attack from the sea, the main part of its defenses was directed outward. On both sides of the island, which was about six miles long and not more than three miles wide at its broadest point, the fortress was flanked by batteries emplaced on rocky islets. In addition, the forts of Sestroretsk and Cape Lissionis had been built on the northern shore of the gulf, as well as those of Oranienbaum and Krasnaya Gorka on the southern coast. These forts and their guns were intended to neutralize the Kotlin fortress in the event that it should fall into an invader's hands.

The town itself, situated to the east of the island, had about fifty thousand inhabitants: ships' crews, garrison soldiers—mostly artillerymen—arsenal workers, officers, officials, artisans. The sea was frozen over approximately five months of the year, from November into April, and communications between the island and Petrograd were maintained along a snow trail on top of the ice.

This ice was to seal Kronstadt's fate.

At the time of the October Revolution the cruiser *Aurora* had steamed up the Neva and dropped anchor near Nicholas Bridge. Her guns had fired a few blank rounds in the direction of the Winter Palace. Hardly anything further had been needed to topple an already moribund authority. But this time the fleet could not land. The combat vessels were immobilized by the ice and the insurgents had no access to an ice-breaker that would cut a path for them.

This fact in itself destroys the Bolshevik thesis of a counter-

sented the Bolshevik elite, had evidenced the same repugnance. "It was only because of the command and encouragement of the *Politrabotniki* (political commissars) and the officers," Uglanov, commissar for the northern sector, wrote, "that the *Kursanty* agreed to take part in the attack under a violent barrage by the artillery of Kronstadt." [3]

In the Omsk division, too, it was necessary to disarm two regiments.

With a view to preventing other desertions, the Bolsheviks adopted ruthless measures: The revolutionary tribunals went into action and shot all who had refused to march. Machine-gunners stationed behind the front opened fire on men who attempted to run away or seemed about to surrender. The delegates from the Tenth Congress, brought up in haste, were distributed among the different units in order to improve their morale. Regiments composed wholly of Kirghizi and Bashkiri were moved up. New units of *Kursanty* were also sent into action.

These young men formed the sacred battalion of the Bolshevik troops. Their six-month course of instruction was given in stages, often interrupted for practical exercises: immediate engagement in battle when the need for this was felt. Barmin, at that time a student officer in Gomel, told in his memoirs how he and his comrades were thrown into battle to stop General Haller.[4]

All seemed lost at that time. All that was left was the armored train "commanded by some insane ex-sailor," when Trotsky arrived and retrieved the situation *in extremis*.

Now Moscow was counting once more on these youths to take Kronstadt. Even before the mutiny had begun in the old fortress, Radek, on assignment from the central committee, had gone to address the Moscow student officers. He spoke for three hours, with an appalling accent that was quickly forgotten in the extreme gravity of the situation that he was describ-

[3] Quoted by Ida Mett, *La commune de Cronstadt*, p. 51.
[4] Barmin, *Vingt ans au service de l'U.R.S.S.*, p. 117.

ing: The working class was exhausted, the party's delegates were being hooted at in the factories, the worst was to be expected. "Shall we give way," Radek asked, "to workers at the ⚹ end of their physical resources and their patience and *less enlightened than we as to their own general interests?* . . . The party believes that it cannot yield, that it ought to impose its will to win on the weary workers, ready as they are to fall back. Grave events are in preparation. Be ready." [5]

Nevertheless, in spite of the courage of the *Kursanty*, new attacks on Kronstadt were driven back. Regardless of cost, the fortress had to be taken before the thaw. The success of the attack was in Tukhachevsky's hands. Trotsky had confined himself to signing the ultimatum. He did not intervene directly in the conduct of the battle, no doubt for reasons of internal politics. Petrograd was Zinoviev's fief, and, since rivalries among Lenin's lieutenants were already emerging from his shadow, the head of the Red Army was not eager to intensify the disputes by moving in to restore order where his rival had been unable to preserve it.

On March 16 Tukhachevsky ordered a concentrated attack for the next day:

To the Commander of the northern group, Kozansky, and the Commander of the southern group, Sedyakin; copy to *Glavkom*. Petrograd, March 15, 1921, 11:45 P.M.:
I order the fortress of Kronstadt to be taken by an all-out attack during the night of March 16–17. With this end in view: 1. Artillery bombardment is to begin at 2 P.M. on March 16 and to continue until night. 2. The northern column is to move out at 3 A.M. and the southern column at 4 A.M. on March 17. 3. The northern group will attack the northeast sector. The southern group will attack the northwest and southwest areas of the town. 4. Both groups should restrict themselves only to the occupation of those forts that constitute the greatest obstacles to their advance. 5. The Commander of the southern group is to appoint a single leader to direct the fighting in the streets of Kronstadt. 6. The Commander of the south-

[5] *Ibid.*, p. 147. Italics added.

ern group is to concentrate his effort on the capture of the north-west part of the island of Kotlin within the time set. 7. The lines of the columns are to be strictly maintained. 8. Receipt of this order and reports of actions taken are to be notified.

(*signed*) TUKHACHEVSKY (Order No. 534/0444, Series B)

The force within Kronstadt amounted to only slightly more than ten thousand sailors and three thousand garrison troops. These men had been fighting for a week without any substantial relief, and the length of the front compelled them to maintain a thin defensive curtain consisting of one man every ten yards. Munitions had to be used sparingly and food was rationed. The final combat set an exhausted garrison against an enemy in a position to bring up unlimited reinforcements.

On March 16 the southern group's artillery opened fire at 2:20 P.M., followed by the guns of the northern group at 5 P.M. Kronstadt's cannon replied, and the artillery duel continued for four hours. At dusk planes flew over the town and dropped bombs. Then it was dark. Kronstadt's searchlights swept back and forth endlessly over the frozen plain in search of possible assembly points.

The pincer attack began at midnight. Once more the guns thundered, gaping holes were opened in the ice, the Bolsheviks' machine guns chattered from the sleds on which they were mounted, men called for help as they drowned. But this time, in spite of their losses, Tukhachevsky's men advanced irresistibly. Before dawn the *Kursanty* had taken by storm a number of forts against which Kronstadt was now concentrating all its fire. Then the attackers drove against the southern sector of the fortress, the weak point in the defenses, and shattered resistance there. At about seven o'clock in the morning the assailants burst into the town itself.

This was the end of the Commune. All day long on March 17, however, ferocious fighting continued in the streets. Men fired from houses, from rooftops, from sheds. The workers left their jobs to lend a hand to the sailors. Many Red soldiers and officers were lost in this combat. During all this time, the municipal printing plant continued work on the current issue of *Izvestia*. But it was never published.

On the same day the northern group attacked the forts in its sector and occupied all of them except one. During the night of March 17–18 fighting continued in the town. But the mutineers' situation was desperate. Those Communists who had remained loyal to the party opened fire at the defenders from the rear. The last resistance points fell.

On March 18 the forts of Milyutin, Konstantin, and Obruchev were still holding out. There too the shooting stopped. The final fighting took place on the island, near the Tolbukhin lighthouse, where 150 sailors were still engaged. In the town a column of some five thousand men and women had been able to flee across the ice and find refuge in Finland.

That same day the government and the party celebrated the anniversary of the Paris Commune.

After the battle the attackers' casualties were put at 4127 wounded and 527 killed.[6] No figures for the defenders' losses were given.

Once Kronstadt had been taken, the *Cheka's* tribunals moved in. There were mass arrests. Petrograd's prisons were jammed. Every night little groups of prisoners were taken out of their cells and shot. Perepelkin, one of the members of the committee, was among them. Those who were spared were loaded onto trains and shipped to the north and the camps of Arkhangelsk. These men would never be seen again.

Virtually nothing was said of those who had taken refuge in Finland. The men who had led this revolt remained almost nameless. Apart from the anarchist press, no one was interested in them. *Le Matin*, which had resorted to big headlines when the revolt began and which had very coolly described the sailors invading Petrograd, where the Bolsheviks "were still resisting" (*sic*), was not to give a single line more to this mat-

---

[6] Statistics released by the Army Medical Corps for the Petrograd sector and probably less than the actual number.

ter once the revolt had been put down. The fate of these defeated revolutionaries was of little moment to the bourgeoisie
once they were no longer a threat to the Bolshevik government. At rare intervals the memory of Kronstadt was evoked
in the publications of the non-Communist left. The world
would have to wait for Budapest, whose revolt was to be likened to that of Kronstadt. But the rising in Budapest had been
born of the agitation of the intellectuals. Kronstadt, on the
other hand, was a typical popular uprising, and its Petrich-
enkos and its Perepelkins were lost in the mass that they had
encouraged into a brief rebellion.

(4)

UNDER THE BLACK
FLAG OF MAKHNO

═══════════════════

ALTHOUGH KRONSTADT had been subdued, thousands of miles to the south, in the Ukraine, Makhno and his partisans were engaged in desperate fighting near the Sea of Azov. On March 14 a sudden cry had gone up from the midst of Makhno's men at the height of combat: "*Batko* has been killed!" *Batko* (Father) was the affectionate nickname that the partisans had bestowed on Makhno. He had merely suffered a bullet wound in the thigh—he had already been shot in the ankle. He could no longer mount his horse. So he was put on a wagon bed. Then followed flight, combat, encirclement, march, and countermarch in an effort to escape from the enemy.

Fifteen hundred horsemen and two regiments of infantry were all that remained to Makhno. On their heels were several divisions of the Red Army and the cavalry of the famous Budyenny. For many months this pursuit across the snowy steppes of the Ukraine had been continuing like a fox hunt. Thanks to his devilish cleverness, Makhno had eluded every trap. Fighting constantly, scaling rocks, slipping to the bottoms of ravines, his men would turn and face the pack that was tracking them, break its encirclement, and cut across the

Ukraine while the enemy hastened up from every direction to seize them. They advanced as far as the borders of Galicia, turned back toward Kiev, wheeled into the governments of Poltava and Kharkov, turned north again toward Kursk before falling back toward the Sea of Azov. Their ranks were thinning. Makhno's lieutenants were killed off one after another. Food, munitions, artillery had to be left behind. But on March 18 they still were able to find a way to put Budenny's cavalry to flight.

Nevertheless Makhno and *Makhnovchina* (Makhnoism) were doomed.

Nestor Makhno, the son of poor peasants, had been a prisoner of the tsar because of his terrorist activities; he had been liberated in 1917 by the October Revolution. His private war began in his native town, Gulay-Polye, with the organization of a guerrilla band to fight the Germans. He displayed amazing ability as a war leader whose tactics were based on thorough knowledge of his theater of operations, the infinite collaboration that he enjoyed among the peasants, and the speed of his movements. Makho's horsemen loomed up where no one expected them, launched a lightning attack, then vanished to attack again somewhere else.

These daring assaults were made easier by the chaotic situation in the Ukraine. Since the October Revolution it had been the prey of armies and guerrilla bands that raced over its soil in merciless, inextricable combats: first the Germans, who imposed the rule of Skoropadsky as hetman, then Kaledin's Whites, then Denikin's, then Petlyura's nationalist partisans, then the Bolshevik partisans, the Red Army, then ordinary bandits. . . . All of them tried at the same time or by turns to impose their shaky authority, occasionally calling a truce or forming some brief alliance that was speedily broken.

As for Makhno himself, who drew his inspiration from the ideology of libertarianism, he called on the peasants everywhere to set up soviets elected and governed by themselves. He rejected any attempt at centralization, any authority established in the form of a party. Thus, as at Kronstadt, the idea of freely elected and freely associated soviets was opposed to the centralism and the bureaucracy of the Bolsheviks.

The Bolsheviks could not tolerate the existence of such autonomous republics, but they needed the military qualities of Makhno's men as long as the peril of the White armies remained. Hence the history of their relations was one of temporary agreements that were hardly respected by either party to them.

Makhno's major achievement was his long march to the west, pursued by Denikin's armies, which ended with a shattering counterattack. This occurred in midsummer of 1919. The heat was tropical. The dusty roads of the Ukraine were crowded with an endless, slow procession: Thousands of peasants were following Makhno in his retreat.

They moved across country, driving their cattle ahead of them, while Makhno's infantrymen, mounted on *tachankas*— carts with two horses, a driver, two soldiers and occasionally a machine-gunner—opened the way for them. Above the leading wagon floated a huge black flag on one side of which was embroidered in silver the slogan, *Liberty or death;* on the other side, *The land to the peasants, the factories to the workers.* The cavalry (two to three thousand men) covered the retreat, and Makhno continually sent out patrols to scout for the enemy's approach.

In midsummer, darkness in the Ukraine lasts only a few hours. Daylight dissipates it with amazing speed, and the rising sun was daily accompanied by the crackle of rifle fire, the thumping of shells, the hoofs of horses. Denikin's cavalry attacked from every direction, and there would be savage combats that would go on until darkness returned.

Makhno's troops were still retreating along a line 360 miles long, and the ring of iron was tightening round them. At the end of September they were trapped in Peregonovka, near the town of Uman.

At this time the main body of Denikin's troops was marching on Tula, and the Red Army too was falling back before this offensive. Makhno decided that, regardless of the cost, a breakthrough must be attempted. He attacked to the east, forced the advance guard of the Whites to retreat, and then himself withdrew as if he were afraid to pursue his offensive. Suddenly his troops attacked anew while his cavalry, erupting from a ravine, hit the enemy's flank and, after a fierce battle, broke the Whites' front. Makhno drove ahead through the breach thus opened. Twenty-four hours later he had advanced more than sixty miles. He overran everything along his route and captured Alexandrovsk. Behind him more than a mile of road was piled with the bodies of Denikin's officers, ruthlessly sabered and mutilated.

This partisan action, like a Ukrainian western studded with heroic deeds, was also sullied by abominable butcheries. Where Makhno passed, everything that had to do with author-ity—police, prosperous peasants, and priests—was massacred. So too were persons who for any reason at all were marked for popular vengeance. Volin, the anarchist who was a member of Makhno's Propaganda Committee, described in his book the trial and execution of one unfortunate priest. He was dis-covered in the belfry of his church, where he had sought to hide, and he was dragged out to the public square. There the villagers accused him of having denounced people to the Whites. True or false? One woman, when the priest begged her to save him, retorted: "If you are innocent, defend your-self. These men are not wild beasts." Whereupon one of Makh-no's soldiers horsewhipped the priest, tore off his cassock— which, the soldier said, would make a fine black flag—and asked whether anyone was prepared to defend the man. No one moved. Apparently it did not occur to Volin that those who might have been tempted to defend the accused were not eager to share his fate. Finally, "repugnant in his underwear" [1] (but how would Volin himself have looked in the circum-

[1] Volin, *op. cit.*, p. 592.

stances?), the priest was disposed of with a few bullets at the base of the skull.

Makhno was not backward about taking a hand in these slaughters. Since the news of the Whites' defeat was not yet generally known, he and some of his comrades disguised themselves in the uniforms of White officers and went to the estate of a rich farmer, who greeted them joyfully. There was great festivity, with toasts to the defeat of "the bandits." Then, to his host's dismay, Makhno identified himself. Everyone on the estate was killed.

Such events were everyday occurrences, it is true, in Russia when she lay open to all the furies of civil war. Neither the Whites nor the Reds boggled at them.

But Makhno was not satisfied with an unrelenting pursuit of his enemies. His intimates were often the objects of his whims and of a temper that was continually sharpened by alcoholic excesses. For all that he was the paladin of libertarian ideas, this man with his hard, suspicious little eyes set deeply under bushy brows led his staff in a group whose only law was its own pleasure. When they were not fighting, they were busy with orgies and drinking bouts.

One day the Council of Education and Propaganda, of which Volin was a member, complained of the abuses by one of the officers. Makhno lost his temper. "He grabbed his revolver," Volin wrote, "pointed it at everyone, waving it back and forth, left to right, right to left, in the faces of the members of the assembly, meanwhile heaping vulgar insults on them. Then he stalked away without listening to any explanation." [2]

Steeped as it was in libertarian theories, the Council probably refrained from reminding Makhno that he was behaving like a hooligan.

Nevertheless it was this man who dealt what was undoubtedly a decisive blow to Denikin's offensive. Having broken

[2] *Ibid.*, p. 683.

his pursuers' front, Makhno pounced on the White general's rear just when Denikin was threatening Tula, and thus he cut off the White army from its supply bases. It was indeed Trotsky who finally shattered Denikin's offensive, but would he have been able to do so if Makhno had not wrought havoc behind the front?

Now this same Trotsky, on June 4, 1919, before Denikin's drive, had issued Order No. 1824 to prevent the convocation of a congress of Makhno's partisans and to place all violators of the order under arrest.

The entire population will have to be warned orally and in writing that participation in the said Congress will be regarded as tantamount to any act of high treason. . . . All delegates to the said Congress will have to be placed under arrest at once and taken before the revolutionary military tribunal of the Fourteenth Army of the Ukraine.[3]

Makhno eluded every trap that was set for him, avoiding arrest, and Denikin's offensive compelled Trotsky to concern himself with other things than chasing Makhnoists. But once Denikin and then Wrangel had been defeated, the Bolsheviks devoted themselves to the liquidation of the turbulent communes that supported Makhno and his partisans. The agreement that Makhno had signed with Frunze and Bela Kun, which contained the implicit promise that the Makhnoists would be allowed to forward their experiment in the territory of two or three Ukrainian provinces, was broken late in November 1920. Frunze ordered that the rebel army be incorporated into the Red Army, and, when this order was not carried out, a new drive against the Makhnoists was launched.

Makhno had been able to preserve his autonomy as long as the civil war was raging. Alone now face to face with the Red

[3] The Congress of Makhnoist Soviets was to have been held in their leader's birthplace, Gulay-Polye, which was the center of his influence. Trial before the revolutionary tribunal was most often tantamount to execution.

Army, with all his tactical genius he was able merely to pro-
long a resistance that was doomed to annihilation because of
the relative strength of the opposing forces. Disabled in March
1921 by his wounds, he nevertheless held out until the end of
August. On the twenty-eighth of that month, under the pressure of his comrades, he crossed the Dniester and fled to
safety abroad. The man who had made the entire Ukraine
tremble was to die in Paris in 1934 after a dozen years of
wretched exile.

Thus the last organized anarchist forces in Russia were liquidated. And it had been the anarchists whom the Bolsheviks
had first had to battle after their seizure of power. In April
1918 Trotsky ordered anarchist clubs in Moscow stormed, and
artillery was called in to accomplish the task. These clubs, the
Bolsheviks asserted, were the haunts of numerous bandits who
held the city at their mercy. The statement was correct. But
above all the Bolshevik party dreaded the growing influence
of these men who had played no negligible part in the seizure
of power.

In the three years between the end of 1917 and the beginning of 1921, all organized political strength was exterminated
by the Bolsheviks.

First the Revolutionary Socialists and then the left Revolutionary Socialists were expelled from the soviets and their
newspapers were suppressed. Their major leaders—Spiridonova, Karelin, Kamkov—were arrested. No one ever knew the
fate of Spiridonova after she vanished into the world of concentration camps. Karelin and Kamkov, of whom there was no
word for many years, reappeared in 1938 to give testimony
against Bukharin at the trial of the rightist and Trotskyite
blocs. They were ghosts from whom Vyshinsky, the prosecutor,
had the utmost difficulty in extracting a few paltry words.
Then they vanished again into the night.

It did not help the Mensheviks that they had sought to remain as the only legal opposition, for the successes that they

had been able to score in the elections to the soviets in the spring of 1918 had been nullified in practice by the activity of the *Cheka*. Since voting had been conducted by a show of hands, it was easy to arrest on a variety of pretexts some of those who had voted for the Mensheviks. Then the elections were voided. In the next election backers of the Mensheviks were rare.

The final attack against them was launched in February 1921, just before Kronstadt. The weary workers in the factories were broadly responsive to their slogans. In the first three months of the year there were approximately two thousand arrests, including the entire membership of the Mensheviks' Central Committee. By the middle of 1922 the party had virtually ceased to exist.

On his return from a visit made by a delegation from the British Labor party in 1920, one of the delegates, Shaw, interviewed in Geneva, offered this summary of the fate of the democratic opposition: "The proletariat has no rights in Russia; it enjoys neither freedom of assembly nor freedom of the press. It does not have the right to choose its representatives. The oppression of the Russian people is as great as it was under tsarism."

"Mensheviks and Revolutionary Socialists are to be shot if they show their faces!" This terse order was Lenin's. At about the same time, in *Terrorism and Communism*, Trotsky mocked at Kautsky, who called for freedom of expression for all varieties of Socialism: "We have smashed the Mensheviks and the Revolutionary Socialists," Trotsky wrote, "and there is nothing left of them. This criterion is sufficient for us." [4] Besides, the civil war precluded any indulgence in such dangerous fantasies as freedom of the press or assembly. "We are making war. We are fighting to the death, not to life. The press is the weapon not of an abstract society but of two irreconcilable camps that do battle with weapons. We suppress the counter-

[4] *Terrorism and Communism*, p. 171.

revolution's press just as we destroy the counterrevolution's fortified positions, storehouses, spy services." [5] But the measures that were being justified by the necessities of war were not to be abandoned when war had ceased to be necessary. Trotsky would soon become aware of this to his cost.

For the strangulation of opposition outside the party was to infect the party itself like leprosy. The left parties denied freedom to the other bourgeois parties; the Bolshevik party denied it to the other left parties. "The general management of affairs," Trotsky wrote, "is concentrated in the hands of the party. . . . What is more, experience has led us to conclude that in all these controversial matters, in all the conflicts that may arise among administrations, the final word must belong to the Central Committee of the party." [6]

Trotsky wrote this in 1920 during his controversy with Kautsky. In fact, under the climate of terror imposed by the civil war, the Central Committee was the last remaining island where free discussion was still possible. But, with the Tenth Congress, its freedom too was quickly to be put on short rein. ✳ This Tenth Congress was a major turning point in the history of the Bolshevik party: it adopted the NEP—the New Economic Plan—which loosened the chains of war Communism; the right of opposition within the confines of the party became virtually impossible; Trotsky's rise suffered a blow the effects of which he would never be able to overcome.

The NEP had already been decided on in Lenin's mind. The mutiny at Kronstadt had made clear to him how urgent it was to take a backward step, to restore to a hungry population the basic freedoms of trade in order that goods could circulate again. Artisanry and small shops could once more develop without too much hindrance. But the major beneficiaries of the NEP were the peasants. Instead of being subjected to merciless requisitions, the peasant once again enjoyed the right to dispose of his farm, to lease his land, and to hire labor for

[5] *Ibid.*, p. 102.
[6] *Ibid.*, pp. 167–168.

its cultivation. Results were not slow to appear. In 1923 total farm production rose to almost three-quarters of the 1913 level.

This retreat on the economic front was accompanied by a further tightening of the political vise. The NEP's program was virtually the same as the Mensheviks'. To permit them to act within the law was to give them the opportunity to assert that they had been right. Similarly, when the huge peasant mass was being given a chance to breathe, for the Bolsheviks there could be no question of authorizing the Revolutionary Socialist party, the traditional champion of the slogan, *The land to the peasants,* to make itself the spokesman for the peasants' demands. All this was very clearly and very cynically explained by Radek at the party's Tenth Congress in May 1921.

Within the party itself, tendencies toward opposition were brutally crushed by Lenin. During the preceding months two such currents had emerged within the party's ranks: Democratic Centralism and the Workers' Opposition. In essence the Centralists called for greater freedom of discussion. The Workers' Opposition, which had begun to develop in 1919 in labor-union circles, sharply attacked the employment of "bourgeois" experts in the productive process and the bureaucratic tendencies of the leaders in the management of industry. The chief spokesman for this group was Shlyapnikov, a member of the Central Council of Trade Unions and president of the Metallurgical Workers' Union.

The strongest opponent of this tendency was Trotsky, who in 1920 had called for the militarization of the unions. A long controversy ensued, in which Trotsky was made to seem an aspirant to dictatorship. Lenin, who was more flexible, triumphed.

Although he rejected the militarization of the unions, Lenin intended to prevent any crystalization of the opposition tendencies. By the second day of the discussions he was insisting: "We have had enough of opposition!" Exploiting the mutiny of Kronstadt and the agitation of the Mensheviks to the full, he vehemently accused the opposition of playing the enemy's game, following a method that has since been repeated hundreds of times.

On March 16, 1920, he won the adoption of a resolution calling for the dissolution of all groups that were seeking to form round a "platform" within the party. One clause of this resolution, which was not revealed until 1923, gave the Central Committee the power to order the immediate exclusion of anyone who might attempt to move in this direction. In the event that a member of the Central Committee should be involved, however, a two-thirds majority would be required for his exclusion.

Furthermore, although the party's by-laws adopted in 1919 provided for completely free discussion, the right of criticism was now confined within very narrow limits. Henceforth its exercise would require consideration "of the form . . . of the party's situation in the midst of the enemies that surround it." And enemies would always be found.

A second resolution denounced the Workers' Opposition as a "syndicalist and anarchist deviation." In practice, then, the positions taken by the opposition were deemed incompatible with membership in the party.

There had been nothing to foreshadow the appearance of these two unprecedented documents that were to stifle democracy within the party. The elections for the Central Committee had ended. Continuation of the discussion on the following day had been scheduled only for consideration of the fuel-supply problem. Nonetheless it was on that day that Lenin exploded these two carefully prepared bombs.

Only twenty-five or thirty votes were recorded against the adoption of these resolutions that silenced all opposition. Discussing them in a speech, Radek displayed both clarity and cynicism. Clarity: "In supporting this resolution, I recognize that it may very well be used against us." Cynicism: "And yet I endorse it."

Both resolutions would later prove to be decisive weapons

in the struggle against Trotsky: He had approved their adoption. Inclined toward authoritarianism, he saw at that time no reason why he should not make use of them. The result of the elections for the Central Committee, however, was the first step taken by him toward his ultimate defeat. During the debate on the function of the trade unions he had committed the error of diverging from Lenin. It is possible that Lenin took offense at this. In any case, the elections for the Central Committee were a clear-cut defeat for Trotsky's backers. Three of them—Krestinsky, Preobrazhensky, and Serebryakov—held the posts of secretaries to the Central Committee. They were voted out and replaced by Molotov as first secretary with Yaroslavsky and Mikhailov as his deputies. Their entrance into the Central Committee was accompanied by those of Komarov, Ordzhonikidze, and Voroshilov. Kirov, Chubar, Kuibyshev, and Gusev were still only candidates. They were the future lieutenants of Stalin.

Now the advancement of these men and the removal of Trotsky's supporters came at a time when the party's apparatus was acquiring body and gaining a weight that was all the more decisive as the freedom of discussion disappeared. One could see the workings of the mechanisms that would very soon make the party a formidable instrument of oppression.

In the beginning the chief power inured to the members of the Central Committee, who themselves derived their mandates from the party congresses. Nevertheless the clandestine preparations for the October days had already constrained the Committee, for reasons of purely practical necessity, to delegate its executive powers to a smaller group of men. What had been purely fortuitous was soon to become institutionalized under the name of the Politburo.[7]

[7] The Politburo, which could be convened quickly to make urgent decisions because at that time it consisted of only five members, played a more important part than the Central Committee during the civil war. From March to September of 1920 it seemed that the situation had been reversed to the advantage of the Central Committee, which met at the rate of four times a month. But, after the Tenth Congress, the meetings

Until 1919 the Central Committee had operated without a secretariat or a staff trained to assign responsible men to any given position. One man alone, Sverdlov, because of his great talents as an organizer, set himself to this task: His knowledge of men served as his filing cabinet. He died in March 1919. It became obvious that his place must be filled. Hence a secretary was appointed and a Committee of Organization (*Orgburo*) was created and charged with assigning men to positions subject to the supervision of the Central Committee. The secretary was Krestinsky, and he lost no time in providing himself with two assistants: Preobrazhensky and Serebryakov. Then the secretaries entered the *Orgburo,* of which they became the virtual masters in 1920. In March of that year the *Orgburo* gained the right to make assignments and transfers without compulsory referral to the Politburo.

No serious organizational effort, however, was feasible without a sound records system. A special section of the secretariat was therefore charged with establishing such a system. By September 1920 the party members had already been divided into three categories: 1. the most active and most reliable; 2. those whose future was highly promising; 3. the rank-and-file militants. In this same month, after its establishment, the *Orgburo* had already assigned twenty-five thousand party members to posts.

At the same time the secretariat was gaining in importance. In 1919 it had 30 employes; in 1921 it had 602. From this it is possible to measure the bewildering expansion of the central apparatus. Soon the secretariat was provided with a code service. All these bodies proliferated in almost automatic fashion.

Little by little the party's administrative machinery was taking the place of the party. Everything made it seem as if the

---

of the Plenum (the Central Committee and the Politburo) were held at greater intervals again. Between June and August the Plenum met five times to take up twenty-seven matters. During the same period the Politburo alone met 24 times to deal with 264 questions. In 1922 the substance of power was definitively transferred to the Politburo.

civil war had been won only to assure its triumph. Only internal democracy could curb its power, and that was effectively disposed of by the Tenth Congress.

Krestinsky and his deputies were conciliatory by temperament. As long as they remained at their posts they made every effort to find compromises and allay resentments. But should men of a different type succeed them, what had been merely annoying constraint would be transformed into tyranny. The technical machinery of oppression having been placed in position, all that was needed was the entrance of a tyrant on the stage.

At first there was only a petty tyrant, hard-pressed and small-minded: Molotov. In August 1922 Stalin appeared. He took Molotov's place as first secretary.

Stalin was already a member of the *Orgburo* (with Molotov, Yaroslavsky, Mikhailov, Komarov, and two future rightists: Rykov and Tomsky). Stalin was the only member of the *Orgburo* who was also a member of the Politburo.

Central Committee, Politburo, Secretariat, *Orgburo*—it was in one or another of these four agencies that every major decision that concerned the life not only of the party but of the country was made. Stalin was the only leading official who was a member of all four. This was a tremendous advantage, the importance of which was ignored by everyone except Stalin.

Backed up by his *apparachiki,* he was at all the command posts. At once he recognized that he held in his hands the instruments of his future triumph, that the conditions of the battle had completely altered, that victories would no longer be decided on the rostrum or at meetings or in newspaper articles, that even the reputations that cloaked men more glorious than himself would in no way prevail against the weight of the apparatus. From now on the weapons of victory in the struggle for power that was beginning in Lenin's shadow were filing cards.

Cautiously Stalin began to maneuver on the lower levels of the party, appointing or removing secretaries, before giving battle on the higher elevations.

(5)

TWO RIVALS

I T WAS NOT until September 22, 1939, that Trotsky
made up his mind to describe in detail his first meeting with Stalin. Eleven months later Stalin procured
his murder.

In itself this meeting came down to a very minor occurrence,
a brief encounter between two destinies that were later to be
joined in a mortal duel. It happened at the end of January or
the beginning of February of 1913, in Vienna. Trotsky was in
the city to visit a Menshevik, Skobelev, who had been his colleague on the staff of *Pravda*. While they were talking the door
was suddenly opened. A rather short, stocky man stood on the
threshold; his face was thin beneath a heavy shock of hair, his
skin was tanned and pitted with smallpox marks. As if surprised at Trotsky's presence, the intruder hesitated a moment,
grumbled something that might with an effort have been taken
as a greeting, and then, going up to the customary samovar,
poured himself a cup of tea and went out again.

"Who is that?" Trotsky asked.

"Dzhugashvili, from the Caucasus. He has just joined the
Central Committee, and, you know, he seems to be getting
somewhere in it."

There was no reason why Trotsky should have paid much attention to this fleeting visitor. Trotsky, who had made a tumultuous entrance on the stage of history in 1905, was one of the luminaries among the exiles. Enmeshed in all the hairsplitting controversies that were destroying the Social Democratic Party, in disagreement as much with the Mensheviks as with the Bolsheviks—though perhaps more with the latter—he had carried on a furious, sarcasm-studded debate with Lenin. He knew Bebel and Kautsky and the Austrian Marxists such as Hilferding, Renner, and Adler; in meetings of the International he associated with Vandervelde, MacDonald, Guesde, Vaillant, and Jaurès, whose splendid rhetoric he admired. But not doctrinal controversies or journalism or political encounters were enough to exhaust the capacity for interest in this man of dazzling talents, familiar with all the cultural riches of Europe: the museums, the novels, the literary discussions, the nascent theories of Freudianism. To Trotsky in his pride Dzhugashvili, whose name he was hearing spoken for the first time, was a militant like so many others, of no real importance.

The fact remained that, twenty-six years later, Trotsky retained an obscurely painful impression of this insignificant encounter. There was something forbidding and surly in that quickly glimpsed face, an evil light in those "yellow eyes," a light that Trotsky would have the opportunity to see flicker many times in brief flashes. He did not yet know, though he may have vaguely suspected, that what had come out in those eyes was hatred.

This Dzhugashvili had a few reasons for disliking Trotsky. First of all there was jealousy. They were barely a year apart in age. But what a difference in their backgrounds! The son of the Jewish settler Bronstein had been a brilliant student, alimented on tremendous reading and contacts with the revolutionary intelligentsia. As early as 1902 he had met Lenin in London. Dzhugashvili, having entered a seminary in Tiflis—the only path to education open to the son of a poor Caucasian shoemaker—though he may not have been a poor student, was always to retain from his education something of the grammar-school boy: He assimilated rather than enriched himself. Trotsky had sprung into the front rank in the tempest of 1905. He was then twenty-six years old. Stalin, a dull speaker, remained outside the great mass movements that he could not govern by words; then he turned to journalism. Trotsky's pen was a dagger that cruelly wounded his adversaries; Stalin launched his career with a clumsy dose of platitudes burdened with inappropriate metaphors.

The gifts that he himself lacked and that he recognized in so many others were already exacerbating in Stalin an animosity that age, competition, and the struggle for power would render unhealthy. Two weeks earlier, in *Pravda*, he had spoken of Trotsky as "an athlete with hollow muscles." Even if Trotsky had had the opportunity to read the description, it would never have entered his mind in those days to reply to so puny an adversary. Many years later, compelled to refute, point by point, the shameless accusations of the "Stalinist apparatus," he was to do so with contemptuous aloofness. "Not an orator, not a thinker, not a writer," he said in his *Stalin*, which death prevented him from completing. In other words, as far as he was concerned, a nothing.

In 1913 Stalin had other reasons, deeper in the last analysis, for resenting Trotsky. At the Congress of London in 1907, at the height of the revolutionary revulsion, Trotsky had condemned the acts of violence organized in Russia by clandestine Bolshevik combat groups and the "expropriations" that augmented the party's funds with money stolen from the tsarist state. Stalin was in fact one of these "expropriators." While he did not directly take part in the incidents of violence, he instigated them. Thus, in Tiflis in June 1907, Kamo, one of Stalin's comrades and a magnificent fighter, had led the attack on a Treasury vehicle that had netted three hundred thousand rubles.

It was at approximately this time that Lenin was speaking enthusiastically in his letters of the "marvelous Georgian." He was the more to be valued because in this period Lenin's disciples were not dazzling in number. Men of action who were experts in underground activities, like Bogdanov and Krassin, were leaving him, and they were followed later by Gorky, Menzhinsky, Lunacharsky. Moreover, after 1907 all the revolutionary forces were in full retreat. And, as was natural, the more reverses they suffered, the more the quibbles and the fragmentations into competing sects proliferated. The exiles' congresses and conferences reverberated with these acrimonious quarrels. Trotsky was never backward about joining them.

That was what Stalin must have been thinking when he found the "athlete with hollow muscles" at the samovar. As for himself, he belonged to those few hundred men who had formed round Lenin, in the isolation of his emigration, that hollow square of *practical* militants that Lenin needed not in order to sustain scholarly discussions in the noisy nights of exile but to execute orders without delay.

Trotsky related that, in the last session of the Congress of London, when the delegates were beginning to depart, suddenly a young man with a clean-shaven face and thick hair leaped onto a chair. This was Zinoviev. In a few seconds his shrill voice had captured everyone's attention. Here was a lad who would be heard from again. All during the Congress, on the other hand, Trotsky reported, comrade Ivanovich (this was one of Stalin's aliases) had never opened his mouth. The conclusion was apparent: Stalin had nothing to say.

This was probably true. But why would he have spoken? He was absorbed in dangerous clandestine work. He was cut out not for oratorical jousting but for the missions and diplomacy of the "underground."

The rancor that shone out of Stalin's eyes in the meeting in Vienna was the same hostility that opposed the militants of the home front to those of the emigration. Concealed or acknowledged, such opposition rends any secret organization whose base is established outside its home country. Later the same conflicts would be experienced by the men of the French

Resistance and, afterward, of the Algerian National Liberation Front: Conflicts between the directing staffs, squabbling in the safe havens of exile, and the executants on the spot whose primary concern is to elude the bloodhounds of the police.

Although Stalin was not rich in ideas, one idea at least was close to his heart: establishing the leadership on Russia's own soil. Analyzing the party's crisis in *Rabotinsky Proletarii* in 1909, he emphasized the gaps that, in his view, could be ascribed "to the old methods of working and the 'leadership' of the party from abroad." As Deutscher observed, the quotation marks in which Stalin enclosed the word "leadership" showed no great regard for it on his part.

A year later he wrote in a most respectful manner to Lenin that the most important thing was not the exiles but practical work on the spot. He declared that a group must be established in Russia that would coordinate legal, semi-legal, and illegal activities, "regardless what it may be called." Twenty-four days later, in a letter to militants in Moscow, he declared, this time without any deference at all: "The workers are beginning to look with disdain on the emigration *in general.*" [1]

"In general": Lenin too, then, Trotsky commented, seeing in this an instance of the duplicity of Stalin, whose tone changed with the person whom he was addressing. But this example was above all characteristic of the patient, stubborn manner in which Stalin pursued his ends. He remained closeted inside Russia and, further, within those hierarchic committees that formed the party's skeleton.

Men like Trotsky, Zinoviev, Bukharin, or Kamenev (particularly Kamenev, whose activity in the Caucasus was better known than Stalin's) might also have known prison or deportation, the ordeals of illegal life, but, through their culture, their knowledge, their contacts, their sojourns abroad, which had opened new horizons to them and brought them into

[1] Gorky wrote to Lenin along the same lines, telling him that Russians were tired of the emigrants' quarrels. Lenin replied, not without some acerbity, that the discussions were indispensable.

touch with the European Socialist movement, they belonged to a universe other than that of the militants of the committees. This was the self-enclosed world of the practitioners, distrustful of initiatives by the masses, hounded by the police, too deeply committed in the routine of subversive activity not to be irritated by the controversies of the exiles, and it was this world that shaped that emotional nucleus composed of the touchy tempers and visceral loyalties of the old Bolsheviks that Stalin was to know how to enlist for his conquest of power. These men would often remember that before 1917 Trotsky had not been one of them, that he had been not only outside the party but also outside their experiences. And the theses of Socialism in one country would not be difficult to transplant into this environment prepared to accept them.

Stalin was the typical product of this harsh school, restrictive in the development of the intellect but productive of vigor. Previously he had known the harsh experiences of life in the Caucasus, ravaged by age-old rivalries and struggles; while young Bronstein was making a brilliant reputation as a student in a preparatory school infused with the liberal spirit, Dzhugashvili was locked away in a seminary where he detested the teachers and their teachings. For seven years this hatred was hidden, except for the brief flash of a smile of scorn or a snicker when the monitors' backs were turned. As an adult, he had to grow up not only in the atmosphere of political rivalries in which Mensheviks, Bolsheviks, Revolutionary Socialists, and Federal Socialists contested with one another while the Okhrana, which had its antennae everywhere in that turbulent little world, kept them all under its surveillance, but also in the environment of those peoples—Georgians, Chechens, Armenians, Turks—who envied and detested one another quite as much as they loathed tsarist absolutism. Here was where one learned that one must look out for oneself, that no blow was too low.

By the time of his accession to the decisive post of secretary general, Stalin's personality had been fashioned quite as much by the experiences that he had undergone as by the innate traits of his character: a gift for deception and trickery, envy, obstinate distrust, concentration on surrounding himself only with persons who would execute his orders and who were his inferiors, complete control of his nerves, indefatigable determination in the service of a "concentrated ambition," the art of concealing his real intentions, progressing only by stages, coordinating his moves, breaking off if his opponent proved too strong—all these qualities were heightened or acquired through almost daily ordeals or practice. And the contempt that he felt toward all men impelled him to see in them only their weaknesses and their baseness, on which he was adept at playing in order to attain his ends.

His time in prison during these years of apprenticeship played a part that throws some light on his rugged personality. Unlike so many other revolutionaries who pursued their studies in prison, Stalin gained nothing there on the intellectual level, not even knowledge of a foreign language. The man whom his schoolmates in the seminary had described as a good pupil, endowed with an extraordinary memory, seemed strangely insulated against everything that might be called culture. A certain laziness gained the mastery of him as soon as effort could no longer directly serve his ambition. Sullen in his deportation, he hunted and fished, avoiding his fellows, and did not write a line. At the height of the war, when he was isolated in Cadiz for six weeks, Trotsky feverishly went through old French and English books, annotated them, and copied out quotations on the Spanish revolutions and counter-revolutions. Everything was nutriment to his intellectual appetite.

To Stalin prison was the place for a different training: that of character. Verechak, a Revolutionary Socialist who was in prison with Stalin in Baku, related that the prisoners played a cruel game that consisted in choosing a victim and exasperating him with taunts or anything else. This was called "putting him into a bubble," as nearly as the Russian expression can be translated. No one ever succeeded in putting Dzhugashvili into a "bubble." Regardless of taunts and provocations he retained perfect composure. He slept during executions, and he went on reading while his companions were being beaten. If the occasion arose, he endured beatings with the same stolidity. At the same time, he was always ready, in this hermetic world overheated by its passions, to make others spread malevolent rumors.

This cold, aloof man, deliberately coarse and brutal, who had the charms of neither style nor speech, was at ease only in the tenacious, silent activity of the "apparatus." He missed all the great encounters of history. His name is absent from 1905. He played no part in the great conflicts of the emigration. True, in February 1917 he was the director of *Pravda*, but he was following an opportunist course that Lenin, on his return, made haste to rectify. During the October days he was nowhere to be found, a fact that was later to create some difficulties for his zealous biographers. Sukhanov, one of the great eyewitnesses of the Revolution, disposed of him in three lines: "A gray spot . . . that is all that there is to be said." Even the civil war did not bring him out of his obscurity. He was forty-one years old.

It was at this period that Victor Serge noticed him for the first time, during a banquet in Petrograd. Stalin was wearing a blue blouse and acting vaguely important.

"Who is that?" Serge asked his neighbor.

"Stalin, a member of the Central Committee. That's all I know."

At this period the names of Trotsky, Zinoviev, Bukharin, Kamenev, Radek, Rakovsky, Dzerzhinsky were blazing at the zenith of the Revolution.

This effacement, this shadow from which he could not (or would not) remove himself, this intellectual mediocrity that was already in such sharp contrast to the adoration of which he would later insist on being the object, were constantly impressed on him with amusement by all his adversaries, Trotsky above all. All of them were to be, so to speak, stunned that this man, of all men, should oust them.

And yet all the criticisms that they addressed to him, all the scorn that they heaped on him came from a few lines out of a document that they would seek, too late, to transform into a weapon against him: the famous "Testament" of Lenin. In this document, prepared when he knew that death was near, Lenin acknowledged Stalin to be with Trotsky the most impressive figure in the Central Committee.

※ Lenin did not specify the attributes that he saw in Stalin. But we know that above all what he valued in the Georgian was his character. Justifying Stalin's appointment to head the Worker and Peasant Inspectorate, Lenin said: ". . . in order to be able to manage properly, there must be a man with authority at the top."

Trotsky no less than Stalin was a man of energy and resolution, and the intellectual brilliance of which his rival was so cruelly deprived and the prestige with which he was invested by the end of the civil war ostensibly assured him of an overwhelming superiority in the combat that had begun between them. But even before the war an excess of pride had made Trotsky a lone rider in the emigrant world. Almost as soon as the perils of counterrevolution had been overcome, he was once again that solitary figure admired but feared and rejected by a whole clan. The party that had made use of him—in other words, the ruling class, whose influence was a major factor because democracy had been virtually abolished—solidified itself into a mass that was hostile to him.

※ We know next to nothing of the first brushes, the first clashes, the first wounds that were to set these two powerful personalities in opposition to each other; Trotsky is strangely reserved on the subject. But we can visualize them in terms of Lev Davidovich's character: proud, full of arrogance, a man to whom the Revolution was a theater and who carried its ways and its idiosyncrasies over into his private life, much given to insolence and contempt and sarcasm. It is enough to read Trotsky. A few lines and a character is completed—that is, executed. On Chernov: "He always had readily accessible an inexhaustible collection of appropriate quotations. . . . There was only one question that this long-winded leader could not answer: Whom was he leading, and where?" On Stalin: ". . . In 1917 he crossed my path like an imperceptible shadow." On Zinoviev: ". . . When things were going badly for him, Zinoviev stretched out on a couch, not in the figurative but in the literal sense, and sighed. As early as 1917 I could see that for him there was no middle ground: either seventh heaven or the couch." On Menzhinsky: ". . . an inept sketch for an unfinished portrait [that] played with papers in the dark." In all Trotsky's work there are some fifty portraits in these colors: terse, acute, and savage.

It may be supposed that in his speech he was no less quick or skillful at the trenchant summation, which, speedily circulated in that ductile world of the Bolshevik leaders, made his victims flush or pale with anger. His rebuffs and his arrogance did the rest of the job.

One day he burst in on Molotov and cut him to verbal ribbons. Molotov, who was militantly mediocre at repartee (and at everything else, for that matter), merely stammered: "Comrade Trotsky, not everyone can be a genius." This was a humiliation that would not be forgot by the bureaucrat with the pince-nez.

Trotsky wrote that Stalin "was most solicitous toward people who had lost their horns." If such was the case, Trotsky did half the job for Stalin, cutting off many a horn—some undoubtedly as a result of the obligations imposed on him by his post of command but many others for no justifiable reason at all.

The first horns were those of the future secretary general. First of all, Trotsky ignored his existence, and this was the initial insult. And he contemptuously brushed aside Stalin's timorous, wary advances. Trotsky himself reported that their first personal talk was held after the seizure of power, in the

Smolny Institute. It was very brief. Through the thin partition they could hear Dybenko, the sailor, romancing Alexandra Kollontay on the telephone—a love affair that was at that time the talk of the entire party. Trotsky wrote,

> Stalin came up to me in a playful manner, and, indicating the wall with his elbow, said with a smirk: "There he is with Kollontay! With Kollontay!" His manner and his snigger, so wholly unexpected, seemed to me to be out of place and intolerably vulgar, especially on that occasion and in that place. I do not remember whether I merely turned away or really said to him: "That is their business." But Stalin sensed that he had made an error: the expression of his face suddenly altered and his yellow eyes had the same evil glow that I had already noticed in Vienna.[2]

The scene was a contrast in characters. One, whose contempt was never reluctant to wound, loathed all gossip—there was never anything low or petty in Trotsky; the other sought to exploit the weaker aspects of the human soul—vanity, disappointed ambition, malice, calumny—and to make them his allies. When his approaches were rejected, he was thrust a little more deeply into his hatred.

The exercise of power and the conflict of competing ambitions were to heighten these antipathies. The great rivalry between Trotsky and Stalin really began with the civil war, and it was revealed in their opposing strategic conceptions.

The creator of the Red Army built an army of the classic type, highly centralized and disciplined, for which he made great use of military experts—in other words, officers of the Imperial armies. Since these men's loyalty was dubious at the very least, they were surrounded by political commissars who were supposed to countersign the orders given by the military leaders before they could be put into practice. At the same time, every effort was being made rapidly to train officers chosen from among the workers whom the party regarded as the most reliable. But it was still the old officers who provided

2 Trotsky, *Stalin*, p. 378.

the major staff structure. By August 15, 1920, when the civil war was approaching its end, the Red Army counted 314,180 military specialists, of whom 214,717 were second lieutenants and noncommissioned officers and 48,409 were former tsarist officers from the rank of first lieutenant up. And in 1919 it had been possible to train only eleven thousand new officers. Moreover, the commanders in chief were, successively, Vatsetis and S. Kamenev,[3] both of whom had been colonels in the Imperial Army.

This bulk integration of "class enemies" (many of whom in fact did detest Bolshevism) naturally aroused suspicions, antagonisms, and conflicts. It went against the grain of the political commissars to have to enforce their orders. At the very time when Trotsky was preparing to launch the final offensive against Wrangel, Rosmer was present at a conference over a map in the candle-lighted house of a priest when a violent controversy erupted between a staff officer and a young major of the Red Army. The major, a Petrograd worker, was losing his temper; he was impatient to begin the attack and found it very difficult to tolerate the objections raised by the "expert." As Trotsky commented, "a classic quarrel."

The suspicions directed against the "experts" were intensified by every reverse. Each defeat gave those who opposed their employment the opportunity to raise the cry of betrayal. Sometimes, in fact, there was treason, as there were desertion and sabotage, on the part of men who had every reason to hate the government and whose families, at Trotsky's orders, had been seized as hostages. Trotsky himself recounted that once, when he was at the front with an officer, the "expert" excused himself for a moment to telephone. In a few minutes the enemy artillery was zeroing in with much accuracy and vigor on the sector where the commissar for war was.

Throughout the civil war, Trotsky's basic conception of the Red Army and its strategy were the targets of unceasing criti-

[3] Not related to the Bolshevik leader.

cism. Thus he had to defend himself against what was called the "military opposition." The members of this opposition group came chiefly from the ranks of the Bolsheviks who, in the disorders that followed the Revolution, had belonged to partisan detachments in all parts of the country. They endorsed, at least in the beginning, the principle of the election of officers by the troops, they were consistently hostile to the "experts," and in opposition to a highly organized military machine in Trotsky's hands in Moscow they favored diffused local guerrilla operations. This tendency can be regarded as the logical extension of the Bolshevik combat groups, those *boyeviki* who in the days of tsarism had operated so audaciously in Latvia, the Urals, and, above all, the Caucasus.

The backers of guerrilla warfare found themselves in collision with the authoritarianism of Trotsky, who minced neither words nor acts and labeled their views "utter infantilism." Now in large measure these men were old militants who already looked askance at the former "Menshevik." Almost everywhere, furthermore, the local organizations of the Communist party had established cells in the army, and these cells' projects and actions interfered with those of the Army Command. Here again Trotsky had to intervene, break down resistances, offend sensibilities. Little by little he transformed the turbulent Bolsheviks of the army into docile instruments of the hierarchy, thus paradoxically contributing to the training of the type of man that would cause his own downfall.

The most serious conflicts occurred at Tsaritsyn (the future Stalingrad). There Trotsky had to confront a former noncommissioned officer, Voroshilov, round whom the military opposition was coalescing. A prolonged insubordination began, secretly nourished by Stalin. In his messages he poured vituperations on the "experts" and encouraged everything that might thwart his opponent. On one telegram from the commissar for war he wrote a cold comment: "Not worthy of any consideration."

Trotsky finally won Lenin's support in the Tsaritsyn controversy. Early in October 1918 Trotsky telegraphed to Lenin: "I insist categorically that Stalin be recalled!" He threatened to put Voroshilov and Minin on trial (at that time military tribunals were fond of shootings), and he concluded: "Tsaritsyn should submit or secede."

Lenin had Stalin recalled. As Stalin was returning to Mossow, his train passed that of Trotsky, who was on his way to the front, and the two men had a brief talk. Stalin assumed the humility of defeat, imploring Trotsky not to be too harsh toward Voroshilov and the others: "They are good boys. . . ." It was a purely tactical retreat. At the first opportunity Stalin and Voroshilov resumed their attacks, and the struggle between Stalin and Trotsky continued and intensified as the civil war went on.

Two resolute wills were in opposition: One was full of ✳ pride, easily driven to extremes, the other was crafty and tenacious. During this period when the fate of the Bolshevik Revolution was being decided, Stalin displayed the capacities that explained his subsequent successes. Sent on missions to various fronts on a number of occasions, he did indeed commit a number of errors (later he was to be chiefly responsible for the Red Army's defeat in its offensive against Warsaw), but he was also an excellent administrator, highly adaptable to new situations and charged with energy to the point of the most extreme brutality; he was already implacable in his purges. "My hand does not tremble," he wrote to Lenin. An old militant woman told Victor Serge: "Stalin is very strong. But he makes too much blood." This blood that he was shedding without trembling was not yet that of his party comrades.

Against Trotsky, whom Lenin most often supported, Stalin elected to operate with already proved methods—that is, by using cat's-paws, thus leaving avenues of retreat for himself. In the controversy over the conduct of the war, he prudently adopted a middle-ground stand, criticizing the resort to "experts" but insisting on the need for discipline, thus avoiding systematized support for the military opposition, which did not enjoy the favor of the ruling circle, while at the same time taking care not to cut himself off from it. At the party's Eighth Congress, where the military question was debated, he and Zinoviev were members of a commission of conciliation whose purpose was to attempt to establish harmony between the opposing camps.

Trotsky came out of the storm of the civil war in a blaze of victories and glory. His name, his slender profile wrapped in the severe military tunic, his sharp-featured face were famous throughout the world. His armored train had become a legend. The members of his bodyguard, wearing the leather jackets "that gave them substance and importance," were a personal guard. On their left sleeves, just below the shoulder, they wore a metal emblem carefully fabricated in the Moscow Mint. On May Day and the anniversary of the October Revolution the people's commissar for war rode out of the Spassky Gate of the Kremlin on horseback to the Red Square, where the troops passed in review. He saluted them in a vibrant tone: "Greetings, comrades!" and he was answered with a tremendous shout: "We serve the Revolution!"

This display of power, this liking for show, further amplified by his eloquence, his flood of imagery, caused eyebrows to go up, and some who contemplated Lev Davidovich's imperious profile muttered: "Bonaparte!"

Could he have seized power by force? Probably. Trotsky then was in the same situation as Boumédienne on the eve of his coup, a Boumédienne who would have had in addition the eloquence and the renown of a Jaurès. There is no evidence, however, that Trotsky ever entertained such a fantasy. His own thinking, moreover, caused him to see a menace in this army that he had developed. Composed principally of former officers of the tsar and of peasants, with a weak admixture of proletarian noncommissioned officers, it was looked on by Trotsky—if it were to act as an autonomous force—as the vanguard of reaction. Employed for a violent overthrow of the government, could it not be turned against him?

But, even before the civil war had ended, he must have sensed that the war of succession had begun even while Lenin was still alive, and he sought to strengthen his position within the party. His views on the militarization of labor were dictated undoubtedly by his concern with rebuilding industry's catastrophically reduced production. But they also presented him with a means of assuring himself of control over the labor unions. As the master of not only the military but also the labor-union apparatus, with his own men in the *Cheka* (Trilisser and Blumkin), he would enjoy a power that could be counterbalanced only by Lenin's.

This, at any rate, was how his rivals were to interpret this attempt. The union leaders, with Tomsky at their head, reacted violently against Trotsky's plans. His arrogant ways did not simplify matters. He and Lenin were men who gave orders, meticulous, precise, bound by strict timetables that conflicted with the deliberately bohemian habits of Bukharin, Zinoviev, and the rest. But Lenin was an expert at the skillful proportioning of praise and blame. This was not true of Trotsky. At a meeting of the General Confederation of Labor he had a violent outburst because the delegates simply ignored the scheduled time for the session. Somewhat later he had a serious clash with Ryazanov, who described the plan for the militarization of labor in terms of an arrogant young officer, his cap cocked over his ear, bursting into a labor-union office and attempting to dictate its decisions.

Lenin did not wish the labor issue to be debated in public. Through some strange blunder Trotsky paid no attention, and the controversy raged in the party's newspapers. Several points of view appeared, threatening the party unity that Lenin wanted to preserve at all costs, and the Central Committee was virtually severed into two camps. On the basic issue involved Lenin's views were hardly different from Trotsky's, but Trotsky infused a much more systematized and extreme character into measures that in Lenin's case were founded principally on a concern with expediency. In any event, the major outcome of the Tenth Congress was the fact that Lenin established himself as the leader of a tendency opposed to Trotsky's. Stalin, in Trotsky's place, would have speedily compromised or retreated, prepared to return later to the attack. But Trotsky had no sense of maneuver. When the question was put to the vote, he was roundly defeated. When the new Central Committee was elected, his supporters disappeared.

This was a decisive turning point. Stalin, as the preceding chapter has pointed out, had begun his ascent. Trotsky was losing positions that he would never be able to recapture.

It is quite likely that in the circumstances Lenin wanted to curb Trotsky's ambitions. Gorky declared that at that time, after a tribute to the people's commissar for war, Lenin added: "And yet he is not one of us." Reporting this story six years later, at the height of the fight on Trotskyism, Gorky was not a reliable witness. But there can be no doubt that the opinion that he attributed to Lenin was that of the "old guard." The reaction of Lenin's associates was identical to that of the brain trust of a company chairman when he enlists the collaboration of a brilliant expert from a competing firm. In such case everyone stands together against the interloper. It is possible that Lenin was not unaware of the muttered resentments of those round him. After all, he and Trotsky had been in almost continual opposition for a dozen years. Their recent collaboration could not wipe out everything.

But Lenin was to lose no time in drawing closer to Trotsky and making an ally of him against the growing power of Stalin. Was Lenin already opposed to the appointment of Stalin to the post of secretary general? Trotsky related that he grumbled: "This cook will never dish up anything but spiced stews." It is dubious whether in his mouth this remark was anything but an ordinary joke: a few days before Stalin was appointed, Preobrazhensky attacked him and asked: "Is it conceivable that one man can be capable enough to meet the requirements of two commissariats and, in addition, those of the Politburo, the *Orgburo*, and a dozen commissions of the Central Committee?" and Lenin replied: "We need someone to whom any representative of a national minority can turn to report on whatever may be happening. Where is such a man to be found? I doubt whether Preobrazhensky would be able to find anyone but Stalin. The same thing applies to the Worker and Peasant Inspectorate. . . ."

As had happened so many times before in his life, Lenin was very soon to change his mind. Virtually shut off from power by illness after May 1922, he did not require much time to see that Stalin was silently concentrating an enormous authority in his own hands.

At every level of the apparatus he was installing his own men and dismissing or exiling to remote posts those who were in his way. The civil war had already sanctified the custom of disposing of militants as it pleased the central apparatus. These measures, initially imposed by circumstances, perpetuated themselves and served now to get rid of men who showed too great a freedom of mind. Such was the case for major militants like Tomsky and Ryazanov. The one was sent to Turkestan, the other went abroad. They had offended.

"One such case among a thousand," Suvarin rightly wrote, "demonstrates how harshly ordinary unknown militants could be brought into step and what treatment would have to be endured by simple mortals outside the privileged Communist world." [4]

The mounting bureaucratization of the party greatly aided Stalin's game. In 1922 one of every twenty-five members of the party devoted all his time to it. In the same year there were 15,325 militants on its permanent payroll.[5] For purely material reasons the full-time functionary enjoyed a major advantage over the part-time militant. On all levels authority and influence ran from the congresses to the conferences and the committees elected by them, then to the secretaries of these committees.

[4] Suvarin, *Stalin*, p. 278.
[5] On this subject cf. Schapiro, *De Lénine à Staline*, p. 362.

The secretary's function, however, was still limited to the extent to which he was still subject to control by the base organs. But as soon as the central apparatus acquired the habit of appointing the secretaries administratively, they tended more and more to form a caste apart whose interests were merged with those of the secretary general.

Nevertheless Stalin's position was far from having attained to that absolute power that he would later enjoy. At the highest levels—that is, in the Central Committee and the Politburo —he was still an obscure individual. He had been able to accede to the post of secretary general only because it was regarded as a routine job of little attraction and apparently obscure. Zinoviev, who reigned over the Petrograd Committee, and Kamenev, who governed that of Moscow, sometimes looked with a certain flicker of irony at that colorless, deliberately taciturn man who could not handle the Russian language without making mistakes. Stalin's intelligence lay in the fact that—undoubtedly ahead of everyone else in the world—he had grasped the capital importance, in a large modern party, of the position that controls its organization and that he had learned to play this instrument like a master. He avoided committing himself to a premature battle at the summit and he limited his concerns to isolating Trotsky with the assistance of Zinoviev and Kamenev. But he maneuvered on the middle levels of the party in order little by little to alter the relationships in it.

Lenin, meanwhile, had made up his mind to cut off this obvious rise. He alone was still capable of doing so. He began by violently criticizing the inefficiency and the cumbersomeness of the Worker and Peasant Inspectorate. Though it did not mention his name, this attack was aimed against Stalin. The Georgian problem precipitated its resolution.

Having proclaimed itself a democratic republic, Georgia had elected a Constituent Assembly. In the elections the Mensheviks had won 640,000 votes, as against 24,513 for the Communists. The Red Army lost no time demonstrating that in its view these 24,513 votes carried more weight than the 640,000 others. In February 1921 the Eleventh Army, commanded by Ordzhonikidze and supported by Budenny's cavalry, launched its offensive, against which the Georgians could muster only ten thousand men. In a week all resistance had been smashed.

The artillery was followed by the administration. The administration was Stalin. Arriving in Tiflis, he began by purging the Georgian Communist party, which was not strong enough to suit him. His old comrades of the underground struggle, including Makharadze and Tsintsadze, paid the price. A year later the secretary general turned his anger against the entire Georgian old guard, earlier accused of nationalist deviation, as well as Mdivani, his childhood companion; Svandize, and Kavtaradze.

This method was perhaps not wholly in accord with the principles laid down in *Marxism and the National Question*, ✳ the author of which was Stalin. But the brutal purge of the Georgian Communist party was an excellent augury of the broader purges that would be carried out on a nationwide scale.

Lenin was informed of what was going on and he made no secret of his indignation. Through Dzerzhinsky he learned that Ordzhonikidze had punched Georgian Bolsheviks. This was gutter behavior, Lenin said. Did he believe that tyranny was intolerable only when party comrades were its victims? In any event, the punches thrown by "Sergo," which were nothing in comparison with the salvos of the *Cheka*, brought Lenin's anger to the boil.

He drafted a long article on the national question. In it he denounced the Great Russian chauvinism that worked to the detriment of the smaller peoples. He spoke of the Ordzhonikidze incident.

What I learned from Comrade Dzerzhinsky, who headed the commission delegated by the Central Committee to "investigate" the Georgian incident, only intensified my fears. If things went so far

that Ordzhonikidze could lose his composure to the point of resorting to physical violence, it is justifiable to wonder into what morass
we have sunk. . . . The political responsibility for this whole Great
Russian nationalist campaign ought to be laid squarely on the
shoulders of Stalin and Dzerzhinsky.

This article was dated December 31, 1922. Three months
later, on March 5, 1923, Lenin sent Trotsky a brief note in
which he asked him to undertake the defense of the Georgians
before the Central Committee against the "persecutions of
Stalin and Dzerzhinsky."

There can be no doubt: Lenin had made up his mind to the
ouster of Stalin. Feeling that his strength was leaving him,
haunted by the dread of a schism within the party, he laid
down a whole series of measures that in his view were such
as to prevent it. The first of these was the enlargement of the
Central Committee.

This period (December 1922) was also the date of the famous document known as Lenin's "Testament." Drawn in a
cautious manner, it afforded no very clear indications as to the
choice of a successor. In particular it emphasized the danger
of schism that was implicit in the rivalry between the party's
two leading figures. While it acknowledged Trotsky's endow-
ment with outstanding qualities, it criticized him for his excess
of self-confidence and his absorption in the administrative aspect of things. What this meant was that he lacked tact and a
psychological sense. On the precise nature of Stalin's merits
the document was mute. It pointed out that, "by becoming
secretary general, he has concentrated enormous power in his
own hands, and I am not yet convinced that he can exercise
it with sufficient caution." [6]

[6] These quotations, as well as those from *The National Question*, were
among the sixteen documents that were not made public until the secret
session of February 25, 1956, when they were communicated to the
members of the Twentieth Congress—after the celebrated Khrushchev
Report. In July 1956 they were published individually in a million-copy
edition. A large part had already been published in the West, some by
Max Eastman, some by Trotsky, some by Suvarin.

If one compares this view with the accusations made against Stalin in connection with Georgia, one is entitled to think that Lenin intended at least to reduce substantially the powers of the secretary general.

But, a few days later (January 4, 1923), Lenin added a dozen or so lines to his "Testament" by way of postscript. It was a sentence without appeal for Stalin:

Stalin is too brutal, and this defect, which is quite tolerable in internal relations among us Communists, becomes intolerable in the person of the secretary general. This is why I suggest that the comrades consider means of removing Stalin from this post and appointing in his stead a man who in all respects differs from Comrade Stalin in his superiority: one who is more patient, more upright, more courteous and considerate of his comrades, less capricious, etc. This matter may seem a meaningless trifle, but I believe that from the point of view of protection against schism and of what I have said earlier of the mutual relations between Stalin and Trotsky it is not a trifle, unless it is a trifle that can acquire decisive importance.

Why did the cautious recommendation of December 22, 1922, become the indictment of January 4, 1923? There had been what could be called a minor incident, one of those incidents that Lenin would perhaps have described as a "trifle" if the victim had not in fact been his own wife, Nadezhda Krupskaya.

In a telephone conversation on December 22 the secretary general had in fact indulged himself in insulting the wife of the "boss." The next day she wrote a letter of protest to Kamenev:

The authenticity of the "Testament" was at first challenged by Stalin's supporters. Trotsky, himself engaged in the struggle for power, thought it politic to reject it. Stalin, however, decided to make it known to a restricted group at the Fifteenth Congress in 1927. But the Stalinists and a large number of progressives persisted nevertheless in accusing Trotsky (who in the meantime had decided to confirm the existence of the "Testament") of having distorted the truth as to Lenin's death and the succession. The publication of the sixteen documents dissipated the last doubts on the matter. It fully confirmed the version that Trotsky had given.

Lev Borissovich:

As a consequence of a brief letter that Vladimir Ilyich dictated to me with the permission of his doctors, Stalin flew into a violent and unaccustomed anger against me last night. I did not join the party yesterday. In all these thirty years I have never heard a vulgar remark from a comrade. The affairs of the party and of Vladimir Ilyich are as dear to me as to Stalin. . . . Better than any doctor I know what can and cannot be discussed with Vladimir Ilyich because I know what does and does not make him nervous. In any event, I know this better than Stalin.

I turn to you and Grigory Zinoviev as old comrades of Vladimir Ilyich and I beg you to protect me against brutal intrusions into my private life, coarse invectives, and base threats. I have no doubt of the decision that will be reached by the investigatory commission with which Stalin has thought it advisable to threaten me. Regardless of that, I have neither strength nor time to waste on this stupid quarrel. I am a human being and my nerves are stretched to breaking.

Informed of the matter by his weeping wife, Lenin reacted secretly at first with the postscript of January 4 and openly two months later in an extremely harsh letter of March 5 to Stalin:

Dear Comrade Stalin:

You have taken the liberty of rudely summoning my wife to the telephone and upbraiding her in a vulgar fashion. In spite of the fact that she told you that she was willing to forget the remarks that had been exchanged, she has nevertheless informed Zinoviev and Kamenev. I have no intention of so easily overlooking what has been done to me, and it is unnecessary for me to emphasize the fact that I regard as directed against me whatever is done against my wife. Consequently I request that you carefully consider whether you are willing to offer a retraction and an apology or whether you would prefer that relations between us be broken.

Sincerely,

✳ There are two surprising elements here. The first is that Stalin, who was consciously brutal and vulgar with his subordinates, had lost his composure sufficiently to strike out at Lenin's wife when he could not have been ignorant of the fact that Lenin was already ill-disposed toward him. This outbreak of anger and these insults, combined with the threat of haling Krupskaya before the investigative commission,[7] belied the self-control that Stalin had demonstrated in so many other situations.

The whole affair would undoubtedly be clearer if one knew the reason for this violent tirade. On this point Krupskaya offered no clue. But it is known that Lenin, who had suffered an attack on December 16, was attempting, in spite of the advice of his physicians, who were urging him to rest, to discover what Stalin was plotting in the secretariat. It was his wife who acted as his intermediary in these quests for information. Hence it is probable that Stalin had "told off" Krupskaya on the pretext that Lenin must not be wearied.[8]

On the same pretext of assuring Lenin's precious tranquility, Rykov, who worked with Stalin in the secretariat, had already suggested that that body should determine who might and might not visit the patient. Lenin angrily rejected this proposal, in which concern for his fatigue certainly played a lesser part than the desire to "screen" his visitors. The skirmish between Krupskaya and Stalin occurred in this climate of mutual suspicion.

The second surprising element was this: Why did Lenin wait until March 5 to take up the matter directly with Stalin? It could be argued that he refused to exaggerate an incident of a private nature. If he decided to act on March 5, it would seem, it was because some other explosion over the telephone

[7] This was highly significant. At that time the investigative commission was all-powerful and no one could escape its inquisition.

[8] Boris Nikolayevsky thought that Stalin had assumed this attitude deliberately. Knowing that what he said would be reported to Lenin, according to Nikolayevsky, he purposely spoke vulgarly in order to irritate Lenin and thus bring on a new attack. It was a very risky procedure and in this case it backfired against him. It is still more plausible to suppose that Stalin merely gave way to temper.

had occurred between his wife and Stalin, who was then in Georgia, and because what was taking place there had inflamed Lenin's anger to its peak.

There is a curious interweaving here between factors of a private nature (for instance, the tone of the letter to Stalin: ". . . I have no intention of so easily overlooking what has been done to me, . . .") and acute differences on political problems. Was it Krupskaya's tears that made Sergo's punches important, or the contrary? It is a question that cannot be answered, but it recurs at the heart of all the quarrels among the Bolshevik rulers, in which rivalries, ambitions, and natural antipathies constantly interjected themselves into doctrinal controversies.

On the same date as his brusque ultimatum to Stalin, Lenin appointed Trotsky as his champion:

Most Secret
Dear Comrade Trotsky:

I urge you at once to undertake the defense in the Georgian matter before the Central Committee of the party. At present this business is the target of Stalin's and Dzerzhinsky's persecutions, and I cannot rely on their impartiality. Quite the contrary. If you would agree to assume the defense of this matter, I could rest easily. If, for certain reasons, you cannot agree to do so, please let me have the entire file. This will be sufficient indication of your refusal.

As might be guessed, Trotsky had no wish to refuse. The reconciliation that Lenin had effected with him, the information that assured him that, according to the physicians, the patient's health was improving and that he would undoubtedly be able to appear at the Congress, the assurances from Lenin's secretaries that for this Congress Lenin was putting together a "bombshell" against Stalin—all these things proved to Trotsky that the secretary general's doom had been sealed. And backed by Lenin without reservation, only Trotsky could reasonably claim to be Lenin's successor.

On March 5, 1923, Stalin's stock was at its lowest. Apparently he had lost the game. But chance intruded brutally into history and knocked all plans askew.

Kamenev was supposed to leave for Georgia on government business. In agreement with Lenin, Trotsky sent for him in order to tell him what "the Old Man" thought on the matter. Kamenev arrived within an hour. He recognized at once that Lenin was making Stalin the direct defendant. Moreover, he had just talked with Krupskaya, who had told him that Lenin was breaking off all relations with Stalin.

According to Trotsky, Kamenev was upset and pale. Like Zinoviev, he was linked with Stalin in the triumvirate that they had established and that was known as the "troika." Stalin's fall was his own as well. It might come at the Twelfth Congress, which was to be held in April.

Trotsky tried to reassure him. "I have no intention of starting a fight in the Congress," he said. "But the policy being followed in Georgia must be changed at once. Let there be an end of administrative repression. As for Stalin, the best thing for him would be to write a letter of apology to Krupskaya."

Kamenev was ready to agree with all of this. "But," he asked, "will Stalin agree? I am afraid that he will get his back up."

"Of course not," Trotsky replied. "What other way out is there?"

Unquestionably this view was correct. Late that night Kamenev telephoned Trotsky. Stalin had accepted all the terms. He had immediately dispatched a letter of apology to Krupskaya. "But," Kamenev added, "Lenin could not read it. He has had a relapse."

It seemed to Trotsky that something had changed in Kamenev's tone. His voice was less faltering than it had been in their earlier conversation. This was because Lenin was worse. The luck of the "troika" was coming up again.

Kamenev went off to Tiflis. During his journey he received a coded telegram on March 9: Lenin had suffered another stroke and was completely unable to speak or write.

Now his proposals for the solution of the Georgian affair were a dead letter. Completely reassured, Kamenev vigorously defended Stalin's position in the conference of the Georgian Communist party.

All that remained to him was the memory of a humiliating approach to Trotsky; all that remained to Stalin was the thought of a letter of apology that, if he had waited a few days, he need not have bothered to write to that "bitch" Krupskaya. Such things are not quickly forgotten. All that Trotsky had been able to derive from the few hours in which his rival seemed doomed to inevitable defeat was a fiercer hatred.

Lenin died eight months later. But by then he was nothing but a living corpse, far removed from all political activity, already resembling that mummy before which uncounted crowds would later pass, and his name was to grow in renown in direct proportion to the use that would be made of it to belittle his ideas.

Trotsky was left alone to confront the machinations of the "troika."

(6)

THE "TROIKA"
AGAINST TROTSKY

═══════════════════════

ONE DAY in January 1924, Victor Serge, who was then employed by the Communist International in Vienna, was riding through mountains and tunnels in a railway car filled with obese travelers. One of them suddenly unfolded his newspaper. The headline was huge: LENIN DEAD.

In the Caucasus, to which the Politburo had sent him for his health, Trotsky had already learned of the event. He fainted. Until the very end he had wanted to believe that Lenin would recover, in the face of all the evidence; Lenin's third cerebral stroke, in March of 1923, had left him a wreck. Unable to leave his bed, he could barely raise his eyelids, and the headlines in *Pravda* had to be spelled out to him letter by letter. Occasionally there would be some improvement, and the doctors nourished a little hope. Their bulletins were read with different hopes by every member of the Politburo. For the bitter struggle for power depended on whether Lenin recovered or died.

Lenin's body was placed on display on January 23, 1924, in the Trade-Union House in Moscow, amid crape-hung lights and red flags. Trotsky was not there. He said later that Stalin

had lied to him about the funeral date; he had remained in
the Caucasus. And on January 26, before two thousand delegates from all the soviets, it was Stalin who in his dull voice
pronounced a series of pledges in the form of litanies: "As he
left us, Comrade Lenin ordered us to stand guard over the
unity of the party as over the pupils of our eyes. We swear to
you, Comrade Lenin, that we will fulfill that command of
yours with honor. . . . We swear to you. . . . We swear to
you. . . ."

The crowds that gathered on the following day to watch the
coffin pass, while sirens wailed from every factory in Moscow,
had no idea that party unity at the summit was already no
more than a myth. The militants themselves did not yet suspect as much; the secret was known only to a very small group.

Zinoviev, Kamenev, and Stalin had constituted a secret
"troika" that was soon to be supported by the other members
of the Politburo. There was only one mortar holding this coalition together: the determination to block the road to Trotsky.
All of them together felt that they were not too many to stand
up to the one-time Menshevik.

Two months later Rosmer arrived in Moscow to take part in
a meeting of the Executive Committee of the International.
During his earlier journeys it had been his habit to visit Zinoviev unannounced for discussions. This time the atmosphere
was no longer the same. Zinoviev, who was in his home with
Bukharin, greeted his visitor with ironic surprise.

"What is going on?" Rosmer asked.

Bukharin laughed. "Simply that one no longer comes to see
Zinoviev just like that. One must make application to the Secretariat."

The Secretariat was Stalin. The successor of Kamenev, Tomsky, and Rykov, he was the newcomer, the "ferret face." Rosmer, of course, could not have guessed it, but the great Russian comrades had to concert a plan of action in time for the
next meeting of the Politburo, at which they could confront
Trotsky with the common front of their objections and their

rejections. Rosmer was politely given to understand that he was intruding, and he was moved out the door.

Trotsky, however, had certain weapons: Lenin's "Testament" and his articles on the national question. Why did he not explode the bombshell against Stalin that Lenin had intended for the party Congress in April 1923? In order to gain time he had made a compromise with the triumvirs: Stalin would take a conciliatory stand on the Georgian question and Trotsky would have full freedom to expound his theories on economic policy.

This was a bargain that was completely to Stalin's liking: Once the commitments had been made, there would always be time to disown them. He too was relying on time, but he was miraculously adept in using it to consolidate his position. Let Trotsky say whatever he pleased, then. It was no longer on the rostrum, amid cheers, but in the unseen operations of offices that power was to be conquered.

In vain the Georgian delegates protested in the Congress against the treatment that had been given to them. Trotsky, who had promised Lenin that he would defend them, said nothing. Only Bukharin intervened on their behalf, amid the general hostility of the Russian delegates.

It is perhaps in this affirmation of Great Russian chauvinism that the explanation of Trotsky's remarkable silence must be sought. Without Lenin's support he did not dare to challenge this current. It would have meant isolating himself even more within a party dominated by Russians. It is possible, too, that Trotsky was afraid that in assuming the defense of the Georgian Communists and their "autonomist" demands he might antagonize a number of army leaders and thus at the same time impair his own position at the head of the only "apparatus" on which he could still rely.

With his customary brilliance Trotsky set forth his theories on economic problems. The NEP and the revival of a certain freedom of trade had made it possible for Russia to slip out of the chains of war Communism. The country was beginning to breathe after the horrors of the civil war and the great famine of 1921, which had brought on incidents of cannibalism.

But already there were visible symptoms of a crisis that Trotsky depicted with clarity. Industrial prices were rising more quickly than farm prices. Lacking the means to buy manufactured goods, the peasants tended to restrict their work to the satisfaction of their own needs. This was what Trotsky called the "scissors" phenomenon. If the gap between the industrial sector and the agricultural sector increased, he said, there was a danger that trade between urban and rural areas would be cut off as it had been during the period of war Communism.

The remedy that he proposed was the planning of production in order to bring down production costs. He made no secret of the fact that this policy would entail sacrifices for the working class. Here was a prime propaganda theme for his opponents, who did not neglect to point out, surreptitiously at first, that Trotsky was trying to go back to his old program for the militarization of the labor unions.

While Trotsky was making the best of his eloquence, Stalin was operating the controls of the machinery. He was already moving against his future rival, Zinoviev. Stalin was not the master of the Politburo, where Zinoviev and Kamenev controlled the majority, as they did in the Central Committee. Stalin's stronghold was the Secretariat with its antennae, the Central Control Commission, and the *Orgburo*. His first concern had been to make himself completely the master of the previous Congress. Many local and provincial commissions had been elected before he became secretary general. It was necessary that he gain control of them. On various pretexts he had matters within the jurisdiction of hostile commissions transferred to the Central Commission. He had other commissions eliminated. When he sat silently smoking his pipe after dinner in his residence in the Kremlin, he must have spent a great deal of time considering the stratagems, the ruses, and the expedients that would permit him to attain his objectives and consolidate his positions in this or that sector. Trotsky, Zinoviev, and Bukharin were not the sort of men who would discipline themselves to such dogged maneuvers.

The condition of the party was favorable to such undertakings. After the civil war it was swollen by a flood of opportunists who preferred the winning side. It had 576,000 members in 1921, against 23,600 in 1917. The purge decided on in 1921, which was to become a permanent system, might make it possible to eliminate the self-seekers and, as well, those who for one reason or another were disliked.

Barmin, who was to become an important Soviet diplomat before he chose to defect in Greece in 1937, told of his own victimization by a purge in the Military Academy after the civil war, on the pretext that he was too young. He went to see Molotov, who arranged matters satisfactorily in a few days. Enjoying the prospect of a splendid career, he was not to be among those who would follow Trotsky when the crisis came. How many others like him there were!

Stalin's control of the apparatus made it possible for him to gain the majority in the Central Committee, which was enlarged from twenty-five to forty members. Only one of them, Rudzutak, reinforced Stalin in the Politburo. But henceforth Stalin could rely on a solid group in the Central Committee.

The success that Stalin scored in the Congress was indirectly reinforced by a serious setback for the Communist International. During the civil war the Bolshevik leaders had thought that revolution would spread like a conflagration throughout Europe. The defeat of the Spartacist movement in Berlin, the overthrow of Bela Kun in Hungary, the defeat of the Red Army outside Warsaw, and the accession of Mussolini shattered that gleaming hope.

Was this a matter of a temporary setback, a last upsurge by a bourgeoisie in its ultimate agony? At the end of 1922 it was possible to believe that the revolutionary tide would flood again. Germany was the prey of inflation, the situation was aggravated by the occupation of the Ruhr in 1923, the masses were in a state of agitation. Who was to be sent to them? Wearied by the stubborn opposition of the Politburo and still maintaining, under his theory of permanent revolution, that Socialism could not be preserved in Russia unless the revolutionary movement was extended to Europe, Trotsky suggested himself.

"Certainly not," Zinoviev, the chairman of the International, replied. "I will go."

Stalin benevolently pointed out that both these comrades were too valuable to risk their lives in dubious battle. Furious, Trotsky left the room. He intended to slam the door behind him as he went, but he failed. It was a very heavy door, he had a great deal of difficulty opening it, and as much again closing it. His theatrical exit was aborted into a movie gag.

The German revolution too was an abortion. In October 1923 the German Communists were smashed. The defeat of a revolution in Bulgaria and of a *Putsch* in Estonia, both incautiously set into motion by Zinoviev, sounded the knell of the offensive in Europe. The Revolution was locked up within the borders of the Soviet state. This setback played into Stalin's hands, and he lost no time in announcing his views on building Socialism in one country.

Meanwhile agitation was reviving in certain party cells, encouraged by the "wildcat" strikes that broke out in factories during the summer of 1923. Small clandestine cells were set up. As early as the end of 1922 the miniature organization called Workers' Truth was denouncing the party functionaries as the "new bourgeoisie." In the leaflets that it distributed, this group contended that "the dictator class is in fact devoid of the most elementary political rights." The next year there was the Workers' Group, which accused the party of having established "not the dictatorship of the proletariat but the dictatorship of the triumvirate."

These organizations were lacking in leaders of major stature. They amounted to hardly more than a handful of men. Led by Myasnikov and Kusnetsov, the Workers' Group numbered no more than two hundred members in Moscow.

No more was needed, however, to fill the Politburo with alarm. The GPU [1] went into action, arresting some twenty persons. Thereupon its leader, Dzerzhinsky, posed this question to the members of the Politburo: "Is it the duty of a Communist who knows of opponents within the party to denounce them to the GPU?" The majority of the Politburo responded: "It is his obligation!"

Thus the police ceased to be an instrument of repression against the "class enemy." Its mission now was to act against anyone in the party's ranks who openly or covertly opposed the line laid down by the leadership. And it was the duty of every Communist to denounce the heretics to the police. This mission was to be carried out later with diligence, reaching even into the highest spheres of the party.

Trotsky, who had not spoken out against the arrests, took an ambiguous position. In his letter of October 8, 1923, to the Central Committee, a long indictment of bureaucracy in the Secretariat, he conceded that it was the duty of every member of the party to identify hostile elements operating in the cells. But it seemed to him, he wrote, extremely serious to make this an obligation imposed statutorily through a special resolution. A most specious distinction, it must be said, and one that showed the precariousness of Trotsky's position. Officially he sat at the summit of the apparatus, sharing a power that he no longer exercised; in his heart he had already joined the opposition.

A week later, on October 15, the opposition came out into the open with an explosive document known as the Manifesto of the Forty-six. This was no longer a matter of little clandestine fly-sheets; it was an open proclamation, signed by well-known names: Pyatakov, Preobrazhensky, Serebryakov, Ivan Smirnov, Ossinsky, Bubnov, V. Smirnov, Sapronov, Mura-

---

[1] The GPU (State Political Administration) had supplanted the *Cheka* in February 1922. Dzerzhinsky remained as its head.

lov, Rozengolz, Drobnis, etc. Radek endorsed it in a separate letter. Others, like Krestinsky and Rakovsky, had not signed because the Secretariat had taken pains to assign them to posts abroad—an excellent method of isolating Trotsky from his best lieutenants.

The Forty-six demanded a return to workers' democracy. Ostensibly they had made their move without any cooperation from Trotsky. But there were far too many points of convergence between their manifesto and his letter to the Central Committee for the two actions to have been fortuitous, and besides Trotsky was in constant contact with such signers as Muralov and Eltsin. But he continued to cloak himself in silence lest he be accused of having sought to bring on a formal schism.

In the Politburo the climate had turned glacial. Now Trotsky ostentatiously took an isolated seat in its meetings, opened a book, and pretended to read and take no interest in the discussion. He acted as if he did not see Zinoviev, who ignored him equally. Stalin, in contrast, made a point of warmly shaking hands with him at the start of each meeting.

In the face of the shock created by the Forty-six, the Politburo, after having protested, deemed it more prudent to open a safety valve, and it announced in December 1923 that free discussion could begin in the cells. Meanwhile the Central Committee had made a point of blaming Trotsky, regarded as "morally responsible" for these deviations.

In actuality, these often Byzantine controversies left the great mass of the population indifferent; its major concern was the solution of its urgent material problems. But in the party cells the talk rapidly assumed a tone that threatened the "troika." The opposition's theses were supported by half the votes in the Moscow cells and one-third of the votes in the army's cells; they won the backing of the students and of the Central Committee of *Komsomols*.

This was a danger signal for the triumvirs. They called out the guard—in other words, the bureaucratic powers of the "apparatus." The Central Committee of *Komsomols* was dissolved. And there was a purge of university circles.

It was at this time that a young man named Malenkov, a former *politrabotnik* (political commissar) in the eastern armies and Turkestan, attracted the attention of the party leadership with his zeal in repression. After his discharge from the army, Malenkov entered the Upper Technical School in Moscow in 1922. It was a time of great excitement among the students. Those who were not Communists were extremely active and formed political clubs that issued underground leaflets such as *The Young Proletarian* (Menshevik) and *Aspirations* (Populist in tendency). All the institutional organizations in the Upper Technical School, such as mutual aid, were in the hands of non-Bolsheviks.

Having become secretary of the Communists cell at this school and then secretary of all the cells in the whole of the *Vuz* (the institutions of higher learning in Moscow), Malenkov devoted himself to preparing lists of opponents of the system, on the basis of which, when the university year opened in the autumn of 1923, it was possible to exclude many students and to make mass arrests. This task completed, Malenkov's energies were directed, within the Communist cells themselves, against the agitation of Trotskyist students.

During the winter of 1923 the Trotskyist students in the Communist cells of the *Vuz* had won 6594 votes against 2790 for the supporters of the "troika." Once again young Malenkov's priceless lists made the required purges possible. It is highly probable that it was at this time that Stalin concluded that so gifted a man deserved to be closely watched: Malenkov was soon to become one of the members of his private secretariat—in other words, the body that in the ensuing years would enjoy the reality of power.

But the leadership was far more perturbed by the relative success of the opposition in the army's cells. In principle there was no bar to participation in controversies by Communist militants in uniform. A blunder by Antonov-Ovseyenko, Commissar for the Army and a supporter of Trotsky, gave the leaders their pretext for action. He had issued an appeal in which he called on Communist soldiers to declare themselves "as one man . . . for Trotsky, the leader, the organizer, and the soul of the victories of the Revolution." The triumvirs purported to see in this an incitement to insurrection, and Antonov-Ovseyenko was removed from his post. Since the leaders had already succeeded in having two of their own men, Voroshilov and Lashevich, appointed to the Supreme Council for National Defense, Trotsky suffered a new loss of backing in this quarter.

It was his further misfortune to be ill at this time, suffering from a malignant fever that was to get the better of him on a number of occasions during his life and of which his doctors were never to be able to cure him. Hence the Politburo held its meetings at his bedside. Through the wall his wife, Natalya Sedova, could hear him arguing vehemently. Cold, aloof voices answered him. His disdainful silence abandoned, he was exhausting his strength in a vain effort to break down a structure of hostility that was held together only by its antagonism to him. These sessions left him weak and bathed in sweat.

All the efforts of the Forty-six were crumbled by the solidity of the "apparatus." The platform of the Forty-six had united Trotsky's friends, some left Communists, and former members of the Workers' Opposition. It was not even the organized faction that it was accused of being, but, rather, a loose clan of malcontents. Furthermore, its facilities for propaganda were pitiful. Trotsky, who had just published *The New Course*—a pamphlet in which he was bitterly critical of the bureaucratic apparatus—was refused authorization for further publication by the state printing plant. But the government's presses were turning out by the millions, newspapers, leaflets, pamphlets that thundered against the heretics. In the party's Thirteenth Congress, on January 16, 1924, the opposition found itself with exactly three delegates. There were only three votes against the motion that condemned Trotsky and his supporters.[2]

Thus Trotsky was a beaten man a few days before Lenin's death. This perhaps was the true reason why he did not return to attend the funeral. A few months later, in the Thirteenth Congress, he was all but excluded. And yet in the interim Lenin's "Testament" had finally been brought to the attention of the Central Committee. The shock of this disclosure and the reading of the famous postscript were a very severe ordeal and a rare humiliation for the secretary general. The focus of every eye, the man who a few weeks earlier had poured out solemn pledges to Lenin's memory was compelled to listen to the recitation of this damning indictment. He sat modestly below the rostrum, not moving, utterly composed, taking the blow. But, according to Bazhanov, one of his secretaries, who was watching him all the time, he looked "small and miserable."

It required action by Zinoviev and Kamenev to rescue him from this dangerous situation. Undoubtedly Lenin's words were sacred, they said, but at the end of his life he was no longer quite himself. Certainly Stalin had his faults. But he had been able to correct them. The "Testament" was cast into the oblivion from which it was not to be exhumed until the Twentieth Congress thirty-two years later.

Trotsky had taken refuge in silence. Zinoviev wanted him ousted; he called for this in the Thirteenth Congress but he could not put it through. In the end Trotsky defended himself with the dignity that was natural to him. "I will accept the party's decision, whatever it may be," he said. "The party is always right, because it is the only historical instrument available to the working class for the resolution of its basic prob-

[2] The elections to the Congress had been held indirectly at successive levels: cell conferences, regional conferences, etc. At each level the secretaries took the requisite steps to skim off the oppositionists. The Forty-six contended that at the regional level they had won 36 per cent of the votes but at the next stage their share had fallen to 18 per cent.

lems." But, in all the uproar and amid all the insults, he said
that he could not acknowledge that he had been mistaken: "I
cannot say it because I do not believe it."

Thus he professed to maintain the right to his own opinion
within a party that was no longer satisfied with outward obedience but that demanded the abdication of conscience itself.
But, committed to respect for its discipline, he forbade himself to carry the controversy outside the party and seek reinforcements. There was nothing left for him but to count on
time to erode the coalition that had brought him down.

He would hardly have long to wait: Already the triumvirs
were contesting subterraneanly among themselves for the monopoly of power. But once again Trotsky maneuvered with
singular ineptness. Thoroughly defeated after the Thirteenth
Congress, he published two books, *1917* and *The Lessons of
October,* that recalled the part that each individual had played
in those decisive times—in other words, the defeatist position
of Zinoviev and Kamenev and the conciliatory proposals of
Pravda (of which Stalin was at that time the director) before
Lenin's return.

This reopened old wounds. A flood of opprobrium swept
over the "former Menshevik," documented with every circumstance in which he had opposed Lenin and accompanied by
innuendoes as to his achievements during the revolution and
the civil war. As before, newspapers, pamphlets, indignant
motions joined the chorus. Certainly Trotsky's needle-pointed
pen could deal with the self-contradictions of a Raskolnikov,
who said that on his return to Russia Trotsky "had not yet defined his position with regard to Bolshevism and Menshevism,"
whereas a year earlier he had declared that "between Lenin's
and Trotsky's tactics there was no difference." But Trotsky's
replies reached a few thousand persons; the accusations
against him influenced millions. One of the outstanding traits
of Stalin's character was his comprehension that in the modern
era the quantity of lies produced by the propaganda machine

would overwhelm the quality of the arguments evolved by a preeminent polemicist.

Trotsky was forced to resign from the Supreme War Council. Immediately Stalin called off his campaign: Now he had to face up to Zinoviev.

The anger of the peasants, subjected to unending bureaucratic persecutions, was mounting steadily. Sabotage was increasing. Physical attacks were made in the rural areas on the party functionaries and the peasant press correspondents, suspected of being informers and therefore hated. One group in the Politburo, under Bukharin's leadership, was inclined toward a policy of conciliating the land workers. Stalin too tended in this direction. Only Sokolnikov supported Zinoviev and Kamenev. "Enrich yourselves!" Bukharin had told the *NEPmani* and the *kulaki,* and to them this seemed defiance, shameful capitulation to the "renascent bourgeoisie." A new crisis erupted.

It came to a head in the Fourteenth Congress in December 1925. Zinoviev and Kamenev, though in the minority in the Politburo, were confident of victory. Zinoviev was relying on his powerful organization in Leningrad. Kamenev's authority was still great in Moscow, where, he thought, he could rely on the organization's secretary, Uglanov. Stalin had a firm grip on the Caucasus, the Urals, and the Ukraine, where Kaganovich was in command.

In theory the citadels represented by the Leningrad and Moscow organizations should have been the guaranty of victory, just as in the United States Congress reactionaries can generally rely on the collaboration between the southern Democrats and the Republicans. But, Bazhanov reported in his memoirs, a few days before the Congress he saw Uglanov going into Stalin's office. What pact was made between them? What methods had Stalin employed to win his visitor to his own cause? We do not know. The fact remains that Uglanov and, with him, the entire Moscow organization defected.

Trotsky's position during this period remains an enigma.[3] During the Fourteenth Congress he maintained an unbroken silence, siding with neither camp. Valentinov, on the basis of rumors that were circulating at the time, offered his own hypothesis: a secret understanding between Stalin and Trotsky, since Stalin needed Trotsky's agreement for changing the name of Tsaritsyn (it became Stalingrad on April 15, 1925). In exchange, Trotsky supposedly obtained appointment to the Supreme Economic Council. According to this theory, it was only when he saw that Stalin was not going to keep his promise that Trotsky would have the chairmanship of this body that Trotsky went back to the opposition in the autumn of 1925.

This was indeed the period during which Trotsky was denying the existence of a "Testament" by Lenin, extracts from which had been published by Max Eastman, the American writer, in his book, *After Lenin's Death*.

Nevertheless it is not clear why Stalin would have needed Trotsky's consent for the rechristening of a city with the secretary general's name. Having himself set the example, on what possible ground could he have contested Stalin's wishes?

It is more reasonable to believe that, in Stalin's combat against Zinoviev and Kamenev, Trotsky could not make up his mind which side to espouse. After all, it was Zinoviev and Kamenev who had most violently attacked him during this period. ("They will kill me," he confided to Suvarin in January 1925). Stalin, on the other hand, had opposed the exclusion of Trotsky.

Barely a year after Lenin's death the idea of murder as a means of resolving the problems of the succession was already in the air. No more than the idea? It is not unlikely that even at that period Stalin had cleaned house in the Commissariat

---

[3] Similarly, it is difficult to understand why Trotsky did not come back from the Caucasus to attend Lenin's funeral. Was he so seriously ill? How is it possible to think that he had allowed himself to be taken in by a telegram from Stalin?

for War by this most expeditious of means. Frunze, a veteran of the civil war and a supporter of Zinoviev, had replaced Trotsky. Did Stalin get wind of some conspiracy under way in the Commissariat, or was the mere fact that the supreme authority there was in the hands of a man who might be pledged to his adversaries enough to incite him to alarm?

Frunze was suffering from a gastric ulcer. His own physician advised against surgery, pointing out that because of his cardiac weakness Frunze could not tolerate chloroform. On Stalin's orders, however, he was compelled to submit to examination by the Kremlin's medical commission. Counter to all expectations, the commission advocated the operation. As a disciplined Bolshevik, Frunze yielded. He went from the operating table to the mortuary table.

After his death, Boris Pilnyak published a long short story with the strange title, "History of the Undying Moon," and the more explicit subtitle, "The Death of the Commander in Chief." The story was laid in an imaginary country but it very obviously resembled the Frunze case. It told of a chief of state, called Number One, or "the man with the stiff back," who ordered his commander in chief to be examined by a medical commission that recommended surgery that was anything but essential. The commander died on the operating table.

The story created a scandal. Pilnyak was compelled to acknowledge his "error." Later he was to vanish during the great purges.

Thus even at this period the bureaucracy maintained a singular grip on the militants, to such a degree that the phrase, "belonging to the party body and soul," was no longer a mere figure of speech. And for the first time the Kremlin's medical commission was openly suspected of being an instrument in the service of political crime. Those devils, the doctors, would have subsequent occasion to draw down on themselves the suspicions of all sides.

(7)

BATTLES WITHIN
THE PARTY

FTER HIS defeat in the Fourteenth Congress, Zinoviev fell back on Leningrad as if it were a fortress from which he would be able to defy the victors. This man with the fleshy proconsul's face, the party's finest speaker next to Trotsky, lived on the illusion of his influence over the masses. How many times at meetings he had reveled in the thunder: "Hurrah! Long live the Communist International! Long live Comrade Zinoviev!"

But he had led the International into the bloody defeats of Hamburg and Sofia and Reval. And the workers of Leningrad had not forgotten how harshly he had dealt with them at the time of Kronstadt. Zinoviev mistook the views of the little clan of bureaucrats who surrounded him for those of a proletariat that he had unceasingly ground down.

Within two weeks the rhetoric was silent and the vestiges of resistance had vanished. Stalin sent Gusev and Stetsky to Leningrad. In a very short time they brought everyone into step.

The Vyborg district was the first to yield. The most determined oppositionists recoiled at the prospect of resisting the decision of that Central Committee, the sanctity of which had so long been impressed on them by Zinoviev himself. The rest immediately went over to the enemy, assuming that this defection would protect their careers. Working with threats, Gusev and Stetsky set up new committees everywhere. The least of these threats was the loss of employment in a country in which more than two million workers had no jobs.

For two or three days Zinoviev's most faithful followers barricaded themselves in the offices of the Leningrad *Pravda*. Then they too surrendered. And Kirov took over the city.

In a "letter from Russia" dated December 1924 (but published by *Proletarian Revolution* in January 1926), a militant who was one of four hundred members of a factory cell in Moscow related that the cell seemed resolved to defend Trotsky against the triumvirs. "What we won't do to the delegate from the Central Committee!" the members were saying. A few days later the cell gave birth to a remarkably shapeless resolution on the subject. When the author of the letter expressed his surprise, he was told: "We decided not to take so definite a position." He asked why, and he was answered: "Why? Look, comrade, we are not children any more. We have families to support, and it would be pretty stupid to have to move to Arkhangelsk or Siberia."

In spite of this, in August the party's Regional Committee invoked the pretext of mobilization for farm work to put all the influential oppositionists' names on the departure lists. "Since then," the letter concluded, "the cell has become 'well behaved and Bolshevik.'"

The Leningrad cells displayed the same wisdom, and for the same reasons. This attitude did not prevent the dismissal of some three thousand functionaries suspected of oppositionism.

Zinoviev's fall was rather warmly greeted abroad. Stalin was viewed at that time as a moderate element. "What is Stalin's aim?" *The Observer* asked. "A good administration. This is a practical policy. This man is not a starry-eyed idealist. . . . Stalin and his associates are now in a position to continue their extension of the NEP."

Rosmer himself, in *Proletarian Revolution* for February 1926, after having criticized Zinoviev, asserted that

Stalin is a man of another temper. He is a revolutionary of character and determination. . . . He is too much the manipulator and the man of the apparatus for his policy to be of a kind that would reassure us. But this should not prevent us from recognizing that he has spoken the language of a man aware of the exigencies of the present moment and concerned to create a collective leadership embracing all the forces of the party.

As for the world's stock exchanges, they viewed the Georgian's triumph with favor. After all, it was generally understood that foreign capital could invest heavily in the Soviet Union.

A year earlier Victor Serge had returned to Russia. In his capacity as an official of the International in Vienna, he had committed the grave error of refusing to carry out a directive from Bela Kun. On his return to Leningrad, one of his friends urgently counseled him to be careful: "Do not get yourself deported for nothing, or for something trivial, a gesture, a refusal to be humiliated. . . . We are at a mysterious turning point, it is a bad time, let us husband our forces. . . ." [1]

Serge paid no attention to this advice. What he saw every day only reinforced his revulsion. Militants were committing suicide: Lutovinov, Glazman, Yevgenya Bosch. . . . Others, in contrast, were establishing themselves in luxury. Invited to a card party by Illin, Serge found his apartment filled with fine furniture dating from the time of Tsar Paul, dinner services with coats of arms, precious tapestries—all the result of the expropriations, municipalizations, and nationalizations of the property of the old aristrocracy.

A well-known writer had just been thrown out of the party: In his apartment someone had found notes such as this: "I've just got eight hundred rubles for the little pile of shit I dropped

[1] Victor Serge, *Le tournant obscur,* p. 54.

on the subject of Lenin. I found two whores and we had a hell of a drunk."

The lowest wage for workers was forty rubles a month. On this meager stipend they were privileged to stare at the fine displays in the shop windows of Leningrad. Yet the only subjects of conversation were speculation and profits and the scandal of Chubarov Lane: Eighteen young men, half of them members of the Young Communists, had raped a girl of their own age in a vacant lot.

On December 29, 1925, Essenin committed suicide in the Hotel England. He had written his last verses in his own blood:

> So long, my friend, so long
> . . . .
> If there is no novelty to dying in this life
> There is certainly no more novelty in living.

The other leader of Russian poetry, Mayakovsky, retorted:

> It is not hard to die in this life
> To make life is truly harder.

But was Mayakovsky himself so convinced that he was right and Essenin was wrong? One night Serge saw him come into the bar of the Hotel Europe, the only one that was open all night. Tall and athletic, the poet took his place at the bar.

"How are things?" someone asked him.

"How are things, shit!"

"Depressed?"

"No, but one day I'll blow my brains out. Everyone's a bastard."

In fact he did kill himself on April 14, 1930.

Victor Serge turned his back on the victors' camp. He joined the Trotskyist opposition. Not long after the trial of the Chubarov Lane rapists, Serge was approached in the Press Building by a militant named Chadayev, who said: "Tarass told me about you." This was a password.

Serge had been accepted. Meetings were held in a militant's room in the Hotel Astoria. They were attended by two or three students, two old Bolsheviks, three or four other militants. Trotsky's first wife, Ivanovna Bronstein, presided.

It was a puny opposition. Serge and Chadayev were members of the Communist cell of the *Krasnaya Gazeta,* which had about four hundred members, pressmen and linotypists. Most of them were men of Lenin's vintage who had been recruited after his death. The oppositionists were of the generation of the civil war. But there were only five of them, and one was probably a police informer.

The meetings always followed the same immutable procedure; They were held every two weeks and attendance was compulsory. The district orator made a two-hour defense of the concept of Socialism in one country. Then a dozen "activists" spoke in rotation, all approving what he had said. This proportionately limited the opposition's time: "Five minutes, Comrade Serge."

Five minutes in which to touch on all the problems that the bureaucracy wanted to hush up: agriculture, the internal government of the party, the crisis that was brewing in China after the interlude of euphoric relations with Chiang Kai-shek. Serge or Chadayev would rise to speak. "We had invented a style," Serge wrote. "We spoke in short sentences that were all questions, statements, or disclosures of facts. Each one had to make an impact, even if it stood alone, if what went before had been shouted down." [2]

For one or the other would barely have begun to speak when twenty-five or thirty voices broke out in interruptions, shouts, howls. "Enemy of the party!" This frenzy stood out against the amorphous silence of the rest of the audience, which was content to observe the unequal struggle.

[2] *Ibid.,* p. 104.

The outcome was always the same. When the time came for the vote, a forest of arms sprang up to approve the party's positions. "Those against?" Serge and Chadayev alone raised their hands; the three other oppositionists in the cell were under orders not to expose themselves.

It was an exhausting business, repeated every two weeks, and it affected neither the believers' hostility nor the neutrals' fear of compromising themselves.

Would the defeat suffered by the partisans of Kamenev and Zinoviev alter the conditions of combat by inducing them to join the Trotskyist opposition? Zinoviev and Kamenev did in fact decide to pay a visit to Trotsky in order to propose that all three form a bloc against Stalin.

They acknowledged their misdeeds: It was the opposition that had been right. Convincingly they informed Trotsky of the details of the secret coalition against him that they had mounted in concert with Stalin. But had not Trotsky himself erred in criticizing their 1917 position instead of attacking Stalin?

They painted a frightening portrait of the secretary general, even imitating his voice and mimicking his postures, and this did not fail to antagonize Trotsky. They depicted Stalin as a cruel torturer, capable of anything. Knowing this, they had deposited in a safe place letters in which they stated that, if they should disappear, Stalin would have to be held accountable. When Trotsky spoke of Stalin's *conceptions,* Kamenev interrupted: "You don't understand at all. Stalin doesn't give a damn for ideas. Only one thing interests him: power. He would gladly have got rid of you in 1923 or 1924. If he did not, it was because he was afraid that someone would rise up out of the Trotskyist ranks to avenge you."

Trotsky could have reminded them that they had adjusted quite well to the companionship of a man whom they described as a devil and that after all Zinoviev had not scrupled to call for Trotsky's head, or very nearly. But it was to his political interest to make an alliance with these men or to attempt to arrive at an understanding with Stalin or Bukharin, both of whom were making advances to him now that he was no longer a threat to them. After having undoubtedly hesitated,[3] he opted for the alliance with Zinoviev and Kamenev, who, like him, were opposed to the party's rural policies.

"With you we are certain to win," Zinoviev and Kamenev said. "It will be enough for the three of us to appear at meetings together, and Stalin will be swept out." They added that Lashevich, Voroshilov's deputy in the Commissariat for War, was backing them. Undoubtedly they expected to receive some support from this quarter.

Trotsky was less optimistic. But he believed that the news of their reconciliation would not only lead to the strengthening of their respective forces but also, operating like yeast, rally a number of the faithful to their side.

Not everyone among his intimates shared this point of view. Antonov-Ovseyenko and Radek would have preferred an alliance with Stalin. Mrachkovsky was opposed to any coalition. "Stalin will betray us," he said, "and Zinoviev will run out on us." Others such as Victor Serge, who had hurried to Moscow, raised arguments of a practical nature. The Trotskyists' underground organization in Leningrad was small in number but reliable. The Zinovievists professed to be able to furnish five or six hundred members in that city. But it would be necessary to effect a fusion with people who hardly inspired confidence, and there would be no guaranties against possible betrayals.

Comparable reservations were manifested on the part of

[3] It would appear that at the time of the Fourteenth Congress negotiations had been initiated with Stalin and Bukharin. Antonov-Ovseyenko wrote to Trotsky: "I know that you were preparing to move against Zinoviev and Kamenev in the Congress. I regretted and deeply deplored the fact that the impatience and short-sightedness of our friends in the fraction impelled you, not without some resistance on your part, to abandon this intervention on which you had previously decided" (quoted by Suvarin in *Stalin*, p. 388). These hesitations in selecting an alliance show how the puny extent to which doctrinal positions that were later confirmed in decisive fashion could operate against maneuvers that derived from the party's internal machinations.

Zinoviev's supporters. For years the Trotskyists had been denounced and now it would be required to make an agreement
with them.

At this point Trotsky fell ill once more and went to Berlin
for treatment. Battle could not be given until he returned in
June of 1926.

The struggle went on for eighteen months, waged with remarkable bitterness on both sides under conditions of complete confusion. Trotsky denounced Stalin as the friend of the
kulaks, but it was Stalin who liquidated them a few years
later. Stalin attacked Trotsky as the champion of super-indus-
trialization, but it was Stalin who, without any mercy for the
sufferings of the country, ordered that everything be dedicated
to the success of the Five-Year Plan.

The party's entire policy, both internal and external, was
made the issue. The outcome of this conflict involved the fate
not only of a country of one hundred sixty million persons
but also of the international Communist movement in the
whole world.

Yet, with infrequent exceptions, the struggle proceeded before an audience that was both formless and muzzled. Within
the party itself, which at that time had seven hundred fifty
thousand members, only seven to eight thousand militants
were mobilized on the side of Trotsky and Zinoviev. Their
Stalinist and Bukharinist opponents, *playing an active part*,
were probably hardly more numerous. But they enjoyed the
tremendous advantage of occupying an excellent strategic position in the "apparatus."

The oppositionist forces openly launched their struggle in
July of 1926 at the summit of the "apparatus"—in other words,
in the Central Committee. Trotsky fired the first round by
stating that Zinoviev, Kamenev, and himself, burying their differences, would henceforth constitute the party's left wing,
which would defend the interests of the working class against
the kulaks, the *NEPmani,* and the bureaucrats. In the realm
of foreign policy this left wing would oppose the opportunist

common front established with the Social Democrats and the reformist labor unions.[4]

It was in this session that Dzerzhinsky, after a long, vehement denunciation of Kamenev delivered in a tone of hysteria, died of a heart attack as he left the speaker's rostrum.

The majority of the Central Committee replied to the criticisms. But Stalin's counterattack consisted chiefly in using the resolutions that had been adopted at the Tenth Congress to accuse the opposition of setting up a fraction. This fraction, he said, tended to establish itself outside the party in order to combat it from without. Furthermore the Central Committee exploited to the full the presence of Lashevich at a clandestine meeting, a *massovska*[5] held in a woods near Moscow. Indeed Lashevich, who was a Vice Commissar for War, had spoken at the meeting. A GPU agent who had been infiltrated into the opposition had reported his presence.

Thus, even at its first public appearance, the opposition encountered a series of obstacles that it could not overcome. Some obstacles were political: If it defended its positions publicly within the party, it was accused of violating the statutes that Zinoviev, Kamenev, and Trotsky themselves had adopted: if it endeavored to seek help outside the party itself, it would then be setting up an anti-party organization. There was also a practical obstacle: It had to deal with a vast intelligence network whose agents had been infiltrated into its ranks.

This first encounter quickly became a defeat. One of the members of the opposition, Ossovsky, a member of the Central Committee, had in fact contended that the opposition ought to organize itself as an independent party. Ossovsky was expelled from the party and repudiated by Trotsky. Lashevich was also expelled from the Central Committee and the Commissariat

[4] Trotsky especially criticized the Anglo-Soviet Council, established through an agreement between the two countries' trade unions, as an abandonment of the class struggle.

[5] *Massovska* was the term used for secret meetings that were held in forests under the tsars.

for War. Zinoviev was expelled from the Politburo, a step that paved the way for his ouster from the presidency of the International. Only Trotsky remained in the Politburo, where Kamenev had already been reduced to the rank of an alternate.

Beaten at the summit, the opposition turned for revenge to the base, distributing pamphlets and leaflets and making speeches at meetings of cells. Smilga went to Leningrad to explain to the Trotskyists why they must ally themselves with the Zinovievists. He spoke in a small bedroom, standing on a stool round which forty persons crowded. Outside the door a gigantic Latvian stood guard.

The leaders of the opposition decided to go into the factories. There they collided with teams of bruisers and hecklers whom Ryutin, one of Stalin's supporters, had recruited and who were moved from one factory to another by truck. At the Aviapribor works Radek was able to speak only three minutes.

Trotsky managed to speak a little longer. But, when it came to the vote, the chairman of the meeting read a resolution that faithfully reflected the views of the majority and then he posed only one question: "Anyone opposed?" Not a hand went up.

Those who might have dared to record such a vote were rare. But the opposition's defeat stemmed from other causes besides the heckling from Stalin's hooligans or the fear of losing one's job. The newspapers did not miss the opportunity to revive the reciprocal insults that Zinoviev and Trotsky had traded. Their sudden alliance seemed as artificial as the later coalition of "no" votes in France against de Gaulle. And, when they called for democracy in the party, there were many who remembered that the men who were championing so virtuous a principle had been the first to suppress it.

A correspondent of *Proletarian Revolution* wrote at this period,

It is true that every Communist opting for the opposition was certain to lose his job if he was a worker and to be sent to Turkestan or Siberia if he was more or less "responsible." But none of this

would have been effective if there had been confidence in the opposition. That it was able to gain only some five hundred votes out
of more than fifty thousand in Moscow or Leningrad was proof not
of a discussion in which the majority had triumphed but of the
scornful indifference of the bulk of the party toward the leaders
giving battle.[6]

Serge, in Leningrad, looked toward the future with pessi-
mism. One day he went to Moscow. He was received by Trotsky, once again a prey to malaria, his skin yellow, his lips
bloodless, his hair already turning white. Serge told him that
in Leningrad the opposition had been able to rally only a few
hundred members and the broad mass of the workers took no
interest in the bitter controversies. "I saw that he knew this
much better than I," Serge wrote. "But, just as a leader ought
to do his duty, so we revolutionaries ought to do ours. If defeat was inevitable, what could we do other than face it with
courage?"

Can we win? This was the question that Serge asked of
Trotsky as the comrades in the cells asked it of Serge. When
Serge was talking with four or five undergrounders who had
changed streetcars several times before they reached the meeting place—an embankment near a road or a little woods near
a cemetery—all that he could say in reply to their anxious
questions was: "The fight will be a long one." Their faces hard-
ened. Their determination mounted. But the same sentence
spoken to a larger audience chilled the air.

As for Zinoviev, he was already discouraged. Trotsky, in
contrast, was inspired by problems. Now that he had emerged
from his silence, he threw all his strength into the battle,
which he was to carry on from deportation and exile and
which would end only with his death.

But for the moment the opposition was in danger of blowing
up. Zinoviev and Kamenev wanted to lay down their arms.
Others, in contrast, especially those who came from the ranks
of the Workers' Opposition, thought that the party had be-

[6] Letter of a correspondent to *Proletarian Revolution* in 1927.

trayed the revolution and therefore a new party must be established. They saw clearly that the bureaucracy had become a
new bourgeoisie. Trotsky himself had not decided to go that
far.

In order to prevent the opposition from disintegrating, Trotsky accepted the notion of a truce, which he and Zinoviev offered in the Politburo on October 4, 1926. The opposition was
not abandoning its positions, but it was pledging itself to ab-
stain from fractional activity. It dissociated itself from the former leaders of the Workers' Opposition, such as Shlyapnikov
and Medvedyev.

Stalin agreed. Thereupon Max Eastman released Lenin's
famous "Testament" to *The New York Times,* which published
it on October 18. Stalin, driven into a rage, raised the cry of
treason.[7] The truce was broken. Debate in the Politburo had
never been so violent. Stalin declared that he was going to denounce the opposition as a Social-Democratic menace. Trotsky
retorted angrily: "The first secretary of the party is announcing his candidacy as the gravedigger of the revolution!"

Zinoviev and Kamenev turned against Trotsky: He should
never have provoked Stalin with such vehemence. Pyatakov
was of the same opinion. Trotsky's wife wrote in her memoirs
that Pyatakov was pale and trembling when he arrived at
their apartment in the Kremlin.

"Why, why did Lev Davidovich say that?" Pyatakov demanded.
"Stalin will never forgive him for it, not even to the third or fourth
generation!" He was so agitated that he could not rationally describe the scene at which he had just been present. Trotsky himself
arrived a moment later. Pyatakov went back to his lamentations:
"Why did you do it? why?" With a wave of his hand Lev Davidovich brushed aside all questions. He was exhausted but calm. . . .
We recognized that the rupture was final." [8]

[7] A few months earlier, when the opposition was still confident of victory, Krupskaya had given the text of Lenin's "Testament" to Boris
Suvarin in Paris. Suvarin passed it on to Eastman.

[8] Victor Serge, *Vie et mort de Trotski,* p. 180.

The next day the Central Committee expelled Trotsky from the Politburo and Zinoviev from the presidency of the International. The party's Fifteenth Congress opened on the same day. Stalin denounced the heretics from top to bottom for hours. The cheers that spurred him on were soon transformed to protests of horror when the oppositionists attempted to defend themselves. "We are no longer in the Middle Ages!" Kamenev shouted. "Witchcraft trials are a thing of the past. . . ." Zinoviev, whimpering, was hooted into silence. Only Trotsky imposed his personality, dominating that sinister mass that could not help listening to him.

Sarcastic and savage, Bukharin resorted to mockery. Let Trotsky say again that Stalin was the gravedigger of the revolution! Did the opposition talk about tragedy? What was going on? It was a farce. It begged the party to avert the crisis of a schism? Why, it was reduced to three men. "There's the entire schism!" The whole audience burst into laughter and Stalin shouted: "Bravo, Bukharin! Perfect! This is no refutation, it is a slaughter!"

The defections began. Shlyapnikov and Medvedyev, bitterly disillusioned at having been deserted by the opposition, rallied to Stalin. Lenin's widow, Krupskaya, did likewise. It was crushing.

The winter was quiet. The opposition was muzzled. Any initiative that Trotsky might have taken would only have isolated him even more from Zinoviev and Kamenev. He must wait for something to happen either at home or abroad: a break between Stalin and Bukharin, for instance—in other words, between the center and the right—on the policy to be adopted toward the peasants. But it was in the domain of foreign affairs that the opportunity arose.

Defeated in Europe, the revolution was apparently certain to triumph in China. In 1924 the Chinese Communist party had gone back into the ranks of the Kuomintang, in which Moscow's agents—Borodin and Blücher—were playing important parts in the guise of technical advisers. But Chiang Kai-shek, perturbed by the mounting strength of the Chinese Communists, was preparing to liquidate them. Informed of this, the leaders of the Chinese Communist party had several times requested permission from Moscow to leave the Kuomintang and organize themselves against a growing danger. Each time they were told to continue their alliance with Chiang.

On April 12, 1927, Chiang took the offensive in Shanghai. Without mercy he liquidated the Communists and the revolutionary workers. The operation claimed many thousands of victims.

A few days earlier, in a speech delivered in a Moscow theater before three thousand militants, Stalin had incautiously boasted: "I will squeeze Chiang Kai-shek like a lemon and then I will throw him out!" He had barely time to prevent the publication of an article that praised the "wise" tactics that he had employed. The crushing defeat of Shanghai turned against him.

As for Trotsky, he had warned a few days earlier that Chiang's violent action was imminent. Immediately he attacked in the Executive Committee of the International.

Stalin responded with his customary administrative measures, scattering the chief members of the opposition among remote provincial assignments and diplomatic posts abroad. He had made up his mind to achieve the expulsion of his adversaries, or at least of Trotsky, before the session of the Fifteenth Congress.

Actually new cracks were appearing already inside the government coalition because of the peasant question, which was constantly deteriorating. Stalin wanted to have a clear field on his left in order to be able to liquidate the rightists.

The violence intensified on both sides. It was at this time—for reasons that have never been fully explained—that Trotsky made his famous "Clemenceau declaration" in a letter written to Ordzhonikidze on July 11:

At the start of the imperialist war the French bourgeoisie was in the hands of a government of incompetents, a government lacking both a head and feet. Clemenceau and his group were members of the opposition. In spite of the war and the military censorship, in spite of the Germans, who were within fifty miles of Paris (Clemenceau said: "Precisely because of that!"), he launched a fierce attack against the weakness and the *petit-bourgeois* indecisiveness of the government and demanded that the war be fought with the utmost bourgeois cruelty and ferocity. In so doing Clemenceau did not betray his class, the bourgeoisie. Quite the contrary: He was serving it, more honestly, more firmly, more resolutely, and more wisely than Viviani, Painlevé & Co. The course of events was the proof. Clemenceau's group took over the government, and, thanks to a more coherent policy—a policy of imperialist pillage—it gained the victory.

This was the model on which Trotsky intended to align himself in the event of war. He believed that Stalin's crew would be incompetent to lead the country to victory. Therefore the opposition would combat it with increased intensity. It would do everything to take over the government.

This document was to prove to be of major importance, for, when the great Moscow trials began, it was to serve as the foundation on which to accuse the Trotskyists of preparing for defeat in the event of war and working in the service of the German government. Thus Trotsky armed his worst enemy with the weapons for his own future destruction.

In any event, the Clemenceau declaration aroused a storm as soon as it appeared, and the opposition was accused of seeking to prepare for a *coup d'état* in the event of war. Somewhat later Trotsky was to explain that nothing of the sort was the case. Clemenceau had acceded to power in the most legal manner possible by a vote of Parliament. There was no Parliament in the Soviet Union. But the decision would be made by the majority of the Central Committee, which, in accordance with its statutes, would overthrow Stalin.

Trotsky's line of argument on this point was not the most

convincing. He had often enough had the opportunity to observe that the Central Committee, composed of Stalin's crea-
tures, endorsed the secretary general by massive majorities on
which his own reasoning regularly shattered. The Stalinists
were therefore led to the conclusion that, since Trotsky could
not seriously count on an about-face by the Central Committee, he was indeed envisaging a violent overthrow. Deutscher
pointed out that at this time, when Trotsky published his famous declaration, a group of military leaders addressed a secret declaration to the Politburo in which they proclaimed
their solidarity with the opposition. It was signed by, among
others, Muralov, who had just been removed from his post as
Inspector General of the army; Putna, Yakir, and other generals. All the three named were to be executed some ten
years later, like Tukhachevsky, who had signed nothing.

Stalin must have thought that there was no need to look
elsewhere for the forces on which Trotsky would rely for support in the event of war.

With a view to the next Congress, the opposition decided
to publish a "platform" that would summarize its positions.
It called on its supporters to countersign this platform. "If we
can gather thirty thousand signatures," Zinoviev asserted,
"nothing will be able to prevent it from being discussed in the
Congress." With difficulty four to five thousand names were
obtained.

It was at this time that the business of Wrangel's officer occurred. Suddenly the press disclosed that on the night of September 12–13, 1927, the GPU had broken into an opposition
printing establishment where militants were at work with
nonparty counterrevolutionaries. A former officer of Wrangel
was mixed up in the affair. Thus the proof was complete: The
opposition was compounding with the White Guards in order
to create a conspiracy.

Trotsky and Zinoviev raced to Menzhinsky, the chief of the
GPU, and demanded that he produce his "evidence." Menzhinsky was compelled to open his records. The printing plant

itself consisted of a place where there were a few typewriters and duplicating machines. The report filed with the GPU came down to this:

On September 12, 1927, the GPU learned that a certain citizen, Shcherbatov, son of a former manufacturer, nonparty, had asked a former officer of Wrangel to obtain a duplicating machine for him. At almost the same time it was learned that one Tversky, an office worker, nonparty, who maintained close relations with Shcherbatov, had informed the same person that a military *coup d'état* would very soon be organized in the USSR.

As a result of this information the GPU had searched Shcherbatov's premises and discovered an "illegal printing plant." The record continued:

"The GPU conceived it to be its duty to impound this literature, and, after the discovery of the connection between Shcherbatov and Tversky, to arrest all nonparty individuals involved in this matter. Given the special character of the matter (the organization of a military *coup d'état*) and the necessity for a speedy clarification, the GPU also felt constrained to undertake searches in the premises of members of the party who, according to what emerged from the searches, were in contact with the illegal organization of Shcherbatov and Tversky. It goes without saying that none of the party members was arrested."

The investigation was continued "in the light of the fact that the declarations of the nonparty individuals confirmed the existence of a group that had assumed the mission of organizing the above-mentioned military *coup d'état*."

But who then was this officer of Wrangel's? Deluged with questions, Menzhinsky refused to answer. All that he could say was that this man "has already assisted the GPU more than once in unmasking White Guard conspiracies. It was thanks to his efforts, for instance, that the weapons storehouse of the counterrevolutionary Savinkov organization was discovered. He has also helped the GPU to find persons who had taken part in various military conspiracies." [9]

It was obvious: The officer of Wrangel was a *provocateur* working for the GPU. There was every reason to believe that it was he who had proposed the idea of a military conspiracy.

But it is also reasonable to suppose that the opposition and certain members of the military apparatus maintained connections that had always aroused great anxiety among the leaders of the party.[10] This had to do with the recruitment of the officers' corps. After the civil war, the majority of its members still came from the officers of the imperial forces, who were replaced progressively as the training of young Communist officers proceeded. And it was well known that Trotsky had always championed the "specialists."

There is no evidence that Trotsky ever wanted to turn to them. His own ideas, at the time when he was Commissar for War, impelled him to reject the notion of a Bonapartist *coup d'état*, which in his eyes was the prelude to a kulak victory. Moreover, it is probable that with a few exceptions the majority of the former officers felt no particular sympathy with him: He had made them march only by taking their families as hostages.

But the genuinely revolutionary sector of the higher ranks of the army was composed of Bolshevik intellectuals who had distinguished themselves during the civil war. They could not remain indifferent to the controversies that were tearing the party asunder. Probably divided among themselves, they nevertheless represented a circle receptive to the thinking of the opposition. Since they were not "safe," they automatically constituted a potential threat to the leadership. Stalin would remember this ten years later.

[9] Cf. *"Contre le courant,"* Nos. 5 and 6, December 30, 1927.

[10] Before the GPU carried out its search, Okhotnikov, a high officer of the Red Army, had appeared in full-dress uniform, the Order of Lenin on his tunic, to disperse the GPU agents posted at the suspect quarters. He accomplished little. The GPU returned in force the next day. On this subject cf. Serge, *Le tournant obscur,* p. 120.

Was it as a result of complicity—this time in the ranks of the militia—that Trotsky and Zinoviev were finally able to obtain a mass demonstration in their favor during an official celebration? Trotsky wrote in *My Life* that he and Zinoviev were wandering through the streets of Leningrad in order to observe the state of mind of the population, which was taking part in a demonstration organized in October for the meeting of the Central Executive Committee of Leningrad. At one point their car was halted by a barricade. "The commander of the troops hurried over to our car and spontaneously suggested taking us to the speakers' stand. We were still trying to make up our minds when two columns of militiamen were already clearing a path for us to the last truck that was still unoccupied." [11] Was this officer really behaving spontaneously? Or had the entire maneuver been arranged in advance? It would seem rather too simple to think that the two leaders had been taken against their will, so to speak, to this improvised platform.

The fact remained that, as soon as they appeared, the tone of the demonstration changed. "The masses moved disinterestedly past the first trucks without replying to the greetings that were made from them and hastened toward us."

In a period of defeat the slightest counter-tendency seems gravid with miracles. Zinoviev was enthusiastic. Trotsky was more reserved. "It was a silent and almost desperate demonstration," he wrote.

Nonetheless the opposition decided to make the most of this success and to go into the streets for the commemoration of October in Moscow and Leningrad. It would parade with banners bearing its own slogans.

The members of the opposition marched in both cities on November 7. In Moscow they unfurled banners on which their "seditious" slogans stood out in white letters against red backgrounds: "Down with the wealthy peasants, the merchants,

---

[11] Platforms for the officials had been mounted on these trucks.

the bureaucrats! . . . Let us carry out Lenin's 'Testament'!" But the Leningrad experience had been a lesson to the leaders. Ryutin's "toughs," the constabulary corps, hastened up, truncheons in their fists. They struck (seven banners were seized). Two shots were fired at Trotsky's car. A drunken fireman made his way out of the crowd, shattered a window of the car, and spat out a torrent of insults. All the groups were quickly and violently dispersed.

Smilga, a member of the Central Committee, had hung two portraits from his balcony: Lenin and Trotsky. The doors of his apartment were broken down. A gang of toughs stormed in, knocked him about, tore the two portraits to bits, and broke his furniture.

That night, with his friends, Ryutin boasted of the success of his methods: "There's nothing more to talk about. Got to break their necks."

In Leningrad the police hurled back the oppositionists' procession between the caryatid gates of the Hermitage and the old Archives building. Caught in the crowd, Serge shouted the names of Zinoviev and Trotsky. He was accompanied only by his wife and their child. His shouts fell into a frightened silence. Activists ran up to him. He was wearing a leather jacket, and only figures of some importance could afford this luxury. The toughs hesitated to let him have it: There might be trouble for them.

In an instant a great void had opened round him. A lone student moved into it. "Walk!" he said. "I'll walk behind you to make sure that no one hits you from behind."

Elsewhere, on the Khalturin Street bridge, mounted militiamen and a few hundred demonstrators were battling. The demonstrators were led by Bakayev and Lashevich. They and a few others dragged a militiaman out of his saddle. Blows were struck on both sides, but there was never any doubt of the outcome.

This day tolled the doom of the opposition.

Serge went to Moscow. Zinoviev was still in the Kremlin,

expecting to be expelled at any moment. Trotsky preferred to take the first step: He was moving out. In another room Radek, among a heap of books, was sorting and burning papers. "We've been idiots," he said with a laugh. "We don't have a penny, and we could have picked up a handsome war chest. Now our lack of money is the death of us. With our famous revolutionary integrity we've been nothing but intellectuals full of scruples."

That night, November 16, Yoffe, one of the leading oppositionists, put a bullet into his own head. The opposition staged its last demonstration behind his coffin. It was a gray, snowy day. The procession was moving slowly beneath a forest of red flags. Trotsky and Ivan Smirnov marched at its head. At the gate of the cemetery the militiamen sought to bar everyone except delegations, but gave up in fear of an outbreak. At the grave a functionary presented the official condolences of the Central Committee. "Out with him!" some of the mourners murmured. Rakovsky began to speak: "We will follow this flag as you have done. Whatever happens. . . ." Many things that Rakovsky did not suspect were going to happen.

Angry murmurs against official speeches had risen in the same cemetery during the winter of 1920 as well, when Kropotkin was buried. Then there were banners that proclaimed: "No poison is worse than power." For that ceremony the Bolsheviks had agreed to extract two anarchists, Yarchuk and Baron, from their prison for a few hours. In those days Trotsky and his supporters were hunting down anarchists. Now they themselves were the pariahs.

Ten years earlier Trotsky had led the insurrection to victory in Petrograd. Now his downfall was certain. He would not speak to the Congress.

A few days later he mounted the rostrum for the last time before the Plenum of the Central Committee and the Control Commission, surrounded by a flood of hate. Below the rostrum fifteen comrades stood as a rampart, at their head the rough Evdokimov. Yaroslavsky hurled a heavy book at his head.

"You cannot read your books any more," Trotsky remarked, ✳
"but they are still good for putting people to sleep."

He spoke with a steady voice. The tumult mounted round
him. Shouts blended from every direction. His words were
constantly mangled by angry outcries. Better than any commentary, the stenographic transcript of this session describes
the ruthless fury.

Petrovsky: A revolting speech, a Menshevik speech. It's really horrible.

Skrypnyk: What infamies you utter, Trotsky.

Voroshilov: This is the limit. . . .

Skrypnyk: What's the point of listening to him? It is only a continuous insult to the Central Committee. [Shouts, yells.]

Baluchin: He reads *The Socialist Courier* [the newspaper of the
Menshevik emigrants in New York]!

Various: Menshevik!

Trotsky: . . . Today we have been served up one of those pepper
pots [12] in the shape of information about the military conspiracy.
[Outcries.]

Various: Menshevik! That's enough!

Trotsky: Under Lenin's leadership . . . the secretary general played
a completely subordinate part. The situation began to change
when Lenin became ill. The selection of men by this secretariat
and the accumulation of Stalinists in the "apparatus" have assumed a character independent of the political line. That is why
Lenin, thinking of his retirement, gave the party his supreme
counsel: Remove Stalin, who can lead the party to schism and
destruction. [Shouts.]

Skovtzov-Stepanov: An old slander.

Thalberg: What a braggart! What a loud-mouth!

Various: Shameful!

Skrypnyk: How low he has sunk! What an outrage!

Petrovsky: You're a contemptible Menshevik!

---

[12] An allusion to Lenin's comment on Stalin: "This fellow will cook
us up nothing but spicy stews." The military conspiracy was the case of
Wrangel's officer.

Kalinin: Petit-bourgeois! Radical!

A voice: Martov! [13]

Various: Down with him! What filth! Menshevik! Traitor! We must not listen to him! What slanders against the Central Committee!

As the tumult mounted, Trotsky gripped the lectern, denouncing the zigzag policy of the center that tended sometimes rightward, sometimes leftward, though in his own view actually rightward.

"A mass for the repose of Trotsky's soul!" Yaroslavsky cried. "Funeral march!" someone else shouted. The catcalls and hoots increased. "Listen to this vileness, Zinoviev!" Voroshilov yelled. More catcalls and hooting followed. "Gravedigger of the revolution! For shame! Down with him! Down with the swine! Down with the renegade!"

"Enrich yourselves [14] today!" Trotsky taunted; "but tomorrow . . . no one will get anything from the kulaks. . . . Behind the bureaucrats the bourgeoisie is coming back to life." Again he was cut off by angry shouts, and Voroshilov cried: "That's enough! Shame!"

The jeers, the hoots, and the whistles increased. It was utter chaos: No one could be heard. The chairman rang his bell, and there was more whistling. "Get off the rostrum!" various voices cried. The chairman announced that the meeting was adjourned. Comrade Trotsky continued with his speech, but now not a word could be understood. The members of the Plenum left their seats and began to depart. [15]

"Yoffe's life, not his suicide, should be the model for those whom he has left behind. The struggle goes on. Every one is at his station. Let no man desert!" This was the call with which Trotsky had concluded his address at Yoffe's grave. Facing the Central Committee and the attack against him he had shown that nothing could hobble his vigor. He would carry on the struggle until his last breath.

[13] One of the major Menshevik leaders.
[14] Bukharin's slogan.
[15] Cf. *Pravda*, November 2, 1927.

Zinoviev and Kamenev, for their part, broke ranks. On December 18 they went before the Congress to make their act of submission. They abandoned their own "erroneous and anti-Leninist conceptions."

Bukharin laughed: "And about time. The iron curtain of history is descending at this very moment."

Nonetheless they were made to do penance for six months. Thereafter the Central Committee would decide whether the offenders had earned release from their purgatory.

Trotsky, who had refused to appear before the Congress, was expelled, and fifteen hundred oppositionists were ousted later. Twenty-five hundred signed a statement of recantation.

Expulsion meant deportation. Trotsky knew that he was spending his last hours in Moscow. His little bedroom lined with books, maps, and papers was bustling with the incessant stir that precedes major departures. Comrades were coming to see him from every part of the country, and the telephone was ringing incessantly. Outside other Trotskyists stood guard, themselves under surveillance by GPU agents. Trotsky and his supporters mingled their hurried talks with his dictation of messages and quick replies over the telephone. His features were drawn and his hair was now almost white; his skin had the yellow of malaria. He was charged with inexhaustible energy.

On January 12 the GPU informed him that, under Article LXVIII, which punished counterrevolutionary activities, he would be deported to Alma-Ata in Turkestan, not far from the Chinese border. The time of his departure was fixed at ten o'clock on the night of January 16.

That day Trotsky and his family waited in vain for someone to come to fetch them. The reason for the delay was explained by Rakovsky and some of his friends. Aroused by the rumors of his deportation, a crowd had invaded the railway station, and men were stretched out on the tracks. The government did not want the departure of its most savage enemy to turn into an uprising.

The GPU men came a day later. They had to break down the door, which Trotsky refused to open. Their leader had been his bodyguard in the days of the famous armored train. When he stood face to face with Trotsky, he collapsed: "Kill me, Comrade Trotsky!" he begged.

"You have orders," Trotsky replied; "obey them." But to the very end he himself offered passive resistance. The GPU men had to dress him and carry him to the police car that took him at high speed to the Yaroslav station.

The station was surrounded by soldiers. Not a single traveler was on the platforms. On one track there was a lone carriage. It was to this car that the GPU squad took former Comrade Trotsky, while his younger son, Serge, traded blows with a guard and his elder son, Lev, attempted in vain to stir into action the few witnesses to this historic scene: a handful of railway workers silenced by indifference or fear.

(8)

"THE TRUST," THE HOPE
OF THE WHITE EXILES

═══════════════════

W HAT WAS happening to the Whites? Their leaders, their officers, and a large part of their troops had been swept up into emigration at the end of the civil war. In exile they had been reunited with all sorts of people who had fled or were still fleeing the Soviet system: leaders of political parties—Cadets, Mensheviks, Revolutionary Socialists, even anarchists like Makhno—; members of the social classes persecuted by the Bolsheviks—landowners, industrialists, financiers, members of the liberal professions, etc.—; and, too, others who had been unable to make an adjustment with the onerous censorship—journalists, actors, scholars. To these were added the representatives of various national minorities—Petlyura's Ukrainians, Armenians, Georgians.

In the years that followed the civil war, the emigration as a whole represented a quite impressive number of people, though the figure has always been approximate rather than exact. In 1932 the Special Refugee Committee of the League of Nations calculated it at 844,000 persons, of whom 150,000 were in Slavic countries, 120,000 were in countries bordering on Russia, and 400,000 were in France. Still others who had

(123)

escaped from Siberia had settled in Manchuria and China.

The majority of these exiles cherished the hope of an imminent return to their homeland after the collapse of the Bolshevik system, of which they were more than confident. This was virtually the only conviction that they shared in common. Otherwise the harsh law of exile only accentuated and exacerbated the inevitable political, philosophical, and religious differences among them, envenomed even more by the classic conflicts of personalities.

The Mensheviks, the Revolutionary Socialists, and the Cadets confined their activities to information, propaganda, and the maintenance of a certain political line. Thus the Menshevik organ, *Sozialitishetsky Vestnik* (*Socialist Courier*), which was published in New York and which counted as its major collaborators Dan, Abramovich, Nikolayevsky, and Slomon Schwarz, became an invaluable source of information on what was really occurring in the USSR.

The monarchists, on the other hand, believed in the feasibility of vigorous activity waged from abroad to bring down the government in short order. Much divided on the choice of a successor to Nicholas II, adhering to rival groups, they had finally established a "Supreme Monarchist Council" in Berlin.

But the spearhead of the active battle against Bolshevism was still the rank and file of veterans of the Volunteer Army. After his defeat in the Isthmus of Perekop in the Crimea in 1920, Wrangel had managed to evacuate some 135,000 persons, including 70,000 soldiers and officers, on 126 ships. The troops had at first been billeted in military camps on the peninsula of Gallipoli and the Island of Lemnos and then had emigrated to Bulgaria, Yugoslavia, and France. Now they were working as miners, factory labor, and taxi drivers. But at night they gathered in their clubs, and for solemn occasions they put on their old, often mended uniforms again, talked about their recollections, and fantasied enterprises of revenge. Under Wrangel's forceful leadership they had preserved their

discipline and their ranks.[1] In September 1923 Wrangel established the ROVS (Russian Inter-Forces Union), which numbered twenty-five thousand veterans of the civil war. Retaining
for himself the political leadership of this organization, he
assigned its technical command to an energetic officer who favored direct action against the Soviets, employing if necessary
the old revolutionary methods of terrorism and sabotage: General Kutyepov, who was established in Paris.

The ROVS recognized Grand Duke Nicholas as the heir to
the throne of the Romanovs, although to these veterans of the
civil-war battles their true chief was always Wrangel. The
ROVS established correspondence courses in military science
for its members, a War College for its higher officers, and
cadet academies for the members' sons. At the same time
young officers crossed the border on intelligence missions. In
1924 Wrangel formed his "Combat Organization," intended
to train a large number of nuclei for the innumerable tasks of
terrorism.

The Baltic states, Poland, Finland, and Persia also felt the
need to keep themselves informed of the situation of their redoubtable neighbor. Nor did the British Intelligence Service
or the French *Deuxième Bureau* evince any less interest in
gathering such information. And what better agents could they
recruit for these dangerous ventures than former White soldiers or officers?

As for Boris Savinkov, he too had not given up the struggle.
During the civil war he had been the semi-official representative of the White armies in Paris and London. In 1920, during

[1] "In Wrangel," Mikhaïl Frunze, who had succeeded Trotsky as Commissar for War, wrote, "our country unquestionably had a most dangerous opponent. . . . In the various operations in which he took part
Wrangel demonstrated not only tremendous energy but a complete grasp
of the situation." Unfortunately, during the greater part of the campaign
he was under the command of Denikin, to whom he was greatly superior both as a combat leader and, especially, as a political strategist. By
the time he assumed command of the operations in the Crimea it was
too late to reverse the situation.

the conflict with Poland, he attempted to create a new organization with the help of Pilsudski, himself a veteran of terrorist combat. From Polish territory he launched a series of terror and sabotage raids against White Russia. His men, the "hardnoses," were recruited among former Revolutionary Socialists, tsarist officers, Ukrainian autonomists, to say nothing of brawlers and adventurers of every cast. They murdered Soviet functionaries, burned crops, and derailed trains. These activities were backed up by the famous Intelligence Service operative, Sidney Reilly.[2]

All these enterprises aroused the greatest apprehension among the Bolshevik leaders, and the GPU, which had succeeded the *Cheka* in 1922, was in no danger of unemployment. At the same time it had to cope with an internal situation that was more to be feared in its development than the emigrants' activities. For the adoption of the NEP afforded a fertile soil for the propagation of counterrevolution. The economic retreat ordered by Lenin created the objective conditions for a political and psychological offensive by the Whites and, at the extreme, for operations of a subversive character. The great majority of "class enemies" had not been able to make their way into emigration. A class of relatively rich peasants was being reconstituted. It entertained no sympathy for the government. Small business and artisanry were growing rapidly, and with them the mentality peculiar to them.

Above all, the government could not exist without specialists (*spets*) for its official services and the administration of the NEP. In order to stay alive the former technical intelligentsia was virtually compelled to make itself available to the government. It took on more and more jobs under the orders of those Bolsheviks who had stripped it of its positions and its

2 A remarkable adventurer of Irish-Jewish origins, Reilly had attempted to overthrow the Bolshevik government on a number of occasions after the October Revolution. In particular he took part in the attempt by the left Revolutionary Socialists in Moscow. Caught subsequently in a trap set by a *Chekist* provocation, he barely managed to flee Soviet territory after a melodramatic manhunt.

rights and whose incompetence and ideology it ridiculed. Liberated from their sufferings, restored to a place in the process of production, the *spets* began to make contacts with one another, exchanging ideas and plans, trying to correspond with the exiles or, if they were sent abroad on behalf of the government, to meet them. It was no great step from this to conspiracies.

As early as the end of 1921 a "Monarchist Union of Central Russia" (MUCR) was formed in Moscow, and its ramifications reached into a number of other cities. Thanks to an informer infiltrated into one of its cells, the GPU soon had detailed knowledge about it. It immediately devoted extreme attention to this movement. In the spring of 1922 Dzerzhinsky called together his chief associates assigned to watching the activities of the Whites: Artusov, the Baltic Baron Pillar von Pilchau known only as Pillar, Kossinov, and Starov. He put them on the alert:

A reasonably large and very well camouflaged counterrevolutionary organization, the MUCR, is at work in the country. Its center is in Moscow and it has branches in Petrograd, Nizhny-Novgorod, Kiev, Rostov, and the northern Caucasus. It is certain, too, that there are other organizations on which as yet we have no information. The MUCR has established direct contact with the leading centers of the White emigrants abroad and with their backing it is preparing an uprising against the Soviet government.

What was to be done? should an attempt be made to "localize" the guiding center of this organization quickly and arrest its members? Dzerzhinsky recommended a slower but more subtle course:

Premature arrests would entail the risk of letting the real brains get away. This is the point of view of the Central Committee as well. The GPU should maintain constant watch over the activities of the MUCR in order to obtain precise information as to its size, its structure, its ideological and field leaders, its composition, its program, its purposes, its tactics, and its means of communication with the emigrants. We must analyze the danger of this organization to the Soviet Republic, and intercept its communications with the emigrant centers abroad. We must make it our business to convert the MUCR into a "peephole" through which the GPU can form an accurate picture of the plans being made by the White emigrants.

A few months earlier, in fact, certain emigrant groups had learned of the activities of the MUCR. Early in November 1921 a high Soviet official on a mission in Sweden had stopped on his way in Reval, Estonia, for a number of conversations of a private character with a former tsarist officer, Captain Artamonov, to whom he had made certain confidences. "Yes," he said, "I am working for the Soviet system, but I hate it. There are innumerable former tsarist officers and officials in the same situation. They are what Lenin called radishes—red outside and white inside. Their numbers and their capacities make it possible for them to exert a subtle influence so that conditions can be completely changed."

The Soviet official who spoke in this fashion was named Yakushev; he was on a government assignment. Captain Artamonov was extremely interested. And Yakushev had excellent reasons for his hostility to the system. In 1917 he had been the director of the development division of the River Traffic Department. His rank was equivalent to that of a brigadier general. He received a large salary and had a car and an apartment among his perquisites. He was already a conspirator at the time of Yudenich's advance on Petrograd in 1919. When his organization was dissolved he had been able to flee to Moscow, where he did not work but lived by selling off his silver.

One day as he was walking along a street he had encountered General Potapov, who had joined the government. Potapov, who knew Yakushev well, was amazed that a man of his abilities should be unemployed. Through the general's inter-

cession Yakushev became a state official again. But his monarchist convictions were unaltered.

Immediately after Yakushev's departure from Reval, Artamonov sent a report on their talks to Prince Shirinsky, one of
the leading figures among the monarchist emigrants in Berlin.
Yakushev, he said, was an important *spets*. He was an intelligent man who knew everyone and everything. He shared the
monarchists' ideas and he was precisely the man whom they
needed. According to Yakushev's opinion, which, he said, was
that of the best men in Russia, the Bolshevik system was leading to anarchy and ultimately, without any midway transition,
to tsarism. It could be expected to collapse within three or four
months. Once the Bolsheviks had fallen, the *spets* would assume power. The government would be formed by those who
were in Russia, not by emigrants. Yakushev insisted that a
counterrevolutionary organization existed and operated inside
the country. He had a very low opinion of the emigrants. In
his view, they would be welcomed back to Russia at a later
date, but he said that a government from abroad was out of
the question. The emigrants no longer knew Russia. They
needed to be reacclimated to the country. It was the monarchist organization in Moscow that ought to set the directives
for the organizations in the West, not the reverse. Yakushev
insisted that terrorist activity was useless. The emigrants must
go back to Russia in as large a number as possible. Officers
and those who were mixed up in politics would have to delay
their return. . . . Yakushev suggested that the emigrants establish a contact with the men in Moscow. He mentioned no
names but he implied that they were people who had some
prestige both at home and abroad.

These disclosures were bound to arouse excited interest.
The existence of a powerful clandestine movement—if it was
confirmed—would substantially enhance the emigrants'
chances. Undoubtedly there were unpleasant aspects to the
views expressed by Yakushev. They already foreshadowed future complications with the internal organization that claimed

the right to run the movement and relegated the emigrants to the rank of followers. The rejection of acts of violence ran counter to many opinions. But all this was secondary if it could be confirmed that something was indeed afoot within Russia.

Weeks and months went by. Yakushev gave no further sign of life. Was he an impostor? Had he been arrested? Suddenly Artamonov heard news of him.

Sometime in 1922 one Kolesnikov, a former lieutenant in the Markov Division of the Volunteer Army of the Crimea, went to see him. Kolesnikov was carrying a message in code from Yakushev. At first Artamonov evidenced great caution toward his visitor. But Kolesnikov was able to provide sufficiently precise details on Yakushev and his activities to dissipate any doubt. And the code message that he had brought confirmed the growing influence of the MUCR. Said Yakushev:

We should like to inform you that the MUCR enjoys good communication with monarchist groups in Petrograd, Kiev, Nizhny-Novgorod, Rostov, Yaroslav, Smolensk, and Tula. We have succeeded in establishing contact with important military groups, staffs, and units that we are not identifying now for obvious reasons. We believe that initially not too much emphasis must be placed on the monarchy. The tactic to be followed should be this: Ardent monarchism within our organization and disguised monarchism in its outside contacts. We are obliged to be especially cautious with the soldiers. . . .

It is extremely important to the staff of our organization to know what armed forces it can count on abroad. We expect real help, not directives, from Berlin. Preparations are under way for the general congress of the MUCR, but they are hampered by lack of funds. It is essential to establish continuing communication with you by creating a transit point on the Estonian border and through the diplomatic pouch.

Artamonov and Kolesnikov decided that the contact would be carried on through the intermediary of the Estonian Legation in Moscow. Roman Birk, its press attaché, would be the man involved. A form of code would be established for telephone conversations that would set dates at which he would meet a messenger from the organization at the Artistic Film Theater.

Kolesnikov went back to the Soviet Union. Yakushev reappeared in November 1922 in Berlin, where he had been sent on government business by the People's Commissariat for Roads and Communications. Under Artamonov's sponsorship he had a number of talks with representatives of the Supreme Monarchist Council, especially Prince Shirinsky, and with trusted agents of Grand Duke Nicholas.

They were delighted to hear that the influence of the MUCR was mounting uninterruptedly. The organization had succeeded even in infiltrating its people into the GPU, where it enjoyed considerable protection, which substantially facilitated travel abroad. In addition, the MUCR had completely absorbed a municipal credit organization in Moscow. This afforded a double advantage: It was in a position to make commercial agreements abroad and to make discreet levies for its clandestine activities on the money that came in from these transactions. Business letters provided, as well, a magnificent means of circulating secret messages both within and without the country.

This was why the MUCR would always be identified in this correspondence under the code name of "the Trust," in which there was no danger of attracting attention.

Yakushev made a very sharp impression on the men with whom he dealt. He was intelligent, persuasive, and clever. He expressed himself with great assurance yet never fell into bravado. Everything that he said seemed perfectly probable. A whole correspondence began to go back and forth between the monarchist center in Berlin and the Trust.

During his journey Yakushev was also able to make contact with Wrangel's organization in Berlin through the intermediary of Wrangel's representative there, Colonel von Lampe.

Yakushev soon saw that this organization had no respect for the old men in the Supreme Monarchist Council, whom the colonel curtly described as "old spittoons." Von Lampe advised Yakushev to forget about them.

Von Lampe also introduced Yakushev to General Klimovich, former head of the tsarist police in 1917 and now chief of information in Wrangel's organization. Klimovich was no more a mincer of words than von Lampe. This time the object of the denigrations was Grand Duke Nicholas, the pretender to the throne. "He is a crackpot," Klimovich said. "It was he and his Montenegrin wife who discovered Rasputin. He is quite capable of finding another magician. . . . Besides, all those Romanovs are exalted nonentities. As far as I am concerned there is only one solution: Pyotr Nikolayevich Wrangel."

Markov, one of the members of the Supreme Council, soon learned of Yakushev's new connections. He was not eager to see so valuable a man taken over by competitors. Consequently Yakushev went off to Paris under the name of Fyodorov, carrying letters of recommendation to Grand Duke Nicholas' intimates in Paris and other letters from von Lampe to Wrangel's representatives there, Generals Holmsen and Miller.

Yakushev received a joyful welcome from the grand duke. He took advantage of the opportunity to restate the positions of the MUCR. From the very start any uprisings or disorders on the Russian borders must be blocked in order to prevent the enemy from unmasking the organization's forces and to keep them intact for the zero hour. Second, after the government had been overthrown it would be the domestic organization that would assume power, naturally under the grand duke's authority. As soon as he was reassured that his own authority would be preserved, Nicholas had no further objection.

During the same journey Yakushev signed an agreement to collaborate with Wrangel's organization. He then went back to Moscow in an aura of tremendous prestige with his asso-

ciates in the Trust. He had succeeded in establishing profit-
able contacts with the emigrants by his supple maneuvers between the rival groups. He had gained victory for the Trust's
views on the primacy of the domestic organization. Furthermore, he brought back important news. Thus far the Trust
had had no major military specialists, a serious lack for any
future uprising. Now General Potapov, who was employed in
the General Staff—this same Potapov who had allowed himself
to join the new class as a specialist—agreed to become Chief
of Staff of the Trust.

Contacts with the intelligence services of bordering countries were also progressing. In this connection a "technical" incident played a decisive part. The GPU had seized a certain
Colonel Yukovsky who had entered the Soviet Union without
the Trust's knowledge. Yakushev immediately sent a violent
protest to Holmsen, Wrangel's representative in Paris. It was
essential, he emphasized, that emissaries sent from abroad use
the "windows"—this was the term used for the transit points
on the border that the Trust had set up. One "window" had
already been opened in Estonia. Another was to be put into
operation in Poland.

It was through this "window" that Yakushev and Potapov
passed in October 1923 on their way to Warsaw, where they
entered into an agreement with the Polish intelligence service.
The Trust pledged itself to guarantee Poland's independence
after its seizure of power in the USSR. In return it obtained
the assurance that Poland would no longer protect Petlyura's
autonomists or Savinkov's "hoodlums"—he had to transfer his
activities to Prague. In addition the Trust would take over
Poland's agents and direct their operations in Russia.

Now the Trust had a virtual monopoly on the work of the
Polish and Estonian intelligence services. In the autumn of
1923 Marya Schulz, General Kutyepov's niece and a former
soldier in the White armies, left for Moscow with her husband
in order to check the true influence of the Trust on the spot.
Both she and her husband were extremely suspicious. Their

doubts were dispelled by the contacts that they made. They then approached the head of the Finnish Intelligence, and it was agreed that postal communication with Finland would be carried on through the Reval "window," beginning in 1925. The traffic was to be virtually continuous in both directions.

In emigrant circles, and chiefly among the young officers impatient for action, however, there was criticism of the Trust's temporizing policy. The Trust was in fact unshakably opposed to any act of terrorism or sabotage. Every proposal of the kind was countered with the same argument: We run the risk of jeopardizing everything by arousing the GPU. It was difficult to challenge the common sense of this argument.

On the other hand, it was true, a question might be asked: How could the activities of an organization as large as the Trust remain long concealed from the vigilance of the Soviet police and continue without interference? This was the only question that General Klimovich had raised on April 23, 1923, during Yakushev's first visit to Berlin, at a meeting attended also by von Lampe, a journalist named Shulgin, and Senator Chebyshev. Klimovich pointed out that "bitter experience has already taught us the strength and the skill" of the GPU.

Very calmly and even with a certain irony Yakushev had replied: "How can you think, sir, that civil war, famine, and the NEP have not sown disillusion and skepticism in Russia with respect to the Revolution? Please do not take offense, but you apparently reason like the mouse in the fable: 'There is no wild beast stronger than the cat.' This cat has taught us many things, particularly the art of conspiracy. We have our own men at every level of the Soviet administration. Thus we are able to ward off any blows."

He went on to emphasize that travel across the border had been organized with the help of foreign governments. Thus all the required conditions on both the Soviet and the foreign sides were such as to assure the operations of the Trust and protect it from attacks and surprises.

After a long silence, von Lampe thanked his "dear visitor"

for his fascinating disclosures. Yes, he could be trusted. As he took leave of his guests, Yakushev felt that he had convinced men who were especially suspicious.

He had barely left the room when Senator Chebyshev burst out: "Gentlemen, this is a very dangerous man! His Trust is nothing but a fraud by the GPU!"

But he was alone in his opinion.

(9)

YAKUSHEV, THE MAN
WHO REALLY CAME IN
FROM THE COLD

THE GPU had arrested Yakushev on November 22, 1921, as he was returning from Reval and those conversations with Captain Artamonov that were described in the previous chapter. He was confined in the Lyubyanka Prison and entrusted to the skills of an agent named Artusov.

Artusov conducted his interrogations without either violence or haste. At the end of each session, according to custom, he gave the prisoner a sheet of paper and urged him to compose a "complete and sincere" confession in the quiet of his cell, when his mind was clear. Yakushev made no attempt to hide his political views. In his final deposition during this preliminary stage he declared:

My convictions have not altered. I remain a Russian nationalist and a monarchist. . . . You asked me what my attitude toward the Soviet government is today. I do not ignore the Bolsheviks' efforts to restore what has been destroyed. But true order can be reestablished only by the crowned master of Russian soil.

I conclude my deposition here. I will not name anyone, but I have admitted everything and hidden nothing of my counterrevolutionary activity.

Apparently Artusov did not insist on the names of these accomplices of a counterrevolutionary, a "class enemy," who would not capitulate. At the end of each interrogation, however, he asked one or two ostensibly trivial questions that were nonetheless of such a nature as to arouse a certain apprehension in the prisoner's mind. Throughout entire days afterward Yakushev was at leisure to turn them over and over in his thoughts, wondering what trap they concealed and to what extent the GPU knew the precise extent of his activities. Sometimes anxiety would bring him out of his sleep at night. Artusov must know that he was a member of the Political Council of the MUCR. But, if that were so, why did Artusov not use quicker methods to make him admit it? Weeks passed in this fashion without resolving these unanswerable questions. This game wore out the nerves.

Obviously Yakushev could not have suspected that he was already a "chosen man," chosen by Comrade Dzerzhinsky, "the faithful paladin of the proletariat." When Dzerzhinsky had called a conference of the brain trust of counterrevolutionary repression in the spring of 1922 to discuss the dangerous activities of the MUCR, he had also explained the means by which he expected to make that organization his "peephole" for a clear view into the emigrants' plans and activities.

"We must find a man who can help our people to get into the very heart of the monarchist organization," he said. "Recently we arrested a certain Alexander Alexandrovich Yakushev. We have established not only that he is an enemy of Soviet power but also that he is one of the leaders of the MUCR. It is apparent that he began working [for the Soviet government] solely in order to cover up his counterrevolutionary activities. . . . Nevertheless we have established that, in spite of his monarchist convictions, he repudiates the inhuman techniques of combat proposed by his companions. He rejects foreign intervention. In so doing he condemns terrorism and espionage for the benefit of the Allies. At the same time he categorically refuses to give us a single name."

Was it not a gamble to try to make a GPU agent out of a man who clung to all his convictions? Nevertheless Dzerzhinsky believed this paradox possible. "Yakushev," he concluded, "can become the key that will open the door of the MUCR to us. This, of course, depends on Yakushev himself. He must declare a secret war, a war to the death against his companions."

One day Artusov summoned Yakushev to a new interrogation. This time Artusov was not alone. A rather short, quite fat man was sitting in his office, apparently absorbed in reading a long letter. This was Pillar, the former Baltic baron. He paid no attention to the prisoner and the questions began.

Artusov had abandoned his indirect approach. The GPU, he said, knew everything. It knew that Yakushev had had talks in Reval with a former tsarist officer, a dangerous emigrant, Captain Artamonov.

Yakushev took the blow with poise. "Yes," he said, "I saw him. But only in order to give him a private letter from a relative. There was no political talk between us."

Pillar broke off his reading and rose. "Listen, Yakushev. Listen carefully."

Slowly he read aloud the letter that Artamonov had sent to Prince Shirinsky in Berlin to report on his conversations with Yakushev, the latter's views of the emigrants, and his analysis of the political situation. Yakushev listened in the stupefaction of terror. "How could you know all that?" he said at last. "It is impossible that Artamonov should have betrayed me. He hates you too much."

Without expression Pillar handed him the letter. It was indeed Artamonov's signature. So the GPU had remarkably long tentacles if it had been able to get hold of this letter so quickly. And what recklessness on Artamonov's part to risk such confidences in writing! What negligence!

It was too much for Yakushev's nerves. He fainted. When he regained consciousness, Dzerzhinsky stood before him, talking in a gentle manner, as to a child or a hospital patient:

"You are upset, Yakushev. Who was it whom you trusted? These gentlemen play at conspiracies like schoolboys. We knew all about your activities in 1919, but we preferred to pay no attention. You could have worked honestly. Many people have joined us and now work with us. Little by little they have recognized that we had only one aim: to rebuild the national economy and make backward Russia the world's first Socialist state. . . . We know all about your counterrevolutionary activity. Give the matter thought."

Yakushev had an entire night in which to think. The next day he drafted his confession. Yes, he had indeed sought to establish communication between the MUCR and the Supreme Monarchist Council abroad. He added that, if he were granted clemency, he would forever relinquish all political activity.[1]

Once he had completed his confession, Yakushev went back to waiting. During the next interrogation he received a shock as great as that of Pillar's reading of Artamonov's letter.

"What would you do," Artusov asked, "if we let you go?"

Could he have expected such a proposal? After a moment, Yakushev said: "I think that I would be loyal to the Soviet government."

"Only loyal?" Artusov was ironic. "But what would you do if a member of the clandestine organization communicated with you?"

"Tell him to go to hell. It's because of their stupidity that I have almost been shot."

---

[1] Soviet disclosures on the Trust are of recent date. They were made in a fictionalized work by the Soviet writer, Lev Nikulin, called *Myortvaya Zeb* (*Groundswell*), which was published in Moscow in 1965. But the various conversations that are quoted in this and the previous chapters are taken from the GPU's archives and transcripts of interrogations. Unquestionably they contain a large measure of the truth, if not the whole of it. In particular, they give Yakushev's "conversion" an angelic aspect that is rather too labored, and, as will become apparent presently, a certain number of mysteries persists. To my knowledge only *Le contrat social* in France has taken notice of this book, in two interesting articles by Delimars (March–April and May–June 1966).

"In that case," Artusov pointed out, "your man would turn to someone else to prepare a terrorist attack. Let it go, however; you have already signed a renunciation of all political activity. We are going to trust you. You are free, Alexander Alexandrovich; here are your papers. Just one condition: absolute secrecy, and this includes your family. Your relatives will not be surprised at your absence. As far as they are concerned, you have been on a mission to Siberia, where you contracted typhus."

When Yakushev returned as a free man to his home he learned that *at the end of November* his wife had received a telegram from Irkutsk saying: "Seriously ill. In good hands. Don't worry. Love. Alexander." As long ago as that, Dzerzhinsky had had plans for Yakushev.

In all probability Yakushev had not yet divined that his release was only a stage, a phase in that slow evolution that, according to Dzerzhinsky's calculations, would bring him from political neutrality to close collaboration with the secret police.

Artusov had told the truth. It was difficult to remain neutral. A week after Yakushev's liberation one of his old comrades went to see him. The MUCR was continuing its activities. Moreover, its Political Council intended to place Yakushev at the head of a new and very active group in Siberia. The group's agent would be in touch with him almost immediately.

Yakushev reported the meeting to Artusov. "Go and talk with him," Artusov said. "Otherwise your old friends will be suspicious of you."

In a Moscow square, then, Yakushev was approached by a tall, red-haired man who spoke with a slight German accent. "To you my name is Staunitz," he said. "To others, depending on circumstances, it's Operput, Upelnitz, Selyaninov. . . ."

Staunitz asserted that he had been evacuated from the Crimea with Wrangel. Then he had wandered through Europe and been recruited by Savinkov. Caught as he was crossing the border, he was sentenced to death. Saved by the abolition of the death penalty, he was placed in a prison camp, then liberated by the NEP; whereupon he returned to conspiracy. His group was ready for any act.

Obviously, if Yakushev did not go along, this man would have him killed. Artusov was right: It was difficult to remain neutral. Yakushev asked him for an appointment.

To his great surprise it was Dzerzhinsky who received him. And Dzerzhinsky was exceptionally friendly. "They are wild animals," he said. "They will never leave you in peace. And it is impossible to send you into the interior; your departure might alarm the leaders of the MUCR. Now we have no intention of liquidating them for the moment. But there is another possibility."

For three hours Dzerzhinsky indoctrinated Yakushev. While it was fine to be loyal to the Soviet state, a man like himself could do much better. He ought to put his abilities at the disposal of the state—in other words, work with the GPU against its enemies.

Dzerzhinsky overlooked nothing in his effort to accomplish Yakushev's conversion. He demonstrated that the tsar and those round him were nonentities. Were they worth dying for? He produced massive evidence of the atrocities committed by the Whites during the civil war. The Soviets had abolished the death penalty. Why had it been necessary to revive it? Because of the atrocities of the Whites.

And the entire people, Dzerzhinsky insisted, stood with the Soviets. "Now no man can be a hero if he goes against his people," Dzerzhinsky argued. "It was Victor Hugo who said that." He had a taste for literary references; sometimes it was Shakespeare whom he quoted.

This was followed by the appeal to conscience. Not all those men in criminal organizations were doomed. Yakushev had no right to abandon them to their fate. "You ought to help to rehabilitate them. It is your duty. For our aim is not to punish but to reeducate. But you will be no less useful if you help us to neutralize an irreducible enemy."

Dzerzhinsky had been fanatically religious in his youth, exhausting himself in the effort to convert those who did not believe in God. He had rejected all religion, but he had kept the talent and the taste for preaching, directed now toward one sole end: to bring the counterrevolutionary, Yakushev, the repentant sinner, to the state of grace of the policeman.

"You have pledged yourself to give up all political activity. But I ask you to resume that activity on our side. . . . You ought to fight to the death against your former comrades. That means that you will be required to continue to play the part of the old Yakushev, the monarchist, the counterrevolutionary, the conspirator, and at the same time examine with us the means of unmasking the monarchists' contacts with foreign countries. I know that it is not easy for you to answer me at once. We will wait for your reply. This is the other possibility that I mentioned at the start of our talk. This is the only solution to the situation into which you have put yourself."

Chewing over his doubts, Yakushev went home, flattered perhaps by the attention lavished on him by the head of the GPU. A few days later Staunitz knocked at his door. He suggested that they plan an "expropriation" operation against a bank. On that same day Yakushev wrote a letter to Dzerzhinsky. He was ready to assume the part that had been offered to him.

Dzerzhinsky sent for him at once. At midnight, in the presence of Pillar, Artusov, and Starov, he laid down a line of conduct for him.

The most dangerous men in the MUCR must be eliminated. As an "honest and upright" leader of the White movement, Yakushev should insist on the expulsion of adventurers and rogues, inform the GPU of all attacks of which he could learn anything, and utilize his influence to introduce GPU agents into the organization. It was not a simple task: Not all the monarchists were stupid, and their ranks included highly experienced and dangerous men.

Second of all, there was no competent soldier at the head

of the MUCR. This gap must be filled. And, finally, the organization must be given a code name. "I suggest 'the Trust,'" Dzerzhinsky said. "The word is in harmony with the times and it has a most innocent ring. Have your political friends adopt this name and make it known abroad."

As for Artusov, he expressed the hope that Yakushev might become, so to speak, the "foreign minister" of the Trust. Pillar would take over the task of finding the competent general. (He turned out to be General Potapov.) As for Starov, he would be Yakushev's permanent contact.

That night Yakushev felt that the terrible Dzerzhinsky had treated him not as a common informer but as a man in whom full confidence was invested, a neophyte snatched from the inferno of counterrevolution and welcomed by his seniors to his new battle station. It took some time for him to perceive that their confidence was not total and that in Staunitz' group another GPU agent was already keeping an eye on his behavior.

Thus the Trust was nothing but a colossal provocation, a fantastic illusion staged by a remarkable director, Dzerzhinsky, and starring an actor of exceptional talent, Yakushev. The part that he played, moreover, was made easier for him by his own beliefs prior to his arrest: the primacy of internal organization, the renunciation of acts of terrorism, the policy of waiting until the situation was ripe. The only difference was that now he was defending these theses on behalf of the GPU. The MUCR was continuing its work in the Soviet Union, but it was more and more infiltrated by GPU agents. The real monarchists were manipulated from within, and the whole organization gradually came to resemble one of those houses gnawed away by termites that suddenly crumble one day into dust.

But it was abroad that the results obtained by the GPU acquired a remarkable importance. Yakushev had succeeded in prevailing on the emigrants to postpone their plans. He sowed discord among their various groups, he became conversant with their plans, their disputes, their various states of mind. Even more, he had gained the confidence of foreign intelligence services, whose agents and correspondence were now under the surveillance of the GPU. At the same time, feeding on the information poured into them by the Trust, these services were in a state of permanent intoxication.

This amazing achievement far outstripped the exploits of the Okhrana. The Okhrana had had remarkable agents such as Azev,[2] Malinovsky, Zhitomir, and Zhuchenko, from whom it had got invaluable information. Never, however, did it succeed in completely controlling an organization as the GPU controlled the Trust.

Only Chebyshev had guessed that Yakushev was a traitor. And Wrangel, though he had not been so definite, had maintained a cautious reserve. In November 1923, it was true, Wrangel had received General Potapov, but he had been suspicious and disclosed virtually nothing of his plans.

Nonetheless the Trust continued to delay the Whites' attacks. The men of Kutyepov's "Combat Organization" who used the Trust's "windows" were taken over as soon as they arrived by the GPU agents, who deprived them of all freedom of action.

In addition the Trust resorted to the most ingenious make-believe to convince the visitors of its remarkable power. In 1924 a White named Mukalov, who had arrived by way of the Estonian "window," was made so drunk in a restaurant by men from the Trust that in the end he was taken off to a police station. He was soon released through the "powerful connections" of the organization. Then he was taken to observe "secretly conducted" religious services; he had equally "secret" meetings with "highly placed officers of the Red Army," etc. When

[2] The leader of the Revolutionary-Socialist party's "Combat Organization" and, as such, responsible for many of its terrorist acts, Azev was in reality an informer for the tsarist police. An extraordinary double agent, he made the Okhrana as well as the party his dupe.

Mukalov went back to Europe he made short work of anyone who expressed unfavorable views on the Trust.

Marya Schulz was no less enthusiastic after her arrival in the Soviet Union. But, like Staunitz and certain monarchists inside Russia who were still in ignorance of the absorption of the Trust by the GPU, she was critical of the refusal to resort to terrorism.

Nevertheless there were strange occurrences in the well-lubricated machinery of the Trust. On August 10, 1924, no doubt confident of the imminence of an uprising in the Soviet Union, Boris Savinkov left Berlin and crossed the Russian border by way of the Polish "window." From there he was taken to Minsk by agents of the Trust and arrested on the spot by Pillar.

Tried and sentenced to death, he was given clemency and his sentence was commuted to life imprisonment. On May 7, 1925, he killed himself by leaping from a prison window. At least, that was the Soviet version. One of the most formidable of the GPU's enemies had been eliminated.

Shortly afterward, Sidney Reilly was picked up. Dzerzhinsky had entrusted Yakushev with the mission of enticing Reilly into the Soviet Union, a difficult task. Nevertheless Yakushev managed to establish contact with Reilly through a Russian agent of the British Intelligence Service in Helsinki, whose confidence Yakushev had gained by engineering the "escape" of the agent's brother, who lived in Moscow.

Yakushev met Reilly in Helsinki on September 25, 1925. Reilly was supposed to be in Stettin five days later; therefore at first he refused Yakushev's offer to smuggle him into Russia.

"What a pity to have got so far and then miss this opportunity!" Yakushev said. "I can guarantee you that you will cross the border tomorrow to go to Leningrad and then to Moscow. You can spend all day on the twenty-seventh talking to the Political Council of the Trust. You will be back here on the twenty-ninth."

Reilly, who was a gambler, thought it over briefly. "All

right," he said, "I'll go with you." Hastily he got off a message to his wife: "I am leaving tonight and will be back Tuesday morning. There is no danger. If by chance I am arrested in Russia, it will be only for some trivial affair. Our new friends are so powerful that they will assure my release."

He crossed the border at the Sestra River. On the opposite bank a border guard was waiting to play the part of smuggler. But his assignment was to kill Reilly if the agent showed the slightest desire to turn back.

Reilly was not arrested immediately. It was important to learn his plans first. He had the political conversations to which he had looked forward, but with GPU agents. Reilly explained to them that in the prevailing circumstances they must not count on subsidies from abroad. He himself had his own plans for obtaining funds on the spot: Russia had magnificent treasures, the value of which could not be estimated, and these must be stolen and shipped abroad for sale at extremely high prices.

He was arrested on his way back to Helsinki and executed on November 5.

The capture of Savinkov and the fate of Reilly, lured into the Soviet Union by Yakushev in person, might have been expected finally to open the emigrants' eyes to the truth about the Trust. In order to prevent this, the GPU set up a mock encounter at the Finnish border between smugglers and a Soviet patrol: shouts, whistles, shots, general confusion. Everything would certainly be audible on the other side, and it would be reported that Reilly had been a victim of this clash.

In complete good faith Marya Schulz convinced Mrs. Reilly that the Trust had had nothing to do with her husband's death.

The plotters in Warsaw congratulated themselves when they learned that at least Yakushev was safe. The Polish Intelligence Service sent automatic pistols and gold watches as gifts to him and Potapov.

Some suspicions, however, were inevitably aroused by the arrest of Savinkov, the disappearance of Reilly, and the cases of other agents of whom there was no word. The GPU saw that it must dispel these suspicions through some sensational enterprise.

The victim was Shulgin, the journalist. For years he had been seeking some trace of his son, who had disappeared during the Crimean retreat. He felt confident that his son was still alive but locked away in some refuge.

So Yakushev arranged a trip through Russia for Shulgin. He visited Moscow, Kiev, and Leningrad, escorted by an army of GPU men calling themselves members of the Trust. The travelers with whom he shared compartments on the trains were also GPU men. Their conversations had been painstakingly rehearsed by the GPU to give Shulgin the picture of the "new Russia" that he was intended to take back to the West.

Of course he found no clue to his son. But on his return he published an enthusiastic account of his journey. In order not to compromise his valorous friends in the Trust, he had sent his manuscript to Yakushev so that he might have the opportunity to make such changes in it as he might think required for the safety of the monarchist organization. Translated into French in 1927 as *La Résurrection de la Russie,* the book appeared in effect with not only the *nihil obstat* of the Trust but also the secret *imprimatur* of the GPU.

One of the men whom Shulgin mentioned in it was a certain Vassily Stepanovich, ". . . a man who was incapable of treachery. He had such good eyes, such a good smile." He was a GPU man named Shatkovsky. This splendid lad of the resurrected Russia had taken part in the capture of Reilly.

Thus for six years the Trust succeeded in gulling the emigrants, assuaging their impatience and forever setting back the time for action. In November 1926 Yakushev had once more persuaded Grand Duke Nicholas that he must wait.

"We must act!" Nicholas repeated. "We must act!"

"Nothing can be done for two years, Your Highness," Yakushev replied.

"That is ridiculous."

"I am merely telling you the truth, Your Highness. We are prevented from working. They send us kids without any kind of preparation. To save them from arrest the Trust is compelled to play nursemaid to them."

Finally the grand duke softened somewhat. And on December 14 Yakushev left Paris with a splendid photograph of the grand duke on horseback, augmented by a flattering inscription, and an appeal from the grand duke to the Red Army.

Yakushev was never again to be seen in Europe.

Someone had in fact made up his mind to bring to light the fantastic story of the Trust as soon as he had the evidence; this someone was Marshal Pilsudski. On May 26, 1926, a *Putsch* restored him to power in Poland. This old fellow-traveler in underground combat, exactly like Senator Chebyshev, had always refused to be taken in by Yakushev and company. One of his first acts was to order the Polish Intelligence Service to ask the Trust—which could do anything—for a copy of the latest Soviet mobilization plan.

Yakushev evidenced no haste to carry out this mission. He replied that "at this moment" the Trust had no reliable contact in the appropriate division of the Soviet High Command. Some other source would have to be tried, and this would cost the earth: at least ten thousand dollars!

"Price means nothing," the Poles retorted coldly.

It took months before the plan was delivered. Polish Intelligence scrutinized the precious document in its most minute details. It came to the categorical conclusion that it was obviously a falsification.

Pilsudsky immediately ordered all ties with the Trust severed. Shortly afterward the other Western intelligence services followed his example.

The end of the Trust was approaching. According to Nikulin's book, the dispatch of a White emigrant, a former policeman named Baskakov, to Russia brought about its downfall. Baskakov became certain that the Trust agent who accompanied him wherever he went was a GPU man. He at once alerted Staunitz-Operput, the man who had resumed contact with Yakushev when the latter had been released by the GPU.

Overwhelmed by the revelation, Staunitz refused to believe in so enormous a provocation. But now all kinds of strange coincidences recurred to his memory. When he himself questioned Baskakov's escort, he too became convinced that the man was in fact a GPU agent.

Staunitz informed Marya Schulz. She must flee at once, through the Finnish "window," before the alarm could be given. Both boarded a train and crossed the border on the night of February 12–13, 1927.

In the ensuing days the GPU threw out a huge dragnet: all the counterrevolutionary members of the MUCR, *all the real monarchists,* were rounded up. On April 21 the Tass News Agency announced that a clandestine monarchist organization operating under the leadership of General Kutyepov had recently been uncovered and liquidated in Moscow. During the following days there were rumors that executions had taken place in a number of Soviet cities.

The Trust that had functioned for six years was annihilated in a few weeks. Meanwhile the originator of this gigantic hoax, Comrade Dzerzhinsky, had died.

The version that Staunitz gave after his arrival in Finland, however, differed on several points from Nikulin's Soviet version. Staunitz asserted that he had made the acquaintance of Yakushev not through the underground but in the Lyubyanka, where he was being held because he had served in Savinkov's organization. He said that he and Yakushev had shared a cell at the end of 1921 and from time to time they had been taken out to see a show: an execution. They saw men struggle and heard them cry out. Then on a number of occasions they were put through the ordeal of mock executions. Yakushev, he said, had undoubtedly been sincere at the time of his first visit to Reval, but this treatment had got the better of him.

Staunitz too had agreed to play his part in the epic comedy

of the Trust, along with Kiakovsky of the GPU (who, under the name of Kolesnikov, had gone to visit Captain Artamonov in Reval).[3]

Staunitz' version of the aims assigned to the Trust coincides with Nikulin's. But what is one to think of the divergences of fact between the account given by Staunitz in 1927 and Nikulin's version of 1955? Was Staunitz, as he claimed to have been, a GPU agent who preferred to flee rather than be liquidated one day or another because he knew too much? But, if that is the case, why did Nikulin still deem it necessary, when he unmasked the entire machination, to portray Staunitz as a genuine anti-Communist?

From another point of view it is completely surprising that Staunitz should have been unable at the time to provide any information on the identities of the agents working for the GPU. Once the Trust had been finally disposed of, was it not to the interest of the GPU to incite the flight of one of its agents who by forging a new "legend" would be able to continue furnishing it with information on the emigrants' activities?

These questions did not escape General Kutyepov.

Nor did they prevent Staunitz, with Marya Schulz and four other emigrants, from crossing the border again, in May 1927, to carry out a double terrorist attack. A "troika" led by Captain Larionov reached Leningrad and hurled two bombs into a room of the party's central office in which a meeting was being held. After this attack, which claimed several victims, the "troika" fled successfully back to Finland.

Marya Schulz, Staunitz, and their companion were never to return. Their mission was to blow up the GPU's quarters in Moscow. On June 10 Tass announced that a bomb containing more than eight pounds of melinite had been "placed" in or near the building but had not exploded. A short time later

[3] According to Staunitz the idea of the Trust was not born of the "genius" of Dzerzhinsky, who was skeptical at first, but was evolved by Kiakovsky.

Tass reported that Staunitz had been killed on June 14 and Marya Schulz and the third terrorist two days afterward.

This is the version that appeared in Nikulin's book. But it is not quite accurate. During the German-Soviet war a White emigrant claimed to have seen Staunitz in Warsaw: He was on his way to Berlin from Kiev. Supposedly the Germans subsequently arrested and executed him because he was working for the Russians.

It is useless to attempt to resolve these enigmas. They are part of that store of mysteries that is always created by the work of secret services.

The other authors or victims of the Trust had varied fates. According to Nikulin, Yakushev died quietly in 1935 (which, however, was the year in which the Great Purge began). Potapov went back to his position in the Military Academy and died in 1946. Artusov, Pillar, and Starov were liquidated by Stalin in 1937 and later rehabilitated. Kiakovsky-Kolesnikov was assassinated by religious fanatics in Mongolia. General Wrangel died in 1928.

After the deaths of Savinkov and Reilly, General Kutyepov was the most redoubtable of the Soviets' enemies. He disappeared from the center of Paris on January 26, 1930. That day he had left his apartment in Rue Rousselet to go to mass in Rue Mademoiselle, as he did every Sunday. The owner of a hardware shop in his street saw him walk by the store. The owner of the Pathé Film Theater, also a White Russian, remembered having greeted him. The final witness said that he had seen the general at the corner of Rue de Sèvres and the Boulevard des Invalides, near the place where the Number 89 streetcar stopped.

The investigation into his disappearance by the French police established that very probably he had been abducted in a taxi from the corner of Rues Rousselet and Oudinot. It was supposed on the basis of certain testimony that the taxi drove to the Norman coast and Kutyepov was put aboard a Soviet freighter that was cruising offshore.

Thirty-seven years after its occurrence no more was known of the circumstances of this abduction. But there can no longer be any doubt as to its origin or the identity of its organizer. In fact, reviewing Nikulin's book in *Krasnaya Zviezda* (*Red Star*), the Soviet Army's newspaper, General Shimanov expressed regret that the author had devoted only a couple of modest lines to Puzitsky, a subordinate commissar in the State Security Service. According to Shimanov it was Puzitsky who was responsible for the arrest of Savinkov, and in addition this talented policeman ". . . briliantly led the operation *for the arrest of Kutyepov* and a series of other White Guards."

In Shimanov's opinion, apparently, it was a mere detail that this arrest was made on the territory of another country, an example that has since had some imitators.

For this double exploit, Shimanov revealed, Puzitsky had twice received the Order of the Red Flag and the police honor badge. It is useless to expect Puzitsky's memoirs to be published. He was in fact liquidated during the Great Purge. But perhaps General Shimanov or Nikulin could publish the story of Kutyepov's abduction and his final fate. This is a contribution to history that would be eminently desirable at this period of French-Soviet cooperation.

TWO

(10)

PEOPLES, BELIEVERS,
PEASANTS

W ALTER KOLARZ wrote in that monumental work, *La Russie et ses colonies*, that Stalin's attitude toward Tiflis might be likened to Hitler's toward Vienna. In each case the man felt a profound aversion toward the city.

The roots for these resentments, however, were different. What Hitler detested in Vienna was the polyglot, cosmopolitan city in which German values were bastardized. Stalin, on the contrary, looked on Tiflis as the citadel of a Georgian nationalism that befogged the international prospects of a class struggle.

One fact was common, however, to both men: Each hated the city in which he had suffered frustration. Hitler had a miserable life in Vienna; Stalin clashed with the Mensheviks in Tiflis, was unable to cut into their power, and preferred to withdraw to Baku and carry on his campaign there.

As we have seen, Dzhugashvili's destiny intersected Trotsky's for the first time in 1913, and in Vienna. Stalin had gone there to collect materials from Bukharin that would help him to write, under Lenin's guidance, his famous little book on *Marxism and the National Question*.

It was a question in which Lenin at that time was deeply interested. The Austrian Marxists envisaged a Socialist state that would guarantee the cultural and linguistic autonomy of national minorities. Lenin was then plunged in a sharp controversy with the Jewish *Bund*, which demanded such autonomy and, with it, the right to constitute a separate sector within Social Democracy, to which it would be linked by some vague tie of federation. Bolshevik centralism could not accept such a solution. That was why Lenin, of whom Stalin was merely the docile pupil, opposed a unitary Socialist state to the theses of the autonomists, although in theory he granted the right of separation to the national minorities that would be a part of it.

This right was always to remain a fiction. Georgia was the first to learn this, and the practical Stalin showed that he paid little heed to the principles set forth in his own book. After the October Revolution, in fact, Georgia had proclaimed itself an independent republic, in which the Mensheviks were the majority. This in itself only flouted Moscow's authority and made Georgia a stronghold of the Second International. For the workers of the entire world the Georgian Menshevik experiment could be contrasted with that of Russia.

The Bolsheviks could not tolerate this challenge. In February 1921 the Red Army drove out the Menshevik government. But the institution of a Bolshevik republic merely transferred the conflict to another arena. Stalin collided immediately with his own Georgian comrades (we have noted the method by which he and Ordzhonikidze undertook to put down the "rebels"). It was Stalin who conceived the idea of creating a Transcaucasian federation that would include Armenia and Azerbaidzhan with Georgia. Within this federation Moscow would be able to play on the ethnic rivalries and impose its will conclusively.

Nevertheless the Mensheviks, who had sixty thousand adherents (against twenty thousand for the Bolsheviks), retained close ties with the Georgian peasants and in intellectual circles.

On August 28, 1924, an insurrection erupted in Georgia. (It may have been provoked.) In a single day half the country was liberated. In twenty days of fighting, the Red Army's troops, reinforced by armor and planes, crushed the insurgents as they were to do again thirty-two years later in Hungary. There were some three thousand victims. In the repressions that followed, distinction was gained by a young architectural draftsman who had joined the Bolshevik party in 1917: Beria. At this time he headed the *Cheka* in Georgia. A former member of that *Cheka* who fled to France, E. Dumbadze, related in a book published in 1930 [1] that in a single night 118 persons were executed. They were taken in trucks through streets that were still except for the noise of the engines. At the end of the procession was a car that contained Beria and members of the Georgian Central Committee.

Although there were no other comparable risings in the Caucasus, the various ethnic minorities were not backward in offering sullen resistance to the central power on the cultural, linguistic, or religious levels. Moreover their diversity raised extremely complex problems. For example, the mountaineers of the Caucasus included no fewer than seven peoples: Kabardians, Chechens, Ingushi, Ossetians, Circassians, Balkari, and Karachais. Under a decree of January 20, 1920, they were authorized to set up an Autonomous Socialist Soviet Mountain Republic, the capital of which was Vladicaucasus. In reality the administration, in Russian hands, was established in Rostov.

The life of this federation did not exceed twenty months. New combinations came into being as several peoples formed autonomous provinces the administrative borders of which were constantly being revised. These changes were purely formal: The reality of power was always in the hands of the Rus-

[1] *Au service de la Tchéka et du Komintern.*

sians in Rostov, and in 1936 only 17 of 1310 functionaries in the northern Caucasus were men of the mountain peoples.

The provisional government laid the problem over for the future Constituent Assembly. The Bolsheviks, being better tacticians, made the claims of the national minorities their own. In December 1917 a proclamation entitled *To All Moslems of Russia and the East* was published in Moscow under the signatures of Lenin and Stalin:

To all of you whose mosques and shrines have been destroyed, whose beliefs and customs have been trampled beneath the feet of the tsars and the oppressors of Russia . . . your beliefs and your customs, your national and cultural institutions are henceforth free and inviolable. You can organize your national existence in full freedom.

There was rather a gap between these promises and the facts. In Turkestan, Bashkiria, and Daghestan the Red Army followed its own example set in Georgia: It imposed Bolshevik power by force of arms. And this power made every effort to undermine the cultural and religious principles of which it professed to be the defender.

Thus in Daghestan the Bolshevik party encouraged the creation of what was called an "advanced" religious group— as is the case of the Pax group in Poland today—in order to bore from within into religious resistance. But that resistance was not so easily to be broken. Until 1930 in some districts 80 per cent of the Communists continued to observe religious customs, and leaders of the Communist party themselves judged it desirable to take part in religious ceremonies in order not to offend the believers' sensibilities.

Among the Chechens, fierce adversaries of tsarism, religious opposition was no less active. In 1931 they still had 2675 mosques and Arab schools, 1250 mullahin, 34 sheikhs, and 250 religious "elders." The Ingushi also remained faithful to Islam, and more than once it came about that teachers who had attacked religion were forced to leave their schools. As for the Ossetians, they were not slow to mount a savage resistance to collectivization.

The language problem was no less thorny. In a territory like that of Daghestan, embracing almost 15,500 square miles, 32 nationalities were living. The most widely spoken of the local languages, Ovar, was understood by only 22 per cent of the population. If it was necessary to adopt an intertribal language for the convenience of administration, the best choice seemed to be Arabic. But to encourage Arabic would be at the same time to strengthen the Moslem religion. Hence the Soviet leaders imposed the use of Turkish, because, as Samursky, the party secretary, explained, this language made it possible for Daghestan to maintain contact with all the nationalities of the Middle East and to incite a revolutionary tendency among the colonial and semi-colonial countries.

The idea of utilizing these nationalities as a point of departure for propagandizing the Middle East ended in complete defeat. By 1927 the Communist party had been able to recruit only 651 members among these 32 nationalities. When these neophytes were in no position to enlist their own compatriots, how could they have become the emissaries of Soviet propaganda beyond the borders?

Many other examples of the more or less strong resistance of nationalities might be adduced. Furthermore, in Turkestan and Tadzhikistan a Turkish nationalist movement, *basmachi*, waged an armed campaign against the government until 1933.

But the region in which national sentiment and separatist tendencies were most violently expressed was the Ukraine. Ukrainian national feeling had already manifested itself with enough force for Tsar Alexander II to prohibit all publications in the Ukrainian language in the nineteenth century. The collapse of tsarism, the German occupation in the First World War, and the civil war delivered the territory of the Ukraine into the hands of factions that vied with one another for power. Out of these bewildering frays the Bolsheviks were not to emerge as the victors until the beginning of 1920.

On December 2, 1920, the Ukrainian Congress of Soviets adopted a treaty that in practice turned over to the Russians the control of military affairs, finances, labor, security, and communications. Theoretically, however, the Soviet Constitution of 1923 allowed the Ukraine the possibility of divorce.

The Ukrainian Communist party itself was composed of a merger of Bolsheviks and Borotbists—[2] that is, former left Revolutionary Socialists who thought that the Ukraine, even though belonging to the Soviet Union, could preserve its national characteristics. Even among the Bolsheviks a man like Skrypnyk, an old comrade of Lenin and a member of the Ukrainian Politburo, retained strong ties to Ukrainian culture.

Initially the Ukraine was the beneficiary of rather broad tolerance on the cultural level. In 1924 Grushevsky, a famous historian of Ukrainian nationalism, returned there and was appointed to head the historical section of the Academy of Sciences of the Ukraine. A large number of books and periodicals in the Ukrainian language appeared, and at the same time a Ukrainian scientific terminology was developed.

Moscow looked on these activities with a favorable eye at first in the hope of winning the population's fealty by fostering the growth of the Ukrainian language. The Twelfth Congress of the Communist party (June 1925) declared that "Ukrainianization was a means of establishing close contact among the Ukrainian masses and above all with the peasants" (Kommunist, a Ukrainian newspaper in Kharkov, 1927, No. 210).

A book published in Kharkov in 1926, Ia Khuylia (The National Question in the Ukraine), showed that, of 15,000 elementary schools, lessons were given in Ukrainian in 11,833. Between 1798 and 1906 only 3214 books had been published

[2] The word was derived from Borotba, the name of a Ukrainian exile publication issued in Geneva beginning in 1915.

in Ukrainian, while between 1917 and 1926 the number reached 6250.

Ukrainianization was substantial in the apparatus of the state. On November 1, 1925, the proportion of Ukrainian functionaries was 52 per cent in the central administration, 60 per cent in the provincial, and 66 per cent in the cantonal. Nevertheless the Russians had taken care to retain the majority in the body that possessed the real power—in other words, the party apparatus. Here there were 60 per cent Russians against 40 per cent Ukrainians.

This tendency toward Ukrainianization lasted until the early 1930s. On December 23, 1929, the Central Committee of the Ukrianian Communist party adopted a resolution stipulating that Ukrainian was to be adopted as the official language as of May 1, 1930, in state and party agencies and in all trade unions.

Skrypnyk evidenced an intention to call in five thousand teachers from Ukrainian Galicia to Ukrainianize the Donbas (the Donetz basin). A Russian living in the Ukraine, Volobuyev, supported the theory of an independent Ukrainian economy in a much discussed article that appeared in *Bolshevik Ukrainy* (1928, II–III).

The defense and the exaltation of Ukrainian culture led imperceptibly into separatism. The elimination of the fractions within the Bolshevik party could not long tolerate such tendencies. Moreover, the former Borotbists were still suspect because of their origins. One of them, Shunski, was soon expelled. In 1930 a purge of arts and letters began. The historical section was dissolved and Grushevsky was exiled inside Russia. In May 1930 Moscow unmasked a nationalist deviation in the Marx-Lenin Institute and the prime mover, Yarosky, vanished.

At the same time the GPU was discovering clandestine nationalist organizations: in 1929 the Union for the Liberation of the Ukraine, in 1931 the Ukrainian National Center, in 1933 the Ukrainian Military Organization. This repression of Ukrainian nationalism more or less coincided with collectivization but it was to go far beyond it.

Thus the relatively liberal policy followed by the central government toward the Ukraine in the years just after the Revolution ended in failure. "Ukrainianization" in the cultural area fostered separatist tendencies among the intellectuals and even among the national subleaders in the party. Nationalism, the major champion of which during the civil war had been Petlyura, was still firmly anchored in many minds. And the great mass of the population, 80 per cent of which was peasants, was still fiercely hostile to the Soviets and to all attempts at collectivization.

There is no occasion for surprise in these phenomena if one reflects that at the time of the elections to the Constituent Assembly in November 1917 the Bolsheviks obtained only 10 per cent of the votes in the whole of the Ukraine. Learning the lessons of this election, Lenin observed that it was in the Ukraine, as well as in Siberia and the eastern Urals (where the Bolsheviks had received only 10 per cent and 12 per cent of the votes, respectively), that the counterrevolution had found its best field of action during the civil war.[3] Denikin had completely overlooked the same lesson.

Under these conditions, domination by a party the majority of whose members were of Russian origin[4] could appear to the Ukrainian population only as rule by a foreign element.

At the same time, efforts to exploit this nationalism abroad, in order to attract populations of Ukrainian origin outside Soviet territory (notably in eastern Poland), had ended in a total fiasco. In 1924, however, the Fifth Comintern Congress had issued the following warning: "The Congress regards it

[3] Lenin, *Works*, Vol. XXIV, quoted by W. Kosyk in *L'Ukraïne sous le joug colonial russe*.

[4] "It is an undeniable fact," the Soviet historian, N. Popov, said in his *History of the Ukrainian Communist Party*, published in 1929, "that in the recent past and even today our party in the Ukraine was and remains in general the party of the Russian proletariat and the Russianized elements" (pp. 9–10).

as necessary that the Communist parties of Poland, Czecho-slovakia, and Rumania issue the slogan of the separation of the Ukrainian areas of Poland, Czechoslovakia, and Rumania in order to reunite them with the Soviet Ukraine and through it with the Soviet Union."

Even in Poland, where the Ukrainian minority was extremely harshly treated, the Communists' ideas had no success. Early in 1928 there was a serious schism in the Communist party of the western Ukraine, and in 1938 that party endorsed the thesis of autonomy for minorities, thus abandoning efforts to bind it to the Soviet Union. This union was to be effected only by force of arms, in 1945, and yet, as we shall see, it in no way broke a savage resistance.

Although the Soviet government was often obliged to indulge the beliefs and rituals of the national minorities that it was trying so hard to assimilate, it did not follow the same course with the Orthodox church, which was treated as an enemy from the earliest days of the Revolution. As early as November 11, 1917, the council of the Orthodox church issued a message denouncing the violences done to the church:

". . . From every corner of Russian soil news comes to us of the unheard-of violences done to the church by various organizations and persons now in power. . . . On the pretext of separating church and state the Council of People's Commissars is endeavoring to make existence itself impossible for the church, its ecclesiastical institutions, and its clergy. Under the color of confiscating church property the decree on this subject is aimed at destroying the very possibility of worship and services. . . .

As a result of the confiscation of the ecclesiastical printing establishments, it becomes impossible even for the church to be in a position to publish autonomously the Holy Gospels and, in general, any of the sacred liturgical books with all the purity and integrity required.

Two months later, on January 19, 1918, Patriarch Tikhon hurled his anathema against the Bolsheviks.

The civil war was accompanied by a pitiless assault on the Orthodox church. Between January 1918 and the end of 1922 twenty-five bishops and archbishops were executed by the *Cheka* or died in prison. After the civil war the campaign was carried forward through the creation of the League of the Godless, headed by Yaroslavsky. At the same time the Bolsheviks were striving, not without success, to undermine the Orthodox church from within by supporting its "popular" fraction that used the name of "the Living Church."

Patriarch Tikhon's resistance was quickly shattered. Arrested in 1923, he submitted a "self-criticism" to the Supreme Soviet Tribunal, ascribing his "faults" (the anathema, his message at the time of the Treaty of Brest-Litovsk, his protest in 1922 against the confiscation of the valuables owned by the church) to his monarchist upbringing:

Acknowledging the valid grounds for the decision of the tribunal before which I have been placed on trial . . . for anti-Soviet activities, I deplore these errors against the established government and I petition the Supreme Tribunal to commute my sentence and release me from imprisonment. Furthermore I declare to the Supreme Tribunal that henceforth I am no longer an enemy of the Soviet government. I am divorcing myself resolutely and definitively from the counterrevolution of the White Army's monarchists within the country.

A subsequent message dated April 7, 1925—the same day on which the patriarch died—marked a further step along the road of abdication. This time Tikhon called on the faithful "to be convinced that the power of the Soviets is in fact the popular power of the workers and peasants and that for this reason it is solid and unshakable." Given its date, the authenticity of this message may be regarded as suspect.

After Tikhon's death, however, the conflict within the church continued between the supporters and the opponents of the government. Tikhon's successor, Metropolitan Sergey, endorsed the government; "every attack directed against the

Soviet Union," he wrote on June 16, 1927, "whether it be war, boycott, some public disaster, or merely a street-corner murder like that in Warsaw, is regarded by us as aimed at ourselves." Other bishops refused to submit. The most intransigent among them had been deported to the camp on the island of Solovetsky in the White Sea.[5] From their detention they denounced the metropolitan's unconditional surrender:

Any government can at times adopt unreasonable, unjust, and cruel measures, to which the church will be compelled to submit and which can neither cause her to rejoice nor obtain her approval. The present government has assumed the task of exterminating religion, and its successes in this domain cannot be regarded by the church as her own successes. . . .

On this internal conflict that divided the Orthodox church we possess among other evidence the testimony of a former Yugoslav Communist, Anton Ciliga, who was confined in the Leningrad prison in 1929 with a number of ecclesiastics and adepts of various sects. Ciliga reported that the opponents refused to insert a prayer for the government in their religious services. The center of this opposition was the Leningrad church, and its elected bishop was the prelate of Rostov, who was looked on as the spiritual leader of the resistance. But Metropolitan Sergey denied the right of religious communities to select their bishops without his approval. "The reason," Ciliga wrote, "was that the question of the internal organization of the church was part of the question of its attitude toward the government." [6]

The opposition itself was split between a "left" and a "right" that was committed to the restoration of the monarchy.

Ciliga emphasized the fact that, even while it was combating religion, the government took an active part in this con-

---

[5] Between 1923 and 1926 twenty-four bishops were confined in this camp; seventeen of them died there.

[6] *Au pays du mensonge déconcertant*, p. 118.

flict within the church. According to him, when the metropolitan's majority in the Synod was shown to be shaky, the GPU reinforced it through a radical procedure: It arrested a few members of the Synod who had the wrong views. Similarly the bishop of Rostov was not arrested until after his election to the Leningrad bishopric. The tactic was obvious: What the GPU wanted was not to exterminate the opposition altogether but to decimate it when it threatened to become dangerous.

The government maintained no less strict surveillance over the sects. Actually they were in general unalterably hostile to any form of statism. They had been centers of opposition to the tsarist system, and at times revolutionaries had sought to make use of them on behalf of their own struggle: Mikhaïlov, the terrorist and one of the organizers of the *Narodnaya Volya*,[7] had in this way joined the sect of the Old Believers in 1876 with a view to destroying it; Sazonov, who led the attack on Plehve, the minister, was also a member of this sect.

The religious fanaticism of the sects and their quality of semi-clandestine organizations were now turned against the Bolshevik system. This phenomenon was all the more disturbing because they had made substantial progress at the expense of the Orthodox religion and because their influence was great in popular circles and particularly among the peasants.

Hence the prisons housed a large number of Evangelists, Churikovtzi—who at that time could claim several hundred thousand adherents—Jehovah's Witnesses, and Old Believers. Some sects refused to have anything at all to do with the authorities or even to speak to a Bolshevik. Ciliga was told that a woman in the Solovetsky prison camp had refused to sign the papers incidental to her release even though she had been informed that, unless she signed, she would not be set free.

The influence that the sects enjoyed over the peasants was naturally to align them against collectivization. In November

[7] The People's Will, a Populist organization that led the terrorist campaign in Russia in 1880.

1929 the Soviet press reported the trial of forty-two members of the Fyodorovtzi sect in the court in Voronezh. They appeared in long white robes bearing the letters X B ("Christ is risen"). Blue crosses were embroidered up and down the backs and fronts of their robes and on the inside of the sleeves. Whenever a question was put to them, the accused fell to their knees and intoned their chants.

They were accused of having paraded among the peasants with a large flag bearing the inscription: "God save the tsar!", distributed calls for an uprising, and stockpiled weapons. But the Fyodorvtzi were above all opposed to the collection of taxes, government loans, and collectivization. This alone was enough to ground their trial. Sixteen of the defendants were sentenced to death, the rest to prison. The court suggested further that thousands of them be deported, for the Fyodorovtzi were very numerous in the rural areas.

The Constitution of 1924 proclaimed that, with the separation of church and state, "freedom of religious and anti-religious propaganda was recognized for all citizens." At least in theory, believers and unbelievers thus enjoyed the same rights. But in 1929 the Congress of Soviets amended Article IV of the Constitution to read: "In order to guarantee genuine freedom of conscience to the workers, the church is separated from the state and the school is separated from the church; freedom of worship and the right of anti-religious propaganda are recognized for all citizens." Henceforth, therefore, only anti-religious propaganda was permitted.

This was carried on essentially by the League of the Godless, which was rechristened the Anti-Religious Association in 1929. Its chief activities consisted in transforming churches into anti-religious museums, holding conferences, parades, and anti-religious masquerades, and issuing publications in thousands of copies.

In its campaign the Association aimed above all at winning over the young. Its regular organ, *The Godless,* laid down guidelines for the participants of the Congress of Red Pioneers

in its issue of August 1929: "Not every young Godless is necessarily a Pioneer, but a Pioneer must be intransigently Godless. . . . The Soviet Pioneer Congress should first of all examine the augmentation of anti-religious activity among children, and especially among the Pioneers."

The same issue reported that in many schools in Moscow
the teachers had instructed their pupils to go to church in order to observe who came in to pray. This procedure was
recommended, and it was noted with satisfaction that apparently gifted pupils had denounced their relatives and class-
mates. The school of the Godless was the school of the little
Bolshevik stool pigeon.

In that year the anti-religious campaign undoubtedly
reached its height *in its visible aspects*. On May Day carica-
tures of religion were paraded through the streets of Moscow.
One of them showed a Protestant pastor whose repulsive face
stuck out of a cardboard collar a foot high. He was followed
by Trotsky on his knees before the British prime minister.

During Holy Week there were street performances of a
kind of mystery play that professed to depict the horrors of
the Inquisition. Platforms were erected in Catherine Square,
opposite the church of Christ the Savior. While the clergy celebrated its rites within, there were singing and dancing on the
platforms, and anti-religious masquerades wound through the
streets.

On the night of July 30 the Iverskaya Chapel, built in 1669,
was torn down on official order. This chapel stood next to
Lenin's tomb. The government could not suffer the simultaneous processions of the faithful of both cults. On November
3 members of the *Komsomol* attacked Moscow's Baptist chapels. In the country as a whole 540 churches, 63 synagogues,
and 18 mosques were closed in the last two months of the year.

On Christmas Eve, as the sound of bells echoed in the
frozen air, the Godless turned out in vast numbers in the
streets. Some of them, disguised as priests, shouted blasphe-
mous songs. Imitation monks cavorted on truck beds, pretend-

ing to be drunk—if indeed they had to pretend—staggering, converting church chants into screaming parodies. Every purchase or sale of a Christmas tree was punishable by a fine of a hundred rubles in order to "extirpate a stupid sentimentality." In the brilliantly lighted shop windows, dolls dressed as workers were poised in the act of hurling down the God of the Christians, the Jews, and the Moslems.

Wagons bore scale models of churches, synagogues, and mosques. When the faithful came out of the real churches, the models were set ablaze to the accompaniment of firecrackers, shouts, and songs.

Such abjectly idiotic behavior was the perfect illustration of Article IV of the Constitution of 1924: freedom of worship was respected, and so was that of anti-religious propaganda.

It was not by sheer chance, moreover, that the intensification of the anti-religious offensive coincided with the collectivization of agriculture. It was actually among the peasants that the Orthodox church found its strongest support. And Stalin had decided to shatter all peasant resistance.

The peasant problem had indeed become acute. The agrarian revolution had distributed the huge agricultural estates— that is, parceled out the land—and in consequence the quantity of marketable wheat required by the urban populations for their subsistence had been reduced. In 1927 total wheat production reached the prewar figure of five billion poods.[8] In spite of this, Russia was producing only half as much wheat for the market as before the war and exporting only 5 per cent as much grain. This was because the small farmers were retaining the greater part of their crops for their own use. Now the number of individual peasant holdings had risen from the fifteen or sixteen million of 1913 to twenty-four or twenty-five million.[9]

The policy that guided the party with respect to the peas-

[8] One pood equals 36.113 pounds.—Translator.
[9] Cf. Stalin's article, "On the Wheat Front," in *Pravda*, June 2, 1928.

ants was that of the right, the chief leaders of which were Bukharin and Rykov. By extending the NEP they intended to make broad concessions to the farmers. Having noted the setback of the Socialist International in Europe in 1924, they had resigned themselves to building Socialism in one country, but, to use Bukharin's expression, "at a snail's pace."

"Granted the possibility of building Socialism in one country," some of Trotsky's supporters, such as Preobrazhensky and Pyatakov, replied, "it must be done not at a snail's pace but by a real leap forward. The country must be industrialized at full speed to catch up with the capitalists."

Where was the capital to be found for the accomplishment of this program? By taking it from the kulaks, Preobrazhensky responded.

Bukharin regarded these notions as "monstrous." An old adherent of the methods of "war Communism" during the period of the civil war, he had come to appreciate their horror. His disciples, who were known as "the young Red professors" (Maretzky, Sten, Slepkov, Goldenberg, etc.), called for the free movement of goods, parallel expansion of heavy industry and consumer production, the elimination of all vestiges of war Communism, and the attenuation of the class struggle in the farming districts.

In 1925 Bukharin issued his famous call: "Enrich yourselves, expand your cultivation, and do not be afraid that you will be seized by the throat!" This policy had been fiercely contested by the left opposition, which denounced it as capitulation to the NEP and the kulaks. Stalin himself had no real agrarian policy. He and his supporters aligned themselves with the right as a matter of tactics while they waited to be rid of the Zinovievists and the Trotskyists.

The right wanted to reduce taxes in rural areas. Nevertheless, beginning in 1926, the Central Committee decided on the contrary to increase them; the total tax revenue rose from 347 million rubles in 1925 to 496 million in 1926 and 759 million in 1927. This onerous taxation, with all the administrative harassments that went with it, led to the disastrous drop in the wheat harvest that was mentioned earlier. Virtually ceasing production for any consumers other than themselves, the peasants threatened the cities with starvation.

Nevertheless the resolution of the Fifteenth Congress in December 1927 contained reassuring prospects regarding the peasant problem. It was stated that the area of land under cultivation had increased and that the quantity of unused land had rapidly diminished. It was added that "the average peasant continues to be estranged from the kulak. . . . A decisive change has taken place against the kulak, tending to isolate him."

But an editorial in *Pravda* on January 15, 1928, took exactly the opposite view: "In the rural areas the kulak has grown rich and strong. . . . He holds back his wheat reserves in order to force up the price . . . he enjoys authority *and he forces the average peasant to follow him.*" (Italics added.)

Stalin's policy was hesitant at first. In the beginning of 1928 prosperous farmers who did not deliver their wheat were made subject to Article CVII of the Penal Code, which provided for one year of imprisonment and the confiscation of property. This decision was accompanied by illegal searches, police surveillance of roads and railway stations, and the prohibition of the sale of wheat in markets or villages.

In July 1928 the government went back to the normal methods of accumulating wheat. Endless lines waited at the doors of bakeries in the cities, and rationing offices had reappeared. In the countryside the peasants were more and more enraged by the persecutions, which recalled those of war Communism. Violence, rioting, sabotage, and arson increased, and Russia seemed to be slipping back into civil war. These disorders became so common that the newspapers had special permanent columns devoted to kulak crimes.[10]

[10] The peasants were divided into five categories:

In a secret conversation with Kamenev in July 1928 Bukharin confided that the GPU had had to put down 150 small, sporadic peasant risings. Insecurity was ubiquitous. Peasant correspondents, who were members of the party, were loathed by the population, which believed them to be informers and often killed them. Bandits were operating in rural areas. Panait Istrati, a writer touring the mountains of the Caucasus, could not move about without the protection of a strong militia escort. Chadayev, Victor Serge's friend, was released from prison and sent to the Kuban to investigate agricultural operations and was killed on a highway even though he was guarded by militiamen (who fled as soon as the attack started). Istrati wrote:

Side by side with passive resistance in the form of a reduction in the sowing of grain and the concealment of harvests, for the past two years there has also been a subterranean rebellion, active but sporadic, like a kind of guerrilla warfare, and it has claimed the lives of a number of real or supposed government agents, most often shot in the back; Soviet crops have gone up in flames reminiscent of the fires of the civil war. In 1928 twenty-four thousand anti-Communist attacks (armed aggressions and arson) have been recorded (*Izvestia,* December 8, 1928). The record for 1929 has not yet been compiled, but there is not a day, in a manner of speaking, when the newspapers do not tell of new manifestations of this nature. The masters of the USSR explain everything as the vengeance of the kulaks savagely opposing the "advances of Social-

---

1. poor peasants;
2. peasants who worked for wages but nevertheless owned bits of land;
3. average peasants, who worked their own land without the aid of hired labor;
4. prosperous peasants, who were well equipped with tools and who occasionally called on hired labor;
5. kulaks, who were regular employers of hired workers. The opposition also regarded the fourth category as made up of kulaks. The majority meant to restrict this term to the fifth category, which amounted to about 5 per cent of the peasantry. In practice, as collectivization increased, the majority's concept of the kulak came to be substantially enlarged.

ism," but who can be expected to believe that an infinitesimal minority scattered over a vast area and drowned in a huge mass of humanity can wage so implacable a struggle without favorable circumstances? [11]

In fact the Soviet press at the end of 1929 was filled with accounts of genuine or provoked conspiracies, and firing squads were functioning without quarter throughout the territory of the Soviet Union. Between October 20 and November 6, 187 persons were executed on charges of counterrevolution. Everywhere the GPU discovered plots in which former officers, manufacturers, landowners, engineers, priests, etc., were involved. At the end of September eight former officers and noncommissioned officers were arrested in Leningrad. In the beginning of October a counterrevolutionary organization with branches in Yaroslav, Ribinsk, Alexandrovsk, and Kinshna was brought to light. The accused included the archbishop of Yaroslav and the bishop of Kinshna. On October 25 it was announced that a monarchist organization preparing for a revolt had been uncovered in Sochi. It was headed by former tsarist officers and the superior of a monastery. They were shot. In Daghestant another underground organization, that of the "agrarians," was discovered.

The shootings included the following: at Kimi on October 27, Kolarov, a priest, with three parishioners and a kulak; at Gori, Voytrin, a priest, with Lazarev, a subdeacon, and two peasants; in Astrakhan, fourteen persons; in the district of Ostrov on October 29, three priests; on November 2, two priests and seventeen peasants. And so on. In Samara on December 3 the government completed the trial of a group of peasants who had stoned government agents. A priest and two kulaks were sentenced to death.

In such a state of violence, disorders, and repression, half-measures were worthless. It was necessary either to apply the policy of the right—that is, disarm peasant anger through

[11] Panait Istrati, *Vers l'autre flamme*, Vol. III, *La Russie nue*, pp. 168–169.

major concessions—or finally smash any attempts at revolt by invoking radical measures, regardless of the cost. This was the alternative elected by Stalin. Since taxes, searches, and requisitions were not enough, since the peasants were threatening to starve the cities by cutting off their sources of food supply, he resolved to destroy the very foundation of their power—in other words, private ownership.

At the time of the Fifteenth Congress in December 1927 it had been asserted that "the party recognizes the urgency of a tremendous propaganda in order to demonstrate to the peasant masses the necessity and the advantage to them of progressive conversion to collective exploitation of the land on a large scale." This slogan, however, had been accompanied by a clause that restricted its application: ". . . while at the same time emphasizing that this conversion can be accomplished *only with the consent of the workers.*" (Italics added.) The events that followed showed that the workers in no way approved this conversion. Collective agriculture (state farms and kolkhozi—collectives) was still quantitatively inadequate. The peasants were moved by no desire to join it. The competition between collective and individual agriculture was working out to the definite advantage of the latter.

Stalin launched his collectivization drive at the end of 1929. On November 17 the Central Committee decided that "through stubborn, systematic action the party should assemble agricultural day laborers and poor peasants into collective farms." Along the same lines Stalin told a conference of Marxist agronomists on December 27 that the government had moved from a policy of restricting the activity of the kulaks to one of completely liquidating them as a class. And on February 1, 1930, the government authorized regional and district Executive Committees to employ "whatever measures they deemed useful to combat the kulaks, up to and including the complete confiscation of their assets and the expulsion of these elements from certain districts and regions."

It seemed that a tornado was howling through the country.

Although no preparations had been made for their accommodation, the peasants were compelled to enter the kolkhozi. Whereas in October 1929 the proportion of collectivized enterprises was only 4.1 per cent, it reached 58 per cent by March 1930: *in other words, in five months more than half the peasant enterprises were collectivized.*

In order to achieve such a result in so short a time, only one method was possible: the application of an insensate terror. When peasants refused to join a kolkhoz voluntarily, village committees escorted by militiamen descended on them. Everything was confiscated: house, food, cattle, even clothing. The peasant and his family were thrown out of their own house, expelled from their district, often deported.

Stalin's brutal policy made such horrors inevitable. On paper it was always possible to draw a line of demarcation between the kulaks and the other peasants. But village realities knew nothing of this technocratic line of division. The village opposed its complex reality to the offensive of the central government. Some kulaks enjoyed authority, authority that was respected, in their villages. Others had blood ties with poor peasants. Very often the villagers instinctively refused to allow themselves to be broken up into categories on the basis of criteria set up by bureaucrats in the cities. This village autonomy was especially strong in the Ukraine. Even during the civil war the village councils, which had existed before the Revolution, opposed their traditional reality to the attempts to implant peasant soviets. In this region as in the Caucasus, moreover, resistance to enforced collectivization was solidly reinforced by national sentiment.

For all its strict orthodoxy, a reading of Sholokhov's novel, *Reclaimed Land,* is enough to make one aware of the profound inhumanity and also the absurdity of these measures. One of the heroes of the novel comes home in anguish from one of these expeditions, his ears still ringing with the cries of children. The justification for these forays is provided by one of his comrades, a party functionary and former officer: "You ought not to feel sorry for a kulak's children. Did the tsarist government take pity on the children of the working class?" [12] In contradiction of himself, the man who makes this statement comes to believe that, once the parents have been liquidated, the young generation will be won over to the government. In reality, as we shall see, this wholesale purge filled its victims' children with bitternesses that would only await an opportunity to burst forth.

Rather than turn over their possessions to a government that they loathed, the peasants preferred to destroy everything: They killed the cattle by the herd, as well as the sheep, the horses, even the poultry; they ate all that they could hold and then, if they had not been arrested, they took to the roads as vagabonds or tried to reach the cities. During the civil war the workers had tried to get to the country in order to find bread. Now it was the peasants who tried to find safety in the cities, at the gates of which squadrons of militiamen were waiting to drive them back.

Clashes occurred almost everywhere, from the Ukraine to Siberia, from the Caucasus to the gates of Moscow, where the peasant rising of Ryazan sowed panic in governmental quarters. Everywhere murders, arson, fighting were on the rise. In the Smolensk region the prosecutor counted thirty-four acts of terrorism in July and August of 1929 and forty-seven in October.[13] Party militants engaged in confiscation operations

[12] An identical repetition of this thought came from a party functionary making searches among the kulaks of the Smolensk region: "In battle there is no place for pity. What does it matter that a kulak's children know what famine is? In the class struggle philanthropy is a curse." Cf. Merle Fainsod, Smolensk à l'heure de Staline, p. 270. (This book is based on archives of the Smolensk authorities captured by the Germans during their advance into Soviet territory in July 1941. These archives, which the local authorities did not have time to destroy, subsequently fell into American hands after the defeat of Germany. Classified and indexed, they were the subject of Fainsod's book. Including records of the GPU as well as the party and the soviets, they constitute a unique source of documentation on the reality of the Soviet system.)

[13] Of the 127 victims of the October attacks, 10 were chairmen and 8 were secretaries of village soviets, 8 were officials assigned to crop

were advised to "stay out of range of windows and not to use village streets after nightfall."

Voroshilov, in spite of his usual docility, refused Stalin's request that the army be used against the rebels: "You are reducing the peasants to desperation, and then it will be I who will have to remedy the situation. I will not march." Hence it fell to special detachments of the GPU to put down the troubles.

They surrounded the rebelling villages and machine-gunned the peasants. Isaac Deutscher told of having met a GPU colonel between Moscow and Kharkov. "I am an old Bolshevik," he said, on the verge of sobs. "I worked in the underground against the tsar and then I fought in the civil war. Did I do all that to come down now to surrounding villages with machine guns and ordering my men to fire blindly into crowds of peasants? No! No!" [14]

Those who escaped the slaughter were most often deported to Siberia or the far north. At the agrarians' conference in December 1920 Larin had stated the kulak problem in these terms: "What is to be done in the future with kulak families? The kulak population amounts to 5 per cent in the rural areas —several million persons. *We do not believe that we must shoot all these kulaks and their descendants out of hand!"* (Italics added.)

The reprieve so generously envisaged by Larin was expulsion from the district without means of survival, or else deportation. The magazine, *Na Agrarnom Frontis* (*On the Agrarian Front*), laid down the methods to be followed for the liquidation of these kulaks in 1929–1930:

1. Confiscation of all the means of production.
2. Confiscation of all liquid wealth.

deliveries, and the rest were "activists" who took part in requisition operations. Of the 122 persons arrested for terrorism during the same month, half were kulaks or prosperous peasants, 45 per cent were poor or average peasants. Cf. Fainsod, p. 271.

[14] *Stalin*, p. 396.

3. Confiscation of all structures, including residences, on kulak farms, as well as furniture and food stocks.
4. With respect to certain kulaks the following methods of banishment were to be applied:
   (a) expulsion from the village but restriction of the kulak and his family to the district;
   (b) expulsion from the district, preferably to the north, Siberia, or the Far East; in the third instance the entire kulak family was expelled, but the expulsion order might also be limited to the head of the family, or to the family without its head if he had been arrested and imprisoned for counter-revolutionary acts.[15]

Some kulaks preferred death, and they imposed it on their wives and children as well. The others were driven out of their districts after they had been stripped of everything that they owned, sometimes even their shoes. Others were shipped to the east, jammed into cattle cars.

A top secret GPU document (March 27, 1931) described one such departure: 437 families—2202 persons—had been herded into reception centers in the city of Rostov. This GPU report stated that the workers approved these measures as a whole. Others adopted "a negative attitude," saying: "None of this would have happened if Lenin were still alive." Groups of women expressed their pity: "Why mistreat these poor people so? They have suffered for two years. One way and another, taxes took away everything that they had. It's a horrible thing to see children and adults sent away with nothing but the clothes on their backs!" [16]

---

[15] Collectivization led to a catastrophic decline in livestock. The animal census (in millions) underwent the following changes:

Year	Horses	Horned cattle	Sheep and goats	Pigs
1929	34	68.1	147.2	20.9
1930	30.2	52.5	108.8	13.6
1931	26.2	47.9	77.7	14.4
1932	19.6	40.7	52.1	11.6
1933	16.6	38.6	50.6	12.2

[16] Fainsod, *op. cit.*, p. 280.

Hundreds of thousands of men, women, and children were deported in this fashion. The journey from the Ukraine to Siberia took some forty days. The prisoners were forbidden to get out when the train stopped. Their only food was what they had been able to take with them. Ciliga wrote:

People died in huge numbers and with terrible suffering, "the living and the dead, their food and their excrement were all piled pell-mell together; desperate fathers were seen to snatch up their starving children and fracture their skulls against the telegraph poles past which the train was speeding.[17]

A letter written by a deportee in Siberia on April 5, 1931, described the arrival of the kulaks:

In the beginning we saw three thousand deported kulaks arrive. Many of them were poor or average peasants. Some had been decorated for their exploits in the civil war, but of course their decorations had been taken away from them. . . . No preparation had been made to receive them. The crowding in the barracks soon led to an epidemic of typhus. In the forests it was worse. They were sent there, I don't know why, with their wives, in the depth of winter without warm clothes.

Victor Serge wrote:

They were preparing for a general rising under the leadership of former soldiers. We succeeded in preventing this fresh tragedy by prevailing on the authorities to cancel the order that they be sent into the forests. All this was very much like sabotage organized on a huge scale. . . . A friend who had seen many kolkhozi told me that virtually nothing was left of the villages of the past and no return to individual ownership was possible without catastrophic upheavals; approximately 15 per cent of the farm workers were solidly in favor of the kolkhozi—these were the young Communists. And they were doing everything, they were working with an energy that seemed super-human.[18]

[17] Ciliga, *op. cit.*, p. 158.
[18] Victor Serge, "De Lénine à Staline," in the special issue of *Crapouillot* (*Trench Mortar*), p. 40.

Another letter, from Moscow, reported that typhus was raging everywhere.

In little railway stations there are patients who have been deserted and who are being eaten alive by lice. They are refused railway tickets for certain regions . . . this is true of the northern Caucasus and central Asia, where there is nothing but typhus: disorders there have reached the proportions of a civil war on a local scale.

The deportations continued until the end of the collectivization campaign—in other words, until 1933. The number of persons deported has been put at five million, but obviously it is impossible to establish exactly the extent of the repressions, for on this subject Soviet statistics, in all other matters so voluminous, are absolutely mute.

The ruthless character of the accelerated collectivization and the disorders that it incited, which threatened as they spread to bring about the fall of the government, led Stalin to sound the retreat. On March 2, 1930, he published an article, "The Vertigo of Success," in which he denounced the excesses of the collectivization campaign. Following his usual custom, he placed the responsibility for them on his underlings. Here and there a few dozen local functionaries and GPU agents paid the penalty: They were shot. In that era of butchery the government could afford a few more deaths.

Stalin's step backward produced a sharp drop in the number of kolkhozi. But it allayed the peasants' anger. The issue of *Pravda* in which this article was printed, and which normally sold for five kopecks, brought as much as ten rubles in the villages. In some places there were processions of peasants carrying Stalin's picture as if it were an ikon.

Later the collectivization drive was resumed and the great mass of the peasants offered no more than an uncohesive passive resistance. "You are frightened by cockroaches!" Stalin triumphantly told the rightists in the Sixteenth Congress. The "cockroaches" were all those persons who came under the label of kulak. Such a remark coming from Hitler would have set off a barrage of indignant commentaries. Inasmuch as its author was Stalin, good consciences ignored it with superb indifference.

The peasants' open resistance had been broken. Enlisted by force into the kolkhozi, they no longer evidenced anything more than a sorry resistance to an undesirable fate. The disorders, the waste, and the incompetence of the kolkhoz bureaucracy caused a drop in production that resulted in the terrible famine of 1933.

The deep feelings of the Soviet peasantry on this way of life were undoubtedly best expressed in a letter that a peasant named Pyotr Gorky sent to a newspaper called *Nasha Derevnya* (*Our Village*):

Every day they send us speakers who ask us to sign a pledge of allegiance to this or that kolkhoz, which means eternal slavery; but we do not wish to give up our nice homes. This may be a wretched cabin, but it is my own; my horse may be spavined, but he belongs to me.[19]

This letter may be compared with the petition addressed to "our dear and respected Comrade Rumyantsev" on July 23, 1936, by three orphans working in a kolkhoz:

Our father was purged as a kulak and sent over the border of our region. He died. Our mother is dead too. We came back from the Urals as orphans.

. . . Our old hut is now in the kolkhoz; there are back taxes to be paid on it; no one lives in it. That is why we, the children, beg you, Comrade Rumyantsev, to look into the matter so that our old hut may be given back to us. . . . I beg you not to ignore our request.

The Smolensk archives [20] show that in fact an investigation

[19] Cf. Fainsod, *op. cit.*, p. 283.
[20] *Ibid.*, p. 420.

was made. But it appeared that, far from being vacant, the house claimed by the children had become the property of the chairman of the kolkhoz. In this circumstance there could be no question of returning property to the children of a kulak. The matter was closed and the house remained in the hands of the representative of the new class.

(11)

BUKHARIN AT BAY

═══════════════════════════

THE PEASANT revolts were shattered one after
another. The peasants' weapons were the sawed-
off shotgun, the axe, and the knife. But the
question of weapons played a much smaller
part in their defeat than the lack of an expert apparatus for
the coordination of their activities. Only one party had succeeded in solidly entrenching itself in the rural areas before
the Revolution: the Revolutionary Socialist party, the heir of
Populism and the *Narodnaya Volya*. But the backbone of this
party had been arrested during the civil war and disintegrated
by deportation and flight to other countries. Obviously the
White Russians' emigrant organizations were in no position to
establish clandestine networks, an undertaking made the more
difficult by the GPU. Besides, as we have seen, all their projects had been neutralized by the provocation known as the
Trust. No more had Petlyura's Ukrainian nationalists had the
time to build up solid organization. Now scattered risings and
individual revolts were doomed to defeat if there was no intellectual nucleus to take over their leadership. Only such a
nucleus would be in a position to direct the anger of the
masses to political objectives, to organize the struggle in terms

of a definitive strategy, to substitute a static defense based on a village or an *izba* [1] for the offensive action represented by the creation of an underground. For lack of such a leadership group, Stalin's tactical retreat disarmed resistance instead of encouraging it.

Here it is necessary to go back and examine how Stalin's opponents inside the party reacted to his policy of collectivization. The right wing of the Bolshevik party, which favored a policy of concessions, was totally incapable of taking advantage of the situation and overthrowing Stalin. The rightists' efforts to alter a policy that they regarded as catastrophic took the form of embryonic actions that were pitifully aborted.

Bukharin, Rykov, and Tomsky, the leaders of the right, could not hope to win in the Central Committee, where Stalin through his supporters held the majority. The situation was different in the Politburo, where Stalin could rely on only three votes besides his own—those of Molotov, Kuibyshev, and Rudzutak. The rightists hoped to be able to gain the backing of Voroshilov and Kalinin. Thus, with five votes against four, they would put Stalin into the minority in the Politburo. In short, they were already seeking to carry out the plan that was to be attempted later by Kaganovich and Molotov in order to overthrow Khrushchev.[2]

Voroshilov's value, furthermore, went far beyond the mere contribution of a vote, because he had the army behind him. In a letter written from his exile in Alma-Ata on October 21, 1928, Trotsky repeated certain rumors and raised the prospect of a Bonapartist armed coup achieved through collusion between the right and the army: "Let us not forget that in the report of July [1928] to the Assembly of Moscow Militants the sorry leader of the right [this was Rykov] said, in allusion to his friend, Klim [Voroshilov]: 'If you resort again to ex-

---

[1] The typical log hut of the peasant.—Translator.

[2] On the later occasion the operation succeeded in the Politburo but was thwarted in the Central Committee, which Khrushchev had managed to alert.

treme measures, the army will retaliate with an insurrection.'
This is a sentence full of meaning—half prediction, half threat.
Perhaps, in fact, the element of threat amounts to three-quarters."

In the same letter, however, Trotsky added: "It is said that
Klim has gone over from the right opposition to a right center
position and that he is supporting the 'chief' [Stalin]." This
"it is said," which Trotsky, because of the time that it took for
news to reach him, had been unable to verify, was correct.
Shattering the hopes of the right, Voroshilov and Kalinin
voted with Stalin.

"Stalin has a hold on them that I cannot explain," Bukharin
was to say later. This singular hold could probably be attributed to Stalin's secret weapons: the files. No one knows what
blackmail he was in a position to practice on Voroshilov. Car-
toons appearing in the newspapers at this period, on the
other hand, showed an unidentified person, who might have
been Kalinin's twin, presenting a magnificent necklace to an
actress. The allusion was obvious: Kalinin had been accused
of dissipating the state's money in sumptuous gifts. The threat
of scandal was undoubtedly enough to influence his vote.

Istrati revealed that Stalin followed an almost identical procedure against Tomsky, who was at the head of the Soviet
labor unions. The committees of the Building Trades Union
and the Union of Government Officials and Employes of Moscow were in fact involved in charges of embezzlement. Stalin
hushed up the scandal at the price of these bureaucrats' votes
against their leader.

The session of the Politburo in which the rightists had seen
their hopes destroyed by the defections of Voroshilov and
Kalinin was immediately followed by a session of the Central
Committee, from July 4 to July 12, that ended in a compromise formula. But the prior discussions had been unusually
stormy. Stalin declared that a tribute must be levied on the
peasants in order to accumulate capital that would make it

possible to accelerate the pace of industrialization. He conceded that collectivization would have to be gradual, but he no longer spoke of voluntary peasant enlistment in the kolkhoz. This was already a significant omission.

Meanwhile Kamenev and Zinoviev, who had offered their total submission at the Fifteenth Congress, had been readmitted to the party. On July 11 Kamenev was in his Moscow apartment with Sokolnikov. A month earlier, by mail, Sokolnikov had informed him that on this date he would have a surprising visitor: Bukharin.

Sarcastic and savage, applauded by Stalin, Bukharin had attacked the left opposition to the utmost. But the visitor who greeted Kamenev now had nothing of the victor. He was pale and trembling, his conversation was disjointed, jumping from one subject to another. From time to time there was a light foam on his lips. He produced the impression of a man with his back against the wall.

He began by describing the stifling atmosphere that prevailed in the Politburo. "We insulted one another to the point of epithets like 'liar' and 'fake,'" he said. "He [Stalin] has given in now, but only in order to strangle us the better: he is maneuvering in such a way as to make us appear to be schismatics. His objective now is to get Moscow, Leningrad, and *Pravda* away from us and to replace Uglanov [secretary of the Moscow organization] with Kaganovich."

As he went on, Bukharin explained Stalin's policy. "According to him, capitalism evolved by despoiling its colonies, issuing loans, and exploiting its workers. . . .

"1. He points out that we have no colonies and that no other nation will lend us money. Therefore the only solution for us is to levy a tribute on the peasantry. This, you understand, is the same thing as Preobrazhensky's theory.

"2. He believes that, the more Socialism grows, the more the resistance to it will mount. This is the illiteracy of an imbecile.

"3. Consequently the tribute must be imposed. If resistance

increases, then there must be a firm leadership. Hence self-criticism should be practiced not against the leadership but only against its executory agents.

"In practice, according to his view, self-criticism should be directed against Tomsky and Uglanov. The result of this would lead to a police state."

"What backing do you have?" Kamenev asked.

"Apart from myself," Bukharin replied, "there are Rykov, Tomsky, and Uglanov. On the whole the Leningrad people are with us, but the mention of deposing Stalin frightens them. Andreyev is with us. But Stalin has bought out the Ukrainians by bringing Kaganovich out of the Ukraine." He also named two GPU men: Yagoda, who was Menzhinsky's deputy, and Trilisser. "They are with us. Voroshilov and Kalinin betrayed us at the last minute. I think Stalin has them bound by some special chain of which I know nothing. The *Orgburo* is also with us."

Kamenev and Sokolnikov listened uncomfortably as he spoke. He said that he had support, but a moment later he demanded: "Does all this agitation of ours amount to anything more than masturbation?" He spoke of backing from Yagoda and yet he voiced a panic fear of being spied on by the GPU. He compared Stalin with Genghiz Khan and cried: "What can be done against such a man?"

His indecision seemed appalling when he analyzed the tactics that should be adopted to combat Stalin. "Our potential forces are vast," he said, "but, first, the average member of the Central Committee has not yet grasped in its entirety the depth of the divergencies of views. Second, there is a tremendous fear of schism. That is why I have followed Stalin on the subject of extraordinary measures [against the peasants], because in this way I have made it more difficult for him to attack us. We do not want to look like schismatics, because then we should be strangled. Our task is gradually to explain the dangerous part played by Stalin and to persuade the average member of the Central Committee to remove him from his post."

"But, while you are waiting," Kamenev pointed out iron-ically, "it is he who is removing you."

Bukharin threw up his hands in a gesture of weariness. "What is to be done? His removal would not be agreed to now by the Central Committee. Sometimes at night I think: 'But do we have the right to be silent? Isn't this to lack cour-age?' Then, considering the matter, I tell myself that we must move with caution. If it is we who open the question, we shall be strangled for it. The Central Committee is afraid of discussion. It will degenerate into a brawl at once. We would say: 'Here is the man who has brought the country to famine and death.' And he would reply: 'They are defending the kulak and the NEP.' "

"On what do they rely for the procurement of wheat?" Kam-enev asked.

"On the repetition of extraordinary measures, given the in-evitable difficulties that will arise. But this is war Communism and throat-cutting."

"What policy do you recommend?"

"They can hunt down the kulaks as much as they like," Buk-harin said, "but it is essential to conciliate the average peas-ant. But there is nothing to be done with Stalin and that brute, Molotov, who tries to give me lessons in Marxism and whom privately we call Stone-Arse."

"So what do you want of us?" Kamenev asked.

"Stalin boasts that he has you in his pocket. Your people are committed to Stalin everywhere. Obviously you are at lib-erty to determine your own course of conduct, but I am ask-ing you not to help Stalin strangle us. It would be terrible. Stalin will probably try to get into contact with you."

"What is going to be done with us?" Kamenev wanted to know.

"I don't know. This question is not raised among us. Either

Stalin will try to buy you off with big jobs or he will put you into posts that will commit you to him."

When Bukharin left, he insisted on the greatest precautions to keep their conversation a secret. "Don't telephone me," he said, "because my calls are intercepted. Only Rykov and Tomsky know that I have come here. Don't mention it to anyone, but find some way of telling your people to avoid attacking us. Good-bye; I will be very busy with the Congress in the next few days and I won't be able to see you."

Immediately after Bukharin's departure, Kamenev drafted a letter to Zinoviev, who was in Voronezh, to give him the essential details of the conversation. A host of new points came back to mind and he hastened to include them. Bukharin's attitude toward Stalin, for example: It revealed absolute hatred and an irreparable rupture. He insisted on Stalin's hypocrisy. Stalin had sought to conciliate Bukharin by way of flattery: "With you we are the Himalaya, the others do not count." But, when Bukharin repeated this conversation in a session of the Politburo that he described as "savage," Stalin began to shout: "You're lying! You invented that to arouse the members of the Politburo against me!"

No shred of trust could be reposed in this man. It was dangerous to provide him with the most trivial scrap of paper, because he was always prepared to use it against the giver. So Bukharin had read aloud, without letting it get out of his hands, a resolution that Molotov denounced as anti-Leninist. But Stalin had asserted coldly: "I can very well endorse nine-tenths of it." Even after the most violent clashes he was capable of any reversal, every possible compromise, without any interruption, however, in his scheming for one's downfall. In order to make it clear what kind of man one was dealing with, Bukharin had recalled the theory of "the sweetness of vengeance." Speaking frankly one summer night in 1923 with Kamenev and Dzerzhinsky, Stalin had said: "To select a victim, meticulously prepare the action, gratify an implacable vengeance to the full, and then go to bed . . . there is nothing sweeter in the world." [3]

After this long conversation, Kamenev had a few infrequent talks with Bukharin, these in the home of Pyatakov. The last took place at the beginning of December, and it brought to an end the wispy understanding between the rightists and the Zinovievists.

Remembering the crushing defeat inflicted on the left opposition, the right decided to adopt a policy of temporization. But Uglanov, who was too bellicose, had compromised this project by a premature attack. "He was under orders to keep his composure," Bukharin explained, "in order not to provide Stalin with some pretext for intervention in Moscow. But in the Ninth Plenum of the Moscow Committee he launched an attack, and he was beaten."

Kamenev was stunned to learn in addition that it was Bukharin himself who had drafted the Politburo's resolution against the rightist movement. "What? *You* wrote it?"

"Of course I did. The right having been brought under attack, I certainly had to make it clear to the party that I was not a rightist!"

Meanwhile the altercations in the Politburo were continuing. At one meeting Bukharin made a number of violent remarks and stormed out. Encountering Tovstukha, one of Stalin's secretaries, in a corridor, he gave her a "note prepared in advance" in which he announced his own and Tomsky's resignations.

"Stalin had come out to find me," he said, "and Tovstukha gave him my statement. He ran through it and went back inside. Rykov said later that his hands were trembling. He was absolutely white, and he stated his desire to make concessions. He insisted that my statement of resignation be destroyed."

---

[3] Written down by Kamenev, these notes on his talks with Bukharin were published in Nos. 25–26 of *Contre le courant,* March 22, 1929. They were also published at the same time in *The Socialist Courier* in New York.

In return Stalin agreed to dismiss a few Stalinists whose resignations were being demanded by the rightists. But these concessions made no great difference: Stalin was applying his policy. The right was growing weaker.

Bukharin then showed Kamenev an eleven-page document on the economic situation, which was clearly farther to the right than his positions of April 1925. "What do you intend to do with it?" Kamenev asked.

"Supplement it with reflections on the international situation and a section on the party's internal affairs."

"Is it a platform, then?"

"Perhaps." Bukharin was irritated by Kamenev's skepticism. "You have drafted platforms too, haven't you?"

At this point Pyatakov joined the conversation. "I advise you," he told Bukharin, "not to launch an offensive against Stalin, who has the support of the majority. Past experience shows that this kind of operation ends badly."

"Yes, that is correct," Bukharin agreed. "But what is to be done?"

This was the question that he had already posed in July with much wringing of hands. Once again there was no reply to it. He left. The alliance between the right and the Zinovievists had been nothing but a dream.

After Bukharin's departure, Kamenev rebuked Pyatakov for having prevented the conflict from proceeding by voicing his pessimistic views. "No one can do anything against Stalin," Pyatakov asserted. "In the present situation Stalin is still the only man who can be obeyed. Bukharin and Rykov imagine that, if they succeeded in eliminating him, they would govern in his place. What a mistake! Kaganovich would take his place. And as for me I have no desire to obey Kaganovich."

A one-time cobbler, Kaganovich was known for his brutal ways. Barmin's book told of his participation in a working session presided over by Kaganovich. He allowed others to speak for two minutes and then cut them off. Stalin did not behave with any less authority, but Stalin belonged to the older generation. This partly excused his coarseness, which on the whole was less shocking to a man like Pyatakov than that of a newcomer.

His observation was nevertheless quite revealing. It demonstrated the preference of responsible party leaders for a man of action over a brilliant theoretician like Bukharin.

"What do you suggest, then?" Kamenev inquired.

"Oh, it's quite simple," Pyatakov replied. "You know I've been put in charge of the State Bank. I will see to it that there is money in that bank."

"Perfect. As for me, I've been placed at the head of a scientific agency. I won't pretend to you that I have any great interest in seeing to it that scientists get into that agency. That is not politics."

They parted on this note. At the end of December Zinoviev and Kamenev reexamined the situation. It was impossible to rely on the right. The only solution was to hang onto the tiller. This could be done only by supporting Stalin. They would have to pay his price.

Kamenev went to woo Ordzhonikidze. He enthusiastically endorsed the Central Committee's line. His friends were ready to support it. So why should he and Zinoviev be left to stagnate in inactivity?

"It is too soon," Ordzhonikidze said. "The right would protest."

"But we are not demanding high positions," Kamenev said very humbly. "Let us just have permission to write for the press."

Ordzhonikidze promised to present the matter to the Politburo, and Kamenev thereupon laid siege to Voroshilov. For two hours he sang the praises of the Central Committee's policy. For two hours Voroshilov listened without opening his mouth. The result of these humiliating visits was disappointment.

The sequel was dramatic. The text of the famous talk between Kamenev and Bukharin came to the knowledge of Stalin.

It has been said that the GPU found the notes. Perhaps the GPU knew of them, but there is no proof of this. In reality the conversation and its tenor were disclosed by a leaflet disseminated in Moscow by the clandestine Trotskyist opposition.

Kamenev had kept Trotsky's backers informed of these talks. As long as the talks had continued, the Trotskyists had kept silent, for they looked on them as a possible means to the overthrow of Stalin. But, when the Trotskyists learned that Zinoviev and Kamenev were trying to make their way into the secretary general's good graces, all their rage against the "capitulaters" revived.

This was a precious windfall for Stalin. Thus far he had been able to reduce the right to virtual silence. He had not succeeded in ridding himself of it. Now he had a frightful weapon against it.

One after the other, Kamenev and Bukharin were called into the presence of Ordzhonikidze, to whom, with some reservations, they confirmed what they had said to each other in their various meetings. On January 30 and February 9, 1929, they appeared before a joint session of the Politburo and the Central Control Commission convened to investigate their case. Obviously they were in a delicate situation: They had pretended to endorse the party's policy and at the same time they had held meetings of a conspiratorial nature. They showed a tendency to constitute a fraction, and this was prohibited by the party's statutes. They had given proof of a flagrant duplicity.

Bukharin attempted to reply by denouncing the abnormal working conditions within the party. "Twelve years after the Revolution," he said, "there is not a single elected provincial secretary. . . . Everything is done from above." His remarks were interrupted by outraged shouts: "Where did you learn that? From whom? From Trotsky?"

In fact these were the same criticisms, made by Trotsky

against the party organization, that had been hurled back in the past with much sarcasm by Bukharin and his partisans.

In April, after an indictment by Stalin, the Central Committee sternly condemned the theses of the rightists. Nevertheless Bukharin and Tomsky remained members of the Politburo and Rykov continued to be Chairman of the Council of People's Commissars. But they were reduced to the rank of figureheads. Any criticism voiced by them now would doom them to expulsion. And this was only a respite. In June Tomsky was replaced by Shvernik as head of the labor unions. A month later Bukharin lost the chairmanship of the Executive Committee of the Comintern. This ouster was a call to hounds. The press accused Bukharin of compromises with capitalist (kulak and NEP) elements and collusion with former Trotskyists.

If he was to avoid expulsion the only course available to him was to denounce himself. Uglanov confessed all his sins in November. After some resistance, Bukharin, Tomsky, and Rykov admitted that their views had been erroneous. Bukharin himself was expelled from the Politburo.

The defeat of the right had been conclusively accomplished, after an uncertain resistance that contrasted with the open opposition by the Trotskyists.

It is logical to wonder why the right wing of the party was so easily vanquished. At first glance, in fact, it appeared to be much more solid than the left opposition. It had rallied many supporters in the rank and file of the party. But above all it could hope to find a basis in tens of millions of peasants fiercely opposed to collectivization and devoted to the NEP. The left opposition could hope for no support from this quarter, and its ties with the working class, with rare exceptions, had never been so strong as it claimed. The workers remembered that Trotsky had wanted to militarize them and that Zinoviev had conducted himself like a satrap in Leningrad.

The essential weakness of the right was brilliantly exposed in an article that Trotsky wrote in November 1928 in his exile in Alma-Ata. In it he said, in part:

In order to give battle, it [the right] would have had to mobilize openly all the property elements and instincts existing in the country. . . . The lack of maturity in the Thermidorian wing of the party, *the lack of political communications between that wing and the reserve represented by the landowners* [italics added] explain the ease with which the centrists [Stalinists] have won their present triumph. There is merely a bureaucratic display instead of military operations, and nothing else!

There is confirmation of this view in Bukharin's observations to Kamenev:

1. If the country loses, we shall perish.
2. If the country comes through, Stalin will gain and again we shall perish.

By this he meant that, if a revolt swept away the government, the right would be liquidated with the rest of the Bolsheviks, and that on the other hand, if the imminent crisis was resolved peacefully—and this, he supposed, could mean only a retreat by Stalin—this too would mean the liquidation of the right. So the eternal question remained: What was to be done?

The only solution would have been for the right to seek support in the resistance of the mass of the peasantry. This was difficult, perhaps, because of the GPU's surveillance. But Bukharin and his associates could hardly make up their minds to adopt this course. They considered it quite likely that they in their turn would have been overthrown after the triumph of the peasant revolts and that a general insurrection would have sounded the knell of the system.

From then on they were doomed to ineffectual debate and inglorious surrenders.

(12)

IN THE GOVERNMENT'S
"ISOLATION CELLS"

I N THE remoteness of his exile Trotsky had not laid
down his weapons. He had been sent to Alma-Ata,
the administrative capital of Kazakstan. It was a
repulsive little town that for a large part of the year
was the prey of mud and floods and, in summer, of clouds of
dust driven by the wind across a torrid sky. Malaria was the
rule in this desolate place. Mad dogs ran howling through its
streets. Sitting outside their little shops, the Kirghiz tribesmen
occupied themselves by picking their lice. In this backwater
of the Soviet Union there was neither regular mail service nor
regular transportation.

Trotsky went hunting and fishing and covered tremendous
distances with inexhaustible energy except when he was incapacitated by malaria. But, as might well be imagined, politics was still the focus of his activities. And for him there was
no question of giving up the fight.

Against that fight there were substantial obstacles. All Trot-
sky's lieutenants had been painstakingly dispersed by the
GPU: Rakovsky to Astrakhan, Radek to Tobolsk, Muralov to
Tara, Mrachkovsky to Voronezh, Ivan Smirnov to Armenia.
The irregularly functioning outgoing mail from Alma-Ata car-

ried a veritable torrent of letters and instructions addressed to
these comrades, who replied and who conveyed their leader's
directives to the other deported Trotskyist oppositionists. This
multiple exchange of correspondence, of course, was thoroughly read by the GPU. But later the Trotskyists succeeded
in maintaining a completely clandestine postal service that
was the special concern of Trotsky's son, Lev Sedov, who was
with him in Alma-Ata.

Trotsky was delighted by Stalin's new "leftward orienta-
tion." In sum Stalin was at last adopting the opposition's program. If he wished to pursue this offensive, which entailed an
enormous economic transformation, he could not be satisfied
with his own apparatus. He would need the reinforcement of
technicians, economists, administrators. Since he could not
count too heavily on Bukharin's supporters, he would be certainly compelled to turn to the Trotskyists and the Zinovievists.

The left opposition's line of conduct, then, in Trotsky's view,
consisted in holding firm until the time when Stalin would
see that he must halt his repression and seek the help of the
Trotskyists in order to get the better of the right.

These optimistic predictions were very easily proved false
by Stalin. Trotsky's criticism had depicted him as the prisoner
of the right—in other words, of the NEP and the kulak—the
prisoner of the new bourgeoisie that was speedily developing,
the hostage of Thermidorian reaction. But he was exerting
maximum pressure for the program of industrialization and
collectivization. Appropriating the policy of Trotsky and his
supporters, Stalin deprived the left opposition of a battlefield.

Trotsky's appraisal was correct, however, in its prediction
that Stalin would need reinforcements. His error lay in be-
lieving that the secretary general would acquire them at the
cost of halting his repressions. Stalin believed, on the contrary, that the policy that he was putting into effect and the
hardships of exile would very soon demoralize many of the
deportees. His emissaries sought out the oppositionists in

their "isolation cells" and argued that, "fundamentally, there is no longer any difference between us. It is time to resume your place in the party. But the party cannot repudiate its past. It is your duty to make the act of submission. Only *petitbourgeois* pride unworthy of a revolutionary can prevent you from doing this."

Confusion began to appear in the ranks of the Trotskyists. Preobrazhensky and Radek were already inclined to yield. In a letter addressed to Radek, Smirnov gave full rein to his bitterness at being reduced to the state of a slave:

You are suffering because we are now outside the party. For me too and for everyone else this has been a real agony. In the beginning I was haunted by actual nightmares. I woke up abruptly in the middle of the night, unable to believe that I had been deported— I, who had worked for the party without interruption since 1899, without taking a single day of rest, and not like some of those shabby members of the Society of "Old Bolsheviks" who deserted the party after 1908. . . .

Dissensions appeared on another level as well. True, Stalin was applying the policy of the left. But it was hardly to be expected that he would reestablish internal democracy. It would undoubtedly be easier to come to an agreement with men like Bukharin and Rykov, who, even though they were preaching a different economic program, would never attempt to impose the suffocating tyranny of the secretary general on the party.

The prestige that Trotsky enjoyed among the exiles, however, prevented the disintegration of their forces. And it was out of the question that he should "go to Canossa," to beg Stalin to forgive him, as Zinoviev and Kamenev had done.

It was still too soon to kill Trotsky. Stalin decided to banish him. On January 20, 1929, Trotsky's house in Alma-Ata was encircled by soldiers in arms. A GPU functionary handed him a document stating that Trotsky was forbidden access to "the entire territory of the Soviet Union."

He was allowed twenty-four hours for his preparations for departure. At dawn on January 22 he and his family left Alma-Ata and traveled to Frunze over a snow-covered mountain road. From Frunze the journey was continued by train. It was only during the trip that Trotsky learned where Stalin had decided to exile him: Constantinople.

He sent a telegram of protest to Moscow. There was no reply. His guards had no orders. Until they should arrive, the train was halted on a siding near a small station no longer in use.

It was a frightful winter. The thermometer fell to fifty below zero. The railway cars stood motionless on their track between two meager curtains of trees. The days went by. Empty food tins piled up on either side of the track. The train seemed to have been forgotten by everyone, lost in the oppressive white vastness. Silence, boredom, waiting. Crows and magpies wheeled in the leaden sky. They were the only things that moved in this frozen universe—they and the locomotive, which panted and breathed out steam and smoke as it rolled endlessly back and forth along the siding in order to avoid being frozen into permanent immobility.

Finally the orders came. The train jerked and lurched and headed south. Odessa: a black night, a deserted port, armed soldiers on the platform. In spite of the high winds of a storm, the steamer *Ilyich* (Lenin's patronymic) weighed anchor behind an ice-breaker that cut a path for her. Her passenger was the famous leader of the Red Army, now a mere outlaw.

In June 1929 the train that was carrying Radek and Smilga back to Moscow halted in a small station in Siberia. A few deported oppositionists were standing on the platform. Smilga, who was ill, stayed in his compartment; Radek got out to talk to his comrades on the platform. Yes, he was going back to Moscow to offer his surrender. There was no other possible way. It was the policy of the left that Stalin was following.

Hence it was a duty to support him at a time when kulak revolts were breaking out everywhere.

"Will you insist that we not be made subject to Article LVIII, which deprives us of all rights by making us counter-revolutionaries?" he was asked.

"Certainly not," Radek retorted. "If you persist in your opposition, you are counterrevolutionaries. You get what you deserve!"

"Will you at least demand the return of Comrade Trotsky, as Preobrazhensky has done?"

"No. I have made a complete break with Lev Davidovich. To me he is a political enemy now. I have nothing more in common with Lord Beaverbrook's collaborator." [1]

He went on denouncing the members of the opposition, particularly the younger ones, who, in his opinion, had nothing of the Bolshevik in them. He would have continued if the GPU guards had not cut him off. "So you are engaging in counter-revolutionary agitation!" they cried. "Back to your compartment as fast as you can make it!"

"Me?" Radek said. "On the contrary, I am trying to convince these men."

But the police were not interested. With considerable vigor they thrust Radek back into his place.

Preobrazhensky and several other opposition leaders had already recanted. In October, after Radek and Smilga, it was Ivan Smirnov's turn, followed by Mrachkovsky and Ter-Vaganian. Raskovsky was one of the last to submit, in the beginning of 1934. All of them attempted to drive bargains with their recantations, to obtain concessions that would salve their pride. Stalin was immovable.

Of four or five thousand oppositionists, three-quarters were former deportees. Stalin entrusted them with no important political posts. But he needed administrators, economists, prop-

[1] From his exile Trotsky had published an article in one of Beaverbrook's newspapers.

agandists in order to accomplish his purpose. He used these men who in the depth of their hearts hated him.

The irreducibles were subjected to increasingly harsh treatment. As we have seen, they had nothing but contempt for the capitulators. Locked in their cells, they remained loyal to Trotsky. They argued feverishly, and their controversies were carried on with the rage built up in them by repression.

In Astrakhan, Tara, Voronezh, Tomsk, Verkhney-Uralsk, every place in European or Asian Russia where there was a colony of political deportees or internees, this empire doomed to silence was dotted with little islands in which the utmost freedom of expression reigned. There, but only there, the right to freedom of speech and writing and association was tolerated—under the eyes of the GPU's henchmen, who did not fail to report everything.

Let us take the instance of Verkhney-Uralsk, where Ciliga was interned in November 1930, and of which he painted an accurate and living picture. The prison was a tremendous three-storied rectangular structure that included 60 rooms into which 250 prisoners were packed. It was surrounded by a wall fifteen feet high, studded with watchtowers, and there were five courtyards, separated by transverse walls, for the prisoners' exercise.

They slept in the north wing, which was the coldest. The rooms, which varied in size, were poorly heated as a rule, and in winter the prisoners wore furred jackets and felt boots. The food was meager: bread (twenty-five ounces) and broth in the morning and evening, varied at noon by a soup of bad fish, tinned foods, and meat, and at night by another soup, but without meat or fish. Once a week the prisoners were entitled to herring garnished with cabbage or beets. This Spartan diet was supplemented by a ration of sugar (two and one-quarter pounds per month) and another of tea. There were also tobacco, cigarettes, and soap.

But the prison routine never overlooked the revolutionary holidays, May Day and November 7, and on those occasions each man received a small slice of white bread. Thus Ciliga, who spent three years in this isolation camp, enjoyed six slices.

For beds there were trestles on which a few boards were laid. At meals the prisoners gathered round large common tables poorly lighted by a single bulb in the ceiling. Twice a day four or five rooms of men—twenty-five to thirty persons—went out into one of the courtyards for an hour. They walked, talked, or exercised, playing football, tennis, and *garbalky*—a Russian variety of bowling. Twice a month they had baths, at which times they turned in their underwear and bedclothes for laundering.

While the food was mediocre and comforts were sparse, the library, on the other hand, was suitably varied. The prison administration had inherited the collections assembled under the tsars, and each new arrival had contributed his small personal store.

In principle the prisoners were isolated in their respective rooms and were not permitted to communicate among them. But there were many ways of getting round the rules. Almost as soon as a new prisoner shipment arrived, the names of its members were passed from room to room and from floor to floor. A note could be passed by way of the flues. Other contacts were made through windows, although this was forbidden. At a signal a rope would be let down from an upper floor with a bag into which the "mail" was placed. Using long poles, the keepers would try to hook it as it passed. But it was difficult to watch all the windows at the same time. Some of the prisoners, using sticks, engaged in regular skirmishes with the guards, the stake being the "mailbag." There was a tacit rule to this game: As soon as the bag reached its destination or was intercepted, the fighting stopped on both sides.

Every left-wing tendency that the government had prohibited was reconstituted here. All were strictly organized, and, except in extraordinary circumstances, none had anything to do with the others. The Communists, who numbered

140, formed their own exercise groups and looked on the Socialists and the anarchists (of whom there were about 50) as counterrevolutionaries. Each group had set up a "black bank," supported by money received from outside, and each bank was managed by a "finance minister."

The Trotskyists, of whom there were 120, represented the great majority of the Communist prisoners. The rest included some fifteen members of the Democratic Centralism group, two or three supporters of Myasnikov's Workers' Opposition, and one lone Zinovievist who had not capitulated (in the debates in which these intransigents engaged, the bitterest insults were "capitulater" and "semi-capitulater"). The non-Communists included Russian Mensheviks, Georgian Mensheviks, and anarchists. There were also five left Revolutionary Socialists, a few right Revolutionary Socialists, a handful of Zionists, and some Armenian Socialists.

All these men, as we have said, were far from agreeing with one another. But it must not be supposed that even the Trotskyists, whose organization was called the Bolshevik-Leninist Collective of Verkhney-Uralsk, formed a homogeneous group: They had a right, a center, and a left. Each of these fractions had evolved its own program—the program of "the three" (drafted by three professors) for the right, the program of "the two" (drafted by Trotsky's son-in-law, Man-Nivelson, and Aaron Papermeister) for the center, and the "theses of the militant Bolsheviks" for the left.

These were endless documents that analyzed the various aspects of the situation in the Soviet Union. In addition the right and the center had arrived at an understanding for the publication of *Pravda in Prison*, while the left's organ was called *The Militant Bolshevik*. These manuscript periodicals appeared monthly. Each issue contained ten to twenty articles signed by their authors. Obviously their "press run" was rather limited: three copies. But each copy went from room to room.

Since there was no other activity aside from exercise and reading, there was endless discussion. Every day the prison was like a big meeting, or, rather, like a club, where everyone's position was debated with much reference to Marx and Lenin. In these sessions the secretary general, who had not yet received the brevet of genius from the official press, was described by all kinds of names.

The bitter criticisms of which Stalin was the object in no way prevented most of these men from regarding themselves as members of the party. This was not Ciliga's point of view: "How can we still consider ourselves members of a party that has expelled us and had us put into prison by the GPU?" [2] Somewhat later he rejoiced at a decline in the production of coal in the Donbas. For this he was sharply taken to task by two Trotskyists, who told him: "It is our duty to be alarmed by anything that threatens to weaken Soviet power."

"But, if production is dropping," Ciliga argued, "that is not defeatism; it shows merely that the workers are resisting bureaucratic despotism."

"No," the Trotskyists insisted, "they are counterrevolutionaries." [3]

In the endless controversies that divided the members of the various groups and fractions, all the discussion focused on the Five-Year Plan, which was then in operation. Trotsky's writings, which arrived from abroad only after long delays, naturally aroused passionate interest in all these men.

On the whole, regardless of the groups to which they adhered, the Communist prisoners remained loyal to the system. Their criticisms dealt only with the deviations to which it had

[2] Ciliga, *Au pays du mensonge déconcertant*, p. 164.

[3] Some idea of the Trotskyists' attitude toward prisoners who were not members of the party can be derived from a prisoner's letter printed in *Contre le courant* (No. 12, June 28, 1928). It reported that in the prison of Butyrky (Corridor 14, Room 63) there were Georgian Mensheviks who were allowed a private washroom, better food, and newspapers. "This," the Trotskyists wrote, "is indeed a spectacle calculated to rejoice the counterrevolutionaries." No. 10 of the same publication declared on a note of outrage that oppositionists' wives were interned with those of NEP.

been subjected. Only certain members of the Workers' Opposition were critical of the one-party principle, and a young member of the Democratic Centralism went as far as to say that there had never been a proletarian revolution in Russia. According to his view the world was moving toward state capitalism in Soviet Russia as in Fascist Italy, in Germany as in the United States, with a new bureaucratic ruling class—we today would call it technocratic. Ciliga justly observed that young Smirnov might be regarded as a forerunner of Burnham. These heretical theses created a scandal and naturally cost him immediate expulsion from the Democratic Centralism group.

At that time this category of prisoners still enjoyed a political status that was to be abolished in 1936. Yet the situation of these men had already grown worse under Stalin. In the beginning, indeed, the "politicals" had the right to circulate in the large rooms and move about freely all day, thus enjoying, as Ciliga pointed out, a status comparable to what Napoleon III had established at Belle-Ile.

Only the Socialists, the Communists, and the anarchists were entitled to the status of "politicals." All the others—the tsarists, the "religious," the workers, the peasants, the NEP—were treated as ordinary criminals. Millions of them were in camps from Solovetzky, where they had built the canal that linked the Baltic with the White Sea, to the shores of the Pacific Ocean. In the forests of northern Russia and Siberia, in the coal mines of Kuznetz and Karaganda, in the copper factories of Balmash, in the electrical powerhouses of central Asia, in the gold mines of Kolyma, and even in European Russia, where they cut through the Moscow-Volga canal, a whole people of slaves represented the basic labor force. It was this huge army of convicts that assured the success of the Five-Year Plan in the Far North, where the average prison life span was not more than one or two years. Their blood was the mortar of the "great accomplishment" that was celebrated by Communist propaganda.

These men had been turned over to the absolute discretion of the GPU, and it hardly entered their minds to voice opinions on the Socialist or non-Socialist character of the system.

The tolerance that was granted to the "politicals," however, was not without limitations. Prisoners could be transferred as a repressive measure to other "isolation cells." Occasionally this step was taken in order to prevent the eruption of a possible conspiracy inside a prison. It entailed—as it always entails—the disadvantage for the government that it made it possible for letters and messages to be transmitted from one camp or prison to another. Besides, the writings of Trotsky, Rakovsky, Radek, and others managed to circulate in places of deportation and exile, where they were impatiently awaited and excitedly discussed.

When too violent a conflict with the administration occurred, the basic weapon of the "politicals" was the hunger strike. There were many of these. Ciliga took part in one in 1931, and it achieved a certain success.

One day a sentry fired on a prisoner named Yessayan, who was standing near the window of his cell, and seriously wounded him. The prison decided to launch a hunger strike as a protest. A strike committee was set up, composed of one right Trotskyist, one left Trotskyist, and one "Decist." [4] The goals of the strike were: (1) the removal of the prison superintendent, Rizyukov; (2) guaranties against new attacks; (3) the release of the wounded man so that he might receive medical care; (4) improvements in the prisoners' legal position.

Three days later all the Communists in the prison were on strike. The committee had sent a telegram to Moscow. After a week the prison superintendent announced that a GPU commission of inquiry was on the way. Therefore he asked the strikers to end their strike, and they complied.

But days and weeks went by and no commission appeared. After two months a second strike was called. At last the com-

[4] A member of the Democratic Centralism group.

mission arrived, headed by Comrade Andreyeva, assistant director of the GPU's political section. Booted and leather-jacketed, she began with the arrogant declaration that she would not negotiate with an illegal committee. But all her attempts to win over the strikers in individual talks failed.

Finally, after the strike had continued for eleven days, the protestants achieved satisfaction on some points. The superintendent would not be dismissed, but the soldier who had fired the shot would be placed on trial. The prisoners would have the right to stand at the windows. The food would be improved.

On the face of it, they had won. The GPU took speedy revenge. Six weeks later thirty-five prisoners, many of whom were left-wing Trotskyists who had taken a particularly firm stand during the strike, were transferred to the Suzdal prison.

Thus, from prison to prison a handful of men kept alive a courageous resistance mired in Byzantine controversies. There was no possibility that their resistance would triumph over the party apparatus or incite it to that return to internal democracy that the resisters sought. And at the same time they had no contact with the subterranean resistance of the workers to the frenzied pace of industrialization. Indeed, most of the time the prison resistance disapproved of the factory resistance; it was no more than a desperate survival, shut out of history.

Trotsky, meanwhile, had embarked on that long journey that was to take him from the Isle of Princes, near Constantinople, to France, Norway, and Mexico. Hated by the Stalinists, under suspicion from the bourgeois governments, he strove in vain to make himself heard by the working masses of Europe. But he was an outlaw, armed only with the *Opposition Bulletin* and those articles and books that he could manage to publish. Whatever his talent, his voice was drowned out in the thunder of the calumnies poured out by all sections of the Comintern.

In the Soviet Union the ranks of his supporters had thinned. As time went on, contact with them became increasingly difficult. Nevertheless, the *Opposition Bulletin,* the press run of which was hardly more than a thousand copies, managed to enter the Soviet Union through mysterious channels. It did not reach the masses, whom in any cases it would have been unlikely to interest. But political figures and high government officials devoured it avidly in secret. Carried in by some diplomat of a European embassy, a single copy would go from hand to hand and, below the apparently even surface of the Stalinist ocean, create invisible eddies.

Stalin was quite well aware of these obscure incursions and of the influence that was still exerted by Trotsky, in appearance so weak, so solitary, so disarmed, an influence that was especially strong among those who had capitulated. Therefore, having amassed evidence that Blumkin [5] of the GPU had had a talk with Trotsky in Turkey, Stalin had the policeman executed on his return.[6] He took other action against Trotsky. On February 20, 1932, Trotsky was stripped of Soviet citizenship. This was an unprecedented measure that thus far had never been invoked even against Menshevik or Revolutionary Socialist emigrants.

In spite of his isolation Trotsky never entertained any doubt of the collapse of the Stalinist system, and he passionately searched for signs of it in every crisis that arose and in the reports that continued to reach him from the Soviet Union in spite of the intense surveillance of the successor to the GPU, the NKVD.

But in Europe his disillusionments were mounting. Undoubtedly he still enjoyed great prestige among many intellectuals. But they represented a poor contribution to his ef-

[5] A former left Revolutionary Socialist, the author of the attack on German Ambassador von Mirbach in 1918. Converted to Communism, he joined the *Cheka* (later the GPU) and carried out a number of missions for it in foreign countries.

[6] According to some sources, Blumkin was denounced by Radek.

forts to organize his supporters in the West. They lost no
time in falling into squabbles over issues of detail. The in-
transigence that never left the imperious Trotsky did the rest.
After a sharp dispute he broke with Boris Suvarin, who had
been expelled several years earlier from the French Communist party. Then he quarreled with Alfred Rosmer and with
Pierre and Madeleine Paz, the publishers of *Contre le courant*.

His own supporters in France were split into two small
groups. One was headed by Naville, the other by Molinier,
and each had its own publication: *La Lutte des Classes* (*The
Class Struggle*) and *Vérité* (*Truth*). These groups had no
roots in the working class, which they claimed to represent,
and the adherents of both together totaled fewer than a thousand.

The contacts that Trotsky made in Italy, The Netherlands,
Germany, and the United States were hardly more encouraging. In Germany, for example, Rosmer found during a journey
there that there were a number of opposition groups but their
basic activity consisted in accusing one another of betraying
the true essence of "Bolshevism-Leninism," which meant Trotskyism.

Trotsky devoted a vast amount of time to efforts to unify
all these scattered tendencies and resolve their various disputes. He failed. The Fourth International, which he decided
to found, never assembled anything beyond embryos of parties. Everywhere in the world these organizations were denounced by the Stalinists as a rabble of renegades and traitors.

Nevertheless Stalin was still afraid of this man who was so
weak and in appearance so cut off. In fact Trotsky still possessed one weapon: an acerb pen directed by an intractable
will. Stalin, at the peak of his power, the object of adulation
of a servile press, was morbidly afraid of this enemy.

Stalin had won. By the beginning of 1934 the Soviet Union
was emerging from the terrible maelstrom into which it had
been plunged. Collectivization was by now an accomplished
fact. After the frightful famine of 1932, unusual climatic con-

ditions had helped to bring the 1933 harvest to a point at which food supplies could be improved. At the cost of innumerable sacrifices the industrialization of the country was assured. More than once the system had brushed elbows with catastrophe, but it had survived every test.

The memory of a four-year nightmare was beginning to fade. Stalin was speedily to plunge the country into another nightmare: the Great Purge.

(13)

THE ORIGINS OF
THE GREAT PURGE

═══════════════════════════════

ON AUGUST 4, 1936, Trotsky mailed the preface for *The Revolution Betrayed* to his publisher and went off on a vacation with his friend, Knudsen. Knudsen was a Social Democrat who had offered Trotsky hospitality after the Norwegian government had agreed to admit him into the country. The two men left Vexhall, thirty miles north of Oslo, for a little primitive island in a fiord where Trotsky could relax with his favorite sport, fishing.

Knudsen had taken along a small portable radio. Every morning he listened to the early news broadcasts. On August 14 or 15 he turned on his radio as usual, and he heard something that stupefied him: Zinoviev, Kamenev, and fifteen other defendants were about to go on trial for conspiracy, treason, and attempted terrorist attacks on the person of Stalin.

The reception was not very good. But Knudsen was absolutely certain of what he had heard: The chief instigator of all these plots was Trotsky, who manipulated his accomplices from abroad. What was even more staggering was the charge that all these crimes had been planned in collusion with the Gestapo.

"It is not possible," Trotsky said again and again. "Terrorism? Terrorism? Yes, that charge I can understand. But the Gestapo? They did say the Gestapo? You are quite sure?"

"Yes," Knudsen replied, "there is no doubt of it: they said the Gestapo."

The witch hunt had begun.

After thirty-one years this somber period is still partly hidden behind a host of mysteries. Since 1930, since the time when all criticism was interdicted, the Soviet Union has been a shadowy nation, walled in by its own secrets. It might be likened to a submarine continent about which our only information is derived from infrequent soundings or from bits of wreckage thrown up by the waves; or to some obscure planet the phenomena of which are observed from a great distance. The "Kremlinologists" are hardly more informed about Russia than the astronomers are about Mars when they examine its surface with the help of their telescopes. The experts on Russia know that between the celebrations of May Day and November 7 the order in which the members of the Politburo were arrayed on the reviewing stand may have undergone two or three changes. They pick their way painstakingly through the newspapers, in which they must learn to read between the lines. With these meager data they endeavor to develop risky appraisals of the favor or disfavor into which this or that high personage has moved.

In this mysterious universe Khrushchev's report to the Twentieth Congress was like a powerful searchlight turned on the sinister epoch of the Great Purge. The report fell far short of dissolving all the mysteries. Such was anything but the intention of either Khrushchev or the other *diadokhoi*. The revelations of Khrushchev's report were limited in their scope by the fact that the underlying motivation for them was not to lay bare the truth (a truth that in its entirety it would have been impossible for these men to acknowledge) but rather to furnish its author with the weapons for a bitter battle of succession.

The story of the Great Purge, therefore, remains in large measure conjectural, and hypothesis, with all the risks of error that it entails, has to operate in order to attempt to explain the causes and illuminate the facts of so bewildering a phenomenon. But at least one major revelation may in fact be derived from Khrushchev's report. *This concerns the date at which Stalin actually wanted to undertake the liquidation of those elements that he deemed hostile.*

From Sochi on September 25, 1936, Stalin and Zhdanov sent a telegram to Kaganovich, Molotov, and the other members of the Politburo, who were all in Moscow:

We believe it absolutely necessary and urgent that Comrade Yezhov be appointed to the post of People's Commissar for the Interior. Yagoda has made it indisputably plain that he is incapable of unmasking the Trotskyist-Zinovievist bloc. *The GPU is four years behind in this matter.* (Italics added.)

Three important conclusions may be drawn from this final sentence. Four years before the end of 1936 Stalin had already resolved on a merciless purge of the Bolshevik ranks. If he had not been able to put his plan into action sooner, it was because he had encountered within the party a resistance that he could not overcome. (This, furthermore, was confirmed by other passages in Khrushchev's report.) Inasmuch as the murder of Kirov occurred on December 1, 1934, if this murder was *in fact* the point of departure for the series of major trials, Stalin's project was substantially prior to it. The murder was a pretext, not the cause.

Four years before—in other words, the end of 1932, a time of major crises in the country. In the field of industrialization a very bitter rancor had been aroused in the working class by the inequalities in wages, the introduction of production norms and Stakhanovism, and above all the inflationary tide in prices.

But the situation was far worse in rural areas. The earlier deliveries of grains requisitioned by the state had completely disrupted the kolkhozi. The granaries of the Ukraine were empty of all the grain required for the subsistence of the peasants and their livestock. The peasants were exhausted and refused to do any work, made no effort to gather their harvests, left the wheat to rot in the fields.

A dreadful famine overran the countryside. In a frightening book, *L'Accusé*, Weissberg-Cybulski, who worked in a physics institute in Kiev, described the sufferings of the victims on their farms, their limbs bloated by their terrible hunger, or fleeing to the towns in quest of food. "Thousands of peasants," he wrote, "died of hunger, and the others, unable to stand erect, lay inside their huts. Every day people were fleeing from the regions where the famine was raging; they fell dead in the Kharkov market. The workers in the towns looked like corpses. Horses collapsed in the streets." [1]

This crisis was accompanied by gigantic inflation. The wholesale price index, on the basis of 100 in 1913, rose from 156.9 in 1927–1928 to 197.5 in 1931. In the same period the purchasing power of the ruble fell in considerable proportion.

None of this prevented Stalin from declaring boldly in 1933 that purchasing power had risen substantially on the sole basis of the rise in money wages.

The various bureaucratic groups, the GPU men, the pretorians of the government, the technicians, and the Stakhanovites were little affected by this catastrophic situation—not so much because they were better paid than the others but because they had access to special shops where they could buy various commodities at low prices.

Nevertheless it was inevitable that the successive waves of discontent aroused in the country should have repercussions even inside the walls of the Kremlin. Men like Bukharin and Rykov had made only seeming submission to Stalin. They

[1] *L'Accusé*, p. 254.

were too thoroughly demoralized and too closely watched, however, to embark on any serious resistance.

It is probable that in this period their hostility was limited to frightened conversations darkened by the shadow of the GPU. They also took advantage of such few legal means as were still available to them. There was a certain way of feigning observance to the party line by passing silently over certain basic subjects in articles or speeches. This sin of omission was soon spotted by the vigilance of the leadership. It too was put under interdict.

Younger circles showed greater boldness. The great leaders of the right were discredited. But between 1930 and 1933 violently oppositionist and even insurrectionist groups emerged.

We have certain knowledge of the existence of only three of these, but it is possible that there were more. The first group, headed by Syrtsov and Lominadze, appeared at the end of 1930. What was remarkable was the fact that neither of these men was a rightist or a Zinovievist: Both were loyal to their inspired leader. Syrtsov had been an alternate in the Politburo in the Sixteenth Congress (1930). Young Lominadze had long been a favorite of Stalin, who had often employed him for special assignments abroad. In particular it was he who in December 1927 had organized the insurrection in Canton.

Now Syrtsov and Lominadze were secretly envisaging a union between the left and the right in order to get rid of Stalin. Syrtsov apparently regarded the great successes of industrialization as a fraud, and Lominadze denounced the "party's feudal attitude" in the face of the peasants' needs. Such comments were made in secret, for, transforming duplicity into a systematic tactic, they made great show of their public support for every act of Stalin.

Their "conspiracy" was swiftly uncovered and both were expelled from the Central Committee in December 1930. Lominadze was to commit suicide in 1934.

Thus Stalin observed that the need for absolute obedience,

which he had imposed, was turning against him. True, he was being obeyed, but at the same time the number of people who merely pretended to be his supporters and who denounced him in secret was growing. Even without the reports that he received from the GPU, he had too keen an instinct not to sense this. The situation that he himself had created fed his distrust. And in turn his distrust engendered a mounting uneasiness round him. In the days when Trotsky and Zinoviev could still express themselves freely it was easy for him to identify the enemy. Now the enemy had been shattered and vanquished. Officially the party was a monolith. But there were those thousands of capitulaters who at bottom loathed him, there was that *Opposition Bulletin* that passed from hand to hand among the *apparachiki*, there were even those Stalinists who were beginning to be doubters. Behind the oaths of loyalty and the intoxicating paeans the enemy was infiltrating.

He had a more serious problem with Ryutin's platform. Ryutin was a brawler who had led the truck-borne teams of bullies who enforced silence on the Trotskyists. But now he had gone over to the opposition. He and a few friends had prepared a 160-page platform in which they criticized industrialization and collectivization and called for a return to internal democracy. What was even worse, they likened Stalin to Azev, the famous double agent of the Okhrana. And in conclusion they called on the party to rid itself of Stalin at all costs.

Another group, led by Eismont and Tolmachev, apparently championed identical views. It too demanded the ouster of Stalin.

When Ryutin's group was brought to light at the end of 1932, Stalin insisted on blood. Ryutin must be executed, he said, because obviously Ryutin wanted to kill him.

Was this really the aim of Ryutin, Eismont, Tolmachev, and their backers? It is permissible to suppose that in calling for the removal of Stalin they were urging the Central Committee merely to replace the secretary general by a majority vote. But the hardly flattering comparison with Azev implicitly embraced the thought that other, more vigorous means were not excluded.

On this subject we have only the indirect testimony of Ciliga. He saw these men arrive in the prison of Verkhney-Uralsk with some young Communists who had been tried with them in closed session. At the trial, it seemed, the prosecution had contended that the chapter in Ryutin's platform dealing with Stalin constituted the "ideological foundation" of a terrorist conspiracy. And, since Ryutin, a former officer, had been the director of the army's newspaper, *Krasnaya Zviezda,* he was accused of having recruited a group of conspirators for the murder of Stalin among the members of the Central Committee's Military Academy.

Tolmachev and Eismont were charged with having prepared a palace revolution. Nothing proves, however, that these charges were any better founded than those that were later presented at the time of the great public trials. Ciliga wrote:

All this talk of terrorism seemed so ridiculous to me that I did not even make the effort to find a grain of truth in it. The rumors that reached us from Moscow were not calculated to dissipate my suspicion. Each of these rumors was more fantastic than the one before it: Blücher was supposed to have been implicated in a plot against Stalin; an ambush had been planned opposite Lenin's tomb, where a well-known member of the military opposition would have to make an attack on the person of Stalin during an official ceremony. But, when I came out of prison (in 1933), I was soon convinced that I had believed Stalin's power better established than in reality it was. . . .[2]

Ciliga learned of the extent of the famine, the ordeals, the appalling death rate, the scenes of cannibalism. . . . "The entire country," he wrote, "cried out in eloquent silence for a palace revolution." It did not seem impossible to him at that time that the idea of a *coup d'état* might have taken root among the ruling circles in spite of the police terror.

[2] *Op. cit.,* p. 219.

Stalin demanded Ryutin's death. On three separate occasions he was refused. In the Politburo he collided with the resistance of Kirov and Ordzhonikidze. He went back to the attack in the Plenum of the Central Committee on September 28, 1932. He failed again. In the next session, on January 7–12, 1933, he again called for the death penalty. Only Kaganovich supported him, but firmly.

The importance of this case must not be underestimated. It revealed a schism between Stalin and his own faction. It confirmed the latent hostility—indicated by Bukharin in his talks with Kamenev—of such men as Ordzhonikidze. The caste established by the Stalinist bureaucracy was already apprehensive at the consequences of the execution of one of its members, lest this prove an initial step that might put its own privileges into jeopardy. Thus there arose the prospect of a conflict between the Stalinist apparatus and the despot himself.

At the same period Postyshev was sent to the Ukraine in order to conduct a purge in furtherance of the fight on nationalism. In the face of this test, Skrypnyk, the old Bolshevik, did not resist: He killed himself.

Many revolutionaries had chosen this avenue out of revulsion, despair, or the fear of deportation: Mayakovsky, Essenin, Yevgenya Bosch—a soldier in the civil war, in which she had gained notoriety by the ruthlessness of her character—and one of Trotsky's secretaries. Now it was the turn of the despot's wife. Her death was a dramatic repudiation of Stalinist policy.

Nadezhda Alliluyeva was the daughter of a revolutionary worker, old underground fighter, and comrade of Stalin, in whose home Lenin had hidden before the seizure of power in 1917. Much younger than Stalin—she was his second wife—she could not help contrasting her own comfortable life in the Kremlin with the lot of the Moscow workers. Continuing her studies after her marriage, she also accumulated the confidences of others. She was a witness to the misery that gave the lie to the vulgar fabrications of official propaganda.

The drama came one night in November 1932. Stalin and

his wife were dining with the Voroshilovs and other members of the Politburo. That night, for the first time in that world in which truth was gagged, in which everything was repression, sycophancy, trickery, and deceit, Nadezhda dared to say what was in her heart. She spoke of the famine, of the population's sufferings, of the terror that reigned in the party.

For Stalin this repudiation by Nadezhda was more than a cruel humiliation. How many of his comrades were muttering in secret what she had said aloud? Even worse, she had not hesitated to speak out even at the moment when "Ryutin's conspiracy" had just been discovered, the moment when Number One was declaring that criminals were trying to murder him. Objectively, according to Stalinist logic, the secretary general's own wife was going over to the camp of his most dedicated enemies. He had been dealt a vital blow.

Was he sincere when he tendered his resignation to his colleagues after this death for which he was morally responsible? It was the third time that he had made the tender. The members of the Politburo must have asked themselves this question, must have sensed a trap laid for any who might answer *yes*, a trap that would be even worse if they turned out to be the minority. Victor Serge has well described the ambiguous character of the scene.

The members of the Politburo looked at one another in embarrassment. Who among them would take it on himself to reply: "Yes, old man, that's right. You ought to step down, there's no other choice." Who? The man who said that without the support of the others would run a terrible risk. No one stirred. . . . Finally Molotov said: "Stop it! stop it! You have the party's confidence." The matter was closed.[3]

The matter was closed, but the infection was there. The mutual confidence between Stalin and his own associates, if it had ever existed, was deeply corroded. They could not know

[3] Victor Serge, *Portrait de Staline*, pp. 94–95.

whether Stalin was sincere in offering to resign; he could not
guess who was honest in asking him to remain.

He was alone. Millions of men in his country hated him. In
the prisons and the camps the hearts of other millions were
charged with hatred. He knew that he could not rely on the
capitulaters, who would hail his downfall with delight. Outside the country, Trotsky, in spite of his exile and the laugh-
ably small audience to which he was restricted, still remained
a threat. And now the enemy had infiltrated the stronghold,
among his own supporters. The enemy's thinking had reached
into his very home. The absolute power at his command, the
cult of which he was beginning to be the object could not
conceal from him the fact that both were founded on reciprocal fear and suspicion.

It was at this moment, perhaps, that his mind conceived
the plan to rid himself of all whom he suspected of disloyalty.

In any event, after his wife's death,[4] he discharged all the
domestic servants who were taking care of his daughter, Svetlana, then seven years old, except for her old nurse. This was
as it were an omen of the purges to come. Everyone who had
known Nadezhda was suspect. Such people might talk. Stalin
removed them, just as, later, he would clap into prison all the
men and women who had had anything to do with a "criminal"—for example, the officers of a general accused of treason.
They were at the very least potential "accomplices."

And Stalin's justice knew nothing of half-measures.

[4] According to a different version, Nadezhda did not commit suicide
but was killed by Stalin in a fit of anger. For lack of specific information on the matter, however, it is advisable to prefer the suicide version
as the more credible.

(14)

TERROR IN THE PARTY

TALKING OF Stalin among themselves, his followers used the familiar appelation of the *Hazyazhin* (Boss). According to Radek, this nickname was not altogether pleasing to Stalin, who would have preferred to be known, like Lenin, as "the Old Man."

His enemies, among themselves, used less affectionate terms. They called him *Ishak* (Caucasian mule) or "the guttersnipe." The more cultivated compared him with Louis XI or one of the Borgias, or even Boris Godunov. Kamenev considered this last much too flattering, even though it irritated Stalin almost as much as Bukharin's scorn-laden remark: "He thinks he is a theoretician." As for Ryazan, who headed the Marx-Lenin Institute in Moscow, he regarded Stalin as a latter-day Caligula.

Must it be thought then that Stalin, like Caligula, was only a homicidal maniac? That the Great Purge, the show trials with their repugnant series of confessions were only the projection of the fantasies of a diseased brain that, beginning about 1935, assumed increasing proportions until the time when the patient gradually recovered his composure and the purge was ended with the elimination of Yezhov? That at the end of Stalin's life he relapsed into his madness? Whence the "plot of the men in white."

There is a passage in Khrushchev's report, it is true, that underlined certain pathological aspects of Stalin's personality. "Stalin," Khrushchev said, "was a highly suspicious man, morbidly suspicious. . . . He was capable of looking at someone and saying: 'Why are your eyes so shifty today?' or: 'Why are you looking away like that today and avoiding looking me in the eye?' This morbid suspicion engendered a general distrust in him, even toward outstanding party workers whom he had known for years. Everywhere and in everything he saw 'enemies,' 'two-faced people,' 'spies.'" Later in this report Khrushchev stated that, after the Second World War, Stalin became even more capricious and brutal; "in particular his suspicions increased. His persecution mania reached an unbelievable intensity."

Nevertheless, a clinical definition of Stalin as a purely pathological case or a comparison with Caligula raises a certain number of objections. It is difficult to establish a close parallelism among a mental aberration, the Great Purge, and the "doctors' plot." The massive purges started in 1936. Stalin's madness, then, would have begun at that time, subsided at the end of 1938, and surged up again at the end of 1952. Now we know from Khrushchev's report that Stalin intended to initiate the purge of the party about the end of 1932. (Cf. his remark, "The GPU is four years behind.") Hence it must be recognized that his mental illness began much earlier.

The argument of Stalin's insanity comes into conflict with another objection: his attitude during the war. When disasters and defeats piled up after the start of the German offensive, Stalin, far from embarking on a universal purge of "traitors" among his associates or the military, closed ranks, appealed to all segments of the nation for help, and even authorized the assignment of important missions to purged generals such as Rokossovsky. How is it possible to imagine that a madman, the prey of an obsession about treason and conspiracy a few years earlier, would not have been persuaded by the brutal impact of events to attribute the enormous avalanche of defeats in 1941 to treason? Would not his already shaky reason have foundered in a new tidal wave of homicidal mania?

Stalin's "madness" must therefore be reduced to its true proportions. That he was distrustful and suspicious by nature, that these characteristics, accentuated by age, turned into an almost obsessive mania—in a word, that he manifested certain pathological symptoms—it is reasonable to concede. On the other hand, similar characteristics are to be found among other people who are not institutionalized on that account, and, if the social consequences of these characterological aberrations are few, it is because those persons in whom they appear do not for the most part control the mechanisms of a formidable power.

At the same time, however, the obsessions peculiar to Stalin's psychological constitution cannot be divorced from his exercise of this power or even from the history of the Bolshevik party. Throughout his youth Stalin lived in the suspicion-ridden climate of clandestinity, in which the enemy was not only external but also hidden in the ranks of the revolutionary parties. The *provocateurs* infiltrated into the revolutionaries' ranks by the Okhrana were not the fantasies of addled minds but an undeniable reality. And the memory of an Azev or a Malinovsky could not easily be erased from the Bolsheviks' minds.

Stalin could not forget that past; perhaps because he himself had been a man steeped in trickery, cunning, calculated perfidies, odious stratagems slowly brought to fruition—in short, a man of utter bad faith. A natural propensity inclines men of such temperament to impute to others the acts and intentions that are their own. Prepared to violate any agreement, to break any promise, Stalin could hardly repose confidence in anyone.

Another source of his distrustfulness was the knowledge of everyone else that he acquired through the police records, a

large part of which was inherited from the Okhrana. Not all
the Bolsheviks had been heroes, nor had some been heroes at
all times. In the hands of the police some had turned traitor.
Others had contradicted themselves in their testimony. These
were so many weapons, so many means of blackmail in the
secretary general's hands. And so many factors to fortify him
in his lack of trust.

But, in all honesty, the obsession with "treason" and "conspiracy" was not peculiar to Stalin. It had impregnated Bolshevik circles since the first days of the Revolution. The Soviet Union grew up in a half-simulated, half-genuine fear of
capitalist encirclement and the secret machinations of imperialist agents. When Rosmer arrived in Russia for the first
time, a British woman journalist stopped to talk to him in the
corridor of his train. They had barely taken leave of each
other when a Russian comrade appeared: The lady was suspect. Besides, Rosmer was told, as a rule foreign journalists
were spies, agents of British Intelligence or the *Deuxième
Bureau.*

A few years later Victor Serge was dining in the home of a
certain Leonidov in Leningrad. One of the other guests was
a Latvian named Otto who was a member of the *Cheka.*
Leonidov himself had formerly been in the *Cheka.* In fact he
had had a brief notoriety when Dzerzhinsky, in agreement
with Lenin, proposed that the death penalty be abolished.
Lenin had signed the decree. The news appeared in the papers the next day, but it had already run through the prisons
and aroused tremendous rejoicing.

Legally, once Lenin had signed it, the decree could be considered effective. Certain *Chekists* did not look at it in this
light. They drove to the prisons in their trucks and loaded
them with men who had thought themselves saved. Three
hundred suspects were shot in Moscow, two hundred in Leningrad. The *Cheka* was liquidating its inventory.

Leonidov was one of these bitter-end executioners. By the
time Victor Serge met him, his moment of glory had passed:

He was in disgrace. He lived in a very fine apartment and collected valuable autographs. The collection mania had succeeded the execution mania, and now it was enhanced by the treason mania. "Treason," he explained to Serge, "has established itself in the heart of the Central Committee. This was true even in Lenin's time. I know names and all the details. It is tremendous and frightening."

He had presented detailed analyses of the immense criminality that he has been tracking down for more than five years to the Central Committee. But he dares speak only to certain men, because treason is really everywhere. . . . C., an engineer, . . . who was assigned to transportation, was really one of them. One of whom? He murmured some foreign names, those of the most powerful capitalists, and others as well that he invested with some secret significance: "Charlestown . . ." I followed his exposition with that controlled anxiety that one feels when a madman starts to reason.[1]

A lunatic? No doubt. But Leonidov, the anonymous bureaucrat, was not the only man who reasoned in this fashion. When Serge left with Otto, the *Chekist,* Otto made no secret of the fact that he took Leonidov's vagaries seriously and was helping him to pursue his investigation.

The ground was already completely prepared for the eventual growth of the Stalinist madness. Moreover, the great trials of Zinoviev and Kamenev, the Anti-Soviet Center (Pyatakov, Radek, and Serebryakov), and the rightist bloc and the Trotskyists (Bukharin, Rykov, Yagoda, Krestinsky, and Rakovsky) in no way represented the emergence of a new phenomenon. What was new about them, what impressed public opinion at that time, was the fact that the spies, the traitors, and the saboteurs had been recruited among the party's celebrities. But the trials that had been held earlier—the trials of Shashty, the industrialists, the Mensheviks—were also constructed on similar scenarios in which sabotage and collusion with for-

[1] *Le tournant obscur,* p. 68.

eigners were the foundation of the script. Though in less extreme degree, these trials too contained the same improbable accusations, the same prefabricated confessions, the same technique of association. In a way they were pilot operations, and it was the job of the sinister Vyshinsky to eliminate their flaws.

It was the same process of Stalinist repression that led to the pouring of the monstrous trials of the 1930s into already prepared molds, utilizing the association technique in ever more intense fashion. Long before Zinoviev and Kamenev were haled before the bar of justice, it was possible to be accused of terrorism without ever having entertained any notion of killing anyone. Article LVIII authorized the most arbitrary interpretations. An angry peasant who slapped the manager of a kolkhoz could be accused of terrorism.

A typical example was presented by the Ryssakov case, which Panait Istrati reported in detail. Ryssakov, who was Victor Serge's father-in-law, was suspect because he was an oppositionist. He sublet some of the rooms in his apartments and he had an altercation with one of his subtenants, a woman. She filed a complaint, and one day Ryssakov was visited by Comrade Svirtsyena, a member of the party who wore the Order of Lenin. They exchanged blows.

In a capitalist country this might be a run-of-the-mill affair to be settled in a police court. In the Soviet Union the reaction was completely different. The Ryssakov case was brought to public attention by an article in *Pravda* of Leningrad:

The execution of Kalganov [the son of a former landowner, he had killed the chairman of a cooperative] was a brutal warning addressed to the kulak and NEP element, whose activity is resurgent. But it seems that Kalganov's fate has not had the expected minatory effect on everyone. . . .

Then there was an account of the actual incident, followed by the conclusion:

Ryssakov is out of the same mold as the Kalganov family. The attack by Ryssakov, armed with his fists, exactly like that by Kalganov, armed with a switch-blade knife, is an attempted attack on our ranks and our creative labor by kulak and NEP elements.

Public opinion demands the immediate arrest of Ryssakov. There must be a major trial that will also serve as an example. . . . We must sternly rout the enemies of the proletariat working on the housing front. (*Leningradskaya Pravda,* January 31, 1928.)

Let us ignore the grotesque nature of this conclusion (in 1928 the grotesque led straight to prison, and Ryssakov avoided this only through Istrati's courageous intercession).[2] What is important is to note that from this time forward a punch was equal to a stab if the victim was an orthodox member of the party. When Stalin concluded that Ryutin wanted to kill him because he had written that the secretary general must be removed, he was merely applying the same logic.

As for the charges of sabotage on which the prosecutions of Shashty and the industrialists were based, the motivation for them was an attempt to attribute the many failures in production to malevolence and conspiracy. The same thing, identically, recurred in the trial of the rightist bloc and the Trotskyists.

It must not be forgotten that the great public trials performed an essential function: that of mobilizing public opinion. They were spectacular propaganda maneuvers and it was the task of the Soviet press and radio and the "apparatuses" of the Communist International to disseminate and interpret them for mass consumption.

The judicial machinery, the definitions of the crimes, and even the technique of the confessions had already been developed in the years that preceded the Great Purge. This machinery, which previously had been employed against the NEP, the kulak, and the *spets* who had to be brought into line, or against the remnants of the old leftist parties (Men-

[2] Istrati tongue-lashed the editors of *Pravda* into mesmerized silence and carried his protest as high as Kalinin.

sheviks and Revolutionary Socialists), *was through Stalin's innovation turned against his own associates with unrestrained savagery.*

This decision must be viewed not as the result of psychological problems but as the deliberate will of one man to establish his own unshared authority regardless of the cost, and to preserve and reinforce a power that he felt was threatened.

He had not been able to carry out the purge that he wanted when the Ryutin affair came to light. His will had clashed with that of the party's ruling circle, concerned with defending its own caste interests. The Conquerors' Congress in 1934, which seemingly celebrated his genius, actually revealed a certain loss of authority.

Every dictator who sees his power and prestige diminished, however slightly, can view this loss only with alarm. He can expect to see new attacks mounted against him.

Stalin had waged a vast war of extermination against the kulaks. He did the same thing against everyone whom he suspected of opposing him. It was easy to get rid of kulaks in great numbers by way of mass executions or mass deportations, neither of which stirred much sentiment in the intelligentsia of Europe, which was little inclined to waste its pity on these "backward" masses. It was another matter if it came to the question of liquidating leaders who belonged to his own group or figures such as Zinoviev, Kamenev, or Bukharin. In order to justify their executions, these men must be convicted of having commited exceptional crimes, and the proof must be adduced through public confessions.

But, in order to take the offensive, to put an end to all the varieties of oppositon that he heard muttering round him, Stalin required a dramatic pretext. This was provided by the murder of Kirov.

Kirov was killed by a revolver shot fired by Nikolayev, a member of the *Komsomol*. On his person the police found written statements setting forth the reasons for his act. They were never to be made public.

Stalin himself, it was said, rushed to Leningrad to interrogate the killer. Some fifteen of Nikolayev's friends had already been arrested. They were shot. So were 116 other persons, arrested previously and thus totally unconnected with the murder. No matter. They were terrorists too, like those other terrorists, the tens of thousands of workers who were deported to Siberia in the weeks that followed and who were known ironically in the camps as "Kirov's killers."

In January 1935 Zinoviev, Kamenev, Evdokimov, and Bakayev were convicted in a preliminary trial in which, under duress, they acknowledged a moral responsibility for the murder. They were sentenced to prison terms. In July there was a secret trial of which nothing was known until later. Kamenev was once more sentenced to ten years' imprisonment.

It was not until 1936 that Zinoviev, Kamenev, Evdokimov, and Smirnov appeared in court for the third time. They looked like broken men in the courtroom. And they confessed. Yes, it was they who had issued the order to kill Kirov, in obedience to Trotsky, who had ordered recourse to individual terrorism. To what end? In order to restore capitalism. And a number of other assassinations were in preparation: Stalin's, Kaganovich's, Voroshilov's, Zhdanov's, Ordzhonikidze's, Kossior's, Postyshev's.

It is to be observed that Molotov's name was not on this list. This omission was to be remedied in the subsequent trial of the Anti-Soviet Center. It is also to be observed that Kossior and Postyshev, whose names appeared on the list of projected assassination victims, were very soon in turn to be transformed into "terrorists and traitors" and duly liquidated.

Trotsky, the focal defendant, the Satan of the Stalinist mythology who inspired the dark conspiracies, replied from his exile with a cogent pamphlet, *The Stalinist Bureaucracy and the Assassination of Kirov*. He accused Stalin and the GPU of having plotted the murder. Twelve years later there was every reason to believe that Trotsky was right: Stalin, thwarted by the majority in the Central Committee, needed this murder

as the detonator that would set off his bloody chain reactions.
Implicitly Khrushchev hinted as much in his famous report.
It is appropriate to quote the entire passage:

It must be admitted that until the present the circumstances surrounding the assassination of Kirov concealed many things that
are mysterious and inexplicable and that call for the most careful
scrutiny. There is some reason to believe that Nikolayev, the murderer of Kirov, was helped by one of those whose task it was to protect Kirov's person. Six weeks before the murder Nikolayev had
been arrested because of his suspicious behavior,[3] but he had
been released and had not even been kept under surveillance. The
fact that the policeman assigned to protect Kirov, who was to have
been questioned on December 2, 1934, was killed in an "automobile accident" in which the other occupants of the car were not
hurt is a remarkably suspicious circumstance. After the assassination of Kirov, very light penalties were imposed on the higher officials of the Leningrad NKVD, but they were shot in 1937. It may
be supposed that they were shot in order to eliminate clues that
might have led to the organizers of the assassination of Kirov. (A
stir in the audience.)

This passage must be compared with the interrogation of
Yagoda during the trial of the rightist bloc and the Trotskyists in 1938:

Vyshinsky: Did you personally take any measures whatever for the
accomplishment of the assassination of Sergey Mikhaïlovich
Kirov?
Yagoda: Personally?
Vyshinsky: Yes, as a member of the bloc.

[3] Kirov had refused to accept an NKVD guard. But he was always accompanied by a certain Borissov, who served as his bodyguard and who
was killed in the "automobile accident" mentioned by Khrushchev. The
NKVD men guilty of "negligence" were tried on January 23, 1935, and
sentenced to short terms in the Kolyma camp. They were Medved, the
head of the NKVD in Leningrad; Zaporozhetz and Fomin, his deputies,
and a few others. In 1937 all except Zaporozhetz were taken back to
Leningrad and executed.

Yagoda: I gave the order . . .

Vyshinsky: To whom?

Yagoda: To Zaporozhetz, in Leningrad. *But that did not happen just that way.*

Vyshinsky: We will come to that later. For the moment, I must clarify the parts played by Rykov and Bukharin in this crime.

Yagoda: I had given an order to Zaporozhetz. When Nikolayev was arrested . . .

Vyshinsky: The first time?

Yagoda: Yes. Zaporozhetz came here and told me that a man had been arrested . . .

Vyshinsky: What did he have in his briefcase?

Yagoda: A revolver and his private diary. And he had let him go.

Vyshinsky: Had you approved of this?

Yagoda: I had made a note of it.

Vyshinsky: Did you then give instructions that no obstacle should be placed in the way of assassinating Sergey Mikhaïlovich Kirov?

Yagoda: Yes, I did. . . *Not in that way.*

Vyshinsky: In a slightly different form?

Yagoda: Not in that way. But it does not matter.

Vyshinsky: Did you give the instructions?

Yagoda: I *confirmed* them.

Vyshinsky: You confirmed them. Sit down.[4]

Yagoda's evasive, ambiguous answers are quite as remarkable as the lack of eagerness displayed by Vyshinsky, who was often more curious, to learn who had given the order that Yagoda claimed merely to have confirmed. One can of course reject the hypothesis that Yagoda might have confirmed an order given by the rightists' and Trotskyists' terrorist center because this center never existed except in Stalinist imaginations. Then there remains only one plausible answer: The order was given by Stalin himself—if not directly by him, at least by one of his trusted assistants in his private secretariat.

This is confirmed by the fact that a subordinate such as Zaporozhetz took on himself the risk of releasing Nikolayev

[4] *Trial of the Rightist Bloc and the Anti-Soviet Trotskyists*, p. 400. Italics added.

after he had been found to be carrying a revolver and a private diary that must have thrown some light on his state of mind. It was only after this action that he made his report to Yagoda. Hence he was already covered by some authority higher than Yagoda. Furthermore, the fact that he should have been the only policeman involved in this matter who escaped the later liquidation is in itself sufficiently eloquent.

Why should Kirov have been selected as the victim? Kirov, it should be remembered, had been Stalin's victorious opponent in the Ryutin case. He was the head of the organization in Leningrad, the second city of the Soviet Union. He was a member of that Stalinist bureaucracy that had mercilessly combated the rightist and Trotskyist opposition. But it is probable that inside the apparatus he was the spokesman of those who longed for a certain respite after the horrors of collectivization, a certain relaxation of police oppression. Moreover, he had just been appointed to the Secretariat, and he had refused to allow himself to be guarded by the NKVD.[5] In 1934 and the circumstances peculiar to the Soviet Union, such an act was of more than individual significance. It amounted in essence to negating the usefulness of the NKVD and demanding the loosening of the police vise.

In no circumstances do privileged groups appreciate any challenge to or diminution in their prerogatives. In a totalitarian state like the Soviet Union, the privileges of the original *Cheka* had never stopped growing. It was the spinal column of the system, and it was on the police much more than on the army that Stalin had had to rely in order to put down the peasant risings.

Kirov therefore represented a dual threat, not only for Stalin, who might have feared him as a possible rival, but also for the NKVD, whose power was more or less flouted by Kirov's refusal. Stalin was killing two birds with one stone: He was eliminating someone who opposed him and he was

[5] The NKVD (People's Commissariat for Internal Affairs) replaced the GPU in 1934.

using this terrorist murder as the pretext for a massive purge at which the Central Committee recoiled.

On the very night of Kirov's murder Stalin took the initiative under a directive signed by Enukidze [6]—it was approved by the Politburo two days later—that was to become the basis for the terror:

1. Prosecuting agencies are instructed to accelerate the preliminary investigations for the trials of persons accused of planning or carrying out terrorist acts.
2. Judicial agencies are instructed not to suspend the execution of death sentences in crimes of this category for purposes of considering clemency possibilities, because the Presidium of the Central Committee no longer deems it feasible to entertain petitions of this nature.
3. Agencies of the Commissariat for Internal Affairs are instructed to execute death sentences against criminals in the above-mentioned category immediately after sentence has been pronounced.

The exceptional swiftness with which Stalin made this decision suggests that it had already been arrived at earlier, at least in his mind.

Yagoda, who lent his collaboration to Stalin so that the murder perpetrated by Nikolayev might be carried out without hindrance, was subsequently to be liquidated for the benefit of Yezhov. There is every reason to believe that Stalin wished to rid himself in this way of someone who knew too much, replacing him with someone else who would be liquidated in turn once he had done his job. But it is also possible that, in direct proportion to the growing clarification of Stalin's plans and their scope, certain resistances manifested themselves even within the NKVD.

The police power, as we have said, had mounted without a break. In theory the concentration of police facilities in the hands of one man endowed that man with formidable power.

---

[6] At this time secretary of the presidium of the Central Committee and subsequently liquidated.

And in fact the NKVD's domination weighed heavily on the whole of the country, including both the militants and the higher officials of the Communist party, subjected as they were to a surveillance that none of them could hope to evade.

It followed that whoever possessed this police power could beome a threat to the dictator himself if he combined all sources of information with the means of surveillance and control over the government. Yet the head of the Soviet police has never been able to gain control of all the power. Dzerzhinsky, the founder of the *Cheka*, certainly had no ambition in this direction. His successor, Menzhinsky, who soon became seriously ill, was in no position, even if he had had the wish, to nourish great ambitions, and during his lifetime the real authority was in Yagoda's hands. One day Yagoda was transferred to the postal ministry and soon afterward shipped off to prison. Yezhov disappeared into a mental institution. As for Beria, after Stalin's death he too was liquidated.

Beria, alone, however, though for only a short period, possessed sufficient power to be really threatening to Stalin's successors. Stalin himself had very early taken his own precautions to counterbalance the police power and had set up his own surveillance in opposition to the ubiquitous surveillance of the police. The little known means for this counter-surveillance was Stalin's private Secretariat. It is important to clarify —on the basis of the sparse information available, most of it provided by Barmin—the part played by this Secretariat.

What it was in fact was a veritable secret government that functioned side by side with the official government. Stalin had a number of private secretaries, each of whom had two assistants. Each secretary had his own theater of operations: foreign affairs, agriculture, finance, military affairs, the international press and propaganda, the Soviet apparatus, the party apparatus. Another division of the Secretariat was assigned to replying to the mail that poured in on Stalin. Not one letter was left unanswered.

Beginning in the 1930s the Secretariat was headed by Poskrebyshev, Stalin's man of all work. He was a rotund little man, rather bald, with a high complexion. He was also one of those few individuals who managed to retain Stalin's confidence to the very end. His predecessors had been Tovstukha and Bratanovsky. Another important member of the Secretariat was Yelena Stassova, who was in charge of the international organizations. Kaminkov saw to the Profintern (the Red Relief), Selitzky looked after the party apparatus, and Grishin dealt with finance and foreign trade.

Radek, after his capitulation, was assigned to international affairs and the international press. Every day he presented a press summary to Stalin, who also received complete information on the course of public opinion in the Soviet Union. In these reports there was no question of concealing anything from him; while the official press resounded with rhapsodic praises for him, Stalin insisted on being accurately informed in secret. It was said even that he had ordered a translation of Suvarin's book about him, which spiced a remarkable body of fact with cruel assessments of the dictator. History does not say what became of the translator.

It followed automatically that the GPU itself did not escape the vigilance of the private Secretariat. In Barmin's time this was the province of one Dvyasky. He maintained relations with a number of NKVD agents whose chief task it was to observe what went on about them and keep Stalin informed of it. Yezhov himself was a member of Stalin's private Secretariat before his appointment to head the NKVD.[7] Thus the private Secretariat became in effect an observation post that kept Stalin informed in a permanent fashion on the country's essential business and that made it possible for him, without the knowledge of the leaders of the GPU and later the NKVD, to keep an eye on the operation of the police system.

Nevertheless the control exercised by the private Secretariat did not guarantee absolute security. It made possible the surveillance of certain operations of the police. This agency, how-

[7] So was Malenkov, who was Yezhov's chief deputy in purge matters.

ever, remained a bastion that preserved a certain autonomy.
In theory it was subject to the orders not only of Stalin but
also of the Politburo. As long as Stalin was in danger from
elements hostile to the Soviet system the police could be
trusted. This ceased to be true as soon as Stalin had to fear
that a conspiracy might be growing among his own supporters.

The titular head of the police, Menzhinsky, weakened by
illness, was no more than a shadow. Authority was exercised
by his first deputy, Yagoda, a former pharmacist, short and
thin and adorned with a Hitler-style mustache. About 1928 he
seemed to be tending toward the right, supplying Bukharin
with information on the misdeeds of collectivization. An opportunist utterly devoid of scruple, he apparently deserted the
rightists as soon as he saw that they had lost. But Stalin's
memory overlooked nothing. He knew that Yagoda's recall was
equally total. Involved in all the maneuvers against the right
and the Trotskyists, he knew too many secrets.

It would appear that Stalin had long sought to be rid of
him. In 1931 Stalin ordered Akulov appointed Menzhinsky's
first deputy. Thus Yagoda was demoted. Four months later
Akulov was removed.[8]

It might be inferred from this that the GPU closed ranks behind Yagoda and forced the removal of an alien element. In a
period as tense as the collectivization campaign, it was difficult for Stalin to proceed to purge the GPU, his major support.

Stalin was adept at waiting. In 1933 he returned to the assault. On June 20 he created for Akulov the special position of
federal prosecutor and instructed him to maintain "surveillance . . . over the legality and fitness of the GPU's operations."

[8] When Yezhov succeeded Yagoda, one of the latter's deputies, Artusov (who, as we have seen, played an important part in the affair of
the Trust), was constrained to deliver a self-criticism. After having accused Yagoda of trying to emulate Fouché, he added: "When the party
. . . appointed the old Bolshevik Akulov to the GPU, we greeted him
with a violent hostility. Yagoda did everything possible to make Akulov's work more difficult" (cf. Krivitisky, *J'étais un agent de Staline*, page
181).

In theory Akulov was thus empowered to call for any record whatever.

This step might be regarded as an attempt to liberalize the system. But it operated also to restrict Yagoda's powers. It is not impossible that Stalin, versed as he was in manipulation, agreed to a seeming return "to legality" solely in order to weaken an agency the complete control of which eluded him.

Nevertheless, when the GPU was converted into the NKVD in July, 1934, it was Yagoda who was placed at its head. Apparently he was retaining all his prerogatives.

It seems, however, that after a certain point he was no longer directly responsible for the protection of Stalin. This in fact became the jurisdiction of Enukidze, the secretary of the Central Committee's executive, who, moreover, was to be purged in his own turn. It is possible that this change was ordered when Stalin, noting the suspicious behavior of one of his secretaries assigned to the library, "unmasked" him and was able to "establish" that he was in contact with certain officers of the Kremlin guard who were planning a terrorist attack. Krivitsky said in his book that the GPU was highly embarrassed that the "conspiracy" had escaped its vigilance.

The other weak point in the Kremlin's defensive system was its medical corps. On two occasions the Kremlin physicians played an important role in Stalin's major spectacles. The first time was in March 1938, during the trial of the rightists and Trotskyists. The defendants included three doctors—Levin, Pletnev, and Kazakov. The charge against them—which they admitted—was that on Yagoda's orders they had assassinated Gorky; his son, Maxim Peshkov; Menzhinsky, Yagoda's predecessor, and Kuibyshev.

While the terrorist schemes ascribed to the other defendants in this trial were extremely vague and incoherent, the doctors, in contrast, indulged themselves in a great luxury of details to explain how they had done away with the patients who had been entrusted to them by resorting to counter-indicated treatments.

Trotsky, in his book on Stalin, expressed the opinion that the murder of Gorky by the doctors, acting in reality on behalf of Stalin, was by no means impossible. His attention was aroused by a statement by Bulanov, Yagoda's secretary, who said that there was a stock of poisons in his superior's office. To quote Trotsky:

During the trial itself, the foundation for which consisted in lies, both the accusations and the confessions of having poisoned the aged, ailing author seemed utterly fantastic to me. But subsequent information and a more careful analysis of the circumstances compelled me to modify this view. Not everything in this trial was a lie. There were indeed men who were poisoned and men who poisoned them, and not all the poisoners were in the prisoners' dock. Their superior was conducting the trial by telephone. (*Stalin*, p. 50.)

Their superior, obviously, was Stalin. At that time Trotsky linked the doctors' case with a confidence made by Stalin to the Politburo during Lenin's illness: Stalin alleged that Lenin, in order to avoid further suffering, had asked him for poison. And Trotsky wondered whether this had not indeed been the means of shortening Lenin's life. Later, it was reported, Stalin similarly suggested to Zinoviev and Kamenev that they get rid of Trotsky by having him poisoned. Why then, Trotsky asked himself, would it be unlikely that Stalin, in fear of Gorky's protests at the extent of the Great Purge, should have decided to eliminate him with the cooperation of certain Kremlin physicians?

Nevertheless, Trotsky's line of reasoning is not very convincing. Gorky had long been seriously ill. He was under treatment by a number of doctors, of whom Levin was the only one to be placed on trial. How was it possible that the others overlooked a counter-indicated treatment prescribed by their colleague? Similarly, the official version, according to which Lenin died after a third cerebral stroke, is still more believable than a death caused by poison.

But the special situation of the Kremlin Medical Corps is not the less worthy of attention. Levin's testimony at his trial showed that, when Gorky went to Italy in the winter for a six-month stay, Levin was ordered to select three doctors, each of whom would spend two months with Gorky in Italy, and that Levin himself was to be one of them. Another, Vinogradov, was a member of the GPU's medical department, and it was Gorky's secretary, Kiryuchkov, who had brought him in to treat the author.

There could be only one explanation for this serial medical care of Gorky abroad: *All the doctors were also policemen;* they were under instructions to keep Yagoda and Stalin informed of Gorky's activities. Lest they be corrupted by their sojourn in the midst of the "enemy," their absence from the territory of the Soviet Union was not to exceed two months.

Furthermore—again on the basis of Levin's testimony—consider the strange working conditions imposed on the Kremlin's physicians. The rulers in the Kremlin could not freely choose their own doctors. It was the Kremlin's Health Department that sent for this or that physician and assigned him to a patient. In the period preceding his trial Levin must have treated twenty-four persons, including Yagoda. Mobilized during the civil war although he was a nonparty man, Levin served throughout in the *Cheka's* medical corps. His treatments of Dzerzhinsky, Menzhinsky, and Yagoda began in 1920.

A summary is in order. The physicians enjoyed no autonomy. The Kremlin's Health Department said to them: "Beginning tomorrow you will take care of So-and-so." They obeyed. Nor had the patients any choice. They were told: "You will be treated by Dr. Such-and-such." Yet these patients were men who held the highest posts in the ruling apparatus. But they, like their doctors, were totally subject to the decision of a functionary.

It must be recalled at this point that it was in this strange climate that the decision was made to perform the operation on Frunze that was to prove fatal. And this decision must also be considered in context with the testimony of the experts called to testify on the deaths of Gorky, Menzhinsky, Kuibyshev, etc., in the trial of the rightists and Trotskyists. The four experts—including Professor Vinogradov, who fifteen years later was to be implicated in the "doctors' conspiracy"—concluded that the treatments prescribed for the patients had been counter-indicated and revealed a criminal intent.

If it is admitted, as Trotsky apparently believed, that the treatments might indeed have been criminal, this means that the doctors served as murderers on the orders of Yagoda, who himself could have acted only as the executor of Stalin's orders. If, as is quite likely, the deaths resulted from natural causes, then the four experts gave false witness on orders from above. Let it not be said that this was less heinous than committing murder: Their perjuries contributed to the imposition of the death sentence on their accused colleagues.

These facts clearly demonstrate that, as a result of duress and fear, the Kremlin's Medical Corps was one of the instruments of the government's crimes. This was not a phenomenon that came into being at the time of the Great Purge; on the contrary, it undoubtedly antedated the purge considerably, as the suspicious death of Frunze indicated.

This was a redoubtable weapon in Stalin's hands—but it was a two-edged one. He himself was subject to the examination of these weird doctors, whose clinical verdicts were subordinate to the political verdicts of the Kremlin's Health Department. Hence the chief of that department had to be an extremely trustworthy man, given the powers at his command. In this connection it is curious to note that in the autumn of 1934 Metalikov, who was the director of this department, was replaced by Khodorovsky, who was later to be shot without trial. It is conceivable that the occupants of this post were frequently replaced as a matter of precaution.

What could Stalin have thought of physicians who were willing to abdicate their professional consciences? If it is true that he made them his docile tools, this in itself would have precluded his placing any shred of confidence in them. If learned professors could gather on his orders and decide that Frunze should undergo counter-indicated surgery, if at a given time Stalin thought that one of them might be utilized to poison Trotsky, then such methods might one day be turned against himself. He knew that he was surrounded by hatred; he knew too that these hatreds were largely emasculated by a fear of giving confidences that might always be betrayed. But no system of surveillance is completely infallible. Men who think that their lives are in danger sometimes prefer to take the biggest gambles. And in the last analysis the poison could equally well come from his own people.

Trotsky likened Stalin's position to the Borgias'. It was indeed the atmosphere of Florentine intrigues that pervaded the Kremlin in these years, which, we must remember, were those of the Constitution of 1936, "the most democratic in the world."

The second trial of Zinoviev and Kamenev, in the autumn of 1936; the charges made against them—no longer the accusation of having through their ideology fostered the flowering of terrorism, but that of having been its direct instigators on orders from Trotsky; their confessions, and the death sentences put a dramatic end to Stalin's preparatory maneuvers.

This time the members of the Central Committee could entertain no further doubt. The tacit agreement that there would be no shedding of the blood of present or former leaders of the party had been breached. Stalin was imposing what he had been unable to achieve in the Ryutin case. And he was not going to be satisfied with the blood of Zinoviev and Kamenev.

During the Bukharin trial, Tomsky and Rykov had been brought into the case. Kamenev, in his statements, had implicated Sokolnikov, Radek, and Preobrazhensky in the "conspiracy." The name of Putna, the military attaché in London, had been mentioned. This was the first public indication of a possible purge of the army.

It was all clear: Stalin was seeking the deaths of the old oppositionists. He was initiating a reign of terror at the summit of the party, that hitherto inviolate bureaucratic preserve. Where would he stop? The time had come to resist him.

Even today there is only meager detail on those resistances that appeared—or, rather, attempted to appear. Some information was contained in Khrushchev's report. The resistances were voiced in the Central Committee's Plenum in February and March 1937. This Plenum had been preceded by the famous telegram sent by Stalin and Zhdanov from Sochi, the dictator's summer residence, on September 25, 1936. Two days later Yagoda was transferred from the NKVD to the Commissariat for Posts, Telephones, and Telegraph.

But the Plenum did not proceed without conflict, if Khrushchev's report is to be believed:

A number of members was in fact questioning the propriety of the line adopted with respect to mass repression on the pretext of combatting "duplicity." Comrade Postyshev expressed these doubts in a most pertinent fashion; he stated:

"After mature deliberation, I believe that the bitter years of conflict have ended; those members of the party who had weakened have either collapsed or joined the enemy camp; the sound elements have fought for the party. These were the years of industrialization and collectivization. I have never thought it possible that, once this harsh period was over, Karpov [a member of the Ukrainian Central Committee] and his like would have gone over to the enemy's camp. And now, according to the testimony, it would appear that Karpov was recruited by the Trotskyists in 1934. . . . I cannot imagine how it would be possible to work for the party throughout the difficult years and then in 1934 to join the Trotskyists. It is very strange (a stir in the audience).

But Khrushchev's report leaves the essence of the matter in obscurity. It is not possible that the case of Bukharin, Rykov,

and their associates would have gone unmentioned in this
Plenum in February 1937. There is indeed every reason to believe that it constituted the heart of the discussions and that
the members of the Plenum had to decide whether these men
were to be placed on trial—in other words, completely surrendered to Yezhov's henchmen.

Actually it would appear that their fate was the subject of
a bitter battle within the party. During the trial of Zinoviev
and Kamenev, the prosecutor, Vyshinsky, asserted that he had
ordered charges lodged against Bukharin, Rykov, and Tomsky
(*Pravda*, August 21, 1936). Tomsky had chosen suicide in
preference to interrogation. It is possible that his death served
to crystalize certain resistances. In any event, on September
10, 1936—a few days before the famous telegram from Sochi—
Pravda announced that the preliminary investigation in the
case of Bukharin and Rykov had produced no evidence and
consequently the prosecution had been dropped.

It is possible to risk a hypothesis: Yagoda, undoubtedly
backed by certain elements in the Central Committee, refused
to cooperate in preparing the case against the former rightists.
Two weeks later Stalin prevailed on the Politburo to remove
him and replace him with Yezhov, who, according to Krivitzky, arrived at the NKVD with a fully trained team of two
hundred men and at once replaced the major division heads.

With Yezhov's accession the campaign against the rightists
was immediately resumed. In the second great public trial,
that of Pyatakov, Sokolnikov, and Radek in January 1937,
Radek once more implicated Bukharin. It was probably then,
or at the beginning of March at the latest, after the meeting
of the Central Committee, that Bukharin and Rykov were arrested.[9]

Apart from Khrushchev's report, which is silent on the main

[9] Bukharin's name appeared on the masthead of *Izvestia*, of which he
was the editor in chief, until January 16, 1937. Furthermore, when he
went on trial in March 1938, he stated that he had been arrested more
than a year before.

matter—for he intended to rehabilitate the memories only of those Stalinists who had become Stalin's victims—there is virtually no other information on the truth of this gloomy period. There are, however, two other sources: *Les Carnets d'Ignace Reiss* and Uralov's book, *Staline au pouvoir*.[10]

Reiss, a Polish Jew born in 1899, was one of those militants whom the Communist International sent abroad to spread revolutionary agitation: He worked in Poland, where he was arrested and tortured; in the Ruhr from 1923 to 1926; in Vienna, where he was imprisoned, and then in other European countries. Stalin's policy toward the left opposition and the trial of Zinoviev and Kamenev shattered his loyalty, and, when he was in France in 1937, he broke with Stalin. Some time earlier he had turned over his notes to certain friends abroad. What is called his "notebooks" contains only a few bench marks, but they throw a harsh illumination nevertheless on the hidden truth of the period. For instance:

Note 10: "Ninety hours of interrogation. The remark by Slutsky [a police official] on Mrachkovsky." (Mrachkovsky, a veteran of the civil war accused at the same time as Zinoviev and Kamenev, had been questioned for ninety hours, undoubtedly by the "relay" method described so dramatically by Weissberg in *L'Accusé*. This method consisted in using teams of questioners who relieved one another without interruption in the interrogation. According to Reiss, Mrachkovsky agreed to confess only when he learned that Smirnov, another defendant, had finally been broken down.)

Note 16: "There is a rumor in the GPU that Yagoda was an agent of the Gestapo. Supposedly the Germans compelled him to work for them by blackmailing him, because he had formerly been an informer for the Okhrana. But he is not even forty years old." (The rumor was indeed ridiculous, and Yagoda refuted it at his trial. "If I had been a spy," he said, "all

[10] Uralov was the pseudonym of Avtorkhanov, a former rightist of Chechen origin.

the foreign espionage services could have gone out of business.")

Note 30: "Messing-Kaganovich: 'Orders are refused.'" (Reiss offered this comment on this note: in a conference in Moscow Kaganovich had made a violent attack on the bad management of the city, sabotage, etc., and demanded exemplary punishments. He had then turned to Messing, a major figure in the GPU, whose reply, "Orders are refused," meant: "I do not assume the task of performing sabotage to order." Reiss' note, however, does not indicate when this exchange occurred. If it is based on fact, it would confirm the existence of resistance elements within the GPU.)

Note 32: "Rykov and Bukharin, brought from their cells and taken before the Central Committee in plenary session, categorically refused to admit their guilt. Stalin said: 'Back to prison! Let them defend themselves there!'" (Again there is no indication of date. One is inclined to think that this refers to the Plenum of February–March 1937, mentioned in Khrushchev's report, but Uralov's book refers to another meeting of the Central Committee.)

Uralov contended that the investigation in the case of Bukharin and his associates was assigned not to the NKVD, which was considered not too reliable, but to the party's Central Control Commission headed by Yezhov. Supposedly he had succeeded in obtaining confessions from Zinoviev and Kamenev and then from Radek, all of whom fiercely challenged them.

According to Uralov, Stalin thereupon decided at the end of the summer of 1937 to convoke a special meeting of the Central Committee to study their case. In this meeting Yezhov acted as the prosecutor. Bukharin answered back—answers that, Uralov wrote, were mimeographed and clandestinely circulated throughout Moscow. Not content merely to defend himself, Bukharin made charges against Stalin and Yezhov. When it came to a vote, only one-third of the members of the

Central Committee supported Stalin: the others either voted against him or abstained. The opponents supposedly included five members of the Politburo—Postyshev, Kossior, Chubar, Rudzutak, and Eikhe—and all the military men in the Committee except Voroshilov and Budenny.

Stalin, Uralov said, yielded and congratulated the members of the Central Committee for their "healthy criticism," by which he pledged to guide himself. When all the delegates had returned to their respective provinces, he at once took the offensive against the redoubtable opposition that had just come out into the open.

What this version contributes is obvious. It explains the extent of the purge: Of 139 members and alternates in the Central Committee elected in 1934, 98 were arrested and shot, most of them in 1937–1938. It also explains the purge of the army. It makes it possible to understand why on September 10, 1938, the press reported that the prosecution of Bukharin and Rykov had been dropped. Finally, seeing the majority of the Central Committee and a number of army leaders arrayed against him and Yagoda's NKVD no longer reliable, Stalin had to take the offensive and carry it through. Hence the telegram from Sochi.

Nevertheless it is difficult to concede that, in the face of these perils, Stalin should have deemed it wise to spend a vacation on the shore of the Black Sea. But above all the strongest objection that can be made to Uralov's version is the fact that there is no official trace of this meeting of the Central Committee. Was it kept secret because it had been unfavorable to Stalin? Undoubtedly this would be a plausible explanation. But to my knowledge there has been no other rumor in confirmation of a session of such importance in which more than a hundred persons took part.

That is why Uralov's version should be considered dubious. It can merely be regarded as probable that at the beginning of September 1936, under conditions of which we know nothing, Stalin suffered a temporary setback with respect to the prosecution of Bukharin and Rykov. He was a man to draw immediate conclusions from this fact and eliminate whoever in his view might threaten his power.

(15)

THE TUKHACHEVSKY
MYSTERY

O N JANUARY 26, 1937, in the midst of the trial of the "Anti-Soviet Center,"[1] Vyshinsky, who was questioning the defendant, Radek, called on him to explain why he had mentioned Tukhachevsky's name in a statement made during preliminary interrogation.

Radek replied: "The government had given Tukhachevsky an assignment for which he needed materials that he could find nowhere and that I alone had. He telephoned to ask me whether I had them at home. I did, and that was why he sent Putna,[2] with whom he was supposed to carry out his orders, to fetch them. Naturally Tukhachevsky had no idea of Putna's part or of the criminal part that I was playing."

Vyshinsky attacked again: "If I understand correctly, Putna

[1] Known also as the "Reserve Center" and the "Parallel Center." According to the Soviet charges, it had recruited a certain number of oppositionists (including Pyatakov, Radek, Sokolnikov, Muralov, etc.) who were to go into action only if the Trotskyist-Zinovievist center (Zinoviev, Kamenev, Smirnov, etc.) was discovered. Thirteen of the seventeen defendants in this trial were shot.

[2] General Putna, formerly military attaché in London, was thereupon arrested.

was in contact with the members of your secret Trotskyist organization and Tukhachevsky's name was mentioned only because Putna had gone to your home on an official mission for Tukhachevsky."

"I confirm that," Radek replied, "and I declare that I never have had or could have had relations with Tukhachevsky dealing with counterrevolutionary activity because I knew from his attitude that he was a man absolutely devoted to the party and the government." [3]

To any Western reader unversed in the mechanics of Stalinist justice, Tukhachevsky had been cleared of all suspicion by Radek's statement. But Walter Ginzburg, alias Krivitzky, one of the major Soviet secret-service agents, shuddered when he read Radek's testimony. He turned to his wife and said: "Tukhachevsky is done for." Then, seeing her astonishment, he added: "Do you think for one second that Radek would have dared to drag Tukhachevsky's name into court on his own? No. It was Vyshinsky who put Tukhachevsky's name into Radek's mouth. And it was Stalin who made Vyshinsky do it. Don't you see that Radek speaks for Vyshinsky and Vyshinsky speaks for Stalin? I tell you again: Tukhachevsky is doomed." [4]

On April 12, 1937, it was learned that Marshal Tukhachevsky, the Commander in Chief of the Red Army, had been downgraded to a secondary post, the command of the Volga military district—sure disgrace. On June 2 it was announced that Deputy Commissar for War Gamarnik, chief of the army's political division, had committed suicide. Nine days later an official announcement stated that the military tribunal had begun investigating "a gigantic case of treason" implicating Tukhachevsky, Yakir, Uborevich, Kork, Eidenman, Feldman, Primakov, and Putna—in other words, the principal army commanders.

[3] *Trial of the Anti-Soviet Center*, stenographic transcript, p. 155.
[4] Krivitzky, *J'étais un agent de Staline*, pp. 257–258.

"All the accused have admitted their complete guilt," the communiqué added. It specified that these men had taken part in "an enterprise against the state in alliance with the ruling military circles of a foreign state that is following an unfriendly policy toward the USSR."

A further communiqué next day announced that these eight officers had been executed.

Of the accusations of treason on behalf of a foreign power—that is, Nazi Germany—nothing remains today. All these men were rehabilitated after Stalin's death as the victims of false charges. In the Party's Twenty-second Congress on October 28, 1961, Khrushchev indicated that the whole affair had been fabricated on the basis of forged documents produced by the German secret service.

"Certain foreign publications," he said, "have published a curious report according to which Hitler, planning to invade our country, had his espionage service forge a document to prove that Yakir, Tukhachevsky, and others were agents of the German High Command. This so-called 'top-secret' document fell into the hands of President Benes, who, apparently with the best intentions, hastened to transmit it to Stalin. Yakir, Tukhachevsky, and other comrades were arrested and eliminated. . . . When we learned that Tukhachevsky, Yakir, and Uborevich had not committed the slightest crime against the state, we addressed ourselves to Molotov, Kaganovich, and Voroshilov: 'Do you approve of their rehabilitation?' we asked. 'Yes,' they said, 'we do approve.' 'And yet,' we cried indignantly, 'it was you who executed these men! When did you act in good conscience? then or now?' But of course they could not find any answer. . . ."

Twenty-four years after Tukhachevsky's execution, then, Khrushchev declared that neither the commander of the Red Army nor the other high officers tried at the same time had committed treason (no crimes against the state) or conspired to carry out a *Putsch* (no crime against the party). Many mys-

teries, however, continue to surround what is called the Tukhachevsky case.

It does indeed seem that it was Heydrich who instigated
the Gestapo's forgery of the documents purporting to establish Tukhachevsky's collusion with certain leaders of the German army. The man who was behind the whole business was
General Skoblin, a White emigrant. He was one of the deputies of General Miller, who had succeeded General Kutyepov
at the head of the ROVS after the latter's abduction.

Skoblin was also in contact with a group of White emigrants
in Berlin headed by Guchkov,[5] and by this means he had established relations with Heydrich's staff, to which he supplied
information. But principally he was working for the GPU, into
whose service he had been brought through the intermediary
of his wife, Plevitzkaya, the Russian singer.

· According to the disclosures made by Walter Hagen[6] in
his book, *The Secret Front*, and the revelations of Walter
Schellenberg of the SS, confirmed in part by his colleague,
Behrens, it was through this triple agent that Heydrich learned
of a conspiracy against Stalin among the leaders of the Red
Army, headed by Marshal Tukhachevsky. This afforded two
possibilities to Hitler and Heydrich. Either they could support
the plot in the hope of overthrowing the Bolshevik government, or, on the contrary, they could inform Stalin of the
preparations and thus bring on a drastic purge of the Red
Army, which in the event of war would be infinitely weakened.

This was the solution that attracted Heydrich. According to
Hagen, Heydrich and Hitler had a decisive discussion of the
subject shortly before Christmas of 1936. It was decided to
fabricate the necessary forgeries and arrange for them to reach
Stalin.

In order to perpetrate the forgeries, however, it was necessary to find original letters from high Soviet military sources.
And such documents were in existence. In actuality, a close

[5] Minister of war after the Revolution of February 1917.
[6] His real name was Wilhelm Hoettl.

collaboration between the *Reichswehr* and the Soviet army had been initiated in 1923, after the Treaty of Rapallo. In order to evade the restrictions in the Treaty of Versailles, German officers were secretly transferred to the Soviet Union in order to test planes and tanks, both of which they were forbidden to build or use on German soil. In return, they played an active part in the technical training of the Red Army. This alliance was quite far-reaching, for certain German war industries were established in Siberia. Hitler's accession to power put an end to this collaboration.

Heydrich began by approaching the head of the *Abwehr*, Admiral Canaris, and requesting the loan of documents in the admiral's possession. Canaris, it was believed, gave him an evasive answer. According to Hagen, the wanted documents were obtained, however, through a well-timed burglary in the archives of the *Wehrmacht*. They were supplemented by a few forgeries intended to establish a record of Tukhachevsky's "treason." The forged papers in combination with the genuine documents, which no doubt dealt only with the purely technical collaboration between the Soviet and German generals, tended to show that Tukhachevsky had sought the cooperation of German generals in the preparation of a *Putsch* against Stalin.

There was still the matter of getting all this documentation to its destination. According to Schellenberg, contacts were made with a friend of Beneš through a German emigrant living in Prague. Subsequently an emissary from Yezhov was supposed to have made contact with Heydrich's people in order to obtain the documents. In April or May they were transferred in consideration of a payment of three million rubles in gold.[7]

If this version is to be accepted, Stalin was thus drawn into a trap laid by Hitler and Heydrich, liquidating imaginary enemies in a dreadful purge that sent the greater part of the

[7] Cf. Schellenberg, *Le Chef du contre-espionnage nazi parle*, p. 30.

Soviet General Staff and thousands of officers to the scaffold and the prison camp. This is a reaction in strange contrast to the distrust that Stalin was later to display toward information coming from abroad. It will be remembered that, in spite of the abundant information from various sources that he received on Germany's preparations for her offensive, he refused to place any credence in it right to the end, regarding it as provocation by the imperialists. At the start of the war he had shown the same incredulity toward reports transmitted by the Roessler network in Switzerland on the German General Staff's plans.

Actually, talk of collusion between Tukhachevsky and the *Wehrmacht* had begun to circulate in a variety of circles even before Heydrich's people had been able to transmit their documents. Léon Blum, testifying on June 18, 1946, before the "commission assigned to inquire into the events occurring in France between 1933 and 1945," declared:

At the beginning of 1936 I had received from my friend, M. Eduard Beneš, privately and confidentially and transmitted through my son, who had passed through Prague, a warning that I should at once adopt the greatest precautions in our relations with the Soviet General Staff. According to his own intelligence service—the Czech Intelligence Service enjoyed a deserved reputation in Europe—the leaders of the Soviet High Command were maintaining suspicious relations with Germany. . . . I do not know whether I told anyone of this. I believe that it is a revelation to my friend, Maurice Violette, and in fact I believe that I am revealing it here for the first time. It was this warning, given to me at the end of 1936, that to a certain degree paralyzed me in the stubborn effort that I had been making for some months to make a reality of the French-Soviet military alliance and bring it to full fruition on the military level.[8]

[8] Report by Charles Serre, Appendixes (*Dépositions,* Vol. I, Paris, 1951). Quoted by Suvarin in *L'Affaire Toukhatchevski in Le contrat social,* July 1959.

The date twice mentioned by Blum—the end of 1936—does not accord, however, with that given by Beneš himself in his memoirs. According to him it was in January 1937 that Trautmannsdorf, a German diplomat, let slip a remark that alerted Beneš to the fact that Hitler was negotiating with certain groups in Russia: Tukhachevsky, Rykov, and their associates. . . . Beneš added that he had immediately informed Alexandrovsky, the Soviet ambassador in Prague. Churchill's version (Volume I of his memoirs) was that Beneš was informed in the autumn of 1936 by a German military figure.

While the dates may vary, the fact seems clear that in late 1936 or early 1937 rumors of collusion between Tukhachevsky and the Germans were already circulating in Czechoslovakia and France and were speedily conveyed to Stalin.

The chronology is an important reference point here. For it was also in January 1937 that Radek in his testimony publicly, though casually, mentioned Tukhachevsky's name. Now the argument adduced by Krivitzky is flawless: If Radek spoke, it was because he had been ordered to do so by Vyshinsky and hence by Stalin. And, since a big Soviet trial necessitated meticulous preparation, it may be taken for granted that Radek's statement had already been prepared, even rehearsed in secret during the preliminary investigation—in other words, several weeks before the opening of the trial.

Stalin, who had not yet received Heydrich's forgeries, was therefore preparing something against Tukhachevsky, and he used Radek to set the machinery in motion. (Obviously it was not by sheer chance that Radek got off with a sentence to forced labor.) Moreover, General Primakov—who, according to Ignace Reiss, had not yet confessed on December 11, 1936—and Putna, the military attaché in London, had already been arrested. So the purge of the Red Army had begun in the closing months of 1936.

Is one to believe that Stalin acted only on the basis of the information that he had received from Beneš? The same question arises again: Why would so suspicious a man have immediately given it credence?

The man who was at the origin of the information supplied to Heydrich on Tukhachevsky's contacts with the *Wehrmacht* was General Skoblin. He informed the Gestapo, but he was above all—and this is known beyond question—the Soviet services' man. Of course it might be supposed that he had invented the Tukhachevsky conspiracy for financial reasons. But it is much more logical to believe that by transmitting his information to Heydrich he was carrying out the mission that the NKVD had assigned to him.

Thus Stalin's secret services appear at the root of this whole business. This was the view of Behrens of the SS, who was the technical director of Heydrich's forgeries. According to Behrens, a former GPU agent who had gone to work for the Gestapo had taken part in the fabrication of the forgeries. Behrens said that in his opinion this turncoat was really working on behalf of the Soviet services [9] and that in this instance Heydrich, in the belief that he was bringing off a stroke of genius to weaken the Soviet Union, was "intoxicated."

This version, which in the end seems the most probable, falls far short, however, of clarifying everything. There was nothing ingenuous about Heydrich. Could he put any confidence in mere remarks repeated by an informer as suspect as Skoblin? Had Skoblin supplied some documents tending to prove suspicious contacts between Tukhachevsky and certain German military circles? Had he gambled on the distrust that might agitate Hitler and Heydrich with respect to possible dealings between Soviet and German military men?

These are questions to which it is dubious whether any answer can be found at present and that are among the mysteries that all secret services always keep inviolate. On the other hand it is difficult to imagine any reasons why Stalin needed documents supplied by Hitler if he wanted to liqui-

[9] This should be compared with Krivitzky's statement: "We have agents even in the heart of the Gestapo."

date his generals, unless one concedes that in order to carry out the decapitation of the Red Army he required these "proofs" to convince the other members of the Politburo.

There is still one further problem: Was Tukhachevsky preparing a *Putsch* against Stalin? Various opinions have circulated on the subject in emigrant circles.

In its issue of October 23, 1947, *The Socialist Courier* published an article by an emigrant named Bobrov who declared that Tukhachevsky, Yakir and some other generals had indeed conspired together. Another version in the same journal (published in the issues of September 8–9 and September 27, 1948) contained confidences allegedly made to the writer of the article (he signed it with only his initials, MN) in the camp of Vorkuta by a former legal consultant to the Council of People's Commissars, Nariman-Narimanov, who said that he had attended Tukhachevsky's trial. According to him, the plotters intended that Petrovsky, the leader of the proletarian division in Moscow, should seize control of the Lyubyanka, the postal service, the telegraph network, and the railway stations. The conspirators had also counted on gaining the support of troops garrisoned in Siberia. Supposedly they were betrayed by Dybenko, the Commander in central Asia.[10]

All these versions, which contradict one another on a number of points, are unverifiable in the present state of available documentation. To tell the truth, no serious evidence of a projected *Putsch* has ever been adduced. The very existence of such a conspiracy was denied by Khrushchev when he stated in the speech quoted earlier that the generals had done nothing against the party.

This denial, obviously, is not conclusive. It was put forward in a very special frame of reference: the conflict with the anti-party group. In his violent attack on Voroshilov Khrushchev

[10] Dybenko was listed among the military judges who tried Tukhachevsky. He was executed a short time later. But there is actually no proof that a trial was ever held.

may have required a complete "whitewash" of the generals who were the victims of *Yezhovchina* (Yezhovism).

Some have occasionally professed to find evidence of the *Putsch* in the haste with which Stalin's police carried out the arrests and liquidations. At the time Trotsky himself appeared to give it some credence. But, from the moment when Radek mentioned Tukhachevsky's name from the witness stand, there can be no doubt that the marshal was doomed in Stalin's mind. Consequently there can be no doubt that his activities were closely watched by Yezhov's police. The margin left to the ebullient marshal for preparations for a *coup d'état* became most tenuous, if not nonexistent. Everyone who was privy to the methods of the apparatus reacted as Krivitzky did: Tukhachevsky was doomed. What high-ranking officer would be willing to compromise himself with a marked man? Though they were possible earlier (but extremely difficult because of the surveillance of the NKVD), preparations for a *Putsch* to be headed by the marshal became tantamount to suicide. After January 1937, Tukhachevsky was a man alone.

A fascinating picture of that isolation was provided by Barmin, a Soviet diplomat who chose freedom rather than liquidation in the Great Purge. On May 1, 1937, while the troops were preparing to parade beneath their red flags in the sunny streets of Moscow, Marshal Tukhachevsky appeared at Lenin's tomb. That was where the generals stood to take the salute. A moment later Marshal Yegorov arrived. He stood beside Tukhachevsky but did not speak to him. Then came Gamarnik. All remained silent and motionless. The parade approached at marching pace, to the obbligato of the tanks. When it was over, the officers did not say a word. Tukhachevsky left. No one saluted. He ignored the others. He kept his composure, but his face was completely gray.

There was nothing left for him to do but to wait for the day when Yezhov's men would come and knock at his door.

If it was impossible for the generals to attempt a *coup d'état*, why did Stalin decide to get rid of them and to launch that tremendous purge of the army? An answer to that question might be found if it was confirmed that Tukhachevsky had voted against Stalin or abstained in that meeting of the Central Committee that Uralov described. But we have seen that that meeting itself was conjecture rather than fact.

Besides, did Stalin need an actual military opposition if he wanted to act? The Red Army had always been a source of anxiety for the leaders of the party. In the beginning the "troika" was afraid that it might serve Trotsky as the instrument for a *coup d'état*. When Trotsky had been eliminated, Stalin got rid of Lashevich, a supporter of Zinoviev and deputy commissar for war; and Frunze's death is still a mystery.

In 1926-1927, when the campaign against the opposition was at its height, the party crisis had its echo among the political commissars and certain young officers.[11] From another point of view the large number of former tsarist officers was also an occasion for concern. Nevertheless their number declined steadily and their influence was very meager at the time of the Great Purge.

Paradoxically, the officer corps taken as a whole had never experienced the kind of purge of its ranks that struck the party itself. It is possible that this fact alone incited Stalin to his repression: *here was a potential danger*. It was all the greater in that the men who looked to Kirov as a pretender to the succession after Stalin must have been inspired by the one

11 Shortly after the Trotskyist demonstrations of November 7, 1927, three officers who belonged to the Military Academy of the General Staff—Arkady Heller, Boris Bulatov, and Enukidze (a relative of Stalin's associate)—were arrested. (Heller, however, had already been expelled from the Academy a few months earlier with four others on a charge of having planned a military conspiracy). The three were accused of having tried to organize a terrorist attack. According to *Contre le courant* (No. 10, March 31, 1928), they were simply paying for their loyalty to Trotsky, for whom they formed a bodyguard at every meeting.

It will also be noted in *The Notebooks of Ignace Reiss* (n. 22) that at an unspecified date, but certainly later than 1930, two officers, Ryubinin and Chernyavsky, were accused of having planned an attack against Stalin. So Red Army circles were hardly ever exempt from Stalin's suspicions.

outstanding personality, the man who had made the Red Army a modern force.

Undoubtedly the mere possibility of conspiracy was enough to make Stalin decide on a preventive measure modeled on the night of the long knives. Afterward, furthermore, he would have a clear field in order to put into practice the policy for which he had the marshal shot: an understanding with Hitler.

On September 24, 1937, a few months after Tukhachevsky's death, old General Miller, who had succeeded Kutyepov at the head of the ROVS, left his office in Rue du Colisée in Paris. As a precaution he left a letter on his desk: It said that he had an appointment for twelve-thirty at the corner of Rues Raffet and Jasmin with a German officer and an attaché from the German Embassy. "This appointment," the letter added, "was made at the instance of Skoblin. It may be a trap; that is why I am leaving this note, just in case."

He was never seen again.

It was not until eleven o'clock that night that Miller's adjutant, General Kussonsky, apprehensive at his leader's disappearance, remembered the letter and opened it. He sent someone to rouse Skoblin, who went very composedly to the office. He was unperturbed until he was told of the letter, which in effect was an accusation of him. But, through a further unbelievable oversight of Miller's associates, he succeeded in fleeing. He too was never heard of again.

There may have been a connection between the abduction of General Miller and the Tukhachevsky case. Krivitzky declared in his book that in December 1936,[12] when he was in The Hague, he was asked for two men who could play the part of German officers for a matter of prime importance that Slutzky was about to undertake. Krivitzky provided the two

[12] It should be remembered that it was at approximately this time that rumors of an understanding between Hitler and the Soviet generals began to circulate and that it was probably during this period that the testimony given by Radek at his trial was put into its final form.

men requested, and they left for Paris. They returned two weeks later. For some unknown reason they had not been able to carry out their mission.

Krivitzky was convinced that these two men had been sent to Paris to abduct General Miller. But for some unknown reason the enterprise had been postponed.

It might be supposed that Yezhov had contemplated abducting Miller at the end of December for possible use as a witness against Tukhachevsky, and this would have presented no great problem once he was safely ensconced in the Lyubyanka. But the abduction of Miller after the execution of Tukhachevsky is no longer understandable.

Was it because he knew certain secrets of the Tukhachevsky affair that his disappearance was desirable? But why had Miller revealed nothing after the marshal's death? Or, if he had permitted himself certain discreet confidences, why is nothing yet known of them after thirty years?

All these questions are still unanswered. And many aspects of the Tukhachevsky affair are still mysteries.

(16)

INSIDE *YEZHOVCHINA*

═══════════════════════════════

T HE ARMY having lost its head, Stalin could now carry through his purge of the party to the end. It was prosecuted especially vigorously against the Communist apparatus in the national minorities. In consonance with the geographical position of their areas, the leaders of these Central Committees were variously accused of being in the pay of Germany, Poland, England, or Japan.

The Ukrainian Communist party, whose representatives, Kossior and Postyshev, had opposed Stalin in the Plenum of the Central Committee in February 1937, suffered especially from the purge. The Ukraine had remained an irredentist region, and it is probable that Stalin utilized the publicly manifested opposition as a pretext for extirpating as much as possible the roots of "bourgeois nationalism."

In the spring of 1938 Molotov arrived in Kiev with Khrushchev. The atmosphere in the city was tense. Troops of Ukrainian origin had been removed and replaced by Siberian divisions and NKVD units. The Central Committee of the Ukrainian Communist party met in the shadow of this threat. Molotov demanded Kossior's resignation and his replacement by Khrushchev as first secretary. According to Uralov, the Central Committee refused its consent, whereupon Kossior, Petrovsky, and Postyshev [1] were summoned to Moscow to discuss the situation with Stalin. There, Uralov wrote, they were imprisoned. Lyubchenko, another Ukrainian leader, opted for suicide. And Khrushchev assumed the post of first secretary to carry out the purge.

An almost identical scene was played out in Uzbekistan, where it was Andreyev who had received a mission similar to Molotov's from Stalin. The secretary of the local Central Committee, Ikramov, was arrested as a "bourgeois nationalist." In 1938 he was to appear as a co-defendant with Yagoda, Bukharin, and Rykov in the trial of the rightists and Trotskyists.

Throughout the territory of the Soviet Union arrests mounted. The prisons were filled. Hundreds of thousands of men were accused of fantastic crimes. In the ranks of the party, at the core of the *Komsomol,* in the factories, in the universities, among the technicians *Yezhovchina* (Yezhovism) raged. In the Ukraine, White Russia, Uzbekistan, Armenia, Georgia, tens of thousands of spies, traitors, saboteurs, and terrorists, all connected through a series of intermediaries with the arch-fiend, Trotsky, were flushed out of their cover. The arrest of one person usually meant the arrests of his associates as well. Anyone who had had anything to do with him was accused of having plotted with him. Denunciations and witch hunts sharpened appetites and alimented betrayals. A whole generation of "Old Bolsheviks" was thrown on the scrap heap of history. New strata, made up of younger men, were recruited by Stalin to take their places. Terror and opportunism have always been congenial bedfellows.

The nightmare intensified. Every night men listened for the sound of footsteps on the stairs announcing the arrival of Yezhov's thugs. Every day, in the offices of investigating mag-

[1] Cf. *op. cit.,* pp. 68–71. With respect to Postyshev, however, Urallov was manifestly in error. In March 1937, in actuality, he had been demoted to the post of provincial secretary of the party in Kuibyshev.

istrates, defendants suffered the torture of the "relay," the endless fire of questions posed by successive teams of interrogators: "Confess, Trotskyist dog! Name your accomplices, tell us about your organization. . . ."

Under the insults, the blows, and the tortures—authorized by a circular letter from Stalin—the avowals piled up. Thousands of people confessed that they had been enlisted by British Intelligence, the Gestapo, Polish, Latvian, Turkish, Japanese spies. . . . They had sought to kill Stalin, or Voroshilov, or Kaganovich, or Kossior. But now Kossior had been arrested in his turn. So the interrogators, too tired to prepare new transcripts, told the accused to replace Kossior's name with Molotov's or Mikoyan's. And indeed, given the situation as it was by then, did it matter what name was used? Take Molotov, then, if this meant an end to further ordeals, unremitting interrogation for endless hours on one's feet against a wall, if this was the price of sitting down at last and going to sleep.

The Communist press of every country took part in the hue and cry: Kill the bandits, the monsters! In its issue of June 12, 1937, *l'Humanité* printed a lengthy manifesto dealing with the "treachery" of the generals. A few paragraphs from it are enough to give the flavor:

> While Socialist civilization under the leadership of the Bolshevik party, the Central Committee, and our great Comrade Stalin is demonstrating its full superiority in the face of unleashed Fascist barbarism, . . . a few miserable wretches in the pay of Hitlerism have tried to stab the young proletarian state in the back.
>
> Carrying their betrayal to the point of joining forces with the Gestapo of the Berlin government, traitors following the orders of Trotsky have tried to conspire against the Soviet Union, the bulwark of peace in the world.
>
> The French Communist party is confident that it speaks for the working population of France when it thanks the Central Committee of the Bolshevik party and Comrade Stalin for having thwarted the plans of international Fascism through their vigilance.

Shame on those who have not hesitated to ally themselves with the agents of Hitlerism!

Shame on those who have not hesitated to become the spies of the *Reichswehr!*

Long live the glorious Bolshevik party! . . .

Long live the Soviet Union, which has raised the banner of hope for the human multitudes over one-sixth of the globe!

Few voices indeed were raised by leftist intellectuals in the name of human conscience, justice, freedom, and truth against this purge madness and the hideous mockeries of the trials. Many approved; others said nothing. It was reported, however, that an attempt was made to explain to Stalin that all these trials were producing a harmful reaction among the Western intellectuals; he is supposed to have retorted: "They'll swallow anything." If indeed he did say this, it cannot be denied that he knew what he was talking about.

It would be fallacious to attempt to reckon the number of the victims of Yezhovism. It is possible, however, at least to catalogue with precision the number of leading party and army figures who were purged.

In 1934 the Politburo had ten members. By 1939 one of them, Kossior, had been shot, and three others had died in suspicious circumstances: Kirov, Kuibyshev, and Ordzhonikidze.[2] Of three alternates elected in 1934—Rudzutak, Postyshev, and Petrovsky—the first two had been shot and the third had been removed. Chubar too was shot, and Yezhov vanished, himself carried off by the purge that he had launched on Stalin's order. As for the members elected to the Central Committee in 1934, four-fifths of them were replaced in the Eighteenth Congress, which was held in 1939.[3]

[2] Ordzhonikidze probably committed suicide after a violent quarrel with Stalin.

[3] In his previously cited book, *De Lénine à Staline,* Leonard Schapiro draws a telling comparison: between 1919 and 1934 the turnover ranged from 7 per cent to 21 per cent (pp. 496–497).

Liquidations in the army accounted for 3 of the 5 marshals, 13 of the 15 generals of armies, 57 of the 85 commanders of army corps, 110 of the 195 divisional commanders, and 220 of the 406 brigadier generals. It is estimated further that some thirty-five thousand officers below the rank of colonel were victims of the purge.

In the period 1935–1937 more than one hundred and fifty thousand members of the party were expelled. (This did not necessarily mean that they were arrested.) Their places were taken by a new generation of bureaucrats. In 1939 most of the party secretaries were less than forty years old.

The offensive waged against the party apparatus in the national minorities similarly led to a change in personnel. In the 1930 decade it became the general practice to appoint a non-Russian as first secretary and a Great Russian as second secretary (exercising the real authority). This resulted in a number of conflicts, heightened by collectivization and the centralized planning that took little heed of the minorities' desires. As a result of the Great Purge, this apparatus, which was still insufficiently tractable, was decimated. In the Ukraine more than half the secretaries of the party were replaced. In Georgia 260 of fewer than 300 first, second, and third secretaries were purged. Thousands of functionaries at lower levels were also removed.

Stalin's successors invented a discreet way of describing this wholesale housecleaning. They called it "impairment of Socialist legality." Many persons were indeed impaired, and some so deeply that the impairments proved fatal.

The apotheosis of this tragedy was the trial of the rightist and Trotskyist bloc that was conducted between March 2 and 13, 1938. This was the dramatic masterpiece of *Yezhovchina,* a unique spectacle painstakingly brought to perfection in the workshops of the NKVD, which starred for eleven days in the ballroom of the former Nobles' Club.

Ulrich, the fat presiding judge, sat on a dais, flanked by two military judges. To his right was the prosecutor, Vyshinsky, in a well-cut dark blue suit, his hard brick-complexioned face with its gray eyes standing out against a stiff collar. The spectators of this *corrida* in the high-ceilinged hall, among its Corinthian columns silhouetted against a light blue background, were a chosen segment of the privileged persons of the government.

Twenty-one defendants filed in through a side door and faced the prosecutor: Yagoda and his medical squad; Rykov with his bushy beard; Bukharin, the "favorite child of the party"—but that was in Lenin's time—Krestinsky, small, thin, and nervous; Rakovsky; Khodzhayev; Ikramov; and others less well known.

The show began. All catalogued their crimes, as repugnant in motivation as they were vague in detail: plans for assassinations, *coups d'état* in alliance with Tukhachevsky, espionage, sabotage . . . the usual routine. Behind these resigned men hovered the malefic shadow of Trotsky, the absent but prime defendant.

The atmosphere was weird throughout. Vyshinsky led the chorus of unbelievable confessions, and created occasions for interchanges of this sort:

Q.: Were there instances in which members of your organization who were involved in various ways with the stockpiling of butter put ground glass into it?

A. [by Zelinsky]: There were instances in which ground glass *was found* in butter.

Q.: Not *found* in butter but *put into* it: do you recognize the difference?

A.: There were instances in which ground glass was put into butter.

Q.: Were there instances in which your fellow-conspirators, accomplices in the criminal plot against the Soviet government and the Soviet people, put tacks into the butter?

A.: There were such cases.

Q.: For what purpose? To make it taste better?

A.: The purpose is obvious. . . .

Q.: What about eggs? Didn't you put tacks into them?

A.: No.

Q.: Why not? Couldn't you manage it? Did the shells get in the way? [4]

According to Fitzroy MacLean, a British Embassy attaché who attended every session of the trial, these disclosures were received by the spectators with cries of anger and amazement —and with great guffaws of laughter in tribute to the wit displayed by the distinguished prosecutor. At last the truth was coming out as to the reasons why food supplies were so poorly handled. . . .

In this fabric of confessions, as formalized as a state document, there were some violent rents. On the very first day of the trial Krestinsky had the insolence to declare that he had never been a member of a "Trotskyist center." But had he not stated the contrary in the preliminary interrogation? Yes. Why?

Krestinsky: I made false statements in the preliminary interrogation.
Vyshinsky: And you stuck to them.
Krestinsky: Yes, I stuck to them because—I was convinced—*until there was a formal trial, if indeed there should be one, I could not impeach my own testimony.*[5]

It was perfectly clear. Krestinsky was implying that he had been at the mercy of the interrogators. If he had persisted in denials to them, he could not have appeared in the prisoner's dock: He would have been liquidated and shot.

Yagoda took a similar attitude a short time later. When he denied all responsibility in the murders of Peshkov and Menzhinsky, Vyshinsky asked him why he had made false statements. Yagoda replied: "Allow me not to answer the question."

The explanation, which was obvious then to anyone who was willing to give the matter thought, was made public some twenty years later by Khrushchev: The confessions had been

[4] *Trial of the Bloc of Anti-Soviet Rightists and Trotzkyists,* p. 351. Italics added.
[5] *Ibid.,* p. 57. Italics added.

obtained under duress. At the second session of the trial Krestinsky gave in: His disavowals of the previous day were perversity and lies. Yes, he was utterly guilty. "The words were uttered," MacLean wrote, "like those of a well-learned lesson. The night had not been wasted." [6]

One man dominated these contrived proceedings from a tremendous height: Bukharin. For all that he had lent himself—under what pressures?—to this mockery of a trial, for all that he had admitted having organized a bloc with the Trotskyists, planned a *coup d'état*, issued instructions to this one and that, his confessions stopped there and amounted, in sum, to acknowledging that he had been an oppositionist. Having conceded this, he evaded skillfully or fought back vigorously whenever Vyshinsky tried to force him into more precise admissions: that he had been a spy, that he had been involved in the assassination of Gorky, or that he had planned to assassinate Lenin. Against Vyshinsky's heavy-handed, savage attacks he deployed his own biting wit and the resources of a disciplined dialectician.

In an attempt to confound him Vyshinsky summoned to the rescue phantoms that he exhumed from the concentration camps: old left-wing Communists like Yakovleva and Ossinsky; the left Revolutionary Socialists, Karelin and Kamkov. They marched gray-faced to the witness stand, recited their fables in embarrassed voices, or even, like Kamkov, virtually refused to play the parts that had been assigned to them. But Bukharin, in spite of incessant interruptions from the prosecutor, always evoked some uncomfortable fact that made the shaky scaffolding of the indictment tremble even more.

The catalogue of his "crimes," however, did not include the contacts that he had had in Paris with Menshevik emigrants. These had occurred in 1935. Bukharin was a member of a delegation sent to Paris by Stalin to negotiate with German and Russian Socialists for the archives of Marx and Engels, which

[6] Fitzroy MacLean, *Diplomate et Franc-Tireur,* p. 83.

the German Social Democrats were keeping in the offices of the *Vorwärts*. After Hitler's accession to power these archives had been saved at the very last minute through an audacious move by Anatole de Monzie after he had been approached by Boris Suvarin. De Monzie enlisted the French ambassador in Berlin, François-Poncet, to tell the German government that the archives had been bought by the *Bibliothèque Nationale*—a complete fabrication. Thus the documents could be taken out of Germany and stored in safety abroad.

Informed of this, the Bolsheviks proposed that these archives be entrusted to the custody of the Marx-Engels Institute in Moscow. The German Social Democrats, who needed money now that they were in exile, agreed to sell some of the documents. On this basis negotiations began in the Hotel Lutétia in Paris: Moscow was represented by a delegation composed of Bukharin, Adoratzky, and Tikhomirnov, and the Mensheviks were represented by Dan and Nikolayevsky. Later, during the negotiations, all the parties gathered for a dinner at which, according to Dan's wife, Léon Blum also was present.

No bargain could be struck. Rather strangely, it was the Bolsheviks who had insisted that the negotiations be conducted with the Mensheviks, even though at the same time Moscow was denouncing them as the worst enemies of the working class. Among the German Social Democrats, when they learned of this insistence, some expressed the greatest suspicion that the whole affair was nothing but a provocation engineered by Stalin.

Nothing would have been easier for him than to make use of this negotiation during the trial in order to make it appear a criminal conspiracy. But no such attempt was made, and the reasons remain obscure.[7]

It was during his stay in Paris that Bukharin had a secret

[7] In 1938 the Popular Front was at its height and it was perhaps anything but politic for Stalin to implicate Socialists in this matter. Nevertheless Nikolayevksy was frequently mentioned during the trial as having had dealings with the defendants.

conversation in Dan's home. It was not made public until March 1964, when Dan's wife Lydia described it in *Novy Zhurnal,* one of the emigrant publications in the United States. Unannounced, Bukharin went to Dan's home one day for a frank talk. Mrs. Dan was present during only part of the conversation. Obviously this did not deal with plans for assassination and sabotage and still less with collusion with the Gestapo. But Bukharin seized the opportunity to paint a savage portrait of Stalin, the virulence of which left Dan stunned.

"You say that you do not know him," Bukharin exploded. "Well, we do know him. He suffers from the inability to persuade everyone, including himself, that he is the greatest of men, and this is his great grief, perhaps his most human characteristic; but what is not human in him, but really diabolical, is the fact that he cannot restrain himself from avenging this 'grief' on others, and specifically on those who in one way or another are greater or better than he. . . . If someone is a better speaker than Stalin, he is done for. . . . If he is a better writer than Stalin, woe to him. . . . To us, Fyodor Ilyich [Dan], Stalin is a shabby, evil man. No, Stalin is not a human being, he is a devil."

As he spoke, Mrs. Dan wrote, Bukharin's features were distorted by horror and indignation—the same expression that Kamenev had observed earlier during their talks. Perhaps Bukharin had gone to Dan's merely in order to unburden himself, to cry out the truths on which he was choking and that could not be uttered in the Soviet Union.

"Well, then," Dan said, "why do you still trust the man?"

Bukharin brushed the question aside with an impatient gesture. "You do not understand. It is not he who is trusted, it is the man to whom the party has given its confidence. As things stand now he is the symbol of the party; the ordinary people, the workers, the nation believe in him. Perhaps this is to be blamed on us, but it is a fact, and that is why all of us throw ourselves into his jaws knowing very well that he will undoubtedly devour us. He knows it, too, and he is satisfied to choose the most propitious moment."

"In that case," Lydia Dan interjected, "why are you going to go back into his jaws? Why go back to Russia?"

Astonishment brightened Bukharin's eyes. He made another gesture, as if rejecting a ludicrous hypothesis. "How can I not go back? Should *I* become an exile? No, I could never live as an emigrant, like you. No. No matter what happens . . ." He shrugged. "And perhaps nothing at all will happen." [8]

Three years later, after Chernov [9] had said: "My crimes are vast and monstrous"; after Ivanov had cried: "I was a defeatist and a spy"; after Krestinsky had repeated: "My crimes are tremendous"; after Rosengolz had let himself go into lyricism: "Millions, tens of millions of men, the children and citizens of the Soviet Union, including my own children, sing: 'How beautiful my beloved country, there is not another in the world where man breathes more freely!' "; then Bukharin in his turn, pallid, rose to make his final statement. At two points he had occasion to use words that, in retrospect, sound like muted echoes of his conversation with Dan.

Once again, and with vehemence, he repudiated the crimes that Vyshinsky had vainly sought to make him confess: "I categorically deny having maintained relations with foreign espionage agencies. . . . I categorically deny having been involved in the murders of Kirov, Menzhinsky, Kuibyshev, Gorky, and Peshkov." [10]

But he acknowledged defeat, paying homage to Stalin, and he disavowed "any personal resentment." *And he rejected the temptation to live if that meant being outside the party.* He continued: "If one says to oneself: 'All right, then, you will not die. Suppose that by some miracle you will go on living: what will be your purpose then? Isolated from everyone, an enemy

[8] On the same subject cf. *Contre le courant* (July–August 1964), with the note appended by Suvarin.

[9] This Chernov should not be confused with the Revolutionary Socialist leader who was then in exile.

[10] *Trial, op. cit.*, p. 818.

of the people, in a situation in which there is nothing human, completely cut off from what gives life its essence. . . .' " [11] Until the final moment he was still the prisoner of his party, he still was bound to it by that visceral dedication that had made him refuse the chance of survival as an emigrant.

The verdict was pronounced at four o'clock in the morning of March 13 under the glaring heat of spotlights while cameras turned. In a quiet voice Ulrich read out the grounds for the decision; the names followed like links in a chain: "Bukharin, Nikolai Ivanovich . . . Rykov, Alexey Ivanovich . . . Yagoda, Genrich Grigorievich . . ." To be shot. . . .

Eighteen names were pronounced by the fat presiding judge as he read the sentence of the Military College of the Supreme Court. Bessonov, Rakovsky, and Pletnev escaped with prison terms.

The great center door opened. Ulrich and the military judges departed. Then the little side door opened. One by one the condemned men passed through it, escorted by NKVD men in their red and blue caps. The last man was Yagoda, who looked briefly behind him. The door was closed after him.

During the trial, undoubtedly because of an operator's error, one of the spotlights had shone for a second on a small window just below the high ceiling of the hall—long enough for MacLean to see behind the window the heavy mustache and attentive face of Number One. After all, it was natural enough that Stalin should come to take a look at a spectacle of which he had been the producer and director.

[11] *Ibid.*, p. 825.

(17)

DEATH TO THE
TROTSKYISTS!

O N SEPTEMBER 4, 1937, the body of an athletic young man, riddled with machine-gun bullets, was found on the Chamblands road near Lausanne. On his body there was a Czech passport in the name of Hans Eberhardt, as well as a railway ticket for France.

The next day a woman went to the police. She revealed that Eberhardt was only an alias and that the victim was actually her husband, Ignace Reiss.

Reiss had made three mistakes that brought about his death. When he fled from the Soviet Embassy in Paris on July 17, he left a message with instructions that it be transmitted to the Central Committee in Moscow. It conveyed his final rupture with Stalin in these terms:

The letter that I am writing to you today should have been written long ago, the day when the Sixteen [1] were massacred in the cellars of the Lyubyanka on the orders of the "Father of the Peoples." I was silent then. . . . My offense is grave, but I shall endeavor to remedy it. . . . Until now I have marched with you. I

[1] The defendants in the trial of Zinoviev and Kamenev.

will not take another step. Our roads are parting. . . . I have fought
for Socialism since I was twenty years old. On the threshold of my
forties I have no desire to live at the mercy of a Yezhov. I have
sixteen years of illegal activity behind me. . . .

The noise that has been made over the exploits of the aviators
who flew across the North Pole was supposed to drown out the
moans and the cries of the victims tortured in the cellars of the
Lyubyanka, in Minsk, in Kiev, in Leningrad, in Tiflis. Nothing
will ever be able to drown out those cries. . . .

The day is not far off when international Socialism will sit in
judgment on all the crimes committed during these past ten years.
Nothing will be forgot, nothing will be forgiven. . . . The inspired
leader, the Father of the Peoples, the sun of Socialism will have to
render an accounting for his actions. I return to you the Order of
the Red Flag with which I was decorated in 1928. To wear it . . .
would be beneath my dignity.

Before his rupture Reiss had made contact with Sneevliet, a Dutch Trotskyist, and, through an intermediary, with
Trotsky's son, Lev Sedov. He had warned them that the purge
was aimed not only at oppositionists within the Soviet Union
but also at the Trotskyists in exile. "It has been decided to use
every means against you—I repeat: every means."

It is probable that the NKVD had been informed of these
contacts even before Reiss wrote his letter. And we shall see
that its agents had already been infiltrated into Trotskyist circles. In any case, when Reiss' letter was delivered to the Embassy in Rue de Grenelle, Spiegelglass, an emissary of Yezhov,
was there, and he ordered the letter opened at once. Reiss'
death was decided on before nightfall. When the purge was
raging in the NKVD itself, a harsh lesson was required that
would discourage any possible defections.

Reiss' second mistake was to keep his rupture with Moscow
secret and to retain his underground identity papers. Thus he
deprived himself of any protection against those who were
planning his murder.

But his most serious error was that, after he had taken refuge in Switzerland, he wrote a letter to Gertrude Schieldbach, a Communist like himself who had been his friend for twenty years. After the execution of the Sixteen she had visited the Reisses and collapsed in tears. Hence Reiss thought that she was capable of emulating his example. And in fact he soon received a reply from her. Yes, the good Gertrude had decided to break with Yezhov and she asked Reiss to fix a time when they could meet. He did so at once. So she went to Lausanne and spent a very pleasant evening with Mr. and Mrs. Reiss.

The next evening Gertrude and Reiss dined alone near Chamblands. After they had eaten they went out to take a walk along the dark road. A car came along and halted. Men leaped out and clubbed Reiss into unconsciousness. Then they tossed him into the car.

His body was thrown out not far away. The killers had done a thorough job: five bullets in his head, seven in his body.

Gertrude was not seen again. Various of her effects, including identity papers with photographs, were found in the hotel in which she had stayed. Her precipitate flight would seem to indicate that she had not expected the murder to be carried out so quickly.

The Swiss police were able to establish the identities of the two chief killers: a Frenchman, Roland Abbiat, and a Monegasque, Étienne Martignat. According to the police records, Martignat was an important NKVD agent and Abbiat had already been involved in a serious crime in the United States.

Collaboration between the Swiss and French police led to further discoveries. The ambush car had been rented in the name of a woman who at one time had been assigned to keep Trotsky's son under surveillance. He remembered that a year earlier this woman had followed him to southern France, stayed in the same hotel, and invited him to go sailing with her. Moreover he had observed on a number of occasions that he was being very closely followed, but this had been abruptly broken off during July and August of 1937. Now the reason for this interruption was clear: The agents had been ordered to pursue another quarry, Ignace Reiss.

At the same time, Alexander Barmin, who had also fled to France after his resignation from the Embassy in Athens, was also the object of close and provocative surveillance. He was followed even into a tobacco shop.

Within the Soviet Union the purge spared no one. It swept up the foreign Communists: Germans, Austrians, Poles, Italians who had fled from their own countries. Suspect because of their militant pasts, they were also members of that revolutionary old guard that in Stalin's view had outlived its usefulness. Or in other cases they simply were not versed in Soviet caution and talked too much. Later, Yosip Broz, the future Tito, who was then living in Moscow, was to reveal what precautions he had to practice in order to survive. Well served by his deeply rooted peasant distrust, he had soon recognized that in order to escape the storm he must keep his mouth shut. He went from his hotel to his office in the Comintern and from his office back to his room, and he avoided all imprudent gossip. It may be thought that this experience was not without value to him in his subsequent dealings with Stalin when he had become the master of Yugoslavia. He at least knew very clearly the kind of man with whom he had to deal.

It was of course much more difficult for the NKVD to eliminate enemies outside Soviet territory. At the same time, it was a matter of putting only a few dangerous figures out of action, and the Kremlin's secret services had already demonstrated their capacities in the battle with the White emigrants. In addition, the Trotskyist opposition abroad suffered from two disadvantages: It was small in number and it was suspect in the eyes of the governments of the countries in which it had taken refuge.

In the case of Spain the difficulties of abduction and assassination were remarkably eased for the Russians. The help supplied to the republican government by the Soviet Union and the influence acquired by the Spanish Communist party left them a virtually free hand. Berneri, the Italian anarchist who lived in Barcelona, was murdered. The principal leaders of the POUM (Workers' Party of Marxist Unification), whose tendency was Trotskyist, were arrested, accused of serving as a fifth column for Franco, and doomed. Their chief, Andrés Nin, vanished after his arrest and was almost certainly liquidated. Erwin Wolf, a former secretary to Trotsky, was also killed.

To Stalin Trotskyism was still the major enemy. But the Ukrainian nationalists were also his targets in the person of one of their leaders, Konovaletz.

Colonel Konovaletz, who had campaigned under Petlyura during the civil war in Russia, was an exceptional organizer. He founded the UVO (Ukrainian Military Organization), which carried out acts of terrorism and sabotage in eastern Galicia (a part of the Ukraine that had been annexed to Poland). Later, in 1929, he played an important part in the creation of the OUN (Organization of Ukrainian Nationalists). And it seems credible that the OUN succeeded in organizing secret cells inside the Soviet Union.

In any event, Konovaletz must have been deemed a dangerous man if the Kremlin issued orders to do away with him. Valyukh, an NKVD agent, managed to make his way into the clandestine organization, and on a number of occasions he met Konovaletz in various European cities.

Their last encounter occurred on May 23, 1938, in the Café Atlanta in Rotterdam. It was noon. Valyukh had traveled as a passenger aboard the Soviet ship *Menzhinsky*. In the café he gave Konovaletz a small parcel that was supposed to contain reports from clandestine centers in Russia.

Their conversation was quite brief. Under one pretext or another Valyukh left. Konovaletz then started back from the café to the hotel in which he was staying. He stopped for a moment at the entrance to a film theater. It was then that the parcel exploded and tore the Ukrainian to bits. Valyukh lost no time in going back aboard his ship, which soon weighed anchor.

In France Stalin's trackers concentrated their attention on Lev Sedov, Trotsky's son, who was exhausting himself without restraint in his father's cause. "The kid doesn't do a bad job," the NKVD people said of him, not without a certain respect, if Krivitzky is to be believed. Krivitzky had deemed it advisable not to go back to Moscow after the murder of Reiss. Having made his choice for freedom, he met Sedov and corroborated the view expressed earlier by Reiss: Yezhov's agents abroad would stop at nothing in order to annihilate the Trotskyists. Under much questioning, Krivitzky finally expressed suspicion of Victor Serge on the ground that after his deportation it had been possible for Serge to leave Soviet territory unhindered.

Sedov knew already that he was in danger. He had been warned by the French police during the investigation of the murder of Reiss.

Sedov was ill, running a temperature, endlessly beset by unremitting problems in bringing out the *Opposition Bulletin,* and nagged to boot by his terrible father, who sent him letters full of reproaches from Coyoacan, in Mexico: Why had the *Bulletin* not yet appeared? Why had Sedov not sent this or that document for the counter-trial that Trotsky was organizing in Mexico in order to gain exoneration of all the crimes ascribed to him by Stalin? Since his attacks of appendicitis were becoming more and more frequent, Sedov decided to undergo surgery.

Very much alone in Paris, where virtually his only contact was the Trotskyist world, and separated from his wife Jeanne, who had joined Molinier's dissident group, he placed all his confidence in a young man called Étienne (his real name was Mark Zborovsky).

Étienne had already been mixed up in a strange business. In 1937 Trotsky had decided to entrust some of his archives to the Dutch Institute of Social History, which had a branch at 7, Rue Michelet, in Paris, managed by Boris Nikolayevsky, a Menshevik. Almost as soon as some of the archives had been deposited there the Institute was broken into on the night of December 6–7. The burglary could have been committed only by the NKVD. But, aside from Sedov, only three persons had known of this deposit: Nikolayevsky, a woman working for the Institute, and Étienne. Sedov had complete confidence in all three, but he could not help wondering whether Nikolayevsky had not incautiously talked too much. The hypothesis of Étienne's guilt had to be rejected: The most precious of the archives were in his home and had not been touched.

When Sedov decided on February 8, 1938, to have an operation, he undoubtedly had no objection to accepting Étienne's advice: Rather than go into a French hospital, where he would have to reveal his true identity—and would he not then have reason to fear an attack?—he should call himself Martin, describe himself as a French engineer, and go into a private clinic operated by Russian emigrants. None of his comrades was to know where he was being treated.

On the day when he wrote his name in the register of this dubious clinic he signed his death warrant. For most of its people belonged to the Society for the Repatriation of Russian Emigrants, which was subsidized by the Soviet Embassy. He might as well have been turning himself over to a French branch of the NKVD.

The operation went off without incident and Sedov's condition apparently improved. Then he suffered great pain and lost consciousness. On the night of February 13 he was seen wandering through the clinic, raving deliriously in Russian. He was operated on again the next day and died a few days later.

His wife, convinced that he had been poisoned, demanded an investigation. It seems not to have been very actively pursued: This was the heyday of the Popular Front. In any event, it never established anything.

Years afterward at least some of the truth about Étienne emerged. Convicted in the United States, he admitted that he was an agent in the pay of the NKVD. He confessed, in fact, that, after he had called an ambulance for Sedov, he had notified his "bosses." Whether there was a crime—as seems most plausible—or whether Sedov's death was due to natural causes, the NKVD could rejoice: Its enémy's son had been liquidated and the old fighter's confidence must naturally be transferred to his son's major lieutenant. Only Sneevliet, the Dutch Trotskyist, had always been suspicious of Étienne. But all his efforts to alert Sedov and, after his death, Trotsky himself, were to prove futile.

The next victim was another Paris Trotskyist, Rudolf Klement, who had been Trotsky's secretary in Barbizon. He disappeared from his home early in July 1938. Two weeks later, in Coyoacan, Trotsky received a letter signed by Klement that denounced him for collusion with Hitler and announced that Klement was breaking with him. Trotsky immediately concluded that the letter was a forgery. Not long afterward Klement's horribly mutilated body was found in the Seine.

It was in the middle of that summer of 1938, either shortly before or shortly after Klement's body was found, that Sylvia Agelova, a young Trotskyist who was studying at the Sorbonne, became acquainted with one Jacques Mornard. Sylvia was a frail little woman barren of any attraction. Mornard, who said that he was the son of a Belgian diplomat, was a handsome fellow in his thirties, a man of great composure. An American girl who was a dedicated Stalinist had introduced him to Sylvia, whose lover he soon became. This romance was only one step in a slow approach that was to lead him at some unknown date to Trotsky, thousands of miles from the Sorbonne. From the moment when Mornard met Sylvia, the machinery began to turn for a murder that would not occur until two years later in the house in Coyoacan.

During those two years the old fighter savagely continued a hopeless battle. His life by now was studded with sorrows. His daughter Zena had committed suicide in Berlin after Hitler's accession to power. His son Sergey, who had never been

1.
Dzherzhinsky (1877–1926), one of the organizers of the October Revolution, later chairman of the *Tcheka*. (Photograph by Roger Viollet.)

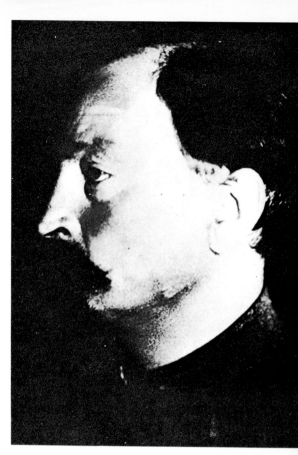

2.
Aerial view of the island of Kronstadt (the island of Kotlin, which seems small in this photograph, is about six miles long), the famous revolutionary center that rose against the Bolsheviks in 1921. (Photograph by Roger Viollet.)

3.
Civil war in the Soviet Union: the flag of the Ukrainian anarchists. (Photograph by Roger Viollet.)

4.
Civil war in the Soviet Union: Makhno, the leader of the Ukrainian anarchists, with his staff. (Photograph by Roger Viollet.)

5.

Sale of religious objects seized from the churches during the early years of the Russian Revolution. (Photograph by Harlingue-Viollet.)

6.

Famine in the Soviet Union during the early years of the Revolution: three brothers—the two youngest are dead and the eldest drags them to their grave. (Photograph by Harlingue-Viollet.)

7.
Victims of the civil war in the villages. (Photograph by Harlingue-Viollet.)

8.
Zinoviev, who headed the Communist International; he was shot in 1936. (Photograph by Roger Viollet.)

9.
Yoffe, one of Trotsky's intimates, who committed suicide in 1927. (Photograph by Roger Viollet.)

10.
General Wrangel, one of the principal leaders of
the exiled White Russians. (Photograph by Harlingue-Viollet.)

11.
General Kutyepov, lead-
er of the exile organi-
zation, ROVS, who was
abducted in Paris by
the Cheka in 1930.
(Photograph by Harl-
ingue-Viollet.)

12.
Anti-religious playing card from the Soviet Union. It shows a Jew at prayer. (Photograph by Roger Viollet.)

13.
Anti-religious gibes. (Photograph by Roger Viollet.)

14.
Trotsky among a group of deportees in 1928; at his right, Radek; above, to the left, Rakovsky. (Photograph by Roger Viollet.)

15.
Victor Serge, the writer deported by Stalin.

16.
Famine in the Ukraine, which claimed several million victims in 1932.

17.
Stalin in conversation with General Shaposhnikov. (Photograph from United States Information Service.)

18.
Yezhov, who carried out the Great Purge on Stalin's orders.

19.
Marshal Tukhachevsky, the famous commander of the Red Army purged by Stalin in 1937. (Photograph by Roger Viollet.)

20.
General Skoblin, a veteran of the White armies who became a double agent and made possible the abduction of General Miller. (Photograph by Roger Viollet.)

21.
Defendants on trial in Moscow: left to right above, Krestinsky, Rykov, Bukharin; below, Yagoda, Rakovsky, Grinko. All went on trial in 1938 in the prosecution of the rightist and Trotskyist blocs. (Photograph by Roger Viollet.)

22.
Lavrenti Beria, who succeeded Yezhov in 1938 as People's Commissar for the Interior. (Photograph by Roger Viollet.)

23.
Assassination of Konovaletz, one of the leaders of the Ukrainian nationalists, in Rotterdam.

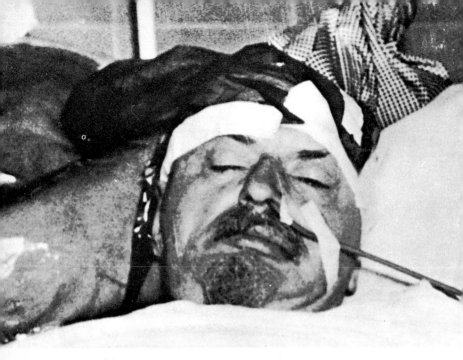

24.
Trotsky, assassinated in Mexico, on his deathbed.

25.
Jackson-Mornard-Mer-
cader, who assassinated
Trotsky. (Photograph
made in the Mexican
prison in which he
served his sentence.)

26.
General Vlassov, who assembled an army of Russian volunteers to fight on the side of the Germans.

27.
Shuprynka, Commander in Chief of the Ukrainian Partisan Army.

28.
An UPA chaplain secretly celebrates mass in the heart of a forest for Ukrainian partisans and civilians.

29.
A group of Ukrainian partisans secretly celebrating Easter.

30.
Political deportees working on the construction of the White Sea Canal (completed in 1933). It is estimated that during Stalin's tenure approximately twenty million persons may have been sentenced to forced labor in Siberia or elsewhere; many died of exhaustion. (Photograph from United States Information Service.)

31.
Balloons intended to carry NTS leaflets to USSR territory.

32.
A priest traveling from village to village with his bundle.

33.
Daniel, the writer: left, before his trial; right, in the concentration camp. (With the permission of *Grani.*)

involved in politics, had been arrested after the trial of the Parallel Center and had disappeared into a concentration camp. His two sons-in-law, Nevelson and Volkov, had also been arrested. His first wife, driven out of Leningrad, had been sent to the province of Omsk. Three of his grandchildren, who were still in the Soviet Union, had been left in the care of an old aunt. For how long? And, after all these griefs, there was Sedov's death.

How many illusions had been shattered in the political combat! Trotsky believed in the awakening of the working class in the West; it had not occurred. In his wanderings through the world he had heard nothing but the cries of hatred of the Stalinists. Finally he had created a Fourth International, but it was a phantom, ravaged by controversies and squabbles. The largest section, in the United States, had only a few thousand members. Moreover, a minority tendency led by James Burnham, the future author of *The Managerial Revolution*, was now challenging the view that the Soviet Union was still a workers' state.

Standing up to the avalanche of calumnies that the Great Purge had unleashed against him, Trotsky had launched a courageous fight for rehabilitation. He demanded the establishment of a tribunal for a counter-trial in which he intended to refute all the accusations made against him and to demonstrate their vanity beyond challenge. A commission of inquiry composed of intellectuals had in fact been set up in the United States under the chairmanship of John Dewey, the American philosopher. It traveled to Mexico, heard testimony for a week, interrogated Trotsky, studied all the documentary evidence submitted to it, and finally handed down its verdict: It was a solemn acquittal.

All this was virtually useless. The Soviet radio thundered against the "mad dog." In every country the presses on which Communist papers were printed turned out the same baseless calumnies in millions of copies. A man who defends his honor

and a few unbiased notables can do little against the power
of a vast apparatus.

Besides, a large part of the intelligentsia was still determined to burn incense before Stalin if not to seal itself into a
cowardly silence. It was to be expected that in the Soviet
Union an Ehrenburg or a Sholokhov would demand Trotsky's
death. In the West, Henri Barbusse, Louis Aragon, and even
Romain Rolland joined the slanderers' chorus. André Malraux,
after a brief tribute to Trotsky as a "great moral force in the
world," cold-bloodedly wrote that "Stalin has restored its
dignity to the human race." Berthold Brecht refused to break
with Stalinism. André Gide and H. G. Wells prudently decided to have nothing to do with the counter-trial. The acquittal by the Dewey tribunal slipped quickly into oblivion.

But, behind his thick lenses, Trotsky's fierce glance was still
sharp. His judgment, which was consistently mistaken when
he turned to political prognostications, was also bitter. The
man was forever ready to wage unending battles, and what
he feared was not so much the killers' weapons as the hemi-
plegia that might render him powerless as it had Lenin.

He lived at one end of Coyoacan in an old house isolated
behind thick walls and transformed into a small fortress:
There were sentries at the gate, armored doors, sandbags
against the walls, alarm signals. Inside, a dozen young partisans stood guard. Outside, there were five policemen assigned
by the government of President Cardenas.

Trotsky emerged from this blockhouse only to drive into
the mountains, where he took short walks. During the ride, as
a rule, he concealed his face behind a scarf. The Mexican
Communist party was powerful; there had been times when
Trotsky had been recognized by a crowd and hooted. Through
force of circumstances his life was not unlike Stalin's. Both
lived walled in behind imposing guards. In order to kill Trotsky it would be necessary either to take his fortress by storm
or to invade it by a ruse.

The attack from outside was made on the night of May

25–26, 1940. At about four in the morning Trotsky and his wife Natalya were awakened by the crackling of violent rifle fire. At first they thought that it was one of those fireworks displays that the Mexicans so often stage in celebration of patriotic or religious holidays. But the room began to fill with the reek of explosives. The Trotskys threw themselves down on the floor at the foot of the bed, and Mrs. Trotsky protected her husband with her own body as bullets pounded into the walls above their heads. The two old people lying on the floor were terrified for their grandchild alone in another room.

The shooting ended. In the villa, where the guards had not fired back, everything was quiet. Then there was a voice: the child's. He was unhurt. No one had been killed, and at first this fact seemed strange to the police chief, Colonel Salazar, who thought initially that the shooting was a hoax staged by the Trotskyists.

Investigation, however, made it possible to establish that the assault had been made by a commando of some twenty Communists under the leadership of Alfredo Siqueiros, a painter and a former officer in the International Brigades. These men, wearing Mexican army uniforms, had overpowered and bound the sentries on duty outside the house. Then one of them must have talked to the man on guard at the gate, Robert Sheldon Harte, a Trotskyist militant, whose suspicions were apparently disarmed by the uniforms and who had opened the gate. Running inside, the attackers had overpowered the rest of the guards and opened fire from all sides. In their retreat they took Harte with them, and his murdered body was found on a farm near Mexico City.[2]

The attack in force had failed. It was now time for Jacques Mornard to appear on the stage.

[2] The exact part played in this affair by Harte is disputed. Colonel Salazar, the head of the Mexican secret police, was always convinced that Harte was in league with the attackers. He was killed because he knew too much. Trotsky, on the other hand, always defended his comrade's memory.

In Paris, when he was courting Sylvia Agelova, Mornard had made a great show of total indifference to political matters, to such a point that he feigned irritation when he had to have anything to do with the little Trotskyist group of which the girl was a part. He also made a parade of boredom when she tried to discuss such questions with him.

In January 1939 Sylvia Agelova went to the United States. Mornard joined her there with a forged passport in the name of Frank Jackson, a Canadian national. He explained that he had assumed this false identity in order to evade military service in his own country. Then he went to Mexico, where, he said, he had to take care of some import-export business, and Sylvia rejoined him there. Since she was well acquainted with the Trotskys, for whom she had previously performed various services as a translator, she often went to their house in Coyoacan. Mornard would drive her there and wait for her in the car, talking with the guards and always, apparently, little concerned with politics.

Through Sylvia, meanwhile, he had come to know the Rosmers, who had been reconciled with Trotsky and were staying with him. It was through them that, at last, in a perfectly normal way, he was admitted behind the defenses of the blockhouse.

At that time his only instructions may have been to spy out the land—a mere gathering of information. In any event, the failure of Siqueiros' assault promoted Mornard to the front rank for the striking of the decisive blow.

Before he acted he made a total of ten visits between May and August of 1940. By then he had emerged from his shell to some extent with respect to political matters. Shyly he began to take part in the conversations. Sylvia having aligned herself with the minority led by Burnham, Mornard took Trotsky's side, arguing that the Soviet Union had remained a workers' state.

On August 17 Mornard-Jackson went to see Trotsky with the first draft of an article that, he said, he had written against

Burnham and on which he wanted Trotsky's opinion. Trotsky led Mornard into his study and read the manuscript, which he found very mediocre.

Mornard's attitude on this occasion inspired Trotsky with something that might have been distrust but that was expressed in vexed surprise. While Trotsky read the manuscript, Mornard casually sat down on Trotsky's desk, his hat still on his head; he held his raincoat tightly against his body.

Mornard left after Trotsky had advised him to rewrite his article, and Trotsky immediately told Natalya of this strange behavior. Natalya was surprised because she had never seen Mornard with a hat before. Both the Trotskys were shocked by his rudeness. It never occurred to them that, by taking a position from which he could dominate Trotsky seated at the desk, Mornard was staging a rehearsal.

He returned three days later, on August 20. The sun was blazing. In its glare Mrs. Trotsky saw him about five o'clock in the afternoon in the garden with her husband, who was feeding his rabbits. Mornard was quite strange that day: His face was gray, his movements were abrupt, he stubbornly kept himself wrapped in his raincoat. Why the raincoat, why the hat, which he was wearing in contrast to his usual habit of never having one, and in that heat? Mrs. Trotsky asked him as much. His stammering response was ludicrous: "It might rain."

Almost immediately afterward he said that he was very thirsty and would like a glass of water. Mrs. Trotsky offered tea, which he refused: He had eaten late, he said, and his food "was still sticking here" (he put his finger to his throat).

Trotsky had no desire to read this pest's revised article, but out of politeness he consented to do so. He closed the door of the rabbit hutch, took off his gloves, dusted his blue shirt, and slowly he, his wife, and Mornard started back to the house. Mrs. Trotsky left the men at the door to the study. Just as they went into the room, she thought fleetingly: "That man could kill him. . . ." But she drove the notion out of her mind. How many times she had had the same fear! The door closed. Three minutes later she heard a dreadful cry and rushed to her bleeding husband, standing at the threshold and clinging to the door-jamb.

Trotsky died at 7:25 P.M. on August 21 from the blows of the pick-ax that Mornard had hidden under his raincoat. The wound was two and three-quarters inches deep, the skull had been shattered, and part of the brain had been destroyed. In spite of this horrible wound Trotsky fought off death for twenty-four hours. Painfully he dictated his final message in disjointed fragments to his bodyguard, Hansen, who spoke only English: "I am about to die from the attack of a political assassin. . . . The man attacked me in my office, where I struggled with him. . . . He struck me. . . . Please . . . tell our friends . . . that I am confident .▾. . of the victory of the Fourth International. . . ."

By this time Mornard-Jackson, who had been disarmed by the guards whom Trotsky's cries had brought to the scene, was in prison. It would require a long investigation to disclose his real identity: His name was Mercarder and he was the son of a fanatical Spanish woman Communist. He was sentenced to the maximum penalty provided by Mexican law: twenty years in prison.

Although it was not known until much later, through the account given by a Vorkuta inmate and published in *The Socialist Courier* (Nos. 10 and 11, 1961), Stalin had begun the liquidation of the Trotskyists inside the Soviet Union in 1938. In Vorkuta they represented an intransigent core and served as the leadership group for the new deportees whom the purge was sending behind the barbed wires. Most of them had already spent years in deportation or isolation camps. Therefore, tempered by these ordeals, they made a fierce resistance to the rigors of the administration.

After the trial of Zinoviev and Kamenev in the autumn of 1936 they organized demonstrations inside the camp in honor of the memories of the condemned men and staged a long hunger strike, in which Sergey Trotsky took part. They were joined by the Trotskyists in the camps in the Pechora region. They demanded an eight-hour working day, the segregation of political from common-law prisoners, the same food for all prisoners, and the removal of the sick, the women, and the old to a less rigorous climate.

They were transferred to barracks about twenty-five miles from the Vorkuta camp and some of their demands were granted. Then their living conditions deteriorated again. Finally the political criminals were taken back to Vorkuta, where they were concentrated in an isolated enclosure. Sentries maintained day and night watch on the entire perimeter.

One morning the guards called the roll. Twenty-five Trotskyists answered to their names. Each was given two and one-quarter pounds of bread and told to get his possessions together. They were going to be transferred once more. They were accustomed to it.

They said their farewells to their comrades and formed a column that marched out of the barracks and through the gate of the camp. The other prisoners watched them trudge across the snowy tundra under a strong guard.

About twenty-five minutes passed. Suddenly, from the direction of a little river known as the Upper Vorkuta, about a half-mile away, the muted echo of concentrated gunfire came through the frigid air. All the men in the barracks rose. A few seconds later there was the sound of scattered shots. Then all was silent again. A quarter-hour later the escort returned.

The next day forty persons were called: They were given bread and told to be ready. Those who remained behind listened to the crunching of their footsteps on the snow until they had gone out of earshot, and then the waiting men listened for the next sound. An hour later they heard the muted volleys.

The same scene was repeated every second or third day throughout April and May of 1938: roll call, bread, departure.

Thirty to forty persons each time, men and women. Then the wait, the counting of the minutes, and finally, each time, the sound of shots.

Only children below the age of twelve were spared.

The same things took place in all the camps in the Pechora district. On certain days thin lines of marchers moved out of all the camps into the tundra, sometimes singing *The International*, to the execution grounds.

At the end of May there were still approximately a hundred Trotskyist prisoners in Vorkuta who were waiting for their turns. Two weeks passed without the sound of a shot.

One morning the guards came for them. There was no roll call. No bread was distributed. They were not told to get their possessions together. They were taken into the mine.

There they learned from the other prisoners that Yezhov had been ousted and that Beria had taken his place. This change gave them a few extra years of life.

PART

THREE

(18)

THE THIRD REICH,
THE OPPOSITION,
AND THE WAR

VOROSHILOV had announced that, in the event of war, the Red Army would assume the offensive and carry the battle to the enemy's soil. In a few weeks the German army made nonsense of these boasts. Breaking through the front, the armored divisions of the *Wehrmacht* plunged deeply into the vast territory of the Soviet Union, occupied White Russia, invaded the Ukraine, overran the Baltic countries, and pushed almost to the gates of Leningrad. Hundreds of thousands of men swept up in gigantic battles of encirclement were carried off into captivity.

The myth of the Red Army's invincibility no longer existed. The troops had fought in very inconsistent fashion. Encircled, they formed flying wedges and tried desperately to break the ring that was tightening on them. But others broke ranks and surrendered. And innumerable deserters made their way to the German lines without having fired a shot.

Under the treads of the German tanks the Soviet empire began to disintegrate and political separatism gained new vigor. In the Ukraine a Ukrainian national government was proclaimed on June 30, 1941, in Lvov (Lviv in Ukrainian).

The German advance guards had not yet appeared and already a Lithuanian government had been established.

In the cities and villages of the Ukraine the local authorities proffered bread and salt to the conquerors. In Volhynia Bishop Polycarp Sikorsky of Vladimir issued statements favorable to the Third Reich. In all the Baltic states a vast surge of hope sent everyone into the streets to greet the German soldiers with flowers—everyone who had not been carried óff by the Russians in their retreat. The bishops of Mittau, Narva, and Kaunas and the Metropolitan of Lithuania sent Hitler a telegram expressing their joy at being "liberated" from the Soviet yoke. Everywhere volunteers tried to enlist in the German army.

Meanwhile Stalin was silent. It was two weeks before he decided to speak.

When the advance guard of the *Wehrmacht* was within sight of Moscow the Soviets' authority in the capital seemed to be wavering. On October 15 the government and the diplomatic missions fled in disorder to Kuibyshev. Two days later there were pillage and rebellions against the militia. Some party members burned their cards. In certain sections parades began to form and the cry of "Death to the Jews!" reechoed. Eyewitnesses saw militiamen take off their insignia.

It is difficult today to measure the precise extent of these phenomena, and there is no clarification to be expected from the Soviet side. It might be thought that hatred of Soviet despotism, the memory of collectivization, and the countless purges played an important part in the defections. But another factor must also be taken into consideration: At the end of 1941 the verdict of battle seemed definitely to favor Hitler. The fall of Moscow and Leningrad seemed to be a mere question of time. Defeats engender defeatism.

Whatever the case, this state of mind provided the Germans with vast possibilities for political maneuver. In immense regions hatred of the Soviet system was reinforced by nationalist sentiment, which yearned to throw off the yoke of Russian domination. Psychological warfare could have furthered military warfare. It is an understatement to say that the opportunities were not exploited. They were deliberately and systematically trampled down.

Not only was the Ukrainian government set up in Lvov by Stetsko refused recognition; its members were quickly arrested and interned in a camp at Sachsenhausen. The Lithuanian government barely escaped the same fate. General von Rocques succeeded only at the last minute in preventing the arrest of its members. In any case, there was no question of recognizing any authority in the Baltic states or even of tolerating an autonomous administration there.

Nothing is more instructive, for an understanding of the idea entertained by the German authorities on their relations with the populations of the conquered Baltic states, than this proclamation addressed by *Reichskommissar* Heinrich Lohse to the population of the former nation of Lithuania on July 28, 1941:

By virtue of a decree dated 17 July 1941 the *Führer* of the Greater German Reich, Adolf Hitler, has designated me as *Reichskommissar* for the *Ostland*. The former state of Lithuania is included in this zone. . . .

I address myself first of all to the population of the region situated to the south of the Duna, within the borders of the former Lithuania, to request its collaboration with all its energies and with firm determination in the mission of maintaining order and work in this region that has been entrusted to me. . . .

At the sacrifice of their blood the armed forces of the German people have conquered the Bolshevik world enemy. Everyone will recognize that it is now the duty and the right of this German nation to take measures so that a similar danger will never again threaten the peoples of Europe.

Those who have given you so many promises of freedom in the past twenty years thought that they could execute their policy by maneuvering between the Soviet Union and the German Reich. . . . In spite of all the wrongs inflicted on the Germans and all the attacks against the National Socialist Reich, the government of the Reich is concerned with your welfare. It will give you bread and work and it will bring you progress. But the German administration has to insist that you carry out all its orders, which have only a single end: to guarantee the security of the country, to guarantee the security of your lives. In case of need the German administration will appoint trusted men among you through whom you will be able to communicate your desires to the *Reichskommissar*, the commissioner general, and the regional commissioners, and it will permit you to set up agencies to assure the security of your labor and your lives.[1]

Eloquent in its own fashion, this document can be summed up in three sentences: "We owe you nothing. We will give you food. Behave yourselves."

It is important to point out that the population of Lithuania, which had just escaped from Soviet tutelage, felt a vast relief. It cannot be doubted that at this time its sympathies urged it toward an occupant who seemed to be a liberator. Many young men were prepared to join the battle. It would have been enough to allow this people and those of Latvia and Estonia to set up their own governments, to give them the opportunity to govern themselves, and they would have been won over.

But, before they were pro-Russian or pro-German, these men and women were above all Lithuanians, or Latvians, or Estonians in their own emotions. They wanted to regain what had been taken from them by Stalin—that is, the right to be nations. Germany intended merely to replace one domination with another.

The whole administration of these countries was turned over to German officials. Since the insatiable needs of the war in the east had mobilized every able-bodied man, this corps of officials was composed of whoever was available: the head of an SA detachment in a precinct of Munich or even a peasant "parachuted" into Estonia with the rank of a general.

[1] Peter Kleist, *Entre Hitler et Staline,* pp. 272–274.

Aside from the inevitable incompetence, there is nothing worse in such lightning promotions than the intoxication that they bring with them. All these men in their light brown uniforms began to pour into the administrations of the occupied countries. Naturally they could not get along without local assistance, but the local people found themselves under the thumb of a German super-administration that regulated even the tips given to cloakroom and lavatory attendants. And everywhere German regimentation was inflexible. "Kaunas, the capital of Lithuania," Peter Kleist wrote, "was given a municipal super-administration consisting of approximately 160 members who instructed the Lithuanian employes even in the right way of using ink and erasers and then were amazed to see the city's services deteriorate steadily." [2]

There were worse things. As soon as the Red Army had been driven out, the former owners of businesses and industries who had remained with their expropriated enterprises as employes of the state ingenuously endeavored to regain possession of their property. To their incredulous stupefaction they found that the expropriations were still in full force. One German commissioner general even applied in the name of Lenin a Bolshevik decree of expropriation that the Russians had not had time to execute.

Why fight the Bolsheviks if even after their departure their system remained in effect? The same question could be asked in the Ukraine or in White Russia, where the kolkhozi continued to operate.

The Third Reich followed a paradoxical policy. Having conquered France, an enemy country, it had left a government and its services in their places. . . . In the Baltic countries that it had conquered, it tolerated no kind of autonomous authority.

Certainly Hitler and Martin Bormann bore the responsibility for having conceived the operations in the east as essentially

[2] *Ibid.*, p. 128.

military undertakings accompanied by administrative measures. The instructions on the conduct to be observed in occupied territory appeared in Section 6 of the "Supplement to Directive No. 33" dated July 23, 1941:

Troops assigned to guard conquered territories in the east will
be adequate for their task, given the extent of these territories,
only when all spirit of resistance has been broken not only through
judicial punishment of the guilty but also by resort to terror, which
alone is capable of purging the population of any desire to revolt.

It is the responsibility of the competent commanders to assure
the maintenance of order in their regions with the troops available
to them. It is not through requests for additional forces but through
the employment of the Draconian methods that are required that
they will find the means of preserving that order.[3]

This was virtually the sole political thinking that appeared
in the military documents dealing with operations in the east.
It can be seen that they were limited to the preservation of
order through measures that the document quoted itself described as "Draconian"; no differentiation of any kind was
made between the Bolshevik system and the populations on
whom it had been imposed, and there was no hint of the conduct to be followed with respect to possible opposition to that
system. Nor did the Supplement mention the non-Russian populations. Nowhere was anything said of their aspirations to independence. Stipulating furthermore that the new states
would have to be purged of their "intelligentsia," Hitler clearly
indicated that, if they ever came into being, these new states
would be mere fronts.

Eastern policy, then, can be summarized as the concept
merely of a military expedition intended to obtain *Lebensraum*
for Germany's children. After the war German colonists would
go in to develop the rich plains of the Ukraine or the territories of White Russia. German schools would be established
in the Baltic countries. Could there be any thought of tolerat-

[3] *Ibid.*, p. 128.

ing sovereign states there with which it would be necessary to negotiate?

What were the origins of this ruthless imperialism? It is probable that they went back to the ancient arrogant contempt for the Slav, "incapable of governing himself." A reverse explanation would apply to the Baltic countries, the majority of whose populations was of Germanic origin. Hence they must be merged in the vast community of blood, and assimilated into the Reich, the ultimate embodiment of conquering Germanism. Here the idea of the independent state came into conflict with that of Nordic unity. Thus the consequence was the rejection of the populations either because they were regarded as inferior races or because they were denied the right to think and feel that they were different.

In the case of the Ukraine, too, Hitler undoubtedly remembered the experiences of the First World War, when the Germans had backed the government of Ataman Skoropadsky. The difficulties that had ensued and the anarchic situation brought on by the disorders of the civil war must have disposed the *Führer* not to repeat such experiences and to eliminate nationalist tendencies in the womb. Superficially it was certainly simpler to settle problems with army orders and police action.

There was a period, however, during which Hitler took a fleeting interest in the Ukrainian nationalist movement, if Walter Hagen's testimony is to be credited. The Ukrainian political leaders in exile regarded the sub-Carpathian Ukraine as their Piedmont, their springboard for the reconquest of independence. Until 1918 this sub-Carpathian Ukraine,[4] which had seven hundred thousand inhabitants, had been part of Hungary; then it had been ceded to Czechoslovakia in 1919 by the Treaty of St.-Germain.

After the Munich Conference of 1938 the separatist tendencies of the sub-Carpathian Ukraine manifested themselves

[4] Also called Ruthenia.

with increased vigor in a Czechoslovakia in which Czech hegemony had been weakened. Two powers kept uneasy eyes on this nationalist revival. One was the Soviet Union, which was afraid that the nationalist agitation would spread into its own territory; the other was Poland, which had in Galicia about five million Ukrainians whose cultural aspirations were stifled. Both countries were sharply apprehensive of the establishment of a Ruthenian state divorced from Prague.

Their fears were all the sharper because during the other war the Germans had encouraged separatism. Now certain National Socialist leaders, especially Alfred Rosenberg, the head of the party's foreign section, and the *Abwehr* were backing the Ukrainian nationalists, whose chief organization was the OUN under the leadership of Melnik, who had succeeded Konovaletz.

For the Germans the creation of a Ruthenian state could be a step in their ambitions in the east. It was probably in the face of this danger that on November 26, 1938, Colonel Beck ratified a five-year extension of the Polish-Soviet nonaggression treaty of 1934.

On March 15, 1939, the German army invaded Czechoslovakia. Two days earlier the sub-Carpathian Ukraine had declared its independence, which was to last only a few days. Hitler had already made an agreement with the Hungarians, to whom he turned over this territory.

Hungarian troops began to invade it. The *Wehrmacht* had occupied Czechoslovakia without resistance. The Hungarians did not fare so well. The Ukrainian Volunteers entrenched themselves round Khust and in the heights of the Carpathians. There they were to carry on their fight until May.

Although the *Führer* had granted his protection to the Slovak state headed by Monsignor Tiso, he made no reply to a request of the same nature that came from Monsignor Voloshyn. On March 15 Foreign Minister Ernst Baron von Weizsäcker merely asked the German consul in Khust to inform Monsignor Voloshyn orally that "the Reich is not disposed under present conditions to extend its protectorate to the sub-Carpathian Ukraine." [5]

Hungary was satisfied and Poland was reassured. So was the Soviet Union. It might be thought that Hitler had merely momentarily exploited the Ukrainians' nationalist ambitions as a pawn in a great diplomatic game. He had just shown Stalin that he did not intend to encourage agitation on the territory of the Soviet Ukraine. This was something that was to facilitate the conclusion of their subsequent nonaggression pact.

After the start of the offensive against Russia, Hitler was not inclined to revive a nationalism that could only interfere with his plans for colonialization. He acted similarly in White Russia.

But why leave the kolkhoz system intact? Here the reasons were of a practical nature. The kolkhoz was an entity that made it possible to expedite crop harvests, at least apparently, and this time in the interest of the German economy. All that was required, the Germans thought, was to put it under German administrators. Most of the military leaders could see only advantages in this, since the restitution of estates to their former owners threatened to cause disorders and disorganize the economy. Goering's economic staff issued a document entitled *The Green Donkey*, which explained that the Reich ought to gain control of industrial facilities and raw materials and keep the kolkhozi running, all in the interest of the military operations.

What was overlooked, however, was that the kolkhoz system was founded on two rocks: the NKVD police and the tractor stations. The Bolsheviks destroyed the tractor stations as they retreated; the oil of the Caucasus was never conquered. Certainly the German police could do the job of the NKVD, but, operating in foreign territory, the Germans would not be able to profit by the same experience.

This shows how much the conduct of operations in the So-

[5] *Akten zur deutschen auswärtigen Politik*, IV, p. 240.

viet Union differed from Bolshevik conceptions. The Bolsheviks seized power and held on to it through political slogans:
immediate peace, land to the peasants. When the peasants
went to see Lenin in Leningrad at the beginning of the Revolution and asked his advice on the distribution of the land,
he more or less counseled them to seize it. He was indifferent
to the disorders that might ensue. Similarly the armed enterprises were part of a broad political strategy. Agitation and
propaganda preceded the troops. The Germans, instead of
encouraging the populations to revolt and shattering a political system by proclaiming the immediate reestablishment of
small business, the distribution of the land, and the restoration
of private ownership, were interested only in conquests and in
the preservation of order behind the front. They relied on the
power of the *Wehrmacht* alone to achieve a speedy victory.

The choice of an eastern policy undoubtedly posed a delicate problem. If the formation of a Russian national government opposed to the Bolsheviks were encouraged, the Third
Reich would disappoint the national minorities that yearned
for emancipation. By supporting the nationalists and declaring
that the German armies had opened hostilities in order to liberate the Ukraine, the Baltic countries, Georgia, Armenia, etc.,
the Germans could anticipate that they would encourage the
Russians to stand firm with Stalin.

Among the National Socialist leaders Rosenberg had long
been favorable to the minorities and in any event the partisan
of an independent Ukrainian state. His views were unquestionably founded on his belief in the inferiority of the Slavs.
In his eyes they represented merely a mass devoid of will that
had been able to construct an empire only under the leadership of Viking invaders who had little by little become Slavi-
fied by language. The fall of tsarism had not substantially altered this state of affairs. The Slavs had come under new
Asian and Jewish masters, who were formidable because they
had effected an alloy of pan-Slavism with world revolution.

This was why Rosenberg thought that in order to do away

with this danger it was necessary not only to shatter the Bolshevik system but also to destroy the Muscovite empire. This
would be achieved by creating a sterile ring of independent
states round Russia: Caucasian, White Russian, and, above all,
Ukrainian.

This is not the place to discuss Rosenberg's superficial think-
ing. Whatever his motives, he in no way rejected the prospect
of establishing independent national states allied with the
Reich. "An alliance between Kiev and Berlin compels recog-
nition as a national necessity for the future German policy."
This was a view that he had put forward as early as 1927 in
Die Zukunft einer deutschen Aussenpolitik (*The Future of a
German Foreign Policy*).

Nevertheless Rosenberg opposed independence for the Baltic countries. Himself a Balt by origin, he argued that these
were Germanic countries and that as such they ought to be
absorbed by the Greater Reich.

It has never been clearly explained to what end Hitler
turned to Rosenberg to head the Ministry for Occupied Territories. Until that time Rosenberg had been restricted to a
secondary position as the head of the foreign-affairs division
of the Nazi party, although he would have preferred to replace Joachim von Ribbentrop as foreign minister. He had no
standing with Hitler, who enjoyed mocking his racist theories,
and the associates of the *Führer* had no respect for a man who
was regarded as a dreamer.

In any event, Rosenberg's ministry swiftly assumed the appearance of a mere simulacrum. Ministry for Occupied—not
Liberated—Territories: even the choice of words seemed remarkably restrictive. Furthermore, Rosenberg, who was totally lacking in character, had absolutely no authority in spite
of his title. If he managed to see Hitler two or three times
during the entire war, that was the maximum.

Everything concerned with the economy depended on the
Four-Year Plan, which was under Goering's direction. By special delegation the police was placed under Himmler's orders.

The army, of course, had something to say. The Todt Organization, assigned to construction and transportation, constituted an independent body. The political department was left to Rosenberg. But, since he was placed on a footing of equality with, rather than primacy over, the economy, the administration, the police, etc., he soon became a pure nonentity devoid of power. Rosenberg reigned, but in reality greedy, arrogant barons carved out fiefs for themselves over which they admitted no supervision. All that was left for the minister for occupied territories to do was to issue circulars that no one read.

Furthermore, Hitler himself chose the commissioner to head each occupied region. In the *Ostland* (the Baltic countries) the post went to Lohse, whose proclamation was quoted earlier. To fill out the portrait of this personage it is sufficient to recall the remark that he made one day to a Dr. Meyer, secretary of state to the Ministry for Occupied Territories, who rebuked him for following an arbitrary policy: "I assure you that no one here is thinking of himself or working in his own interests. For myself, I am not working for me, I am working in order that the son who has just been born to me may one day place on his head the hereditary crown of a grand duke." [6]

Lohse, however, was far from the worst of the commissioners. Under the irresistible pressures of war he came round, in fact, to modifying his feudal notions. There was, on the other hand, Erich Koch. On Goering's suggestion, Koch had been foisted off by Hitler as *Reichskommissar* for the Ukraine. Rosenberg was not enthusiastic about him, but, as was his invariable practice, he gave in.

Koch had been a railway worker: he had a bull neck and a brutish face in which it was not difficult to descry the stubborn arrogance of the upstart and the lack of scruple of the opportunist—the kind of man who uses power as if it were an axe. In temperament he was the diametrical opposite of Rosen-

[6] Kleist, *op. cit.*, p. 131.

berg, who was riddled with hesitations and always ready to compromise.

Koch soon showed the regard in which he held his minister. His eyes ominous, he walked into Rosenberg's office without knocking and emerged a quarter-hour later. Cranz, the press officer, stopped him for a brief conversation. "You are about to embark on an interesting task," he began.

"What? What task?" Koch demanded, his face flushing.

"The liberation of a people as valiant as the Ukrainians."

It was too much for Koch. He glared at Cranz with immeasurable contempt. "My dear sir, in what country newspaper did you read that? Your Ukrainians are nothing but primitive Slavs. They will be ruled with the knout and vodka. In the meantime you in your Ministry will have plenty of time to pore over the Slavic soul. As for me, all I want from you is a cash advance. I will pay it back in a year and we'll be quits. Good-bye."

Koch could allow himself the indulgence of loud talk and the manners of a lout before he acted like a beast. He had sized up Rosenberg. He knew that he had Bormann's support. He began by purging his staff of the German scholars who were thoroughly familiar with the Ukrainian problem. He negotiated the discharge of Cranz, who had taken the liberty of censoring one of Koch's speeches lest it lead to repercussions abroad. He also arranged the dismissal of Dr. Leibbrandt, the director of the political department, who favored the creation of a Ukrainian national state.

His only thought was to make the Ukraine disgorge, to feed the gigantic German war machine. And he could harass Rosenberg at his leisure. He forbade his subordinates to obey a circular letter from the Ministry that merely called for the restoration of elementary schools. Having received a general order dated December 14, 1942, he did not reply until March 16, 1943, in a note charged with sarcasms, the least of which was of this level: "It is a surprise to be asked to treat Ukrainians in a form that is not only correct but cordial in conjunction with an unremitting good will." When Professor Mende, Rosenberg's emissary, suggested moderation to Koch, the *Reichskommissar* threatened him with a slap in the face.

Yet, even though the Germans decided on August 1, 1941, to incorporate Galicia into the Government General of Poland—thus amputating the most nationalist elements of the Ukraine—Ukrainian sentiment continued to be favorable. Volunteers poured in. A whole series of newspapers appeared. A writers' union began to take form, and schools were reopened.

But the cargo of the *Wehrmacht* trucks included German intellectuals. They assumed the direction of archeological explorations. Dr. Johansen was appointed to head a National Library. Another German, Brückner, was placed in charge of the opera house, which ordered everything performed in German exclusively. An article by Koch's right-hand man, one Dr. Pfafrath, which appeared on July 10, 1942, in the *Deutsche Ukraine Zeitung*, could have been regarded as a warning to the Ukrainian intelligentsia:

In the Ukraine today there exists only one will, that of *Reichskommissar* Erich Koch, the trusted agent of Adolf Hitler and Alfred Rosenberg [the latter name was included merely for the sake of form], minister for the east. . . . Our agrarian policy in the Ukraine, guided by the needs of the front and the war as a whole, should envisage as its goal the Europe of the future and the future of our nation. This German point of view leaves no room for the chatter of theoreticians of public law.

The theoreticians of public law would certainly have had a few comments to offer, for example, on the activities of Fritz Sauckel. Appointed in May 1942 as director of the foreign labor supply, he was instructed to draw on the reserves of the east to replace the working force that had been siphoned off from Germany by military mobilization. Kleist, who was working for Ribbentrop, attempted in a conversation with Sauckel to explain that the designation, *eastern workers*, was altogether out of place when one was dealing with Ukrainians,

Great Russians, and White Russians, each of whom insisted on not being lumped under a general label with the others. But in particular, Kleist added, it would be much more advisable to appeal for volunteers than to resort to constraint. Isolated behind his borders, every Soviet citizen was eager to know other countries, even in wartime. And, if it were possible for him to allot part of his wages to be sent home to his family, the appeal might be expected to make a certain impact. Such language made Sauckel's eyebrows go up. "If volunteers come, so much the better," he said. "But I do not have time to concern myself with the state of the *muzhik*'s soul. Hitler has given me a job to do, and I will transfer millions of workers from the east without asking them for their opinions."

Nonetheless the people clearly preferred that their opinions be taken into consideration. They fled from the conscription commandos that rounded up men everywhere—in the streets, in film theaters, in taverns. Two million abducted Ukrainians were sent to swell the ranks of German labor. But many others who succeeded in escaping joined the underground. They provided the fighting force for the guerrilla groups organized by Ukrainian nationalists disillusioned by German policy. Their armed operations began at the end of 1942. In White Russia the fugitives organized their resistance in tremendous forests, while Moscow parachuted its own Partisan groups to join them or endeavored to absorb those that had been spontaneously organized in the occupation areas.

A new front was opened behind the German lines, threatening their supply dumps and their communications system. This new front was never to be completely broken. The army, under instructions to crush with terror every attempt at resistance, in order to assure security in the rear, saw that precisely what was feared was growing. Raids and executions were ineffectual against this proliferation of guerrilla attacks.

It is probable that initially the German High Command was not opposed to the directives laid down by Hitler. It had huge logistical problems to resolve, and, like all general staffs, it sought only one thing: the maintenance of order. It must have looked on the kolkhoz system as both advantageous and convenient. Any other considerations were the business of the politicians. Officially politics was no concern of the army. It was the domain of the *Führer*. The army's task was simply to defeat the enemy, and all that it could hope for was that it be supplied with the physical means to do so. Its conceptions were to evolve slowly, in direct proportion to the mounting defeats and the growing difficulty of winning with only the resources of the German war machine.

Theories determined everything. Once the German government decided that it was following a policy of extermination for the short term (without any clear distinction between the Soviet government and the peoples under its domination) and a policy of colonization for the long term, it had created a machine that would be fatal to Germany herself. The purposes of the war determined the choice of the means that would be employed, and the means in their turn entailed control by one group of men rather than by another. Once all these things had fallen into place, any possible change in the objectives of the war would have entailed a most difficult revision of the methods and a most careful replacement of the men applying them.

There was no lack, however, of men who believed from the outset that the Third Reich had taken the wrong road. But for the most part they were isolated or relegated to secondary positions, if not indeed under the government's suspicion.

Some of them regarded the problem of the war to be waged in the east from a basically utilitarian point of view. They believed that, in order to win the war, it was necessary to invite certain collaborations instead of forcing the populations of the occupied territories into savage resistance. This was the reasoning of such men as the quartermaster-general of the German High Command, General Wagner, who was concerned with the guerrillas and the sabotage behind the lines, and General Köstring, the son of a Moscow family of German merchants, who had a thorough understanding of Russian problems.[7]

Others reacted as politicians primarily. They were the first to conclude that the war could not be won without the collaboration of the various populations. But this collaboration could be obtained only on specific political bases, creating in opposition to the Stalinist system a government of a free Russia with which it would be possible to collaborate after the war.

Most of these men were highly qualified experts on Slavic matters. Such was the case, for example, of Friedrich Werner Graf von der Schulenburg, the last Ambassador to Moscow. He had disapproved of the war in the east, as for that matter had General Köstring, once the colleague of General Hans von Seeckt.[8] As soon as hostilities began, Schulenburg had championed the view that Germany ought to announce that she had no territorial ambitions and that her interest lay in fostering the creation of local governments that would be able to form a federation and establish a government for a free Russia. This group was supporting the principle of a Russian government opposed to Bolshevism, the government of a *free Russia*, rather than the cause of the separatists.

Other officers came to identical conclusions. They were to

---

[7] Goebbels ultimately came to entertain almost identical views. "The SD [*Sicherheitsdienst*—Security Service]," he wrote in his diary, "has sent me a police report on conditions in the east. The danger created by the Partisans in the occupied territories is still substantial. The new slogan, *Land to the peasants*, has been extremely successful among the rural population. We could have achieved this result much sooner if we had had a more intelligent policy and broader views. But we relied too heavily on a campaign of brief duration, and we regarded victory as being so near that we did not deem it necessary to concern ourselves over much with psychological problems" (Goebbels, *Diary*, p. 181). On the other hand, Goebbels seems to have had little respect for Rosenberg, whom he dismissed as a dreamer (cf. *Ibid.*, pp. 187 and 246).

[8] Commander of the Weimar Republic's army after the Treaty of Versailles and a leading figure in the collaboration of the 1920s between the *Reichswehr* and the Red Army under the secret protocols of the Treaty of Rapallo.—Translator.

be found chiefly in the army's propaganda sections. They insisted that vague anti-Bolshevik slogans were ludicrously inadequate in the titanic conflict that was under way. The first defeats of the *Wehrmacht* confirmed them in their conviction that this war could not be won without the collaboration of the peoples.

This was the reasoning of Lieutenant Colonel Gehlen (after the war he was to become the head of a major intelligence service in the Federal Republic of Germany); Dr. N. von Grote, the director of propaganda in the east; [9] Lieutenant Colonel Schmidt von Altenstadt, head of the administrative department; General von Treschkov, already an opponent of Hitler in 1939, and Lieutenant Colonel Claus Graf von Stauffenberg, the future leader of the July 20, 1944, plot to assassinate Hitler. Many of the advocates of a free Russia, in fact, were involved in that plot. In large part, too, it was these men who had argued against the war in the east and who as a result were of little influence.

Stauffenberg himself was a dedicated champion of the formation of a Russian army of liberation. When the German Sixth Army drove toward the Caucasus, it was he who obtained authorization from the High Command for the creation of the Caucasian and Turkmen legions. On this occasion he had a meeting with Field Marshal General Wilhelm Keitel, the chief of the High Command, to whom he pointed out that "not only are the Caucasians fanatical enemies of the Soviets and the Russians; they are pure Aryans, almost as pure as the Germans." Actually Stauffenberg cared little about the ethnic purity of the Caucasians. Chiefly he was employing the kind of argument that he regarded as best suited to overcome the High Command's hesitations.

[9] Formerly director of public relations for the federation of German heavy industry and today the head of an international intelligence and propaganda service in Munich suspected of CIA connections and based largely on former eastern European Fascist collaborators with Germany who fled westward with the German armies.—Translator.

While Keitel allowed himself to be persuaded, Hitler, on the other hand, never had any confidence in the Caucasians.

I regard only the Mahometans as reliable [he said on December 12, 1942]. I consider it extremely risky to create battalions composed of purely Caucasian soldiers, whereas I see no danger at all in raising purely Mahometan units. Those fellows will always attack, and I feel fairly sure, given the fact that Stalin himself is a Georgian, that many of them are carrying on a determined flirtation with the Communists. The Georgians are not Turkmens but a purely Caucasian stock, probably even with some Nordic blood. Consequently, and in spite of all the statements that have been made to me, as much by Rosenberg as by the military, I have no greater confidence in the Armenians. The only ones that I regard as reliable are the pure Mahometans—in other words, the real Turkmen peoples.[10]

At this time two hundred thousand men from the eastern regions were serving in the ranks of the German forces with the status of auxiliaries. They were called *Hiwis* (*Hilfswillige* —volunteer auxiliaries). In the beginning this was not known to Hitler and the High Command. The men were deserters or civilians who of their own volition had joined German army units and who had been accepted into their ranks by the field commanders. They served as drivers, guides, and artisans, and they were scattered among various units.

"All the Russian volunteers are part of the 'black' forces of our army," Gehlen said in the spring of 1942 to a Major Heere, who had had an opportunity to observe the appalling methods of dealing with prisoners of war. ". . . The Russians were ready to receive us as allies, except, of course, for the Communist party's organizations. Unfortunately all the orders from the Army High Command forbid us to exploit this attitude. God alone knows what will happen if Hitler or the people round him find out what is going on, if they learn that there are Russians wearing German uniforms. But we have to carry on

[10] *Hitler parle à ses généraux.* Stenographic transcript of the High Command's daily reports to the *Führer,* 1942–1945, pp. 44–45.

this struggle. . . . Our aim should be not to colonize Russia but to liberate the Russian state from the Soviet system." [11]

Stauffenberg's idea was to assemble all the volunteers into a huge army of liberation. During a conversation at virtually the same time with Major Heere, he assessed the policy—or, rather, the lack of policy—in the east in unbridled freedom of language. "We have a colonialist policy," he said. "Consider the fact that the Estonians and the Latvians are not entitled even to fight in our ranks. Hitler and the SS are dreaming of a German empire stretching to the Urals." He was sharply critical of Rosenberg, whom he attacked because of the minister's desire to destroy Russia and break it up into little states. But, where according to Stauffenberg it was necessary to create independent states—that is, in the Baltic nations—Rosenberg and his associates would not listen to a word. The only man who had any good ideas, Stauffenberg said, was Dr. Bräutigam, the liaison officer in the Ministry for the East, although he cherished the dream of an independent Ukraine.

"He argues that we ought to find a Russian de Gaulle," Stauffenberg explained, "and put him at the head of a free opposition government and an army of liberation." [12]

"What does the Army Chief of Staff think?" Heere asked.

"Halder?" Stauffenberg shrugged. "He thinks like a soldier. Have no illusions on this subject, Heere: Our allies' names are not Halder and Keitel, they are Military Necessity and Defeats!"

The idea of an army of liberation had already been supported by Treschkov. As early as October 1941 he had obtained authorization from Marshal von Bock to prepare a project for an army of two hundred thousand Russian volunteers.

A short time earlier the Smolensk city council had petitioned the marshal to authorize the creation of a free Russian govern-

[11] Jürgen Thorwald, *Vlassov contre Staline*, p. 37.
[12] *Ibid.*, pp. 40–41.

ment. Bock forwarded the petition through the hierarchic channels. The High Command announced its answer in November—a typical military reply: "As a matter of principle army groups are not to concern themselves with politics. Furthermore the *Führer* will not tolerate even the mention of such notions."

On his own, another officer, Captain Strik-Strikfeld, who was later to play an important part, had transmitted to Marshal von Brauchitsch a plan for a "liberation government." Strik-Strikfeld had spent his entire childhood and youth in Russia. Later he had fought as an officer in the White Army against the Red Army before settling in Riga. Mobilized into the German army, he was placed under the orders of Treschkov, who was a member of Marshal von Kluge's staff. Both regarded it as essential from the very start of operations to establish at least an autochthonous administration and to create a Russian army of liberation.

Brauchitsch, it was said, approved the plan for a liberation government. But he dared not mention it to Hitler, and in December 1941, at the same time as Bock, he was removed. The project was buried with them.

The Sixth Army's advance toward the Caucasus, however, was to make it possible to apply a somewhat more liberal policy in this area. The mountain peoples of the Caucasus, whose last resistance to the Soviets had not been broken until 1934, hailed the German troops as liberators.

It was agreed that there would be no repetition of the stupid policy of preserving the kolkhozi and that the mountain men would regain possession of their land. In addition, General Köstring was dispatched by the High Command to enlist fighting men among the population.

The Kabardians received Köstring in their capital, Nalchik. They were dressed in their richest costumes, with the silver sabers that the Soviet authorities had forbidden them to wear, and they pressed round the general in a reception hall adorned with torches. When he left after a banquet, he was given a tremendous ovation. Strong hands took hold of the old general; he was tossed into the air like a balloon and caught again. Then came the presents: sheep, cows, and horses for his army. Then there was another great feast in his honor; sheep were roasted whole on spits. To the sound of song the Caucasian wine flowed like water.

The reception in the Balkir capital had the aspect of a religious festival. The chiefs wore black. There was an unending succession of wild dances and sports. Finally the chiefs presented the gift intended for Hitler: a pure gold harness.

The Chechens, who had always resisted the Bolshevik grip, had mounted a fresh insurrection in 1940 under the leadership of an intellectual named Israilov, a former student in the Bolsheviks' agitation school for eastern peoples. Israilov's assumption of the leadership of the insurrection was encouraged by the difficulties of the Soviet army's war with Finland. His supporters had liberated a number of villages and in 1942 they set up a provisional government.

When the Germans advanced on the Caucasus, the delegate of the Chechen insurgents, apprised of the policy being followed in the Ukraine, informed the Ministry for the East that, if this policy were to be followed in the Caucasus, the Chechen partisans would turn their weapons against the Germans. Stalin had abandoned the idea of a general mobilization among the Chechens and in 1942 his planes had heavily bombed the villages even before the Germans had entered the Caucasus.

The junction between the Germans and the Chechens, however, could not be achieved. German troops crossed the border of Chechen territory but occupied only the frontier point of Magabek; then they were forced to withdraw. Only a few Chechens succeeded in joining the German forces.

Nonetheless at the end of the war Stalin ordered the deportation of the entire population, although it could not have been accused of collaboration with Germany. But this was his punishment for the rebellion by Israilov's supporters.

During this time General von Weichs' army group was advancing across the territories of the Cossack tribes toward the Volga. Colonel Freytag-Loringhoven, the army group's Chief of Staff, took advantage of the opportunity to enlist auxiliary units among these tribes. Groups of Cossacks who had at first gone into hiding in the forests came flooding in to the outposts with their old uniforms and a motley variety of weapons. Among them was a man who had long been thought to have died: Ataman Kulskov. He was conducted in triumph to Poltavo. During the civil war he had lost both his legs. Hidden in a cave, he had fashioned two artificial legs out of wood. His reappearance impelled many vacillators to enlist. Freytag-Loringhoven organized all these volunteers into a single corps.

Kalmuks too joined the *Wehrmacht*. The Soviet authorities had confiscated their flocks, and they hated the Bolsheviks. They were daring horsemen but difficult to discipline, and they were inordinately devoted to pillage and atrocities.

Many German officers, however, looked on these men only as so much cannon fodder, whose greatest possible value was that they could save some German blood on a few sectors of the front. Turkmen and Caucasian battalions had been put together in Poland. There they had the opportunity to observe how the Poles and the Russian prisoners of war were treated. They themselves enjoyed certain physical advantages but were hardly better treated. A German, Colonel von Heygendorff, on his way out of Warsaw, saw on a siding a train on which someone had chalked: "Poles, Jews, and legionaries, last car."

The defeat at Stalingrad led to the precipitate retreat of the Caucasian troops. It required all the energies of Rosenberg's deputy to prevent the Germans from abandoning men who had risen against Bolshevism to their fate. Early in January 1943 the exodus began. In one night thousands of men had to gather their families and their possessions, load them on to trucks, and flee.

This retreat was carried out under dreadful conditions.

Some of the fugitives could not avoid falling into the hands of the Russians. Long lines of Kalmuks fell back into the Ukraine with their wives and children, stealing and murdering as they went. German officers tried to disarm them and separate them from their families. Ultimately they were reassembled in Silesia. The Cossacks formed two cavalry divisions, which, under the command of General von Pannwitz, were to be employed later not in the east but in the war against Tito's Partisans in Yugoslavia.

And yet, in spite of the Germans' behavior, at the end of 1942 there were almost a million volunteers serving in the German army, either as auxiliaries for various units or grouped into national legions of Cossacks, Georgians, Turkmens, Kalmuks, Tartars, Ukrainians, Latvians, Estonians, Lithuanians, etc.

Their enlistment was certainly to be viewed with a certain skepticism. Some had joined in order to escape the harshest of captivities; others preferred service in the army to employment in forced labor as *Ostarbeiter* (eastern workers). Still others were motivated by a desire for adventure or aggressive instincts. Still there were also those who sincerely wanted to combat Bolshevism or liberate their countries from Muscovite rule.

It is impossible to assess the proportionate influences of regular meals, a less rigorous life, a modicum of freedom, and political conviction in the decisions that these men made. But, when one reflects on the unbelievable clumsiness of the leaders of the Third Reich, stained with incalculable brutalities, the number of these volunteers constitutes impressive testimony against Soviet rule. A million men under arms waging war against their Soviet "fatherland" are still a million men.

These million men, however, employed on a trial-and-error basis, without any coordinating plan, without any all-inclusive thought, these stopgap battalions and divisions that lacked any specific war aim, could provide only modest aid to an army that had heard the knell begin to ring at Stalingrad.

It was then that men who believed that the war in the east could not be won without political action received news that revived their hopes.

(19)

HITLER REJECTS VLASSOV

═══════════════════════════════

"**Y**OU WILL see him tomorrow," Captain Strik-Strikfeld said. "He is as tall and strong as a tree. History has put this man into our path. It will not present us with another. We must seize the opportunity at once."

Strik-Strikfeld opened a folder, took out a number of photographs, and laid them out on the desk in front of Dürksen. They showed a gigantic Russian, appallingly thin, his features ravaged by exhaustion. The asymmetrical face was ugly with its excessively high forehead, its prominent thick lips, a long nose that ended in an eagle's beak and that seemed even more conspicuous because of the gauntness of the face. The eyes behind their thick-lensed glasses were strange, and their expression might be found either disturbing or fascinating.

Lieutenant Dürksen worked in army propaganda. Under the command of a Colonel Martin, he was assigned to contacts with the representatives of the NTS (*Narodno Trudovoy Soyuz* —Union of Russian Solidarity). The NTS had been born of a revolt among the young emigrants who believed that their elders had demonstrated their bankruptcy with their inability to offer a coherent doctrine in opposition to Bolshevism. In

July 1930 a conference held in Belgrade had resulted in the creation of the National Union of Russian Youth, which was later to become the NTS. As soon as the war began, a number of its leaders established contact with the Germans, particularly Kasantsev (who prepared pamphlets and newspapers for the German army's propaganda staff) and Baidalakov, one of the major NTS leaders. As for Dürksen, he believed that the NTS represented the only active force among the emigrants and consequently he was favorably inclined toward the notion of a free Russia.

In the beginning of September 1942, Dürksen had been summoned to Vinnitza. There he had heard sensational news: General Andrey Andreyevich Vlassov, the leader of the Volkhov army, had just been taken prisoner.

It was known that at the time of the Great Purge Vlassov had been military attaché in China. Recalled by Stalin, he had made a model division of the Ninety-ninth and his name was cited with praise in Soviet military publications. When the Germans launched their offensive, he mounted a savage resistance at Kiev. Subsequently, like Zhukov, he played a major part in the winter battle round Moscow.

Thus he had become a national hero. Ehrenburg glorified him. France's Ève Curie, who met him in Moscow, wrote that he constantly complained against those who neglected their patriotic obligations. "Everyone, everyone," he said, "ought to take part in the struggle against Fascism."

Now the struggle was over for him. But Captain Strik-Strikfeld, after a number of conversations with the captured general, thought that the Soviet hero was ready to turn against Bolshevism and return to the battle, this time in the German ranks. The captain was convinced of Vlassov's sincerity.

"When he was captured," Strik-Strikfeld told Dürksen, "General Lindemann ordered that he be treated with full military honors. But then he was put into a prisoner-of-war camp and there he had a chance to see how his compatriots were treated. It took me days and days to erase the disastrous impression of that terrible experience. I asked him for a report; he refused to write a word. The Russians are very reluctant to put anything in writing, and there are good reasons for this. His very hesitation convinced me of his sincerity. The more a man hesitates, the more one can be sure of his good faith."

Little by little Vlassov had begun to impart confidences to Strik-Strikfeld. He was the son of a poor peasant of the Niz-hni-Novgorod area. Like Stalin, he had entered a seminary before the First World War, since this was the only means by which a poor boy could gain a solid education. The Revolution had opened the door of the army to him, and he had speedily advanced through the hierarchic ranks in his transition from the black to the red. He had no reason for hostility to the system that had given him an unhoped-for career.

But, according to what he said, he had been profoundly shaken by a phenomenon that was creating upheaval throughout the Soviet Union: collectivization. When he visited his home he heard the peasants' complaints. Some of his friends and relatives had been arrested.

Later he always emphasized the shock that this terrible period had been to his mind and he attempted to date the origin of his revolt against the system from this time. It might also be observed, however, that it was also at this time that he joined the party. Was this opportunist precaution against the possibility of suspicion attaching to his peasant connections?

His second crisis occurred at the time of the battle of Kiev. He had run up against the absurd orders of Stalin and Bud-yenny and the result had been defeats and slaughter.

But the determining shock was the inferno of the Volkhov. In an effort to relieve Leningrad in January 1942 Stalin unleashed an offensive in the loop of the Volkhov. The operation almost succeeded. Through the snow-filled forests the Soviet divisions drove into the Germans' lines and tried to break through in the direction of Leningrad. The Soviet supply lines, however, were wholly dependent on a log road called the Erika Road. The German counterattack concentrated on this artery. The Germans launched a pincer attack from the north and the south against the Soviet Second Army's rear. On March 19 the jaws of the pincers closed on Erika Road. The Soviet supply line was cut off, and the Second Army was caught in a trap.

Two days later a plane deposited Vlassov in the loop of the Volkhov and, on Stalin's orders, he assumed the command of seventeen divisions and eight brigades. His task was to break the Germans' lock at all costs. He launched one attack after another. At the price of heavy losses he succeeded in opening a breach one and one-quarter miles wide in the German lines. It was not enough to permit a breakthrough. Every attempt to enlarge the breach failed.

The spring came, and with it the thaw. Then the inferno began. Torrents of water rolled out of the forests and swamps. In their trenches and blockhouses men stood in water up to the navel. Thousands of mosquitoes appeared. Vlassov's troops were caught in this sodden universe.

Supply became impossible, and cases of cannibalism were rumored. Tens of thousands of men died. As the weather grew warmer, a frightful stench arose from the corpses piled in the clearings, the woods, and the swamps. Enormous swarms of flies buzzed round the charnel house. Capture saved thirty-two thousand men from this rotting morass.

Vlassov told Strik-Strikfeld that on a number of occasions he had been critical of Stalin's orders. This was regarded as provocation and cowardice. One day he received a letter from his wife—only two words: "*Vyli gostyi* (We have had guests)."

"Do you know what that means?" Strik-Strikfeld asked Dürksen.

"Certainly: a search by the NKVD."

The battle of the Volkhov ended with the month of May. But Vlassov had vanished. The Germans searched for him everywhere. They distributed thousands of leaflets with his description and promised a handsome reward to anyone who contributed to his capture.

On July 11 the German Thirty-eighth Army Corps was informed that Vlassov's body had been found. Captain von Schwerdtner, an intelligence officer, went to see for himself. At the place mentioned he found a corpse about six feet three inches tall and wrapped in a general's coat.

This was indeed Vlassov's height. But the body was so badly decomposed that any identification was impossible.

Von Schwerdtner was preparing to write his report when the mayor of a nearby village asked to see him. "In a barn," he told the German, "there are a man and a woman. They must be Partisans. I've locked the door. Do you want to see them?"

Schwerdtner went to the barn with the mayor. His men took up positions at the door, their automatic weapons trained on it. The mayor stepped forward, unlocked the door, and shouted: "*Vykhodi* (Outside)!"

Nothing happened for a second or two. Then, out of the darkness, a bearded giant in an officer's tunic, so thin that he was almost a skeleton, slowly emerged. The harsh light made him squint, and he was wearing black-rimmed glasses with thick lenses. He saw the weapons trained on him and raised his arms.

"Don't shoot," he said in bad German. "I am General Vlassov."

All round the barn the flies were buzzing.

The day after his talk with Strik-Strikfeld, Dürksen met Vlassov. They talked of the Volkhov battle, and the general compared the fate of the Soviet Second Army with that of the tsar's Second Army, annihilated in the battle of the Masurian Lakes by Hindenburg and commanded by Samsonov, who commited suicide after the disaster.

"Some of your comrades have followed his example," Dürksen said cruelly.

It was some time before Vlassov replied. "I have often had

a revolver in my hand," he said finally in his frighteningly cavernous voice. "Why did I not kill myself? Why? Samsonov believed in his tsar. He believed in the worth of the system for which he was fighting. But what about me?"

Then he inquired what the Germans planned to do with his country. He had heard that Russia was doomed to destruction.

"Only a lunatic could propose such a thing," Dürksen assured him. He was very careful not to add that such lunacy might very well represent the intentions of the leaders of the Third Reich.

Ten days later Gehlen ordered German planes to drop over the Russian lines thousands of leaflets dated at Vinnitza on September 10 and signed by Vlassov:

Comrade Commanders,
Comrades of the Soviet intelligentsia,
    I, the undersigned, General Andrey Andreyevich Vlassov . . .

There followed an enumeration of his titles, a summary of his exploits, the story of his capture, which had made him Prisoner of War No. 16,901. Then the leaflet described the tremendous sufferings of the Russian people, for which Stalin and his associates alone were responsible. The leaflet continued:

Stalin's gang has ruined the country with the kolkhoz system. . . . It assassinated the flower of the army in 1937–1938. . . . It is no longer capable of organizing the defense of the country. . . .
There is only one solution. History offers no other. All those who desire the prosperity of their people should join the struggle with all their energies and with every means in order to overthrow the universally hated Stalinist system. . . .

In actuality the leaflet had been written by Captain Strik-Strikfeld. The effect of its distribution was immediate: Several thousand deserters crossed over to the German lines and asked to see Vlassov.

He had been moved to Berlin, where he lived in semi-liberty at Viktoriastrasse 77 with Dürksen and Strik-Strikfeld. Colonel Martin and his deputy, Captain von Grote, a Balt by origin, exploited the success of the leaflet in report after report to the General Staff. They said that a government of free Russia and a liberation army commanded by Vlassov must be established.

The reports came back with annotations by Keitel. The gist of the notes was always the same: Politics was not the business of the army.

But Strik-Strikfeld persisted. He was convinced that Germany was letting her opportunity elude her. Then he decided that the leaders of the Third Reich must be confronted with an accomplished fact: Vlassov should appear in the territories under German occupation and in the prisoner-of-war camps and stimulate adherence to him personally, igniting a mass movement that would require nothing more than legalization.

So, in all but clandestine fashion, Vlassov began to visit other Russian officers in the camps, with only moderate success. A few agreed to back him in his undertaking. Most wanted to know what guaranties he had on the future of Russia, whether he had been able to see Hitler; when they heard his hesitating or negative answers they refused to have anything to do with him. One of his shortest conversations was that with General Ponedzhelin, who attempted to spit in his face.

Nevertheless Vlassov set up a Russian National Committee with the help of Malyshkin, a former Soviet Major General who had been imprisoned during the Great Purge in 1938, and Captain Zykov, who claimed to have been the editor in chief of *Izvestia* and who some Germans suspected of being a Jew. Zykov was later abducted by the *Sicherheitsdienst* and killed.

This committee issued the Manifesto of Smolensk. Its thirteen points called for the replacement of the kolkhoz by private property; the reestablishment of trade and artisanry; the end of terror; the reinstatement of freedom of worship, the press, and assembly; the release of all inmates of concentration camps; the reconstruction of destroyed towns and villages at the expense of the state; etc. The document contained no allusion to either the *Führerprinzip* or racism. On another connection, while it called for a return to private enterprise, it said nothing of the future status of big industry. Subsequently, in a speech on April 12, 1943, Malyshkin dealt with that point, saying:

We believe, further, that all the industries that were created under Bolshevism at the cost of the blood and sweat of the people as a whole ought to belong to the state and become national properties. . . . If, however, it appeared preferable and such was in the interest of the people, the state would not oppose participation by private enterprise. . . .

This showed that the Vlassov movement's program was far from rejecting all the gains of the October Revolution. Though it did not describe it in any very clear terms, in sum it hinted at the coexistence of a public and a private sector. Elsewhere Vlassov was supposed to have frequently emphasized that the solutions adopted in Germany could not be transplanted unaltered into Russia.

The Smolensk Manifesto, of course, did not escape the knowledge of the High Command, which raised no objection to its dissemination among the Soviet troops. But in the High Command's view Vlassov's activities ought to be restricted to stirring up trouble in the enemy's ranks. There could be no question of his establishing a point of departure for a movement inside the occupied territories, in the prisoner-of-war camps, or among the *Ostarbeiter*.

Strik-Strikfeld deliberately ignored these views. In Smolensk itself leaflets embodying the Manifesto were quite widely distributed. As if by accident, aviators who agreed with him dropped certain quantities of the same leaflets over the occupied territories.

This led to much agitation among the battalions of volunteers, some of whom demanded to be allowed to see Vlassov. Rosenberg soon learned of this. Inasmuch as he supported the separatists and was hostile to any resurrection of Russia, he flew into a rage and demanded exemplary punishments. But the battle of Stalingrad was then at its height and the leaders of the Third Reich had other concerns besides men as unimportant as Vlassov.

Himmler had learned that Vlassov had been invited to dinner by a German general during a journey to northern Germany. During the dinner Vlassov had said that Leningrad would again become St. Petersburg and that he would regard it as a pleasure to return the German general's hospitality there.

This kind of dinner conversation did not exactly match Hitler's plans, which envisaged the destruction of the city. "This Bolshevik who comes from nowhere has the gall to play ally!" Himmler stormed, and he promptly informed Hitler.

Himmler's reasons for detesting Vlassov were different from Rosenberg's. At this time Himmler had ordered his subordinates to distribute a pamphlet called *Untermensch* (*Subman*), in which he pointed out that the Slavic peoples were led by degenerates. And here was Vlassov saying everywhere that the Soviet army could not be vanquished without the assistance of a national army of liberation: "Only Russians can defeat Russians." To the *Reichsführer* such remarks constituted unbelievable insolence.

On October 14, 1943, he was to come back to the Vlassov affair with unconcealed exasperation. Addressing a group of SS officers, he made an all-out attack on the Russian general:

Torn apart by intrigues, the Slavic peoples have never been capable of managing their own affairs. In this connection I should like to mention specifically General Vlassov. Great hopes have been invested in this General Vlassov. . . . These hopes were not well founded. With a complacency characteristic of the Russian and the

Slav, Mr. Vlassov began telling a fable, contending that Germany has never been able to conquer Russia and that Russia can be conquered only by Russians.

If now a Russian turns up from who knows where—last week, perhaps, he was a butcher's salesman and yesterday Mr. Stalin made him a general—and if this Russian gives us lessons with typical Slavic smugness, saying that Russia can be conquered only by Russians, then there is only one thing I can say: such a remark in itself shows that he is a *skunk*. If he were really as great a patriot as he claims to be, he would not have allowed that remark to come out of his mouth, regardless of his feelings toward Mr. Stalin. Should we entrust hundreds of thousands of our men to such a man and say: "Please, Mr. Vlassov, would you be good enough to fight the Russians?"

Vlassov's verbal violences, in the meantime, had brought on a severe reprimand from Keitel to Colonel Martin:

After the unpardonable and insolent remarks made by the Russian prisoner of war, General Vlassov, during a visit to the Army Group North, a visit made without my knowledge or that of the *Führer*, it is ordered that the Russian General Vlassov be immediately transferred under special surveillance to a prisoner-of-war camp. The *Führer* insists that henceforth the name of Vlassov is not to be mentioned again *unless for purposes of pure propaganda*. Only in such case, if necessity requires, will it be permissible to use Vlassov's name, but never his person. If General Vlassov dares to show himself in public once more, the authorities, whoever they may be, will be compelled to hand him over to the Gestapo. . . . (Italics added.)

At this very moment Gehlen was preparing to have eighteen million leaflets dropped over the enemy's lines. Special camps had already been prepared for the reception of deserters. Vlassov was to appear and accept their enlistments.

Keitel's decision sowed consternation among the officers who were backing Vlassov—Gehlen, Scheckendorf, Treschkov, Altenstadt, and Heere. In this connection it is interesting to note that the first three played important parts in the officers' conspiracy against Hitler.

At this time—that is, about the middle of 1943—there were approximately six hundred thousand, *Hiwis* and more than two hundred thousand combat volunteers. The official rule was to use them individually or in separate corps under German officers. The evacuation of Soviet soil led the High Command to employ them in Croatia—this was the case of the Cossack cavalry divisions under the command of von Pannwitz—Italy, the battle of Warsaw—in which the Kaminsky Brigade was employed—and France when the Allies landed.

These troops were very inconsistent in their behavior. Some broke ranks and went over to the enemy. Others fought without flinching. The defeats consistently suffered by the Germans contributed to the demoralization of these men and to their growing doubt whether they had opted for the winning side. But there were also other reasons for their low morale. To the better informed it was clear that, aside from propaganda slogans about Bolshevik barbarism, this war was being fought without any positive political goal. Others had to cope with German officers who regarded them as common mercenaries. Still others learned with bitterness that their women, working in Germany, had to wear the notorious armbands labeled *Ost* (East) and were not permitted to go into film theaters or restaurants with them.

Sometime in 1943 Peter Kleist, the diplomat, attempted to persuade Hitler to modify his position. He was received by the *Führer* in his military headquarters in Wolfsschanze at about two o'clock in the morning. Hitler listened quietly to Kleist's exposition. Then he reiterated his refusal, which he based on two arguments quite different in nature.

First of all he said that it was impossible for him to alter his policy during a period of defeats in the field. "It would be regarded as a weakness, and the consequences could be disastrous." Later, perhaps, when victory smiled again on the *Wehrmacht*. . . .

Suddenly, Kleist wrote, Hitler's expression changed. His features seemed to harden, there was a brilliance in his eyes, and it was "as if his thoughtful, contemplative mood had suddenly been driven out of him by a wave of more violent emotions."

"I do not have the right," Hitler cried, "to sacrifice the future for ephemeral successes. In a hundred years the German people will be a nation of one hundred twenty million persons. I need open space for them. It is impossible for me to grant rights of sovereignty to the peoples of the East and replace Soviet Russia with a national Russia even more solidly integrated." [1]

It was this concept of living space that had probably prevented him from initiating this war with the catchwords of a war of liberation. It emerged again when defeat was in progress, occasionally commingled with more practical considerations on the untimeliness of a new policy. And certainly there was a major risk in assembling a Russian national army just when the tide of battle was favoring the Soviet Union. If success were to be possible, it would be necessary not only to gamble on the continuing loyalty of the Russians but also to modify the entire policy pursued in what remained of the occupied territories and to treat the Eastern workers as human beings. Undoubtedly Hitler had speedily seen that one concession would compel the other. In time of war initial errors are very difficult to rectify.

During all this time Vlassov, constrained to inactivity, filled his days and nights with conversations with friends, card games, and vodka. Captain Strik-Strikfeld had become the laughing-stock of the army; he was known everywhere as "Vlassov's traveling salesman."

Nevertheless certain members of Vlassov's group began to contemplate other possibilities. Thus one of his deputies, Kasantsev of the NTS, had a talk in the Tiergarten of Berlin

[1] Peter Kleist, *Entre Hitler et Staline,* pp. 186–187.

one day with Baidalakov, who also belonged to the NTS.
Baidalakov said that contacts had been established with the
Americans in Switzerland; then he asked whether these talks
could be pursued in Vlassov's name. Kasantsev reported this
to Vlassov, who sensibly refused to be drawn in.

"There is nothing to be hoped for from that direction," he
said. "The Anglo-Americans have been hoodwinked by the
Soviets. Look what they are doing in Yugoslavia: They are
supporting Tito against Mikhailovich."

Was he being sincere? Did he think that it was premature
to enter into talks when he did not yet have at his command
a solid force that could be a trump in the event of a future
conflict between the Anglo-Americans and Stalin? Was he expecting an imminent overturn in Germany that would put an
end to the war in the West without on that account interfer-
ing with the hostilities against the Soviet Union? The course
of events compels one to raise these questions even though
they cannot yet be answered.

Meanwhile the idea of employing Vlassov to head an army
of liberation was secretly gaining ground. It was progressing
in *Hitler Jugend* circles, whose publication, *Will and Power*,
issued a special edition that contained Vlassov's manifesto,
while Baldur von Schirach invited him to Vienna, where he
was received with the honors appropriate to the commander
in chief of an allied army. But above all the idea was soon to
gain ground in the group that had initially been the most hostile to it: the SS.

Considerable influence in the SS was wielded by Dr. Riedweg, a Swiss surgeon who had emigrated to Germany and
joined the SS. In 1941 he was in charge of the *Führungshaup-
tamt,* and he had encouraged the recruiting of foreign nation-
als by the SS. He had to resign in 1942 and accept transfer to
the Eastern front, but his policy was continued by Sparmann.
In this way the SS acquired Flemish, Dutch, Danish, Swiss,
Swedish, Walloon, French, Latvian, and Estonian volunteers;

the Estonians and Latvians were commanded by Banzhersky.[2]

At the beginning of the war Dr. Fritz Arlt had encouraged the creation of Ruthenian and Ukrainian committees. He favored the formation of a Ukrainian army of liberation. Transferred later to the SS, he immediately became a fanatical advocate of the establishment of SS units raised among the Soviet peoples, and in the end he endorsed the views of his colleague, Berger.

Arlt began by assembling a Ukrainian division under the command of Schandruk, won Banzhersky's agreement for the Latvians and Estonians, created a Turkmen division, and persuaded Pannwitz to allow his Cossacks to be incorporated into the SS. Arlt believed that all these units should be brought under the authority of a personality powerful enough to cement them together. Although he, like Rosenberg, was favorably inclined toward a policy of minorities, it seemed to him that only Vlassov possessed the prestige required to head the collection of volunteers.

At the same time one of Himmler's favorites, Günther d'Alquen, was coming to the same conclusions. The son of a Ruhr industrialist, he had joined the SS when he was sixteen. Thrown out of his father's house, he had worked as a laborer in a Krupp factory and then as a miner, taking an active part in all the brawls with the Communists. Finally he had founded *Das Schwarze Korps*, the SS publication, and then he had been placed in charge of all war correspondents. From the start of the hostilities he had espoused the idea of opening the SS to all Europeans.[3]

He had not yet divorced himself from the prevailing prejudice on the inferiority of the Slavs. But the course of the war slowly altered his thinking. When Himmler showed him the famous pamphlet, *Untermensch*, d'Alquen could not restrain himself from commenting: "There is a danger that this will

[2] Riedweg wanted to make the SS a European corps. On this subject cf. St.-Loup's book *Les Hérétiques*.

[3] Cf. Thorwald, *op. cit.*, pp. 153–154.

not be properly understood by our units. In battle our men do not feel that they are up against submen."

Himmler did not take kindly to such impertinence. But d'Alquen made contact with some of the officers round Vlassov—Trukhin, Zykov, Zhilenkov—and in June 1944 he once more explained to Himmler that the only solution was Vlassov. Only with him could an army of liberation be created, and such an army was necessary to the winning of the war.

"What about the effects on our ideology?" Himmler objected. "Have you thought about that?"

"May I speak frankly?"

"Go ahead."

"The only choice left is between victory and defeat. Ideology will have to wait until later."

One could not take a chance on the instability of the Slavs, Himmler grumbled. Nevertheless in the end he promised to bring up the matter with Hitler. Finally he announced on July 17, 1944, that he had won Hitler's assent and that he would see Vlassov four days later.

But one day before the appointed meeting Stauffenberg placed his bomb in Hitler's headquarters. One man immediately feared the worst for Vlassov: Captain Strik-Strikfeld. By July 21 he knew that in addition to Stauffenberg the plot had involved Treschkov and Freytag-Loringhoven. These men had always supported the idea of mobilizing Russians alongside Germans. And Gehlen too, Strik-Strikfeld said to himself, might also be a member of the conspiracy. Would not certain ramifications be discovered among Vlassov's associates and might it not be found that Vlassov himself was implicated in this affair?

Strik-Strikfeld hurried to see Vlassov. He found him, in a black mood, with Malyshkin. It was obvious that the giant had been drinking.

"Wilfred Karlovich," Vlassov said, "we had placed all our hopes in this day. A few more hours and the day will have ended."

"Andrey Andreyevich," Strik-Strikfeld replied, "the man whom you were going to meet is one of the great victors of this day. After the attack on the *Führer* he now has increased powers. But we have lost a number of friends who had helped us in the bad times. Stauffenberg is dead."

Expressionless, Vlassov stared into space. "Stauffenberg?" he said at last in surprise. "Stauffenberg? I don't know any Stauffenberg."

"Look, Andrey Andreyevich, you remember: The colonel who did everything on behalf of your cause."

Vlassov rose. "You must be mistaken," he said in a completely composed manner.

Strik-Strikfeld was dumfounded. How could Vlassov contend that he did not know even the name of Stauffenberg? A moment later Malyshkin left. Vlassov waited until his footsteps on the stairs could no longer be heard; then he said: "One should never again speak of such friends. One should no longer be able to say that one knew them. One knows nothing of them. Do not forget, Wilfred Karlovich, that I come out of the Soviet school. There I learned that one can trust no one. I cannot say everything to Malyshkin or Zhilenkov. I could not have complete confidence even in my own brother."

The episode was a brutal illumination of Vlassov's mentality and his position. He was the product of a totalitarian system. His personality had been fashioned by that system. He had learned to repress the most sincere thoughts, to accomodate himself at a moment's notice to every change in the "line." Such conduct had become second nature to him and nothing could erase it, for in going over to the Germans he had merely traded one totalitarianism for another. Perhaps in the beginning he thought that it was less dangerous to speak freely in his new environment. After all, he had seen how it was. The remark that he had made to a German general when he offered hospitality in Leningrad after the war had gained him nothing but insults from Himmler and semi-sequestration. Such a conversational divagation under Stalin would have got him a bullet at the base of the skull. Nonetheless he was living in a universe of distrust, troubled by subterranean scheming, in which the chief rules were still caution, temporization, and deceit.

Was Vlassov in some way involved in the maneuvers that ended in the July 20 conspiracy? The Gestapo could uncover nothing of the sort, and to my knowledge no evidence has since been found.

On the other hand it may be wondered what goal was truly in the minds of men like Stauffenberg, Treschkov, Freytag-Loringhoven, etc., when they advocated the idea of a Russian national army from the start of hostilities. Of course it may be argued that, persuaded that the creation of this army was essential to winning the war in the East, they came to the conclusion, when all their efforts proved vain, that it was absolutely necessary to get rid of Hitler. But this hypothesis does not jibe with reality. We know, in fact, that as early as August 1941 Treschkov and his adjutant, Schlabrendorff, were conspiring to abduct the *Führer* during one of his journeys. Hence they could be in no doubt that the accomplishment of a *coup d'état* in the midst of a victorious offensive against the Russians would destroy that offensive. Now the plan for the organization of a Russian army of liberation that Treschkov submitted to Bock dated from October 1941. This then is the question that arises: Why did Treschkov in October believe that the Russian contribution was necessary for a victory that he was not afraid to compromise a few months later?

Perhaps the conspirators planned to continue the war on other bases after they had achieved an accord with the West. But it would seem that such views did not match Stauffenberg's conceptions. He, on the contrary, seemed rather to favor, if his own confidences are to be believed, an understanding with the East. And perhaps Ambassador Schulenburg and General Köstring, both of whom had disapproved of the invasion of the Soviet Union, also tended in the same direction?

Why then did men like Stauffenberg and Treschkov so tenaciously strive to establish an army of Russian volunteers? There are two possible hypotheses. This corps structured on carefully selected officers could be a mass with which to attempt a *coup d'état*. After the coup, it would represent a major lever in any possible negotiation with Stalin.

There is no less mystery in Himmler's about-face from denunciation of Vlassov and the *Untermensch* to an agreement to confer with him. Here it can be seen that Himmler was no longer altogether unchanged. He had probably ceased to believe that Germany could win the war. It is probable that he knew of the preparations for July 20 and did nothing to hinder them. In any case it is known that, through the intermediary of a lawyer named Langbehn, he made contact with Popitz, one of the plotters, and that on August 26, 1943, Langbehn and Popitz called on him for a talk.[4] After this meeting Langbehn went to Switzerland in order to establish contact with the Allies, but he was arrested on his return to Germany. In circumstances of which nothing is known Himmler managed to extricate himself from this dangerous pass.

Himmler's about-face with respect to Vlassov occurred after these meetings, and obviously it may be wondered whether Himmler was not pursuing through other channels the project of an alliance with the West after Hitler had been evicted from power and the continuation of the battle in the East with the assistance of a Russian national army.

In any event the conspiracy of July 20 merely postponed the talk with Vlassov for a few weeks. On September 16 he was received in Himmler's headquarters in Rastenburg. When Vlassov entered, the SS ignored his protests and prevented Strik-Strikfeld from going in with him.

No doubt Vlassov avoided reminding the *Reichsführer* that a year earlier Himmler had called him a criminal. But, according to what he later reported, Vlassov did speak to him about his famous pamphlet on the *Untermensch*.

[4] General Wolff of the SS was also present.

"We were wrong to generalize," Vlassov quoted Himmler as confessing. "There are submen everywhere. Except that in your country they are in power; in ours they are in prison or institutions. It is up to you to change this state of affairs."

Himmler gave Vlassov two divisions. In the light of the armament situation, he could not have done more. In addition, Vlassov would have full power to negotiate with the leaders of the national committees and constitute a national government with them.

More than two years after the capture of the Soviet general the army of national liberation was finally constituted. On paper.

At the same time the collapse of the volunteer units of Soviet origin that the Germans had committed to the Western front was reaching its climax. It was General Köstring who had decided to transfer them. This was the only remaining solution apart from their dissolution, which Hitler had demanded. But Vlassov's name had become so popular among the fighting men that they wanted to know whether he approved of this transfer.

Vlassov screamed when the Germans asked him to sign a proclamation to that effect. He said that he had been basely deceived and that in no case should the volunteers be used in the West. But, after several weeks of argument, he finally gave in.

It is certain that, if he had been informed that a plot against Hitler was under way, the decision by the *Führer* to use volunteers of Soviet origin in the West upset Vlassov's plans. Did he agree because he thought that the elimination of Hitler would occur before the Allies landed? Or did he simply give in out of weariness and fatalism, or because in the final analysis he still preferred to live cloistered in a villa rather than disappear into a prisoner-of-war camp?

There is an eloquent document on the fate of the units committed to the Western front. It is the journal of a Major Hansen, a staff officer from the volunteer divisions with the commander in chief of Army Group West:

June 11: New rebellion feared in 717th Georgian Battalion. A captain (a German) murdered.

June 15: The new commander, General Ritter von Niedermeyer, has just arrived. He is an old Russian who takes only the Russian units seriously (and therefore has a dim view of the Georgians).

June 24: British and American loudspeaker propaganda promises that deserters will be sent to Canada and not turned over to the Russians.

July 10: Malyshkin [5] is extremely worried. He considers all the units in the West doomed by Vlassov's plans.

August 4: Colonel Bunichenko has received orders from Berlin to appear before Rosenberg with a delegation. This move has little chance of leading to anything, in view of Rosenberg's incompetence.

August 10: Niedermeyer is of the opinion that it is not possible again to throw Russians into the major battles that are now going on. *The fight that they would be asked to make against an enemy that they do not regard as such would be waged without conviction* [italics added].

August 25: There have been repeated murders of German personnel.

August 26: The Americans announce that they have taken twenty thousand volunteers prisoner.

August 28: Niedermeyer at Verdun. We are amazed that there are still volunteers who fight. Fear of being handed over to the Russians may be one of their motives, but that does not explain everything.

September 1: Disorderly flight. Incredible scenes. Our police is setting up barricades to stop the fugitives.

September 6: An assembly camp for our units set up in Wahn. No one has any further desire to be bothered with our battalions. Commander in Chief West orders all units dissolved and disarmed, then used to build fortifications. If there is still anything to salvage,

[5] One of Vlassov's adjutants, he had been Chief of Staff of the Soviet Nineteenth Army before his capture in 1941.

they say, it will be only because of Köstring. He promises by telephone to arrive in Simmern on the twelfth.

September 20: Saw the aide-de-camp of the Volga-Tartar 627th
Battalion, which is completely disorganized. . . . The division to
which it was attached was cited on several occasions, but the battalion itself, on the other hand, was not cited once. No decorations,
no recognition. . . . No one gave them a thought. Apparently
everything is avenged in this world.

September 21: General Westphal on his own initiative dissolved
the Russian units. With considerable trouble we were able to cancel this order in time.

September 30: Niedermeyer taken under guard to Berlin to clear
himself.

October 2 (evening): The height of irony, the propaganda department of Commander in Chief West informs us that the propaganda directives with respect to Vlassov have been changed 100
per cent. Supposedly there has been an agreement between Vlassov
and Himmler. The first Russian divisions will soon be created. Our
soldiers will be regrouped in these divisions. Is it possible? Is there
still time? What is one to believe? [6]

There was not much longer to wait for the answers.

[6] Quoted by Thorwald, *op. cit.,* pp. 186–191.

(20)

THE STRANGE FATE
OF VLASSOV'S ARMY

T HE SS had made up its mind to play its Vlassov card. This was supposed at the same time to overcome the resistance of the national committees that rejected the authority of a Russian general.

One day in October 1944, Khedya, one of the most influential of the Caucasian leaders, was summoned to SS General Kaltenbrunner's headquarters for a talk with Vlassov. The conferees met in a tense atmosphere round a large conference table. Vlassov and Trukhin,[1] one of his deputies, sat facing Khedya and Dr. Arlt. At one end of the table were the three arbiters who had already made their decision: Kaltenbrunner, Schellenberg, and Ohlendorf, all of the SS.

Kaltenbrunner opened the proceedings, addressing Khedya in a cold voice: "Mr. Khedya, have you made up your mind to take part in the creation of a Russian army of liberation under General Vlassov's command?"

Khedya had the reputation of always maintaining his com-

[1] Former Deputy Chief of Staff of the Baltic army, captured in 1941.

posure. No doubt it was the word *Russian* that made him lose it. In a loud voice he replied: "Never!"

"Would you be good enough to state your reasons?"

"Because we Caucasians have not been fighting thus far merely in order to surrender again to a Russian imperialist." And suddenly he began to shout: "I still prefer Stalin's arse to Vlassov's face!"

After this outburst Vlassov agreed to change the name of his committee. Thereafter it would be known as the "Committee for the Liberation of the Peoples of Russia."

The Caucasians' reaction had been the most violent. As soon as Vlassov's plans had come to their knowledge, they had issued a manifesto [2] in which they reiterated their hatred of Bolshevism and the catalogue of their losses, which, they said, had by then reached fifty thousand men. Pointing out that in 1942 Vlassov was still an implacable enemy of Germany, they added: "The Caucasians are prepared to concede that the Vlassov movement created with a view to the liberation of Russia is also combating Bolshevism, but they will never accept General Vlassov as their chief. To accept such an offer would be a betrayal of all the sacrifices that they have made. . . ."

Among the Ukrainians the opposition was no less strong. In the end the Germans had released Dr. Stetsko, the premier of the transitory Lvov government, and a Ukrainian leader named Bandera, both of whom had been thrown into concentration camps, but both stubbornly refused to join Vlassov's ranks.

Most of the leaders of the national committees had addressed petition after petition to Rosenberg. He was infuriated by projects that tended to create a Russian national army, but, lacking all authority, he could do little against Himmler.

Actually it was always possible to find a few men who would agree to stand surety in the name of the national mi-

[2] Signed by Mirscha, Khedya, Kantimer, Alibegov, and Chamalzha.

norities for Vlassov's operations. But these men represented no one but themselves.

Vlassov himself had agreed to make concessions. Some idea of what they were may be derived from a comparison between the resolution adopted on August 1, 1943, in Smolensk and the speech that Vlassov made on November 14, 1944. Almost every line of the resolution emphasized Russia and the Russian people, and the resolution concluded:

> Russia belongs only to us alone.
> The past of the Russian people is in our hands alone.
> The future of the Russian people rests in our hands alone. . . .
> Arise and restore the prosperity of the Russian people in battle!

Vlassov's speech of November 14 began thus: "The *peoples* of Russia have been fighting for more than twenty-five years against the shameful dictatorship of Bolshevism." He continued:

> The terrible situation imposed on the populations of the Soviet Union, the rise in discontent, *the combat of the peoples in the territories occupied by the Red Army for their national independence—* these are the factors that assure our victory and the fall of Bolshevism. . . . Nevertheless . . . the struggle of the peoples of Russia against the Bolsheviks would be impossible if we did not group all the forces of these peoples and did not give them a single leadership. . . . (Italics added.)

The Manifesto of the Committee for the Liberation of the Peoples of Russia, adopted on the same day, offered an ambiguous formula purporting to define the future relations among the peoples. On the one hand, it did indeed assert that one of the Committee's purposes was

> . . . to create a new *state* without Bolshevism and without capitalists, belonging to the people

but on the other hand the same document stated that the
foundation of this state would be

equal rights for all the peoples of our fatherland and recognition
of their absolute right to develop and govern themselves as they
might choose in full sovereignty.[3]

The creation of the Committee [4] was consecrated by a solemn ceremony on that same day, November 14. The Germans
had at first planned to stage it in Potsdam. Vlassov insistéd
that the formal creation of the Committee take place in
Prague—in other words, on Slavic soil. Finally he got his way.
By that time German troops were occupying only a sliver of
Soviet territory.

It was Frank, the *Gauleiter* of Bohemia and Moravia, who
received Vlassov in the great hall of the Castle in Prague, beneath the huge crystal chandeliers whose reflections shim-
mered in the mirrors. Everything had been arranged to create
a Slavic atmosphere: The footmen, the butlers, the orderlies
were Russians. The vodka flowed in torrents. In spite of all
this contrivance it was a dreary ritual.

Frank delivered his address in a monotone. Obviously he believed nothing of what he was saying. There was no other important person at the banquet given in Vlassov's honor. In
spite of the toasts, the songs, and the laughter that rose all

[3] On another point, it is interesting to note that this manifesto intended to restore "the rights gained during the Revolution of February
1917."

[4] The Committee for the Liberation of the Peoples of Russia (KONR)
had approximately twenty-four members, civilian and military, at the
end of the war, and it was headed by a presidium of a dozen members.
Four generals ran the major sections: administration, Malyshkin; military
affairs, Trukhin; prisoners of war and *Ostarbeiter,* Zakutny; propaganda,
Zhilenkov. Five national councils had been created: Russian, Ukrainian,
Caucasian, Central Asian, White Russian. The KONR issued two publications: *Volya Naroda (The People's Will)* and *Za Rodinu (For the Fatherland).* Established in Berlin, the KONR's headquarters was moved in
February 1945 to Karlsbad and later to Füssen, in Bavaria, near the
Austrian border. The German Foreign Ministry had promised a subsidy
of a hundred million marks to finance the KONR's work.

during the feast, the hall was filled with an oppressive uneasiness, a reciprocal distrust that nothing could dissipate. All these men were laboring under the burden of defeat.

Himmler had promised earlier that he would provide Vlassov with sufficient arms to equip two divisions. These divisions were now being organized, one at Münsingen in Württemberg under Colonel Bunichenko and the other in the camp of Heuberg in Baden under Colonel Sverzhev. Vlassov's headquarters had been established in Berlin with no fewer than seven hundred officers, and it might well be thought, in view of their number, that many of them were looking for nothing more than a soft job.

In order to fill out the first division Vlassov began sending Bunichenko the men of the Kaminsky Brigade, who had taken part in the suppression of the insurrection in Warsaw. They were a pirate corps dressed in a wide variety of uniforms, accompanied by women covered with jewels, and wearing three or four watches on each wrist. Himmler had ordered the arrest of their leader. Alerted in time, Kaminsky fled, but he was finally arrested in the Carpathians and shot by the SD (*Sicherheitsdienst*—Security Service).

Bunichenko, a thick-set, completely bald Russian, raged that he was being given nothing but gangsters. Other volunteers were detailed to him. But difficulties arose almost daily. The troops of his division were in constant conflict with the civilian population, and whatever time was left over from drilling they spent in brawling with the Germans. Bunichenko brought these hordes under an iron discipline.

But no arms arrived. Bunichenko's complaints overwhelmed Colonel Hesse, a German officer who had been recalled from Italy to supervise the operation. One morning, wearing his tunic over his pajamas, Bunichenko received Hesse in his office. Among the vodka bottles and mustard jars on his desk there was also his breakfast: thin slices of sausage mixed with a large quantity of onions. He filled a glass to the brim with vodka and offered it to Hesse with a toast. This was followed by his demands: "You do not want to give me helmets. You do not want to give me munitions. . . ." Then came the eternal reproach: "You do not trust us."

In Heuberg, Colonel Sverzhev, slender and elegant, as polished as Bunichenko was uncouth, made the same criticisms.

Defeats were accumulating for the Germans, and they led to new desertions. On the Dutch island of Texel the Georgian First Battalion established contact with the Resistance and through it with the British, then rose, killed all the Germans on the island, and waited for the British to invade. But in vain. The Germans reoccupied the island and exterminated all life on it. The last survivors blew themselves up with the lighthouse in which they had fortified themselves.

Christmas came. The Germans refused the Russians' request for a bottle of champagne and a bar of chocolate for each of their soldiers. The supplies were stored in Ulm. The Allies bombed that city with phosphorus and everything was destroyed.

In January, however, the first division was almost ready. There were almost thirteen thousand men in its ranks. What would it be worth in combat? The Eastern front was crumbling. Soviet troops had crossed the Oder, Berlin was in a state of alarm, Silesia was virtually occupied, and Breslau was threatened. Two words were heard everywhere and always: "Too late."

On March 2 Hesse was finally ordered to move the first division to Army Group Vistula. At first Bunichenko refused to obey. It took four days of talk and a firm order from Vlassov to convince him. At last the division began to move.

In the meantime Himmler, who was in command of the forces on the Vistula, where he had demonstrated his incontestable unfitness for his task, had resigned. His successor, General Heinrici, knew virtually nothing of Vlassov's army. Initially he was suspicious of it. But after all the *Wehrmacht* was in desperate need of bodies. It was decided to send the first division to Erlenhof.

This was a bridgehead on the Vistula occupied by Soviet troops. At the end of March two Junker regiments had vainly attempted to blow it up. Bunichenko's division had not been given an easy first assignment.

The start of the attack had been scheduled for the night of April 12–13. Dive-bombers were to go into action before the infantry attacked. There was no gasoline: The planes stayed on the ground. Only the artillery went into action, and then the first division moved forward.

Bunichenko had taken up a position at the top of a little hill to direct operations. During the night he saw a rocket, which meant that the artillery should lift its fire. Twice more the darkness was broken by rockets. Nothing more happened.

Four hours later the regiments returned to their starting points. After their advance they had encountered heavy barbed-wire entanglements and suffered heavy losses. Their attack had disintegrated at the same point as that of the Germans before them.

From that time on, under the pressure of history, relations between Bunichenko and the Germans deteriorated at lightning speed. The High Command had ordered the first division to fall back toward Kottbus. Meanwhile the division was placed under the command of Marshal Schörner, a fanatical disciple of Hitler. Bunichenko refused to obey his orders.

When Schwenninger, the German liaison officer, conveyed this news to Schörner, the marshal burst out: "Does this Russky want to fight or not? Tell him that I will have him shot if he does not want to carry out my orders."

"That is not so easy," Schwenninger replied. "He has seventeen thousand men behind him."

Bunichenko soon learned of Schörner's intentions. His response was to conceal his men in a forest. Let them try now to dislodge him! As for himself, he would obey no one but Vlassov, and he would move only toward the south.

There could no longer be any thought of putting down the first division's mutiny by force. The German front was disintegrating. The siege of Berlin had begun on April 16. In the end Bunichenko and his men were able to retreat into Czechoslovakia. There he and his officers conferred, and immediately afterward they initiated contacts with the Czech Resistance.

During this period the effects of the German disaster were making themselves felt also in Münsingen, to which the second division had been transferred after the departure of Bunichenko's force. When the Alpine redoubt was beginning to seem the Germans' last hope, the officers of the second division were feverishly working on plans of their own. There was talk of marching southeast and joining forces with the Cossack units, Schandruk's Ukrainian division, the Croats, and the supporters of Mikhailovich, who was in command of the army of Yugoslav nationalists opposed to Tito. By continuing the war after the defeat of the Germans they hoped to demonstrate that the struggle against Bolshevism, and not collaboration with the Germans, had been the basic motivating force of Vlassov's army. In this way, perhaps, it would be possible to influence the point of view of the "Westerners."

Hesse was consulted and he shattered these illusions. Thereupon the second division was ordered to fall back on Landsberg.

The last-chance conference was held on a farm near Linz. Hitler was dead. Admiral Dönitz had succeeded him, proclaiming that the struggle would be carried forward in the East—a frail and futile hope to which these men clung. The conferees included two Germans, General Archenbrenner and Captain Strik-Strikfeld, and Vlassov, Malyshkin, Zhilenkov, and Bozharsky.

Lost causes are the mothers of mad notions. One of the conferees suggested seizing Pierre Laval, who was supposed to be hiding in the area, and turning him over to the Western powers in exchange for a guaranty of the Russians' safety. The insane proposal was hardly even debated. Archenbrenner declared that any idea of continuing the fight in Czechoslovakia or Yugoslavia was doomed to failure.

There was only one solution: to send emissaries to the Anglo-Americans, to try to convince them that for them an alliance with Russia was against nature and that it was to their interest to intern Vlassov's troops and hold them in reserve in the prospect of a future conflict.[5]

[5] Was the idea of substituting the Anglo-Americans for the Germans as allies in the fight against Bolshevism born as a desperate way out in the final days of the German disaster or did it considerably precede the defeat? The question seems difficult to answer. The preamble to the manifesto adopted by the KONR in Prague contained a passage directed against the Anglo-American plutocracy: "There are the forces of imperialism, with the Anglo-Americans at their head. . . ." Y. Pismennay, in an article published in 1950 and quoted by Schatov in *Matériaux et Documents sur le Mouvement de Libération des peuples de Russie*, asserted, however, that the passage attacking Anglo-American imperialism was merely a sop by Vlassov to German demands.

"Those who were close to General Vlassov at the time when the manifesto was promulgated have reported that he was ordered by the Germans to insert two points in the proposed manifesto: attacks on 'world Jewry' and the 'Anglo-American plutocrats.' When Vlassov categorically refused, the Germans offered a compromise: The elimination of either of these attacks that they had suggested. They indicated that the insertion of only one of these attacks would be the last concession that they would make. . . . Vlassov preferred to strike the anti-Semitic statements out of the manifesto and was compelled to retain the attacks on the Anglo-American plutocrats," Pismennay wrote. He added that in the autumn of 1944 neither Vlassov nor anyone else in the leadership of the KONR could still believe in a German victory. "It is obvious that Vlassov and his closest comrades in arms fully expected that England and the U.S. would quickly transform their war against totalitarian Germany into a fight against the totalitarian Soviet Union. This represented the only chance for the liberation movement at that time, and certainly it was openly discussed in General Trukhin's subcommittee in Hoiberg, as well as in the subcommittee of the presidium of the KONR."

As far as Bunichenko is concerned, it is quite apparent that he demonstrated manifest reluctance to take part in any battle, and his efforts to get to Czechoslovakia may support the belief that contacts had already been initiated with the Czech national Resistance. Vlassov's attitude is more enigmatic. After the war his defenders obviously had every reason to depict him as a man who had never been hostile to the Anglo-Americans. In any event it may be assumed that reservations and second thoughts must have been many on both the German and the Russian sides.

Vlassov asked Strik-Strikfeld whether he was willing to undertake this mission. The German hesitated. He did not know whether his name was on the list of important Germans whose extradition would be demanded by the Soviet Union. Finally he said: "Andrey Andreyevich, I will do it."

The conference broke up the next day. Vlassov and his staff left to join his troops in Czechoslovakia. Strik-Strikfeld and Malyshkin set a course for the northwest and their meeting with the Anglo-American forces. Making contact with United States units presented no difficulties. They were taken to General Patch in Seventh Army headquarters.

In the general's presence Malyshkin described the situation of Vlassov's army. Patch did not grasp any part of the picture. He had never before heard of Vlassov. All that he knew was that during the fighting in France his troops had captured Russians who were combatants in the Germans' ranks. Nevertheless the two men in his office were telling him that those soldiers on the Western front had nothing in common with Vlassov's army. It was all very complicated.

Finally Patch referred the problem to Eisenhower, who in turn referred it to Washington. A few days went by. Then Strik-Strikfeld and Malyshkin were informed that they had lost their status as emissaries and they were placed in a camp. The mission to the West had failed.

On May 1 Vlassov had rejoined Bunichenko. The latter, in the meantime, had made considerable progress in negotiations with officers of the Czech national police, who, envisaging an uprising against the Germans, suggested that the Russians cooperate in the liberation of Prague. Weary and completely demoralized, Vlassov listened as Bunichenko explained his plan:

"Attempts to bargain with the Allies have failed. We still have one chance. Only one. The Czechs are about to revolt. But the Czech Resistance is split between a pro-Soviet committee and one favorable to the Western powers. The pro-Soviets are waiting for the Russians' arrival. The nationalists are banking on the Americans. They do not have enough weapons to take over the city, though this would enable them to set up a provisional government before the Soviet units arrive. We have the weapons. If we make it possible for the nationalists to assume power, they will grant us the right of asylum in exchange."

When Vlassov did not reply, Bunichenko resumed: "On what can we rely? Continuing the fight alongside Mikhailovich? Look, he too has been liquidated. Tito has won, and he has the backing of Soviet troops. And how would we get to Yugoslavia? Here we are on the spot. Once we have liberated the country, no American will dare to turn us over to the Russians."

At this point a message was brought in, and Bunichenko read it. "Hitler is dead," he said. "Are you still hesitating?"

"I already knew that," Vlassov replied. "What does it change? Everyone looks on us as traitors. Do you want us to behave like traitors?"

"Haven't the Germans betrayed us?" Bunichenko retorted. "Didn't they regard us as submen? You have no right to think of the Germans now, Andrey Andreyevich. Think of our own soldiers. It is our last chance, don't destroy it."

"I have no faith in it. But I don't want to prevent you from acting." [6]

The last chance was slipping away: Eisenhower had been ordered to halt the advance of his troops on a line running from Karlsbad to Pilsen to Badweis. Prague was abandoned to the Soviets. All the plans of the Czech nationalists were collapsing.

Like Bunichenko, they were still ignorant of the order to Eisenhower. The Czech Communists, however, had been informed of it by Soviet liaison agents parachuted into their lines. That was why they offered no opposition to the scheme evolved by the national police and Vlassov's division. The

[6] Cf. Thorwald, *op. cit.*, pp. 266–267.

renegade Russians would pay for the battle against the Germans. When the Soviet troops entered Prague, they would have only to liquidate them.

The revolt erupted on May 5. The Czechs occupied Radio Prague and the German munitions dumps, and, in the afternoon, most of the bridges, the railway station, and the main telephone facilities.

The next day the Germans counterattacked and the Czechs had to send an SOS to Vlassov's division. It entered Prague on May 7 and seized control of the airport. In the city itself, furious fighting broke out between SS men and Vlassov's troops, both sides inspired by a hatred that burst forth in sudden violence. The Russians were taking their revenge for a long surfeit of humiliations; the SS men looked on them as the perpetrators of a loathsome betrayal.

At five o'clock in the afternoon, while the fighting was still intense, the Czech flag and the banners of St. Andrey and the Vlassov division floated side by side in many windows. Young women were hailing the fighters who had come to their deliverance. Pictures of Vlassov appeared on walls.

The next day's news was a bombshell: Germany had surrendered. Then came another bombshell: The American army had voluntarily halted its advance. Soviet divisions were on their way at top speed. Prague understood. In the windows red flags appeared.

The Czech nationalists still had one last hope. Hastily they signed an armistice with the Germans. By forming a national government they might be able to incite the Americans to come.

Prague then experienced what had happened in Paris. The Communists refused to recognize the armistice. Sporadic fighting continued as the SS fell back toward the west. Vlassov's pictures were quickly removed, and Stalin's appeared. These changes were like a visual knell for Vlassov's division.

On May 9 one of Bunichenko's officers in the center of the city sent a telegram to his superior. Soviet troops would be

entering the city in a matter of hours; already he had been
sought out by a parachuted Soviet officer who had told him
that "Stalin is confident that all these men will go back to
their mother country."

A quarter-hour later Bunichenko was visited by the police
officer with whom he had conducted his negotiations. All was
lost: The Red Army was invading Czechoslovakia and the
Americans were not budging. It was becoming impossible to
adhere to the terms of the agreement.

Bunichenko ordered his troops to evacuate Prague at once.
So the same roads were clogged with SS units, Vlassov's
troops, and Todt Organization workers. All these men cherished the same hatreds toward one another. But they had
other problems more immediate than fighting.

On May 10 they reached the American lines and they were
allowed to pass through them without difficulty. Vlassov was
taken before the American general in command of the sector
at Schlüsselberg, a city that was partly occupied by Soviet
troops as well. Finally Vlassov was placed in the custody of
an American captain, who told him that the American forces
were going to evacuate the city but would take him along. In
resignation Vlassov agreed to exchange his uniform for civilian
clothes.

Under the guard of four American soldiers he left the house
in which he had been kept, heading westward. After about
three miles his car was halted by a Soviet column. The officer
in command of it thought at first that the car contained Germans captured by the Americans, and he was about to order
it to go on. Suddenly a Soviet soldier shouted: "Take another
look! That's Vlassov in that car!"

There was a sharp dispute between the Soviets and the
Americans guarding Vlassov. No one knows how it might have
ended if a jeep had not come up the road. An American officer got out and asked the reason for the argument. Vlassov's
guards explained that they had been ordered to take their
prisoners westward but the Soviets wanted to detain them.

"Look, boys," the officer said, "this is all a fight among Russkies. Don't get involved. Leave the car and the men and go back where you came from."

The Americans obeyed. Soviet soldiers with machine guns jumped on the running-board of Vlassov's car. The American officer got back into his jeep and drove off to the West.

It was not until August 12, 1946, that anything more was known of Vlassov. On that day a brief item in *Pravda* reported that he had been hanged in Moscow "as a traitor to the fatherland and for his esponiage, sabotage, and terrorist activity as an agent of the German intelligence service against the Soviet Union." The same sentence was pronounced against eleven of his associates turned over to the Soviet Union after his capture, in particular Malyshkin, Zhilenkov, Trukhin, Meyandrov, Maltsev, Bunichenko, and Shatov.

In contrast to the practice during the Great Purge, there was no public trial. Why then did Stalin deprive himself of the pleasure of seeing these men appear in court, parade their crimes, voice their penitence, and hail the military genius of the master of the Kremlin?

There is an answer to this question, and it is the only answer: Any public trial would inevitably have revealed the vast number of defections. Stalin preferred to wash this dirty linen in private.

(21)

THE CAMPAIGN OF THE
UKRAINIAN NATIONALISTS

FTER GERMANY'S collapse hundreds of thousands of men who, like Vlassov, had no desire to go back to their Soviet fatherland headed east against their wills. They had fought in the ranks of the German army or fled with their families before the Red Army's advance. Former prisoners of war feared that they would be penalized for having been captured; deserters expected that they would face exemplary punishment. *Ostarbeiter* knew that they were suspect because they had contributed to the German war effort, or, comparing ways of life, they had preferred to remain in Western Europe.

Sooner or later these men and women, thrust into displaced persons' camps, were loaded on trains and trucks in spite of all their supplications. The time of the Cold War had not yet arrived. The Allies wanted to maintain good relations with Stalin. Not only was the Soviet Union a member of the victors' camp; in its own way it was also an incarnation of democracy—a democracy that was undoubtedly rather peculiar, somewhat more rugged than the Anglo-American model, but, it was thought, perfectible. In those days anyone who voiced skepticism toward this myth was looked at askance. And who-

(351)

ever refused repatriation to the great sister democracy was suspect. Beseeched—sometimes with rifle butts—to accept, many of the suspects chose instead to kill themselves.

General Denikin, in exile in the United States, described their fate in a letter to Senator Arthur Vandenberg:

A hundred thousand displaced persons are living in camps in occupied Germany and Italy. These people are deprived of the most elementary human rights of freedom and free labor. . . .

Now that so many things concerning what happens behind the "iron curtain" are becoming clear again and so much living testimony has been adduced to expose the unspeakable cruelties of the Communist dictatorship, there is a duty to help American public opinion understand why these Russians are more opposed than ever to repatriation. Has history ever seen such a phenomenon? Tens and hundreds of thousands of persons exiled from their native country, where they lived, where as a result all their interests were concentrated, where their families and their friends remain, not only resist return with all their strength but are threatened with collapse into madness or suicide. . . .

Of course you are aware of the horrible dramas enacted in the camps of Dachau and Plattling when American soldiers resorted to force against Russian prisoners who resisted, mad with terror, covered with blood, throwing themselves beneath the wheels of trucks, slitting their own throats and veins. . . .

I know that the Yalta agreements are invoked to justify the occurrence of these scenes. . . . But such an abandonment cannot be justified by any political negotiations. For there is something that stands above politics: Christian morality, human dignity, and honor. . . .

The few repatriates who have succeeded in escaping from the camps in the Soviet Union have recounted all their sufferings to the press. These were so appalling that foreigners find it difficult to believe them. Meanwhile, those Russians who lived outside the camps, sheltered by the Red Cross or in barracks in the American occupation zone, live in constant dread of being turned over to the Soviets. . . . They appeal to all our hearts, their SOS signal is heard everywhere, in the indomitable belief that their right to live will be recognized. . . .

The worst fate, obviously, was reserved for those who had fought in German uniforms; a great number of them had been transferred to the SS at the end of 1944. The Cossacks of General von Pannwitz, who had fought side by side with Croat units against Tito's Partisans, were interned by the British at Lienz and Graz. At the end of May 1945 they were turned over to the Russians by the British—with their families they numbered some fifty thousand persons. The British kept only their horses, which received permission to emigrate to England.

The Nineteenth SS Latvia Division, which had been recruited in the country that gave it its name, was isolated in Kurland when General Bagramian reached the sea to the south of Memel. With their backs to the coast, the SS men threw themselves into remarkably fierce fighting. When Admiral Dönitz ordered the evacuation of civilian and military personnel after Hitler's death, the Latvian SS covered the seaborne operation, which continued until May 11. Some of the SS men also boarded ships and made their way to Denmark. But others joined the underground forces that had battled the Germans and were now fighting the Soviets.

Another Latvian division, the Fifteenth SS Settland, was encircled in Pomerania. Only a few of its men were able to break out of the ring at Divenov; they reached the outskirts of Berlin. There they were annihilated in some of the last of the fighting.

The Twentieth SS Estland, composed of Estonians, gave battle to Vlassov's first division in Prague. This was one of the most remarkable paradoxes of the war. These men who had been allies against the Soviet army were now at grips with each other in a savage battle that gave free rein to the national hatreds that arrayed the Estonians of the SS against the Estonians and Russians under Vlassov. The greater part of the Estland fell into Soviet hands. Only a small number reached the American lines at Pilsen, and they were turned over to the Russians a short time later.

The Thirtieth Weissruthenien Division, composed of so-called *Volksdeutsche*, White Russians, and Great Russians, was defending the approaches to Moravia at the time of the surrender. Few of its members escaped the Soviets and the Partisans. The division disappeared virtually without a trace.

The Fourteenth SS Galizien Division, created in 1944 with Ukrainian volunteers, was interned at Rimini at the end of the war. But some of its members, trapped in the collapse of Army Group Schörner and cut off from the rest of the army, fell back with the Germans into the Carpathians. It is possible that in the end they joined the most powerful opposition group: the UPA, the army of Ukrainian independence.

There is hardly any precedent for the remarkable story of the UPA. It began its organization and its fight against the Germans who were occupying the Ukraine, for its members saw that one occupation was merely taking the place of another. In this phase the UPA had also to face groups of Soviet Partisans. When the conquered Germans fell back, the UPA had then to resist the assaults of the Red Army and the NKVD.

The Second World War ended in the West. But the UPA carried on the fight. It had to face not only Soviet troops but the Czech and Polish armies. It could expect no help from the West. No one was backing it. The entire world, with a few rare exceptions, knew nothing of its desperate struggle, which nevertheless went on for years. And even after 1950, when the UPA's headquarters was found and wiped out, small groups continued a hopeless guerrilla fight.

No clandestine undertaking, whatever the quality of its organization, could have maintained such a campaign without the support of the population. But even the support of the Ukrainian peasants and townsmen cannot explain everything. The UPA's long battle was the result of a political and military effort pursued with dedication by the nationalists between the two world wars.

Colonel Konovaletz, whose death has already been described, played a major part in this respect in the creation of the UVO (*Ukrayinska Vyiskova Organizatsia*—Ukrainian Military Organization). The UVO functioned in Rumania, Czechoslovakia, and even the Soviet Union. But its chief theater of action was Galicia, annexed to Poland and inhabited by Ukrainians. As early as 1920–1923 the men of the UVO engaged in assassinations, sabotage, and "expropriations" of banks and large Polish landowners.

The establishment of the UVO made it possible also to assure military training for men who would later become the backbone of the UPA in the fight against the Germans and the Soviets. Beginning in 1929, the OUN—the Ukrainian nationalists' political arm—came to the support of the military undertaking. In Poland the OUN fought for cultural autonomy for the Ukrainians, calling for Ukrainian schools and universities.

The city of Lvov (Lviv in Ukrainian, Lemberg in German) was the seat of this nationalism. The struggle against Polish domination, moreover, contributed to the revival of nationalist feeling in the area of the Ukraine occupied by the Soviets, where police rule, however, made clandestine activity extremely difficult.

In Poland the struggle took an increasingly violent form. The repressions resorted to against it led in turn to OUN acts of reprisal. On June 15, 1934, Pieracki, the minister of the interior, was murdered in Warsaw by a member of the OUN. Subsequent to this attack, at the beginning of 1936, one of the major leaders of the secret Ukrainian youth groups, Stepan Bandera, who was then twenty-seven years old, was arrested and sentenced to death, but his sentence was commuted to forced labor for life.

He was not released until the Germans had occupied Poland. Meanwhile, the first government of the sub-Carpathian republic, proclaimed at the time of the partition of the Czechoslovak state, had had only the most fleeting of existences. In this respect the position taken by the Third Reich was a bitter disappointment to the Ukrainian nationalists.

The start of the war, the attack against Poland, and the preparations for the invasion of Russia opened new prospects for the Ukrainian guerrillas. They had prepared for this struggle. In 1941 the Second Congress of Ukrainian Nationalists had elected Bandera to the presidency of the General Executive of the OUN. Special units were formed and trained in camps in Poland in order to be able to act as soon as hostilities began against the Soviet Union. All the members of the OUN —approximately six thousand—gathered in the territory of the Government General of Poland were ordered to cross the San and the Bug as soon as the offensive had been launched. In addition, the Ukrainian Legion, placed under the command of Roman Shukevich, took part in the invasion alongside the *Wehrmacht.*

The dissolution of the provisional government set up in Lvov on June 30, 1941, the arrest of its premier, Stetsko, Bandera, and other members of the government in July, their internment in the concentration camp of Sachsenhausen, and the roundups of nationalists that began in September showed that their hopes were doomed. The Ukrainian Legion was soon withdrawn from the front and its commander, Shukevich, a tall, long-faced fellow, vanished into the underground. He was to gain renown under the name of Tarass Shuprynka.

In 1941 the divorce between the Ukrainian nationalists and the leaders of the Third Reich became final. Koch's policy, the massive reprisals, and the deportations of workers, as in other countries, were to create the objective conditions for armed revolt.

The first battalions of the UPA *(Ukrayinska Povstancha Armiya)* were created in the autumn of 1942. In the early part of 1943 it began its first operations: sabotage, executions of members of the Gestapo, attacks on railway lines. The UPA was divided into four large armies: North, South, East, and

West.[1] In coordination, independent units operated in the regions of Kharkov, the Donetz, Dniepropetrovsk, the Crimea, and Odessa.

Beginning in 1943 the UPA launched a series of attacks against various cities: Volodymyrets (in Volhynia), Stepan, Derzan, Dubno, Lutsk, Rovno, Kovel, etc. In May, on the road between Kovel and Brest-Litovsk, a UPA detachment fatally wounded Victor Lutze, one of the principal leaders of the SA, in an ambush.

The Germans reacted. In the same month General Hintzler attempted in vain to annihilate the UPA units. Then SS General von dem Bach launched a series of raids in July against villages that were supposed to be strongholds of the nationalist troops. The fighting went on into 1944, when the German armies were in full retreat.

From then on the UPA had in effect to fight on two fronts. Moscow had quickly recognized that the growth of a nationalist army, while it contributed to the enfeeblement of the *Wehrmacht*, also represented a threat to the Soviet empire.

That was why detachments of Communist Partisans, shifted from White Russia in February 1943, under the command of General Kovpak, attempted to cross the western Ukraine in order to establish themselves in the Carpathians. This led to a series of clashes with UPA units.

Early in the summer of 1943 the UPA-North did battle with the Soviet Partisans under General Kedotov and Mikhailov. Kovpak's units, encircled in the Carpathians, were compelled to retreat.

The UPA and the OUN became the targets of both German and Soviet propaganda. German leaflet No. 43/7/G. 26, distributed in the Ukraine, declared:

[1] North: the province of Polisye and the northern part of Volhynia; South: the northern part of Bukhovina and the provinces of Kamenyetz-Podolskye and Vynnytsia; West: Galicia and the Carpathians; East: the sector northwest of Kiev.

Orders and secret directives that have fallen into our hands show that the Jews in the Kremlin are in contact with the OUN, which says it is fighting Bolshevism. . . . The OUN and Bolshevism are the same thing, and that is why they should be annihilated. . . .

Khrushchev, on the other side, in an appeal distributed from Kiev on June 12, 1944, accused the *banderovtzi* (Banderists) of being German agents:

Your enemies are not only the German bandits. Your enemies are also the bands of German-Ukrainian nationalists. They are all those *banderovtzi* who have sold out to Hitler and are helping him to subjugate our people, our Ukraine. . . . These mercenaries pretend to fight against the Germans . . . the Ukrainian nationalists are in reality accomplices of Hitler. They want to break the fraternal bonds that unite the Ukrainian and Russian peoples, to sever the Soviet Ukraine from the family of Soviet peoples. . . .[2]

The attitude of the Ukrainian nationalists in the face of such accusations was stated in the resolution adopted in the Third Congress of the OUN's leaders, which was held in secret from February 17 to 21, 1943. It was the intention of this resolution to express complete opposition to both German National Socialist and Russian Bolshevik imperialism:

In opposition to the reactionary and anti-popular aims of the Russian and German imperialists who, having launched the current war, continue to wage it at the cost of the sufferings and the lives of millions of human beings and who, under the cloak of lying phrases such as *the new Europe* or *the proletarian revolution,* are seeking to achieve the lasting subjugation of the peoples of all Europe, . . . we propose the idea of independent national states composed of all the European peoples within their ethnic borders, which is the most progressive idea of our epoch, the idea of order based on the principle of freedom for peoples and for man. . . .[3]

[2] For both these texts cf. *Les Problèmes actuels de l'est européen,* No. 13, January 1963.
[3] *Ibid.,* No. 12, December 1962.

This principle of peoples' struggle for their independence, of national states erected on ethnic foundations was one that the leaders of the OUN made every effort to translate into practice. They did so above all by trying to win over from the German army the foreign volunteers of Soviet origin whom the Germans were using in their battles against the Partisans. Beginning in 1943 the High Command of the UPA addressed a series of appeals to them as well as to the other national minorities mobilized into the Red Army: "To the Uzbeks, Kazakhs, Turkmens, Tadzhiks, Bashkirs, and Tartars . . ." (June 1943); "To the Armenians and other peoples of the Caucasus . . ." (in the same month); "To the Georgians . . ." (September). When the German retreat from the eastern front began in the summer of 1943, German, Italian, and Rumanian deserters joined the Ukrainians' ranks, though perhaps because they had been cut off from their units. In 1943–1944 the Ukrainian nationalists claimed that a thousand to fifteen hundred foreigners in all were serving in the ranks of the UPA—an obviously unverifiable figure.

The UPA and the OUN did not stop there. On November 21–22, 1943, they held a secret conference of oppressed peoples. It met in the forests of Zhitomir in the center of the Ukraine under the protection of UPA detachments. The deliberations were attended by thirty-nine delegates, including six Georgians, six Azerbaidzhanians, four Armenians, two White Russians, and so forth. The resolution adopted at the end of the conference reiterated the principles already laid down by the OUN: war on both fronts against both imperialisms.

The attempt to group the subjugated peoples into a third force against the two giants, carried out as it was with meager means, may seem presumptuous, except for the extent—which we do not know—to which the leaders of the OUN expected to receive support from the Western powers. Doomed to failure without such support, betrayed by the historical circumstances of the time, it was nevertheless founded on solid bases that are still valid.

The Germans' retreat from the Ukraine left the UPA at grips with the Soviet armies. At this time the UPA was a powerful guerrilla force, well organized, and abundantly supplied with war materials abandoned by the Germans: light and heavy machine guns, mortars, bazookas, etc.

Organized into battalions each of which comprised three or four companies, which were again subdivided into an equal number of platoons, the UPA was established on a territorial foundation. Each company was supposed to act in a specific operational area from which it seldom strayed. Living in forests, where camps and a number of underground shelters had been constructed, these units used the neighboring villages as bases of operations. Each village was itself organized under a clandestine leader, assisted by a deputy assigned to maintain supplies for the combat forces and by communications workers to assure contact with the men in the forests. The clandestine village organization imposed taxes on the population; requisitioned clothing, shoes, etc.; and saw to the fighting men's supplies of food and medicines.

The UPA also had a security and counterespionage branch with agents in the Soviet administration, police, and army. Its propaganda section issued a number of leaflets and periodicals: *I Shyns* (*Idea and Action*), the OUN's ideological magazine; *Somostynist* (*Independence*); *Za Ukrayinska Derzhova* (*For a Ukrainian Nation*); *Povstanats* (*The Insurgent*), the UPA's official newspaper, and even a humorous publication, *Peretz* (*Pepper*). In order to combat this satirical publication the Soviet authorities had to call on a Ukrainian humorist, Osta Vyshnya, who had been deported to Siberia in 1930 and who was now placed at the head of a Kiev publication called *Red Pepper*.

The UPA's technical section was in charge of the clandestine printing plants and radio broadcasting, the food stockpiles, the ammunition dumps, and the manufacture of explosives. The military-training division dealt with the difficult problem of officer training. It established schools for commissioned and noncommissioned officers and developed a 360-page *Practical Handbook of Guerrilla Warfare.*

Furthermore, the UPA was equipped with an exceptionally well-organized Red Cross service that recruited a large number of women and girls as nurses. In addition it had many underground hospitals.

Describing the discovery of one of these hospitals, *Glos Ludu,* a Polish newspaper, reported that corridors and operating rooms had been hollowed out at a depth of more than thirty feet below ground. Access from above was completely concealed. When it was discovered the hospital became a fortress. The doctors and nurses defended themselves until they had no more cartridges; they were killed where they stood or committed suicide. What the press reports today on the Viet Cong's underground installations had its predecessor in the Ukraine twenty years earlier. But these tragedies remained virtually unknown.

What was the exact strength of the UPA? The Ukrainian nationalists asserted that the number of fighting men exceeded two hundred thousand during the German occupation, a figure that seems exaggerated unless one also includes sympathizers. The Soviet authorities, on the other hand, have always clung to their ritual version of "handfuls of criminals," which is certainly ridiculous if one reflects that these "wrecks" were able to continue their armed resistance at least until 1950.

It would seem more reasonable to adopt the figure provided by a former NKVD officer, Yona Liron, a Polish Jew who emigrated to Israel in 1954. In an interview with Leo Heiman,[4] he spoke of three hundred thousand *fighters and sympathizers.* From this it may be deduced that the actual fighting forces of the UPA undoubtedly numbered several tens of thousands of men.

[4] "J'étais un expert soviétique de contre-insurrection," in *l'est européen,* No. 34, October 1964.

The UPA's field of activity was essentially limited to the western Ukraine—that is, a territory bounded by the Carpathians on the south, the Pripet on the north, the Bug on the west, and the Dnieper on the east.

In the central and eastern Ukraine, in contrast, it would appear that the UPA's activities, with the exception of a few groups operating in the regions of Kiev and Odessa, were very weak. The nationalists explain that the topography of the Ukraine, devoid of mountains and large forests except in the west, made it impossible for their men to operate as they did in Volhynia, Galicia, and the sub-Carpathian Ukraine. There is certainly some truth in this argument, but it is dubious whether this was the only reason for the UPA's weakness in that area. In the western Ukraine the nationalists' activities between the two wars had been able to expand on a large scale and to establish a solid popular base, under difficult conditions, it is true, but these were in no way comparable to the repression organized by the Soviet government. In addition, the nationalists in the west could rely on two other supports between the wars: the church and private property. In the Soviet Union the first had been reduced to a spectral existence and the second had been eliminated. The three years of German occupation and all their sequels could not have been enough to enable the nationalists to establish themselves firmly among the population of the Soviet zone and gain support as resolute as that in the west. The statistical table (below) of the operations carried out by the UPA [5] gives a clear picture of the areas of its strength and weakness.

[5] Table published in *The Ukrainian Insurgent Army in the Fight for Freedom,* pp. 44–45.

GUERRILLA OPERATIONS IN THE UKRAINE

(July 1, 1946–June 30, 1949)

A. *By Regions (in alphabetical order)*

Region	1946–47	1947–48	1948–49	Total
Brest-Litovsk	1	2	0	3
Chernigov	1	1	1	3
Chernivtzy	32	9	15	56
Drogobych	164	330	254	748
Kamenyetz-Podolsky	7	5	4	16
Kiev	1	0	2	3
Lvov	110	205	170	485
Rivne	87	61	41	189
Stanislavov	219	318	353	890
Ternopol	191	181	206	578
Trans-Carpathia	16	2	1	19
Volhynia	54	46	14	114
Zhitomir	29	45	12	86
TOTALS	912	1205	1073	3190

B. *Details of Operations*

	1946–47	1947–48	1948–49	Total
Defensive	464	694	532	1689
Offensive	136	118	82	336
Assassinations	117	91	112	320
Sabotage	109	175	231	515
Against kolkhozi	10	51	70	131
Propaganda action	76	76	47	199
TOTALS	912	1205	1073	3190

Victims of their own propaganda, the Soviets thought at first that they would have no trouble liquidating these "bands." In 1944 they believed that it would be enough to call on the Soviet Partisans trained in guerrilla warfare to liquidate these unimpressive adversaries.

They were completely mistaken. The Soviet Partisan battalions of three or four hundred men each were highly adept at attacks on the Germans' fixed lines of communication and installations. But this time they were called on to penetrate very deeply into the forests, engaging and destroying the UPA's mobile units there. Now the nationalists had the double advantage of perfect knowledge of the area and the support of the population. It was a total defeat. The Soviet command was compelled to use these troops for the defense of fixed points.

The guerrilla struggle was waged under conditions of extraordinary chaos. In the beginning of 1944 the SS had succeeded in recapturing Kovel, a pivot for the German troops in White Russia, the Ukraine, and Poland. While the armor swirled round Kovel in a titanic battle, the forests on both sides of the front resounded with the crackle of machine guns and the explosions of grenades: the Soviet Partisan units were fighting the UPA. But the UPA had also to defend itself against the Polish Partisan movement, the AC (Army of the People), which was pro-Communist, and against the AK (Army of the Interior), which was nationalist in tendency. In the beginning the AK cooperated with the Soviets against the Ukrainians but fought the AC.

The UPA was also at times obliged to battle the Ukrainian anarchist Partisans (the heirs of Makhno), who themselves were fighting the Soviets. Ultimately the Germans recruited ordinary criminals into bands of pseudo-partisans who engaged in a campaign of extortion in order to discredit the UPA.

In this period a UPA-North detachment had scored a spectacular success on January 29, 1944, in a clash on the Koretz-Rovno road, mortally wounding the famous General Vatutin, who had defended Voronezh, taken part in the battles of Stalingrad and Kursk, and commanded the first Ukrainian front. As it entered a village Vatutin's column was caught in an ambush. He got out of his car to join in the fighting against the guerrillas, who were attacking from all sides, and a bullet caught him in the kidney. His troops managed to get him away and to effect a withdrawal. But Vatutin died of his wounds in a hospital. The announcement that the UPA was responsible for his death was greeted with skepticism in the West. It was necessary to wait twenty years for Moscow to confirm the accuracy of the story. In the April 5, 1964, issue of the magazine, *Ogonyok*, General Krainyukov reported the circumstances of the fight, which differed only on minor points from the Ukrainian version.[6]

In order to put an end to the UPA the Russians were compelled to call on NKVD units. A broad offensive directed by Khrushchev and led by General Ryasny was launched in the autumn of 1945. At the same time the Soviet authorities proclaimed an amnesty. A second campaign was initiated in December 1945 and pursued into June of the next year. Armed engagements were of course accompanied by encirclements of villages and deportations. Nor did the Soviets hesitate to resort to other methods, it was said, such as infiltrating the bacilli of various diseases into the medicaments sent to the insurgents.

The attack compelled the UPA units to fall back into the Carpathians. In addition to its offensive and defensive battles, its assassinations, and its sabotage activities, the UPA was waging a political fight at the same time: It urged the villagers to boycott the elections, distributed leaflets and oral slogans, and organized armed raids on official meetings.

The UPA units were also endeavoring to sabotage collectivization: They attacked tractor stations and burned kolkhozi. While physical destruction was necessarily restricted, the raids on the kolkhozi nevertheless represented a political threat to Moscow: collectivization, in fact, was eliminating one of the principal operational bases for armed resistance, the individual farm. Hence it was essential to guarantee the safety of the

[6] The UPA's communiqué spoke of an attack on an armored column. The Russians, on the contrary, say today that Vatutin was traveling with only a small escort.

kolkhozi and their offices. Therefore the guards of the kolkhozi were substantially reinforced beginning in 1947. It became more and more difficult for the UPA to attack them.

For a guerrilla force that cannot count on receiving help from without and that is confronted with an enemy who can constantly increase his means of pressure, there is no other resort than dispersal. Hence the UPA was compelled to fragment its troops in order to minimize the enemy's opportunities.

But it was also striving to expand its theater of action to all the areas in which it hoped to obtain collaboration: in other words, especially to Poland (where it could find support among the Ukrainian minority in the southeast) and Slovakia. Furthermore, the Polish nationalists who had bitterly battled the UPA might become allies now that they were being hunted down by the Communist government.

The UPA's action took the form of raids by mobile columns in the direction of Poland and Slovakia. In June 1946 a UPA column penetrated into the interior of Slovakia, where it was favorably received by the population. Even some of the Slovak contingents sent out to repel it fraternized with it.

In the autumn the UPA-North, under the command of Colonel Eney, launched a raid from Volhynia that covered 250 miles into the Kiev region with 21 clashes along the way. This column had been broken up into small squads that advanced separately, making night marches of thirty to forty-five miles.

In the spring of 1947 the UPA-South, under the command of Major Khmara, repeated the exploit, but this time in the direction of Odessa, which it reached after a march of more than six hundred miles across Bukhovina, Moldavia, and Bessarabia. It managed to establish contact with local insurgent groups, destroying kolkhoz silos along its path and distributing the grain to the people.

In Poland accords were signed with the clandestine organization called WIN (Freedom and Independence) and the NSZ (Central Poland). During a raid that got as far as Breslau, other accords were concluded with the national organization, WRN.[7]

In 1947 another operation under the command of Captain R. Prirva carried UPA detachments into East Prussia and enabled them to make contact with the clandestine Lithuanian organizations. On March 29, 1947, an ambush near Boligrad brought about the death of General Swerkewski, a Polish Communist.

Continually shifting its theater of action, taking advantage of the favorable geographical situation created by the Carpathian forests and mountain ranges, enjoying the support of the local populations, crossing and re-crossing borders in such a way as to throw off pursuers, the UPA had succeeded in prolonging the life of a campaign that had seemed doomed to speedy destruction. For the whole world persisted in drawing a cloak of silence over the heroic battles of these men. The Western governments had found themselves compelled indeed to alter their views on Stalin's devotion to democracy. The Cold War was under way. Yet there was never a thought of furnishing material assistance to the UPA, or even of giving it

[7] On the scope of the resistance carried on in Poland it would be enough to quote Pierre Courtade's article of June 30, 1956, in *l'Humanité:* ". . . Let us say merely that the workers' party lost thirty thousand of its people in this struggle against the White Guards." But the study by Polish Communist Ignace Blum, *Contribution de l'armée polonaise à la défense des intérêts nationaux et sociaux du peuple polonais et à la consolidation du pouvoir populaire dans les années 1944–8,* published by the Polish Academy of Sciences (Warsaw, 1959, pp. 241–265), provides more detailed information. It appears from this study that some fifteen illegal organizations took part in resistance between 1945 and 1948. Between May and October 1946, for example, 5458 attacks of a political nature were recorded. Between June 1945 and April 1948, according to this source, the army recorded thirteen hundred persons killed and a thousand seriously wounded. The security corps of the Ministry of the Interior, which began operations in February 1946, registered approximately three thousand killed and two thousand wounded. Among the opposition the toll amounted to seventy-five hundred killed and approximately two thousand wounded. The famous Polish film *Ashes and Diamonds,* moreover, corroborates both the extent and the bitterness of this conflict.

moral support. It is possible, however, that the leaders of the
UPA and the OUN had based their hopes on the imminent
likelihood of a Third World War. For them it was a question
of holding on.

But the combat conditions were growing steadily more rigorous. On May 12, 1947, the governments of the Soviet Union,
Poland, and Czechoslovakia concluded an assistance treaty
directed against the rebels. Furthermore, the Polish government decided to create a vacuum for the UPA by deporting
the Ukrainian population from southeastern Poland. Since not
all the fish could be caught, it was necessary to drain off the
water in which they swam.

The population of Polish origin that was concentrated in the
theater of operations bounded by the villages of Krasno,
Sanok, and Lisko, and the Dukla Pass on the Czech border was
evacuated to the west and settled along the Oder-Neisse line
in the territory taken from the Germans. The evacuated villages were burned and the crops were destroyed.

Village by village, the inhabitants of Ukrainian origin were
deported to central Asia or Siberia. Those who did not report
to the assembly points or who managed to slip through the
encircling troops were regarded as bandits.

The UPA was able to score a few tactical successes by destroying communications lines and attacking convoys in order
to free its compatriots, as well as the prisons and camps in
which they were quartered. These were transitory victories
that could not overcome a procedure backed by all the power
of the state.

Thus the UPA lost a base that was essential to its survival.
"Because of this scorched-earth policy," Ion Lira asserted,
"the Krasno-Sanok-Liso triangle in southeastern Poland is like
an uninhabited desert even today, eighteen years after the
event." [8]

And yet in this desert, deprived of the support of the popu-

[8] *Op. cit.*

lation, of food, of weapons supplies, and decimated by typhus, hunger, and cold, UPA units performed the miracle of holding out for two years more. In the clearings of the forests the men nursed meager farm patches and attacked the Polish army's supply depots. By the end of 1947 these groups had been all but annihilated.

Only a few handfuls of guerrillas still held out in the mountains. They burrowed into bunkers carved out twelve to thirty feet below the surface. Their resistance had literally gone underground. NKVD troops made every effort to locate these shelters and flush out the occupants. From time to time men emerged from these holes, their faces hollowed by privation and pale for lack of sun; they moved silently through the forest, struck a swift blow at a kolkhoz, a tractor station, or a granary, and raced back to their lairs.

These incidents continued for almost three more years. On March 24, 1950, the Tass agency was at last able to distribute a victory announcement: An MVD unit had discovered the underground bunker in which Tarass Shuprynka, the commander of the UPA, and his staff were hidden. Finally trapped, they were destroyed.

Shuprynka (whose real name was Shukevich) was born to a comfortable western Ukrainian family in 1907. In his early youth he became a member of the OUN and took part in the assassinations in Poland; then, in 1938, he helped to organize the national army of the sub-Carpathian Ukraine. Entering the Ukraine proper with the Germans, he soon went over to the underground. As commander of the UPA, he had spent years in a merciless combat that has virtually no equivalent in the history of guerrilla warfare.

No details as to his end are available. Thirteen years later, in a book published in Kiev in 1963, *Des ruines de la guerre à la paix stable,* Leshchenko, a Soviet writer, said only:

In March 1950, in a hiding place near Lvov (to be precise, at Biloshorchi), Tarass Shuprynka, the principal leader of the nation-

alists and known as the "commander in chief" of the UPA, was discovered and liquidated with his entire bodyguard. In this inglorious
fashion an end was made to one of the greatest postwar adventures
of international imperialism directed against the Soviet Ukraine and
the neighboring people's democracies.

Thus, deep in a bunker amid the bursts of grenades and the
crackle of machine-gun fire, the life of the commander in chief
of the UPA came to an end. It is believed that even afterward
a few fighters still carried on the struggle. It was a struggle
without quarter. During the last months of 1944 alone, Lira
estimated, sixty thousand Soviet soldiers under the command
of Moskalenko (who was later to become an expert in rock-
etry) killed fifteen thousand nationalist "bandits" in five weeks.
"Our military hospitals were full," Lira wrote. "General Moskalenko himself was wounded in an ambush mounted by the
UPA, and a number of officers was incapacitated." [9]
Lira calculated that altogether the losses suffered by the
Ukrainian nationalists—including combat deaths, executions,
imprisonments, and deportations—amounted to a million men.

While the UPA's forces were giving battle in the forests of
Volhynia and the Carpathian mountains, Lithuanian guerrillas in other forests in northern Europe were mounting an
equally fierce resistance to the Soviet occupant. This armed
conflict had begun during the German occupation.
A number of organizations, the largest of which seems to
have been the LFA (Lithuanian Army of Liberation), were
operating in the forests in which they were hiding, living in
carefully camouflaged tents. Their officer staffs as a rule were
concealed in underground shelters on farms.
In part these forces' operations were based on the resistance
experience that they had gained earlier under the first Soviet
occupation and then under German occupation, and in addition on the conviction that after Hitler's death an Anglo-Amer-

[9] *Op. cit.*

ican-German coalition would drive out the Russians. For some years the guerrilla leaders persisted in the hope that the Cold War would degenerate into the Third World War.

These units were as well armed as those of the UPA. But, in contrast to the UPA, they usually avoided combat with the Red Army. Principally they attacked the NKVD, the officials of local soviets or kolkhozi or government, and persons collaborating with the Soviets. In addition they made every effort to assure the safety of the population.

As perilous as their activities were—on the average a militant combatant's career did not last more than two years— their ranks were continually sustained by the enlistments of new volunteers, victims of the Soviet system or under its suspicions. In addition the forest fighters enjoyed widespread support among the clergy, Lithuania being an essentially Catholic country. Certain priests served as chaplains in the guerrilla forces, and the fighting men took an oath that was religious in its nature.

The leaders of the movement came in large measure from the Lithuanian intelligentsia, which the Russians were systematically eliminating. A great number of reserve officers in particular, who had fought earlier against the German occupation, continued to serve as resistance leaders.

The Russians had expected to encounter difficulties in imposing their system. That was why the Kremlin had appointed Suslov, who had commanded Soviet Partisan groups during the war, to take over the party and administrative "apparatus" in Lithuania. The Russians' initial intention was to annihilate the resistance movement before going on to collectivization. They were unable to do so. Hence they decided to proceed with collectivization in order to deprive the guerrillas of their chief bases of operations: individual farms.

The leadership of the repression was entrusted to Kruglov, who would later succeed Beria. Arriving in September 1944, Kruglov created within the NKVD in Lithuania a special department assigned to combat "banditry," organized a local militia, endeavored to infiltrate his agents into resistance groups, and directed the publication of forged editions of underground newspapers that supposedly had been issued by the resistance. Searches on farms and dragnet raids in forests became frequent.

In *Guerrilla Warfare on the Amber Coast,* which tells the story of the LFA's campaign, there is a description of one of these searches, the purpose of which was to detect the site of a subterranean shelter. With long pikes the NKVD men probed ceilings, walls, and floors. Four or five breathless men in the hideout waited fearfully for the end of this exploration. When they saw the pikes drive through the ceiling just above their heads, they blew themselves up with anti-tank grenades.

By the end of 1945 Kruglov's campaign, backed up by offers of amnesty, had obtained certain successes. Nevertheless the clandestine struggle had not been abandoned. Other operations were initiated, and they persisted until the middle of 1949.

The guerrillas concentrated their attacks on the establishment of kolkhozi, the settlement of Russian colonists, and deportations. In this campaign the Lithuanians were able to gain some tactical victories. In the long run, given the fact that they received no help from outside, their defeat was inevitable.

At the end of 1947 there were only twenty kolkhozi in Lithuania. At the end of the next year there were five hundred. By the beginning of 1950 collective farms represented 65 per cent of the total.

Some groups, however, went on fighting until 1952.[10] The range of the struggle is sufficiently shown by the extent of the losses. According to nationalist sources, some thirty thousand guerrillas were killed.

Beginning in 1946 some guerrillas, rather than submit to capture, killed themselves with grenades that they exploded

[10] Guerrilla groups functioned also in Latvia and Estonia, waging the same bold campaign. Just as in Lithuania, collectivization led to the diminution of their forces.

at face level. This prevented identification of their bodies, and thus the NKVD could not take reprisals against their families. They disappeared without a trace, unknown to the police and to the West as well. The vast majority of the Western public is still ignorant of the sacrifices made by the fighters in the forests.

FOUR

(22)

THE LAST YEARS
OF A TYRANT

EFORE EVERY audience in the Kremlin there
was a telephone call from Pavlov, the interpreter. How many persons were in the group? What
was the identity of each? What were the makes
and license numbers of the cars? What were the drivers'
names?

On the scheduled day the cars started out, along a specified
route that had already been cleared for them. About 150 feet
from the entrance to the Kremlin a car was waiting. It led
the procession to the Baranovsky Gate, the southeastern entrance to the Kremlin.

Foreign visitors of note were always passed through this
gate. As soon as they crossed the threshold a photoelectric cell
set off a bell. It continued ringing as an MVD major wearing
a white-bordered cap led his officers quickly out of their sentry posts beneath the arches. The drivers' papers were checked
and the interiors of the cars were examined.

If there was nothing suspicious, the bell was silenced. The
cars rolled along the silent, empty driveways of the Kremlin.
They crossed the east wing and the Red Square, passed the

Kommandatura, the central headquarters of the guards, and stopped outside the Kazakov Palace.

In the entrance hall a colonel and other MVD officers who were waiting for the visitors escorted them to the elevator. It rose two floors. There were vast corridors filled with the heavy aroma of *mashorka* (Russian tobacco). In every niche a guard was posted. There was absolute silence.

Now the massive leather-covered doors to the antechamber opened. This was the post of the final guard, commanded by a general. It was whispered that, when the master's intimates, the all-powerful lords of the Politburo, were received, they had to submit to a formality reserved as a rule for suspects and criminals: They raised their arms and the guards ran their hands over the visitors' bodies to make sure that they were carrying no weapons. These humiliations were confined to comrades, and of course they were not imposed on a foreign chief of state.

Finally the guards opened the last door, which led into a paneled room. At the very end an old gentleman, soberly dressed in a gray tunic whose only ornament was the gold star of a Hero of the Soviet Union at the throat, was sitting at a desk.

Marshal Stalin rose and went forward to welcome his guests, who were often surprised at his short stature. His coarse dark hair was thinning and turning gray. His unhealthy skin, usually powdered in order to conceal the scars of smallpox, was deeply lined. Four years of a terrible war had left their mark on this face in which the long, prominent nose of the Georgians seemed all the more conspicuous because of Stalin's habit of squinting.

He bowed to his guests. His handshake was firm. His smile revealed his bad yellow teeth. He was cordial and courteous, unless he was planning some calculated offense to his guest. When Field Marshal Viscount Montgomery brought him as gifts two of his own books and a case of whisky, Stalin cut him short before he had even finished his greeting: "Yes? What do you want from me?" As his mood changed he could switch instantaneously from affability to arrogance.

Stalin seated himself facing his visitors at a long green-covered table beneath portraits of Suvorov and Kutuzov. Drawing on his pipe, he spoke in a slow, low voice, monotonous in its rhythm and marked by a strong Georgian accent that he had never been able to conquer. Russians found this accent rather ludicrous, and in music halls it was imitated in jest, as the Brooklyn accent is in the United States. Quite possibly Stalin was wounded by this when, as he rose to speak in party congresses, he saw faces trying to repress the hated condescending smiles. But those who laughed at the secretary general were dead men.

And those who survived were more apprehensive than ironic when Stalin and his fellow-Georgian, Beria, began to converse in their native tongue during meetings of the Politburo. What were the master and his chief thug cooking up?

Obviously Stalin's guests did not think in terms of such questions. More than one person who met him in the Kremlin or in the conferences in Yalta or Teheran allowed himself to be taken in by his good-fellow mask. Roosevelt viewed him as a fine democrat who must first of all be reassured in order to make it possible for him to acquire polish. "I would gladly entrust him with the upbringing of my children," Roosevelt confided to one of his biographers, Emil Ludwig. Former Ambassador Joseph Davies—who was convinced of the genuineness of the confessions in the Moscow trials—painted a picture of the dictator that would bring tears to the eyes:

A child would like to sit on his lap, a dog to crouch at his feet. Imagine a man who would be the exact opposite of the idea of him that a fanatical anti-Stalinist has, and you have Josef Stalin.

A Parisian reporter once saw Stalin in his box at the Moscow Opera with the other members of the Politburo. This glimpse was an illumination:

He had taken his place among his comrades of the Presidium, in the second row, at the back—really. He literally frolicked, and very cordially in the midst of his peers. I am choosing my words very carefully: He was not the tyrant.

When these lines were written, the "doctors' plot" was on the drawing board, and behind their smiles Stalin's peers undoubtedly had only one question in their minds: Who among them would be the first to feel the jolly scalpel?

Stalin trusted no one, except his secretary, Poskrebyshev, and everyone feared Stalin. When the telephone rang with a summons to the Kremlin or the country house, no one ever knew what fate was awaiting him. "It has happened," Bulganin told Khrushchev one day, "that a man has had a friendly invitation to Stalin's and gone from him to the Lyubyanka." Such confidences were made when the two men were sharing a car safe from microphones.

In his memoirs de Gaulle painted an impressive picture of a banquet given in his honor in December 1944, before the signature of the French-Soviet treaty, in a dining room in the Kremlin. Sparkling with silver, the table was crowded with food. Stalin was the first to pay tribute to it, gobbling everything with a ferocious appetite and pouring himself generous glasses of Crimean wine. As usual, he made jokes, his mocking remarks lashed with down-to-earth common sense. His retainers watched him closely, tense and deferential, alert to the slightest cue.

Then came the time for toasts. Stalin raised his glass in honor of Molotov, Beria, Malenkov, the generals and high officials present. In a few words he sang the praises of each. Here is de Gaulle's account:

He cried to the artillery commander, for example: "Voronov! Your health! Yours is the job of executing the strategy of our big guns on the battlefield. It was thanks to this strategy that the enemy was smashed in breadth and depth. Fire away! Go to it with your guns!" He turned to the Chief of Naval Operations. "Admiral Kuznetzov! Not enough is known of what our fleet is doing. Patience! One day we will rule the seas!"

After each toast, he shouted: "Come here!" to the man whom he had toasted, and they clinked glasses. But sometimes there was a hint of menace in the compliments. Stalin addressed Novikov, the air force Chief of Staff: "You're the one who uses our planes. If you use them badly, you know what to expect." One wonders whether another of the guests, whom de Gaulle did not identify, was very reassured when Stalin pointed to him and shouted: "It's his job to get men and munitions up to the front. He had better try to do it right! Otherwise he will be hanged, as is the custom in this country." [1]

Of all the dictator's close associates it was Molotov who still maintained a certain familiarity with Stalin. Yet, when de Gaulle refused to recognize the Polish Committee of Lublin [2] at the end of the banquet and left the room, "Molotov rushed up. Pale, he accompanied me to my car. . . . He stammered a few syllables, unable to conceal his dismay." When Molotov went back to the banquet, Stalin greeted him with a snicker: "They took you in." It was a bad mark for Molotov that might be exploited by his rivals if the treaty was not signed that night. Everyone resumed eating and drinking. Later, after de Gaulle had returned and the treaty had been signed, it was the subject of further toasts. When all the farewells had been made, Stalin turned to the interpreter who had been present at all the negotiations: "You—you know too much. I have a good mind to send you to Siberia." A threat? A heavy-handed joke? At this point the Frenchmen left. "Stalin," according to de Gaulle, who had looked back as he was leaving, "had begun to eat again."

Other persons had observed the same vacillation between

[1] *Mémoires de guerre*, Vol. III, *Le Salut*, pp. 74–75.
[2] Established by the Polish Communists.

familiarity and curtness in his behavior, and without the discretion enforced by the presence of foreign leaders. After Tito's first talk with Stalin in 1944, Dimitrov gave him a warning. "Walter, Walter," he said, using Tito's underground alias, "the *Hazyazhin* (boss) is in a towering rage at you: that telegram made him hopping mad." The telegram was one that Tito had sent during the war: "If you cannot give us any help, at least don't put obstacles in our way." Stalin's reaction can be imagined. His generals bowed to his orders without raising an eyebrow and swallowed all the master's moods. And this insignificant Walter, barely the head of a gang, sent him messages in such a tone! [3]

Worse still, in his first meeting with Stalin Tito took the liberty of contradicting him. "Careful, Walter," the *Hazyazhin* had warned: "the bourgeoisie is very strong in Siberia." Tito replied: "I don't agree with you on that, Comrade Stalin. It is very weak."

Silence and stupefaction followed. Molotov, Zhdanov, Malenkov, Beria could not conceal their fright.

In the spring of 1946, when Stalin and the Yugoslavs were discussing the status of mixed societies, Stalin suddenly turned to Tito, Kardelj, and the other Yugoslav delegates and asked: "What are you doing tonight?"

"We have made no plans, Comrade Stalin."

"Very well! We'll go and have a bite in my house in the country." Stalin called one of his secretaries, in a colonel's uniform, and ordered cars. The colonel went out. There was some exchange of banter in the next few minutes, and then Stalin rang for the colonel: "What about those cars?"

They were not yet ready, the colonel spluttered. And the storm broke. Dedijer, one of the Yugoslav delegates, was to remember this outburst by Stalin. The *Hazyazhin* howled, his face was distorted by his anger, his hands made motions of

[3] Tito was to hear him telephone to Malinovsky: "You're asleep in your corner. You're asleep. You say you have no tanks. My grandmother didn't need tanks to fight. It's time you got moving. Understand?"

smashing something, and the room rang with his insults. The colonel had gone white.

Later, when they were eating, Stalin's mood was somewhat more serene. He made summary judgments on the foreign comrades: Togliatti was an intellectual incapable of rousing the people. Thorez and Duclos were all right, but Stalin indicated one grave flaw in Thorez: "A dog that doesn't bite shows his teeth when he wants to frighten someone, but Thorez can't do even that." La Pasionaria could not control herself. As for Pieck, he was in his dotage, or on the verge of it.

The meal ended·in a pleasant atmosphere. Stalin rose, selected some records of old Russian folk songs, and placed them on the machine. Suddenly he began to dance, and the courtiers' chorus went up from all sides: "What strength, Comrade Stalin!"

"Not for much longer," Stalin said.

"We need you," the chorus responded. "You still have a long life ahead of you."

Even then he must have been haunted by the thought of dying, by the crushing feeling that his vigor and his faculties were declining. Suddenly he grabbed Tito under the armpits and lifted him into the air three times in succession. The chorus was in raptures. The records were still playing.

These brotherly love feasts, however, were darkened by a mysterious uneasiness. The gaiety was factitious. One never quite knew how to take the master's compliments. At one point he recalled that Churchill had spoken very well of Tito to him: "I said: 'If you say so, it must be true.'" A dubious compliment: Did the Soviet potentate really find it praiseworthy that Comrade Tito should enjoy the esteem of the chief of an imperialist state?

What distinguished the victorious marshal, bending a vast empire beneath his yoke, from his prewar self? Irritable hypersensitivity, accesses of anger, distrust, contempt for others, brutality toward his associates, a propensity toward trickery and deceit when he knew that he had to manipulate something or someone, the vanity that is undoubtedly the mask of an inferiority complex—all these traits had already shown themselves. But his years and the rapidity with which he had aged, probably as a result of the tremendous tensions of the war, had intensified them to the extreme. His distrust turned into that pathological obsession that Khrushchev emphasized in his report. The cult of the superman assumed colossal proportions. In the beginning, perhaps, he had lent himself for political purposes to the delirious praises of his genius; in the end he had undoubtedly become their complete victim. It was said that toward the end of his life he would often stop in front of the statues of himself that peopled the Kremlin and that he would be lost in dreams before his own image.

The West was dreaming too—of a *détente* that would be impossible without immediate shock to the system on which Stalin relied. And it was not only the Allies who fed on dreams. In order to be certain of victory Stalin had had to relax the grip of the system to some extent and to encourage certain hopes. The peasants thought that the end of the war would be the end of the kolkhoz as well. Millions of repatriates, returned to the Soviet Union by choice or by force, took with them their dangerous exposure to life in the West. In the heart of Moscow thousands of Jews one day hailed the ambassador of Israel. Marshals and generals, perhaps inflamed by their victories, might be secretly nursing ambitions. For all that the leaders of the satellite countries had been brought into line, this Tito who stood up to the boss was setting a revolting example for them. The peoples of central Europe were longing for free elections. In the Ukraine, the Baltic countries, and the Caucasus the embers of rebellion were burning. And in the Stalinist universe, which ran now from the Elbe to the Pacific, millions of men and women who had known the ordeals and horrors of the war were yearning for prosperity and the amenities of a less harsh rule.

All these people were threats to the absolute power of Stalin the victorious.

It was true that, once the destruction of the war had been repaired, thought could be given to improving the scale of living, and, after all, credits from the capitalist countries would be of considerable help. But the choice to be made was very like that of 1929 on the eve of industrialization: build up heavy industry or consumer industry? Stalin opted for the first. On February 9, 1946, he laid down the economic program of the Soviet Union:

It is the intention of our party to set in motion a new and powerful advance in our national economy that will make it possible to increase its level to three times what it was before the war. Our industry must produce fifty million tons of cast iron a year, sixty million tons of steel, five hundred million tons of coal, and sixty million tons of petroleum. Only when we have succeeded in doing this can we be sure that our country will be armed against every contingency.

Hence new sacrifices were required to place the Soviet Union in a position to defend itself against the imperialist countries and enable it to resist "encirclement." And the system would be more monolithic than ever.

Dictatorship was more necessary than ever for the assurance of this effort and the compulsion of a wearied population. Vigilance at home and abroad was required. At home a number of problems remained to be resolved. Dedijer reported [4] that the national-minority and peasant problems were perpetual headaches to the men in the Kremlin. During the first session of the Kominform, Malenkov presented a report on the preparations for the forthcoming party congress. This was in 1947. But the congress was not held until 1952, only a few months before Stalin's death. That the preparations required so much time attests either to Stalin's unqualified contempt for palavers in which he saw no point or to a deep-rooted disquiet.

[4] Cf. *Tito parle.*

Where were the major points of tension? First of all among the national minorities, which had been profoundly agitated by the war. The Soviet press was unremitting in its denunciations of bourgeois nationalism and in its exaltation of the progressive parts played by Russian scholars, artists, and writers.

The peasants stubbornly resisted the kolkhoz system and farm production was consistently insufficient. It was in order to resolve the difference between the city and the rural areas that Khrushchev proposed the solution of "agrovilles," which would make it possible to exercise closer party control over the peasants. But this effort proved abortive.

Dissensions and conflicts of interest appeared in the class that was now the chief foundation of the system—that is, the technical and administrative intelligentsia. Beginning in the 1930s industrialization had led to a rapid increase in the number of technicians and specialists. Even before the war their proportion in the ranks of the party was increasing to the detriment of the proletarian elements.

The backbone members of the apparatus of the state up through the important levels, directors of trusts and factories, were of course members of the Communist party. But side by side with them there existed a purely ideological party apparatus that exercised a controlling function on the administrative and industrial functionaries. It could not be denied that this led to many frictions that were often echoed in the Soviet press. Sometimes the party apparatus was accused of meddling too intimately in the machinery of government and industry; sometimes it was accused of insufficient vigilance and inadequacy in its task. Frequently, too, there were denunciations of a climate of "clubbiness," as well as family ties that fostered the burgeoning of little feudal baronies. Criticism of the functionaries was especially sharp in the months that preceded the Nineteenth Congress—a premonitory sign of a coming purge.

Just before the Nineteenth Congress opened, carefully

phrased newspaper accounts revealed that the machinery was creaking. In September 1952 *Izvestia* observed that local and regional party leaders were hesitant to criticize the economic officials either because the latter were well connected in high places or because there were material advantages in silence. On September 26 *Pravda* accused the functionaries of having tolerated "deception of the party and prejudice to the general interests of the state on the part of the directors of industrial and commercial enterprises." Almost identical charges had already appeared in both newspapers as early as 1950.

Did these tensions in the upper levels of the system lead to major rivalries among Stalin's lieutenants? Such was the thesis propounded by one of the greatest experts on Soviet matters, Boris Nikolayevsky. As he saw it, Malenkov was relying on a politicalized technocracy, the numerical size of which was constantly growing. The party's ideologists, whose number was smaller but who held more important posts in the party's hierarchy, felt threatened by this increase. The postwar period was a time of bitter conflict between these two groups: the administrators and technicians of whom Malenkov was the field commander and the *apparachiki* properly so-called, the champions of absolute control in all sectors of the state, whose particular stars were Zhdanov, Voznessensky, Kuznetzov, Rodyonov, and Popkov. This group, according to Nikolayevsky, was smashed by Malenkov, who set in motion a rigorous purge in Leningrad after Zhdanov's death.[5] But, just before the Nineteenth Congress, the *apparachiki* counterattacked with Stalin's support.

In this area we are still restricted to hypotheses, but it is probable that Stalin's increasing age had led to a savage struggle among his possible successors. Such competition was in no way incompatible with the despotic authority of the master of

[5] Khrushchev frequently mentioned the Leningrad purge in his attacks on Malenkov. But no clarification was ever furnished on this matter, the aspects of which are still a mystery. It is not certain that the purge of Voznessensky, who was shot on orders from Stalin, had any connection with the Leningrad business.

the Kremlin. Stalin himself was to encourage it in order to create dissension among those who directly assisted him and to prevent any one of them from acquiring too much power.

The absolute submission that his subordinates practiced in his presence, furthermore, was in no way symptomatic of a passivity that would swiftly have assured their dismissal. Hence each was led to take initiatives in his own area, to compete with the others, prepared to accept the consequences if Stalin intervened. Thus an article by Khrushchev on the agrovilles would be followed by a note in *Pravda* next day pointing out that it had been published only for purposes of discussion. The note had been written by Stalin himself, who had missed Khrushchev's article and flown into a towering rage.

The rivalries among Stalin's lieutenants are still matters of controversy today. Many observers, like Nikolayevsky, make much of a fierce conflict between Zhdanov and Malenkov. As evidence they cite the fact that Zhdanov presided over the first meeting of the Kominform, while, according to some of them, Malenkov's supposed absence from the meeting bore witness to his effacement at this time.

In actuality Malenkov was present at the meeting. It is true that it was dominated by Zhdanov, who led the discussion and drew the conclusions. It is certain too that Malenkov played only a very subordinate part in it. But the report that he submitted dealt with the situation in the Soviet Union and the problems posed by the organization of the party. This does not support argument as to the relative strength of the two men. It is possible that their respective parts represented a mere division of labor.

Regardless of the competition within the closed circle, it certainly did not threaten the absolutism of Stalin's power. Everything changed perhaps not with the "doctors' plot" but with the Nineteenth Congress; more precisely, with the transformation of the Politburo into the Presidium and the reinforcement of the Secretariat.

We have seen how, after the early years of the Bolshevik government, *de facto* power moved from the Central Committee to a body that was at first provisional, the Politburo. Now the decisions of the Nineteenth Congress led not only to the change of name from Politburo to Presidium but also to radical alterations in its composition. The Politburo of 1946 with eleven members and four alternates became the Presidium with twenty-five members and eleven alternates. At the same time the Secretariat was bolstered. It rose to ten members—Stalin, Aristov, Khrushchev, Malenkov, Mikhailov, Ponomarenko, Suslov, Brezhnev, Pegov, and Puzanov.

The meaning of these changes could not have escaped the old guard in the Kremlin, wise in the secrets of the "apparatus." With its twenty-five members the Presidium was an overly weighty body in which, to boot, the veterans were swamped in the flood of new men who belonged to another generation. On the other hand the Secretariat of the Central Committee was strengthened, and in that body Stalin retained only two members of the late Politburo: Khrushchev and Malenkov.

The conclusion to be drawn from these manipulations was clear: Stalin intended to base himself on a younger team, the more docile because it was obligated to him for its rise. And this was not a matter of a mere change in personnel. Other signs showed that a purge was under way.

The changes of the Nineteenth Congress in fact coincided with a violent "anti-Zionist" campaign, of which the most dramatic indication at that time the Slansky trial in Czechoslovakia. In the Soviet Union itself various trials had been organized in order to put an end to economic offenses. Jews were well represented in the prisoners' dock. The press intensified its attacks on the "economic" leaders—in other words, the administrative apparatus and the technical intelligentsia.

Other measures tended in a direction that made the members of the former Politburo uneasy: Kosygin, a technician, had been downgraded; Molotov's wife, elected an alternate to the Central Committee in 1939, had not been reelected. And for good reason: Stalin had sent her, like Kaganovich's brother, to Siberia. Both, as it happened, were Jewish.

Was this the start of a new *Yezhovchina?* All doubts were eliminated when it was announced on January 13 that a group of "murderous" doctors had been discovered in the Kremlin. Two days later the press identified some of them as Professors Vinogradov, Kagan, and Yegorov, who, "as has now been established," had been "the agents of the British spy services for many years." Among other things they were accused of having acted on behalf of a Jewish relief organization, the Joint Distribution Committee, which was described as Zionist, and of having treacherously murdered Zhdanov and Shterbakhov. Naturally they had confessed their crimes.[6]

This "doctors' plot" seems to have been the exact replica of the accusations lodged against the physicians indicted with Yagoda for identical "crimes." It was undoubtedly the signal for a tremendous purge that would reach into the highest spheres. A Tass dispatch eliminated any doubt on that question:

The state security agencies had not unmasked this terrorist organization of doctors in time. These agencies, however, should have been exceptionally vigilant, history having already afforded instances of murderers and traitors acting in the guise of physicians, as for example Drs. Levin and Pletnev.

At this time the Ministry of the Interior was divided into three branches: the MVD (Interior), directed by Kruglov, a member of the Central Committee; MGB (State Security), directed by Abakumov, who was appointed by the Eighteenth Congress but who after the Nineteenth no longer appeared

[6] The precise date of the doctors' arrests is not known. In retrospect, however, it can be presumed to have been December 2, 1952. On that day, in fact, Vinogradov was listed among the participants in the fourth annual conference of the Partisans of Peace, which was held in Moscow. In the Slansky trial earlier a Czech physician had been accused of an attempt to assassinate President Gottwald.

among the members or alternates of the Central Committee; and the State Control, headed by Merkulov, a member of the Central Committee after the Eighteenth Congress and reduced to the rank of alternate after the Nineteenth.

Thus two of Beria's three deputies had been apprised of their falls from grace. The state security agencies were therefore accused of lack of vigilance at the very time when *Pravda* was warning that "the disguised enemies, assisted by the imperialist world, *will also continue their miserable work in the future.*" (Italics added.)

New conspiracies meant new purges. Under the logic of the system it was impossible to entrust them to officials of the apparatus of repression who had been inadequate to their tasks. And what of the man who was above them all, Beria? would he be able to retain the master's favor?

Beria and his acolytes could not have failed to put these questions to themselves. Neither Molotov nor Kaganovich could feel especially safe when the one thought of his wife's fate, the other of his brother's. Malenkov had every reason to fear that the purge already initiated in the economic apparatus would extend to him.

But on March 6, 1953, the world learned that Stalin was dead.

The news was broadcast by Radio Moscow at 3:07 A.M., Moscow time. Stalin had died in his private apartment in the Kremlin at 8:50 P.M. on March 5, Moscow time. The broadcast said:

The heart of our comrade, the inspired successor in Lenin's work, the leader and teacher of the Communist party and the Soviet people, Josef Vissaryonovich Stalin, has ceased to beat.

Khrushchev was later to describe the dramatic circumstances in which he was summoned to Stalin's country house. It was late on a Monday night when the telephone rang in the

Khrushchevs' apartment. The voice that Khrushchev heard
was that of the chief of Stalin's bodyguard: "You are asked
to come at once on an urgent matter to Comrade Stalin's
dacha."

Such a summons was never answered without a constriction
in the heart. Why was the old man summoning him at that
hour, when the wind was howling outside and a heavy winter
snow was falling? Khrushchev's wife insisted that he wear extra clothes, and she poured him a large glass of vodka as he
was leaving.

His car had difficulty proceeding through the snow and on
the sheet ice beneath it. As he approached the *dacha*, he suddenly saw that other cars were moving in the same direction.
He understood: He had not been the only man summoned to
this nocturnal conference. After that he breathed somewhat
more easily.

In fact, Beria, Molotov, Voroshilov, Bulganin, Malenkov,
and Kaganovich were getting out of their cars outside the wall
that girdled the master's villa. They were shown in and
searched by the guards—Beria as well as the others. Then the
chief of the bodyguard explained: "It was I who asked you
to come. Since dusk Comrade Stalin has been inside without a
sign of life."

Every evening Stalin withdrew into a wing of the *dacha*,
once the residence of Prince Orlov, which had armored doors
and windows. There he slept alone. From the bedroom that
was his retreat he could control the electrical system that
opened the doors.

As usual, he had ordered his dinner for eight o'clock. But
three hours later he had not yet sent for his tea. Since he had
been neither seen nor heard from, the chief bodyguard had
decided to summon the members of the Presidium.

There was no choice but to crash the armored door with ice
axes. The job took a long time, and then it was necessary to
break down a second door that gave directly on Stalin's room.
Then they went in.

In his marshal's uniform Comrade Stalin lay on his back on the floor, motionless. Silently the men jostled one another in their efforts to see better. Suddenly Beria's strident voice rose: "The tyrant is dead, dead, dead!"

His joy exploded. He danced where he stood. The others were silent. Khrushchev bent over the body. "And then," he told W. Averell Harriman, "I saw his big open eyes looking at me. Not a dead man's eyes. The eyes of Stalin alive."

That is Khrushchev's version. On some points, depending on the man to whom he was telling it, it would vary, as the story of Beria's death recounted by the same very loquacious fellow was to vary later.

There were other versions. One rumor had it that Stalin had died of a cerebral hemorrhage that followed an angry quarrel with Kaganovich in a meeting of the Presidium on February 28. This was the story favored by Ilya Ehrenburg. He made much of an embryonic plot to get rid of the despot. Supposedly, the members of the Presidium had learned that they were in danger, and hence they had alerted important comrades in the party and the government.

According to this theory, they had decided to act on February 28, when an important discussion of farm problems was scheduled to be held. Stalin supposedly attended the meeting without any idea what was going forward. Zhukov, who was involved in the conspiracy, allegedly had had Poskrebyshev arrested.

Kaganovich took the floor, the story went on, and tore up his party card in a terrible outburst of anger, then turned to Stalin: "You have disgraced the party of Lenin [the said party had been disgraced before, and by Kaganovich]. You are nothing but a rotten murderer."

Stalin's rage was such that he had a stroke, Ehrenburg's account said. He died instantly, without any medical aid. This story is a bit too flattering for the inheritors. It makes them look heroic: They revolted. It clears them of any responsibility for the death of their boss.

Was it a natural death? Was it brought on by a rebellion
among underlings who let their leader die? Or was it a pure
and simple liquidation growing out of a conspiracy?

"It was clear to me that my father was ill," Svetlana Alliluyeva, Stalin's daughter, was to say years later in New York,
thus corroborating the theory that death came from natural
causes. And indeed it is probable that Stalin was already seriously ill. A photograph of him taken at the time of the Nineteenth Congress shows a certain asymmetry in his face, as if
he had already had an earlier stroke. In any case the picture
is that of a man whose physical and perhaps mental deteriora-
tion was well under way. But at the same time his physical
and psychological decline might equally well have facilitated
a conspiracy against a man who no longer possessed the resources of energy and guile required for the successful accomplishment of a second *Yezhovchina.*

Regardless of what caused Stalin's death, there can be no
doubt that, from the moment when it became plain that he
was preparing a new purge, he had created the conditions
for a real or potential coalition: a coalition of fear. In this instance opposition was only a mere defensive reflex devoid of
any political considerations.

Stalin's death put an end to the new Yezhovism. It did not
put an end to all apprehensions. The new menace was named
Beria. And, if it was he who had liquidated Stalin, this made
him all the more redoubtable.

But Stalin's death had another major consequence, the effects of which are still being felt today: It caused a radical
change in the objective facts of the exercise of power in the
Soviet Union. For the end of Stalin meant the annihilation of
a basic instrument in the exercise of this power: *his private
secretariat.* As we have seen, it was through the men in this
small secret apparatus that he imposed his personal control
on the army, the police, and the major instrumentalities of the
state and the party and that he managed the accomplishment
of various undertakings. For the most part the men who made

up this secretariat did not know one another. Each operated in his own sphere of activity, reporting only to Stalin and, undoubtedly, Poskrebyshev. In every respect their authority was only the reflection of Stalin's.

As soon as Stalin died and Poskrebyshev disappeared, the substantial power enjoyed by this secretariat ceased to exist. This miniature general staff was left without instructions. The real command post of the government had been destroyed.

At the same time the various arms of authority regained a kind of autonomy. Government ceased to be an absolute monolith and was automatically parceled out into a series of fiefs. Beria was unchecked in his retention of the police power (but of this power alone). Malenkov had the political and administrative apparatus under his control, but, for reasons that have not yet become known, he soon had to relinquish the Secretariat of the party in favor of Khrushchev and be satisfied with the apparatus of the state. Molotov retained the diplomatic apparatus and Bulganin controled the political apparatus of the army.

Without an interlude of transition the omnipotence of one man was replaced by a temporary equilibrium, a certain balance of power among the heirs. This balance was fragile, precarious, susceptible to constant threat, unless one of these men should succeed in acquiring an authority comparable to Stalin's. The battle among the successors had in effect begun.

(23)

STRIKES AND REVOLTS
IN THE CAMPS

O NE DAY the loudspeakers in the Vorkuta camps announced an interesting news item: Stalin was ill. From then on, the prisoners crowded round the loudspeakers at news time, seized by the most intense anxiety. Four days went by. Then the radio announced that the patient was being given oxygen.

"Can that save him?" someone asked Dr. Scholmer, a German who had been arrested in East Berlin.

Scholmer shrugged. "If the radio is telling the truth, he is probably dead already and they are busy forming a new government in Moscow."

Soon afterward the radio announced that Comrade Stalin was dead. The announcement wiped out every dread. "I have been here nineteen years," a Georgian said, "and that is the first good news I've heard."

Somewhat later Scholmer met an old Uzbek in the main street of the camp. The Uzbek did not speak a word of German, and his Russian vocabulary was of the most primitive. His face was radiant with a great joyous smile. Scholmer, whose own mood was no less gay, gave him a hearty clap on the shoulder. The Uzbek went through the motions of twirling an imaginary mustache, closed his eyes, and rested his head on one hand. "*Spit* (He's asleep)," he said. Then he opened his eyes and his smile grew broader. "*Kharasho* (That's good)."

At the same time the Communist intelligentsia of the entire world was being measured for mourning clothes. A lonely poet labored over a dirge:

> Think, think of Maurice [1] in Moscow in tears. . . .
> Something is giving way in the heart of Jacques.[2]

In a Parisian printing plant the presses were turning out a special edition of *France-Nouvelle* with a headline in huge type: STALIN'S IMMORTAL HEART HAS CEASED TO BEAT.

Picasso was to sketch a casual portrait of Stalin that would appear in *Les lettres françaises* and be judged a scandal by the Central Committee. Aragon would have to make his apologies for having published this sacrilege.

But in Vorkuta and all the other Soviet concentration camps the delight was in direct proportion to the impatience of years, the many years through which millions of slaves had been waiting for this death. They had noticed that Stalin's public appearances had become more and more infrequent. They had pored over the photographs in *Pravda*, trying to find indications of senescence. They had observed that in the Nineteenth Congress he had spoken only once, and then very briefly.

Perhaps the end of Stalin was the end of their suffering. In any event it would be difficult for their fate to be worse.

Vorkuta was a complex of camps north of the Arctic Circle on the boundary between Europe and Asia. There were 105,000 prisoners distributed among 30 camps of about 3500 men each; most of them worked in the mines that supplied the coal for Leningrad.

One hundred twenty thousand released prisoners and

[1] Thorez.
[2] Duclos.

twelve thousand guards and NKVD officers made up the population of the city and the surrounding area. The number of
persons who had voluntarily settled in this desolate region of
tundras, swept by fog and snowstorms during eight months of
the year, was extremely small.

It was here, in the very heart of the Soviet system of oppression, that revolt was to erupt a few months later.

In direct ratio to the major crises that the government had
had to confront, fresh batches of prisoners had been shoveled
into the camps, the existence of which the Soviet authorities
denied. The first generation had been made up of the losers
of the civil war and the members of the opposition parties
(Mensheviks, Rovolutionary Socialists, Cadets, anarchists,
etc.). The kulak campaign, the Great Purge, and the occupation of the Baltic countries and eastern Poland had produced
further bulk shipments. During the war countless suspects had
been sent to the camps, and after the war they were joined by
supporters of Vlassov, members of the UPA and of national
minorities suspected in the mass of sympathies with the enemy, and Germans and Japanese taken prisoner in combat.

It was estimated in 1941 that there were more than eighty
penal-servitude camps on Soviet territory, all of which were
complexes of various size. It has never been possible to establish accurately how many prisoners they held, and no doubt
even the Soviet authorities, so prolific of statistics in all other
matters, would be unable to prepare a precise inventory of this
huge enterprise of repression.

Estimates arrived at by authors who have studied the matter vary substantially. David Dallin put the figure at two million at the beginning of the 1930s. Naum Yasny spoke of three
million prisoners in the middle of that decade. Warren W.
Eason, a demographer, believed that ten million men and
women were in prison camps in 1939.

The variations are substantial, and this is hardly surprising
in the light of the fact that the estimates deal with different
periods and the methods of reckoning are necessarily empiric.

Thus Dallin based his calculations on the Soviet publication, *From Prisons to Reeducational Institutions*. Page 171 of this work shows that prisoners on Soviet territory were receiving four hundred thousand copies of various periodicals, and page 259 reports an estimate of five prisoner readers for each. Co-ordination of these two figures gives the estimate of two million. In the period that followed, Dallin and Nikolayevsky estimated, the number of prisoners must have been somewhere between seven and twelve million.

Weissberg-Cybulski adopted a different method of calculation. According to him, 5 per cent to 6 per cent of the population of Kharkov was arrested during the Great Purge. Extrapolating this percentage, he reckoned that during this period alone nine million persons, including seven million "politicals," must have been arrested.

Yasny starts with a Soviet document entitled *State Plan for the Development of the National Economy of the Soviet Union for 1941*, which fell into the Germans' hands during their advance. This plan established the share of the NKVD in the total outlay (with the exception of the Commissariats for Transport, Defense, and the Navy). Taking as his base the amount allocated to the NKVD, which was in control of the labor force in prison camps, Yasny estimated that the total number of prisoners must have amounted to three and a half million.[3]

But the question is further complicated by the interpretation that is placed on "forced labor." Most of the released prisoners were in fact assigned to residence in the same areas in which they had been imprisoned. According to Scholmer's testimony, the number of prisoners at Vorkuta who were transformed into "free" workers was greater than that of the unreleased prisoners.[4] While these men could move about freely in a restricted area and received higher wages, they were

[3] This figure does not include persons in ordinary prisons or in transit camps.
[4] Scholmer, *La Révolte de Vorkouta*.

nonetheless subject to a certain degree of constraint. The same limitations were imposed on deported populations, which, though they did not have to endure the severity of the camps, nevertheless underwent all the hardships of exile in a land in which they had not chosen to live and a generally hostile climate that was the cause of an appalling death rate.

While the total number of deportees since the October Revolution (former prisoners transformed into so-called free labor, as well as deportees since the beginning of Bolshevik power) cannot be established, it is probably twenty or thirty million. Recent corroboration on the extent of this repression, without equal in the world—for the Soviet camps were in operation before, during, and after the German camps—has come from a source that can hardly be suspected of systematic anti-Communism: namely, Claude Roy, who wrote:

It was only in the Soviet Union itself . . . that I was able to measure accurately what the long, silent terror of this people had been. . . .

In spite of everything I had had a tendency to believe that at least in their statistics informed Communists and anti-Soviet Kremlinologists were exaggerating. I thought that Aragon was exaggerating when on November 30, 1965,[5] he gave me the appalling figure of eighteen million deportees, three million of whom had died. I thought that Suvarin and Branko Lazich were exaggerating when they cited higher figures, to say nothing of some Soviet citizens at international congresses who spoke of twenty-five to thirty million deportees and five to six million dead among them.

Between Moscow and Erivan I met hardly a single Soviet citizen whose family had not lost one or two members during the war against Germany and one or two members more through imprisonment, deportation, shooting, or being listed as missing during the great purges of 1938 and 1948.[6]

Let us not forget that Soviet society was as bitterly tried by

[5] In other words, after the Budapest insurrection.
[6] Claude Roy, *Du culte de Staline à l'idolatrie de Mao*, in *Le Nouvel Observateur*, November 16, 1966.

its own government as by a war against Germany that entailed terrible losses.

The part that the camps may have played in the Soviet economic system has aroused no less controversy. Some observers believe that their function was not so much to isolate persons regarded as dangerous or suspect as it was to provide the state with a cheap labor force that made it possible to exploit the riches of Soviet Asia. Others, however, believe that the savings were offset by the cost of the gigantic apparatus of surveillance, the very high death rate, the low productivity of slave labor, and the loss incurred by the state when it made unskilled laborers out of technicians whose professional training had been very expensive to it.

Without solid facts it is impossible to resolve this controversy. At the very least there is no doubt that the camps played a substantial part in the phenomenon of colonization. The best evidence is the fact that beginning in 1936 the entirety of the migration and colonization programs was removed from the People's Commissariats for Labor and for Agriculture and transferred to the NKVD.

An especially striking example of this forced colonization is provided by the territory of Kolyma, with an area six times as large as that of France. Before 1932 it was virtually an uninhabited desert. Its winters are eight months long, and the temperature falls to sixty-five degrees below freezing. Summers are brief and torrid, and swarms of insects make life there unbearable.

It was in this gehenna that the *Dalstroi*, an agency under the management of the NKVD, undertook to mine gold from the Kolyma River in 1932. Fifteen years later the industry had assumed substantial dimensions; There was a new port, Magadan, which had approximately seventy thousand inhabitants shortly after the war; a major highway linked the port with Yakust on the Lena River, and there were *sovkhozi*, fishing and fish-canning establishments, power stations, and metal foundries.

In every Soviet textbook this transformation of virgin territory is hailed as Socialist progress. The same books say nothing of the other side of the ledger of this Pharaonic miracle: of the hundreds of thousands of men whose bodies were worked to death on the shores of the Kolyma River. Side by side with their tributes to the great victories of Socialism, these textbooks unfailingly recall the "dreadful" days of tsarism and the gloomy lines of convicts leaving the prisons of Moscow and Leningrad for relentless exile in Siberia.

But the distance between the tsarist and the Soviet systems of repression is in a sense astronomical. Krupskaya herself is authority for the fact that, when Lenin was in prison, he was able to receive masses of reference works that made it possible for him to write his first book, *The Development of Capitalism in Russia.* When he was deported he was billeted on a peasant family, was decently fed, and went hunting and fishing. Like him, hundreds of deported revolutionaries were able to escape without too much difficulty, whereas escape from Soviet camps has always been an exploit verging on the unique.

Nor is there any comparison between the numbers of prisoners. On February 13, 1913, Francis de Pressensé, a Socialist friend of Jaurès, president of the League for the Rights of Man, delivered a violent indictment of tsarist oppression before the Learned Societies under the chairmanship of a former terrorist, Vera Figner. He said that in five years, from 1906 through 1910, sentences for both political offenses and common-law crimes had risen to 37,260 (purely political offenses accounting for 19,145) and 8100 persons had been sentenced to death, 5735 of them for political offenses (of whom 4366 were actually executed).

He denounced the rise in repression after the failure of the 1905 revolution. Whereas prisoners of all kinds totaled seventy-seven thousand in 1898, the figure had risen to one hundred eleven thousand by 1907 and one hundred eighty thousand by 1911, and this did not include prisoners in transit, in police-station detention, or serving sentences for misdemeanors—some six thousand persons.

At the height of its repressions, then, the tsarist government was holding a maximum of two hundred twenty thousand persons. Pressensé found such a state of affairs abominable, and he pointed out that in the seventy years between 1825 and 1895 death sentences of every kind had totaled only 1008 and executions, most of them on political charges, had totaled 525.[7]

The "terror" unleashed after the revolution of 1905 and the part played by the Okhrana made the liberal Europe of the period tremble with horror. That system seems mild in comparison with the measureless persecution carried out in the Soviet Union in the name of revolution.[8] It was in that universe subjugated by unmerciful oppression, however, that resistance would spring up.

After the extermination of the Trotskyists the sorry nation of slaves that was exerting all its efforts for survival fell into resignation. Yet to them no hope, no attempt at revolt seemed useless. The NKVD busied itself in spying on them and spreading dissension among them, and in addition it had highly effective allies: the common criminals. The politicals lived under a terror imposed by the real criminals, who played cards for the lives of the other prisoners. Elinor Lipper, who spent eleven years as a prisoner in Kolyma, has painted a striking picture:

[7] "Tolstoy tells us that the death penalty had become so alien to Russian customs that for many years that vast empire . . . had only a single executioner." (From Pressensé's speech.)

[8] Will it be argued that account must be taken not only of prisoners but also of the number of the victims of repressions after the 1905 revolution? There again Pressensé offered statistics based on an investigation undertaken by *Le monde contemporain:* 21,183 persons killed in five years in pogroms and punitive expeditions and 31,117 wounded. Certainly there can be no comparison with the crimes committed by the Soviet police during and after the civil war, during collectivization, behind the front during the war, in the Baltic countries, and against the Ukrainian nationalists.

It was a typical practice among the prisoners to thrust themselves under their bedclothes whenever they could, in such a way that not even their heads could be seen. They did this not only because they could keep warmer in this way but also because no one wanted to see or hear that outer world that made everyone afraid and from which everyone wanted to flee.[9]

Thoughts of revolt did not begin to form until after the end of the war. This was because the very conditions of the Soviet system of oppression had begun to change. It was also because new elements that had had other experiences besides the Soviet citizen's resignation were beginning to arrive in these camps.

Paul Barton has ably described this evolution in his book *L'Institution concentrationnaire en Russie.* Some improvements in living conditions in the concentration-camp system began to appear in 1948: Politicals were as a rule separated from common criminals, the food was somewhat better, and so was medical care. Beginning in 1950 the prisoners even received a modest wage.

And a genuine effort was made to reduce the death rate. A physician held in a Siberian camp provided Barton with statistics on deaths that had occurred in his ward (for tuberculars): whereas sixty-eight deaths had been recorded in 1950, the figure fell to thirty-six in 1951 and to five in 1952. Autopsy in every case of death became obligatory in Vorkuta in 1951, and a detailed report had to be submitted. Before that, in Norilsk, the authorities had been satisfied to smash the deceased's skull with a sledge-hammer by way of precaution against possible escapes. In Vorkuta, for the same reason, it had been the practice to run a bayonet through the heart.

There were good reasons for the sudden humanitarianism of Beria's underlings. They were economic and demographic reasons. The human capital represented by the prisoners had become valuable: In fact, the system was having tremendous difficulties in enlarging it.

[9] Elinor Lipper, *Onze ans dans les bagnes soviétiques,* p. 201.

Collectivization and its sequels had led to a decline in the birth rate. In addition, the war had been a frightful bloodletting. Furthermore, the concentration-camp system and the deportations had led to grave imbalances between the sexes that varied according to regions. In the camp regions there were substantially more men than women. The opposite phenomenon was observed in the countryside, either because the peasants had been deported or because they had been absorbed into industrial production.[10]

There was no abatement in police repressions, however, because of the demographic conditions. A major purge of the party's ranks took place in Leningrad in 1948. Similarly, in 1951–1952, a wave of "economic offenders," most of them Jews, went on trial. But these phenomena were limited to regions or to specific social categories. It was becoming increasingly difficult to operate massive roundups like those of collectivization or the Great Purge of 1936–1938 without further worsening the country's catastrophic economic disequilibrium.

The new human wealth contributed by the return of the prisoners of war, the deportations of the inhabitants of the Baltic countries, and the arrests in the satellite countries had been used up. Hence there was only one solution: a certain pampering of the slave labor available in the camps. The humanization of the system was a fact of economics.

Everyone knows that a time of grave economic crisis ac-

[10] A perceptible decline in the number of specialists coming out of the professional and technical schools was observed beginning in 1949:

1948	1,000,000
1949	723,000
1950	494,000
1951	363,000
1952	326,000
1953	320,000

The statistics began to rise again in 1954 (570,000). The 1949–1953 period was that of the low point in the young-adult population as the result of the massacre of the peasants twenty years earlier, 1929–1933. On this point cf. Lucien Laurat, *L'économie soviétique en 1955*, cited by Barton, p. 256.

companied by mass unemployment does not incite the working class to make excessive demands. The fear of losing their
jobs saps the workers' will to fight. But let the conditions improve and the strike spirit, stimulated by its long depression,
will revive. So in the camps the lack of any prospect, the
frightful living conditions, and the dread of dying paralyzed
any spirit of revolt. As soon, however, as the yoke that pressed
down on millions of prisoners became less heavy, the idea that
further concessions might be exacted began to germinate
among a minority of the prisoners. Thus the various improvements created the objective conditions for launching the battle. *But it could be waged effectively only by men who had
already fought that same battle outside the camps.*

The war had served as a leaven: Men had deserted the Red
Army. Others had fought in the ranks of the German army.
The Baltic deportees showed a fanatical hatred of the Bolshevik system. National minorities had welcomed the invader.
Even the prisoners of war in German camps and the deported
laborers had known a world different from Stalin's. The upheaval that resulted was a phenomenon of far broader scope
than the opposition of a few thousand Trotskyists to Stalin.

But one category of new arrivals in particular entered the
camps with an exemplary will to fight: the Ukrainian nationalists. They had fought the Germans, the Soviets, and the
Poles with guns in their hands. They had enjoyed the backing
of their people. In this combat they had obeyed the orders of
a political-military general staff and practiced every form of
illegal struggle in pursuit of a specific objective: the independence of the Ukraine. By that very fact this generation
was inspired by a spirit quite different from that of the peasants who between 1929 and 1933 had resisted only locally
when they were attacked by expropriation. They knew virtually nothing aside from the fact that they did not want the
kolkhoz. They had no political goal. The members of the
UPA knew very firmly, even if only superficially, why they
were fighting.

Many persons in the West believe that the great strike that broke out in Vorkuta in 1953 was the first attempt at revolt against the oppression of the concentration camps. It was nothing of the sort. It is possible that there were insurrections as early as 1946 at Kolyma, and in 1947 at Karaganda and Ust-Vym. Only very fragmentary clues to these are available, provided sometimes by a single source. Thus it is questionable even whether they took place.

Somewhat more is known of the democratic movement in northern Russia, which was organized as early as 1947 in the camps of Pechora. This movement was supposedly created by seventy-five Soviet officers who were studying at the Frunze Academy in Moscow. After their arrest and confinement, they set up in the camps an organization that in the beginning would admit only Soviet military men. Later it was opened to Poles, Hungarians, Czechs, and even Germans.

In 1948 these prisoners obtained weapons and seized control of one of the camps. Apparently their objective was also to occupy the town of Vorkuta in order to be able to release the other prisoners in the region. This attack collapsed. The defeated rebels retreated toward the Urals in the hope of hiding in the forests and operating there as partisans. But during their march they were located by aerial observers and machine-gunned or captured. Only a handful of them, it was believed, reached the Ural forests.

There is very probably some connection between this rising and the Berlin blockade. The insurgents must have thought that the Third World War was about to start. Their drive toward the Urals was undoubtedly based on the hope of creating a dissident zone there that would be supplied with weapons by American parachute drops.[11]

The intention of the Pechora insurgents was only to organize a military raid, a commando operation, and then flee. Later

[11] Cf. Barton, *op. cit.*, p. 305.

movements,[12] however, were as a rule organized on the spot, with formal lists of demands that were aimed at gaining some changes in the camp rules or even, in extreme instances, the elimination of the camps. In other words these later groups operated like strike committees, negotiating with the authorities and exerting pressures on them in order to win concessions from them.

The battle against the concentration-camp system from within presupposed the prior creation of clandestine networks. These were organized on ethnic bases. Language and customs established an automatic solidarity. Furthermore, it was easier for men who shared a common language to identify reliable persons and, conversely, flush out the stool pigeons. For this reason alone the Ukrainians were destined to play an important part because as a rule they were the largest ethnic group in any camp. Scholmer indicated that in his camp some 1800 of the 3500 prisoners were Ukrainians, and 60 per cent to 70 per cent of these came from the western Ukraine. The next largest groups were the Lithuanians, with 800; the Latvians, with 300; the Russians, also with 300; the Estonians, with 200; and the Germans, with 190, 70 of whom were Germans from the Soviet Union.

The Latvians and Lithuanians also constituted especially active groups, inspired by a savage hatred of the Soviet authorities (they too, as we have seen, had waged a vigorous struggle against the Soviet occupant). Scholmer cited the case of a Latvian who, after six years of imprisonment, consistently refused to speak a word of Russian. Since he worked at the bottom of the mine, it was the Russians who had had to learn to speak his language.

[12] In 1950, supposedly, there were a rebellion at Salekhard, near Vorkuta, and a strike in Camp 015 for women at Taishet. In 1951 there were reports of a strike in the Kolyma camps, a rebellion at Dzehekaz-gan (in the Karaganda region), and another at Karaganda. On this subject cf. W. Kosyk, *Camps de concentration en URSS. Pourquoi et pour qui existent-ils?*, p. 45.

This ethnically based organization was not devoid of friction. Undoubtedly there were contacts among the trusted representatives of each group. But there was deep antagonism between the Russians and the Ukrainians, between the Ukrainians and the Poles, between the Poles and the Lithuanians, who saw red whenever Vilna was mentioned. The Russians were not inclined to overlook the destruction and slaughter wrought by the Germans, who were the targets of the national minorities' anger too—but in this instance because Germany had lost the war.

In spite of their seeming isolation the clandestine organizations were fairly well informed of what was going on in the other camps, in the country as a whole, and even in the West. In fact the public-address systems carried radio news broadcasts, and newspapers circulated inside the camps.

Since members of the intelligentsia constituted a large proportion of the prisoners, there was no lack of men who knew how to read between the lines of a newspaper or analyze a broadcast by Radio Moscow, to examine the events that came to their knowledge, and even to evolve programs or put the final touches to detailed plans to be carried out in the event of war. For war was the great hope of these men doomed to rot behind barbed wire.

Transfers from one camp to another, furthermore, made it easier to exchange news. When strikes and revolts began to erupt, the MVD men took the opportunity to move those whom they believed to be the leaders to other camps in order to smash internal resistance. At the same time they were helping to spread the spirit of revolt to these other camps.

The free population also provided a broad base of support and sympathy because in large part it was made up of former prisoners. Its assistance made it relatively easy for news and messages to be conveyed. Bernhard Roeder cited [13] the case of a physician in Vorkuta who received an underground leaflet

[13] In *Der Katorgan*, pp. 188–189.

only a few days after it had been distributed in Moscow. It had been relayed by groups of railway workers. In other circumstances it was truck drivers who served as postmen.

Within a single complex of camps there were certain areas that were especially useful for communication. These were the central hospital, to which all the ill were sent; the post office, where the prisoners picked up their letters and parcels; and the construction areas, where they could talk to truck drivers.

Occasionally a network would be formed without regard to ethnic lines, though with very few members; thus a "troika" was created in Vorkuta by a German, a Ukrainian student, and a Polish barber. The German, who was a male nurse, could reach many of the ailing. The barber also practiced his trade with a number of the prisoners. The student was in frequent contact with free workers, through whom contacts with other camps were established.

"The condition precedent to any attempt to provide political leadership for the men in the camps," Paul Barton wrote, "was the overthrow of the dictatorship of the criminals." [14] This obstacle varied with the degree to which the common criminals had been segregated from the politicals. This segregation was not a universal practice, however, and in certain instances the MVD deliberately mingled criminals with politicals in order to put down agitation.

There was one method, and only one, of putting an end to the dictatorship imposed by the *blatnoi* (criminals) on the other prisoners, whom they systematically despoiled of their meager possessions. Repatriates from Japan in Camp No. 13 at Taishet told how life in the camp had been changed when some fifteen Ukrainians who had taken part in the Norilsk strikes were moved to Taishet, where a gang leader was the law. One night he was so severely beaten that he had to be sent to the hospital. He was never seen again in Camp No. 13, and the other *blatnoi* took the lesson to heart.

[14] *Op. cit.*, p. 312.

In Camp No. 2 at Vorkuta *blatnoi* were at one time distributed among the barracks of the politicals. The first day one of them laid his cap on the table and said: "I want that filled with rubles when I come back in an hour." Many terrorized prisoners complied. This encouraged the criminal to repeat the procedure over the next few days.

Soon [a former prisoner related] even the cowards had had enough. We drew up a plan. The men who worked in the mine stole copper wire, the electricians confected alarm bells with the material at hand, and these were connected to the barracks. Then, about three o'clock one morning, the bells rang all through Camp No. 2. In no time the handful of *blatnoi* in each barracks was overcome by all the prisoners, and their axes and knives were taken away from them. We emptied one barracks and locked all the *blatnoi* inside it. The barracks was then doused with gasoline that had been stolen for the purpose, and we set it on fire. If it had not been for the guards, who put out the fire and released the *blatnoi*, they would have been burned to death for their crimes. But in any case we were rid of them. They were all removed next day.[15]

If a movement were to gain momentum inside a camp, it was not enough that the politicals be relieved of their fear of the *blatnoi* and that the MVD be unable to make the criminals its willing accomplices. There was another kind of enemy who had to be eliminated or neutralized at all costs: the spies of the prison administration. Infiltrated among the politicals, they were in a position to learn their secrets and prevent their activities.

The only means of eliminating a stool pigeon was to kill him. This is the law of every clandestine organization. Its effect is not only to rid the group of a dangerous element but also to serve as a persuasive deterrent to those who might be tempted to follow the stool pigeon's example. This in itself tended to weaken the police procedure. When such a killing became known, it served also to encourage the enlistment of

[15] John Noble, *I Was A Slave in Russia*, p. 139.

men who might be afraid to join the movement lest they be betrayed.

Japanese testimony gathered by H. Passin [16] showed how these principles were applied by a group of Ukrainians transferred to Camp No. 5 in Norilsk for having taken part in a strike in Karaganda in 1952:

One night shortly after their arrival four prisoners known to be informers in the pay of the prison administration were killed. Their executioners were never identified. What was most significant was the fact that they were killed with pick-axes, a fact that permits the inference that there was a certain complicity on the part of the guards; for each prisoner, on his return to camp from the day's work, was subjected to a rigorous search, and under the rules all tools were supposed to be turned over to the guards. Hence it was necessary to have a real organization or extensive complicity in order to be able to bring an axe into the camp. There were a number of purposes behind this execution of informers, and it led to broad consequences. It weakened the administration's surveillance over what went on in the camp, it aroused anxiety among the guards and their agents and placed them on the defensive, and it made the prisoners aware of the boldness and the efficiency of the Ukrainian group.

Other testimony told of identical executions, which in 1953 compelled the MVD to make each prisoner sign a notice that the murder of a prisoner would be punished by execution.

But often the struggle against the stool pigeons was confined to finding and then neutralizing them. Anyone suspect was immediately put under the surveillance of dozens of watchers. If circumstances dictated, he was given certain information by way of putting him to the test. If as a result there was police action, the proof was deemed conclusive. Throughout the camp complex in any given region the informer became valueless to his employers.

[16] *Bulletin d'Information de la CICRC,* No. 4.

Obviously it is impossible to calculate the number of either resistants or stool pigeons. Scholmer, however, estimated that in his camp there were 120 *stukachi* (stool pigeons) among 3500 prisoners, and the ratio seems credible. According to Scholmer, most of the informers were Russians, but he himself amended this interpretation by pointing out that among the Russians there were many convinced Communists who had not lost their loyalty to the government. Many of them were deeply angered when there were strikes in the camps. To them such disobedience was unbelievable.

This was why the MVD sought its trusted agents among them, agents who enjoyed various advantages within the camp's administrative system. "Even here," Scholmer wrote, "the camp is a miniature Soviet Union whose 'government' seeks to dominate the peoples with the Russians' help." [17]

The MVD men who represented the backbone of the system of repression were not in themselves very numerous. Their number did not exceed 3 per cent to 5 per cent of the prisoner population.

Sometimes the battle to smash the dictatorship of the *blatnoi* was on a scale broad enough to lead to a veritable rebellion that affected an entire camp. Such was the case in Karaganda in 1952. That complex was dominated by a gang of Caucasians who enjoyed the backing of the administration. The fight against them was initiated by members of the UPA, and this battle in turn developed into a genuine insurrection. Its result was the final elimination of the terror imposed by the gang.

The amnesty decreed by Beria after Stalin's death was to introduce a new phase in the struggle. The amnesty applied only to prisoners sentenced to loss of liberty for not more than five years and to those convicted of administrative and economic offenses; it also released male prisoners over the age of fifty-five, women over fifty, and the incurably ill. It did not affect persons condemned to more than five years for counter-

[17] *Op. cit.*

revolutionary activities, thefts detrimental to Socialist property, etc.

A large number of ordinary criminals benefited by it. Many of them, however, committed new offenses because they were unable to find jobs or housing, and soon they were back in their old residence, the camp.

But the number of political prisoners released was minuscule. Their anger mounted in direct proportion to their awareness of the tremendous rise in thefts and burglaries committed by the released criminals. The decree of amnesty began to seem a deliberate provocation.

The strike that broke out in Camp No. 5 of Norilsk in May 1953 was provoked by shots fired by a guard who was trying to prevent the prisoners from communicating with one another. Several men were wounded. The strike began soon afterward. It spread to Camp No. 10 and the women's camp (No. 6). The administration's threats proved futile. Each time the strikers retorted that they would negotiate only with someone sent from Moscow. A general flew to the camp from Krasnoyarsk but he had no more effect.

The next day a high official of the MVD arrived to embark on preliminary talks with the strikers. He asked the prisoners to select delegates for the purpose. This request posed a delicate problem. Indeed, the clandestine networks that directed activities in the camps had to take maximum precautions to protect the identities of their members: otherwise they would be immediately scattered among other camps. That was why seven or eight persons were chosen to represent the clandestine strike committee.

This committee drew up a list of demands that became known later through repatriated German prisoners. There were fourteen main points:

1. A guaranty that there would be no firing on the prisoners.
2. The removal of prisoner numbers from clothing.
3. A reduction in working time.

4. Unrestricted authorization to send letters.
5. The removal of the ailing from Norilsk.
6. A rise in wages.
7. The elimination of window bars and of the practice of locking doors at night.
8. The remission of two or three days of sentence for every day of good work output.
9. Humane treatment by the guards.
10. Common work areas and identical work hours for men and women.
11. No reprisals against the strike leaders.
12. The expulsion of informers.
13. The extension of the amnesty to political prisoners.
14. Better food and clothing.[18]

Almost identical demands were presented by the rebels who became active in Vorkuta and Kinghir. Hence their objectives were limited. The prisoners did not demand the end of the system but its improvement. In reality these concrete demands attested to their recognition of the possible and to the obvious political maturity of the clandestine leaders who had evolved these demands in secret. The armed revolt that broke out at Pechora in 1948 led in sum to a collective escape by the inmates. It was a desperate undertaking whose chances of success were infinitesimal.

In this respect the limited-objective strikes at Norilsk, Vorkuta, etc., represented obvious progress. They were stages in the long battle against the administration, they contributed to its insecurity, and they supported the work that other clandestine groups were carrying on outside.

Finally, after various negotiations and trickery to which the MVD resorted in order to deceive and divide the prisoners, troops smashed the resistance in the Norilsk camp: one day they surrounded it, broke in with shouts, and opened fire.

A short time earlier the foreign prisoners had been separated from the others and collected in Camp No. 7. From there

18 Cf. Barton, *op. cit.*, pp. 326–327.

they could see the black flags raised by the strikers over Camps Nos. 4, 5, and 6 and the construction area. These flags waved for six days. On the night of the seventh day the foreigners heard the noise of shots. By morning the flag over Camp No. 5 had vanished. Two days later the flags disappeared from No. 6 and the construction area. The flag over No. 4 waved for another day.

Then the foreigners were removed to Dudinka. When they left the train there, they saw approximately 120 prisoners who had been their workmates being embarked on a ship. This was the last ever heard of the insurgents of Norilsk.[19]

In Vorkuta there was a dramatic echo of the revolt of East Berlin. This was what gave that strike its special significance. The blow dealt to the system of oppression in a satellite country ignited a revolt thousands of miles away in frozen areas of the Arctic.

The prisoners of Vorkuta had learned of the East Berlin strike from a copy of *Pravda* posted in the canteen. The newspaper admitted that disorders had broken out in East Germany. They were, of course, a "vile provocation" by Chancellor Konrad Adenauer of West Germany, and they had collapsed.

Prisoners jostled one another to read the article, and an old Ukrainian read it aloud. Then he read the report of the Socialist Unity party,[20] which was "now about to turn to the working class and show its true face." This sentence was greeted by an outburst of laughter.

"What has it been showing until now, then?" one prisoner shouted. "Its arse?" Like everyone, he knew that it was the working class that had rebelled.

Not long afterward, on a hot evening in July, Scholmer was enjoying a circumspect chat with a Russian friend, Georgi. From the bench on which they were sitting they could look out over the monotonous expanse of the tundra. A few hun-

[19] Reports of German repatriates quoted by Barton, *ibid.*, pp. 467–483.
[20] The East German Communist party.

dred yards away was the road that led to another camp; beyond the road was the railway. At a certain point the track forked, one line leading to the mines, the other continuing across the tundra to a port on the Arctic Ocean.

Georgi pointed out that for twenty-four hours not a single coal car had come out of the mine. Some technical accident? This was hard to believe, since the railway served three separate pits. How could all three of them have been paralyzed?

At about one thirty in the morning a miner appeared. He said that a strike had begun in Pit No. 7; a locomotive driver had told him of it.

The news exploded at once. In the next few days it was learned that the strike had spread to Camps Nos. 14, 16, and 29. It had been launched by prisoners arriving from Karaganda, because the living conditions there were much better than those in Vorkuta, where they had spent only one day before deciding to call the strike. It was joined by Scholmer's camp. No. 6.

The demands presented by the various camps were virtually the same as those of Norilsk. In addition, all the Vorkuta camps demanded the remission of all or part of sentences in excess of ten years at forced labor.

The MVD spread the most diverse rumors in order to demoralize the prisoners: An amnesty was imminent, the strikers would be tried by a summary court, their fellows in the other camps had been convicted and shot. Then the leaders were arrested—five Russians, two of them Jews. Scholmer added:

This action threw an interesting light on the importance of the part played in the camps by the stool pigeons. They had approached only Russians and Jews, and they had been unable to establish relations with the real leaders of the clandestine movement, almost all of whom were Ukrainians and Lithuanians.[21]

The camps were painstakingly isolated by the MVD. In Camp No. 6 the clandestine strike committee ordered all the

[21] *Op. cit.*, p. 183.

prisoners not to report for the *razvod* (the roll call conducted outside the barracks). Every effort undertaken by the guards and the soldiers—with considerable force, moreover—ended in failure.

All activity in Camp No. 6 had halted. That July was very hot. Naked to the waist, the prisoners lay stretched out on their beds, reading, sleeping, or drinking tea. But a few of them dislodged the bars on the lavatory window and went outdoors to get some fresh air.

The prison administration made a special approach to the brigade assigned to maintain ventilation in the mine. Without ventilation all work was impossible. The camp commander's representative endeavored to persuade the men to resume work. He was not a bad fellow. He had never mistreated anyone. If he failed to win them over, he might very well be in danger of severe punishment. "Try to understand," he said, "that the mine is required to deliver a certain tonnage. If you do not work now, you will only have to make up for lost time later."

"We have nothing against you," a Ukrainian replied. "But should we just accept doing twenty-five years in prison and not even protest?" [22]

So the strike continued. It included five of the thirteen camps. The old Bolsheviks among the prisoners were dumfounded. To them such a rebellion against authority was a stupefying phenomenon. Scholmer asked one of them, Amstislavsky, what he thought of it. The Bolshevik was literally terrified. His whole system of thinking was crumbling.

For the former prisoners who were now free workers in the Vorkuta region there could be no thought of joining the strike: They would at once be arrested. But they demonstrated their sympathy by smuggling newspapers, tobacco, wine, and money to the strikers.

Moscow decided to send a commission of inquiry to make an on-the-spot investigation. Its members questioned arrested

[22] *Ibid.*, p. 183.

strikers and leaders, recorded their replies, and left after a week.

One day there was a great crackle of gunfire from the direction of Pits Nos. 7, 14, 16, and 29. That evening one of the camp's surgeons, Blagodatov, was taken off to an unknown destination. When he returned a week later he told what had happened at Pit No. 29.

The strike committee there had taken over the administration of the camp. It had refused to deal with the local authorities. Soon the camp was surrounded by troops with batteries of machine guns and mortars. General Derevyanko sent an emissary to the strikers; he was so provocative that they insulted and struck him. A last appeal was made to them over the public-address system.

The strikers did not yield. They had gathered before the main gate in a compact mass that sometimes shouted, sometimes sang Ukrainian hymns. Derevyanko ordered an attack. The soldiers broke down the gates and opened fire.

"When I arrived," Blagodatov reported, "I found two hundred men seriously wounded. They had been shot in the belly or the chest. Sixty-four had been killed instantly, including four Germans. I did nothing but operate all week long. The wounded died by the score."

Little by little the strike collapsed in the various camps. One day the inmates of Camp No. 6 saw coal cars rolling along the railway across the tundra. The next day everyone went back to work.

Could it have ended otherwise? Analyzing this experience, Scholmer emphasized the critical conditions under which the movement had had to evolve. There was no public opinion to back up the strikers. Each camp was isolated and carried on its own strike in its own way. Most of the prisoners were taking part in a strike for the first time in their lives.

Scholmer concluded that the major error was that the strike had not been a sit-in in the depths of the mine.

Not one guard [he wrote], not one "red" or "blue" officer who wanted to stay alive would have taken the chance of going down into the mine. In the mine it would have been possible to carry on effective outspoken propaganda. Small meetings could have been organized, which were out of the question above ground where the informers were. And the strikers' shock groups could have taken control of strategic points and key positions such as the principal elevators and the coal cars, thus imposing their control on the entire mine.[23]

But Scholmer still overlooked one point: How could strikers in the depth of the mine have provided for their food supply?

Two months after the end of the strike, the strikers heard from students of the Leningrad School of Mines who had arrived to work in Vorkuta how the city had reacted to their struggle. "We learned very soon that you were on strike," the students said. "Coal deliveries were sharply reduced and we had no reserve. We follow a plan, that's all, and everyone knows how brittle plans are." At the same time, the crews of the coal trains had spread the news, which had run through Leningrad.

Scholmer took this occasion to emphasize how highly vulnerable the Soviet economy was because of its fundamental dependence on slave labor. A simultaneous prolonged work stoppage in all the camps would undoubtedly have been enough to paralyze production. But this was a theoretical view. It was naturally beyond the realm of possibility to launch a general strike in camps that were thousands of miles apart from one another.

Other agitations occurred in Kinghir in January and May and June of 1954, and during the same year in several camps in Kazakstan, in Karagash (forty thousand strikers), Itna, Kolyma, Krasnoyarsk, and Taishet; there were new strikes in 1955 at Vorkuta and at Solikamsk in the Urals. In the same year a wave of strikes and insurrections swept through the camps in the Far East (Magadan, Kharbin, etc.), and in Sep-

23 *Ibid.*, p. 197.

tember there was a further strike in Vorkuta. In 1956 there were strikes and disorders in the camps for Japanese and Chinese near Taishet; in August insurrection flared in Krasnoyarsk and Tomsk. In 1957 there was word of new strikes in the camps near Vladivostok, Chelyabinsk, and Svyerdlovsk.

After that year the already sparse reports became more and more difficult to collect. Actually the Soviet authorities had taken care to isolate citizens of other countries in special camps where they had no communication with the mass of the other prisoners. Hence repatriates could bring home no information. Besides, such facts were hardly noticed in the West. The heroic combat waged in the very heart of the concentration-camp system under the worst conditions was virtually cloaked in silence.

Yet it attained a remarkable dramatic intensity. It showed that the prisoners were endowed with a courage, a resolution, and a dedication that had their roots in the innumerable clandestine struggles that they had waged before their arrests in the cities and countrysides of the Soviet Union: in Moscow and Leningrad and Kharkov, on the steppes of the Ukraine, in the mountains of the Caucasus, in the vast reaches of Kazakstan.

There is no better illustration than the great insurrection of Kinghir in May 1954. Once again the Ukrainians took the lead in the struggle.

They had embarked on the liquidation of a number of spies and thus aroused the anger of the administration and, at times, the shots of the guards. But, since it was impossible to suppress the agitation that prevailed among the politicals, the MVD sent a contingent of six hundred common criminals to the camp in April.

Things turned out differently from what had been expected. The leader of the criminals, a man called Gleb, made contact with the politicals' clandestine committee and entered into an agreement with it.

There were high fences separating the various sections of

the camp. One of these was the women's section. On May 16 the criminals, immediately followed by the politicals, attacked the fences, which were destroyed at a number of points. Soon forty-five hundred men and thirty-five hundred women had joined forces. All the guard troops were driven out and four hundred persons in the camp's punishment cells were set free.

The repatriates' reports are silent on the scenes that may have been enacted when the prisoners of both sexes found themselves together and under no surveillance. But this gap is not difficult to fill. There is every reason to believe that in the next few hours the prisoners' sexual starvation ended. That there was a certain number of rapes may equally be assumed without risk of being carried away by fantasy.

During the night of May 17–18, MVD detachments invaded the women's camp and opened fire on the men who resisted. It was reported that sixty-six prisoners were killed during the night and their bodies were removed in such haste that the prisoners were disposed to believe that the prison administration had called in the troops without first consulting the higher authorities.

In reprisal the strike call was issued by the clandestine committee, headed by Anatol Zadorozhny, a Ukrainian. A broader committee composed of all nationalities was created under the leadership of a Russian, Colonel Kuznetzov.

Two days later, General Bichkov, deputy commander of the *Gulag* (Supreme Camp Division), arrived from Moscow with General Dolghich, a deputy attorney general. The prisoners submitted a sixteen-point list of demands, which the generals accepted on condition that work be resumed.

But, when they returned from their jobs the next day, the prisoners saw that MVD troops had been brought into the camp and that the fences were being rebuilt. The soldiers posted in the watchtowers were under orders to shoot anyone who went near the fences. Anger reigned, but so did uncertainty. Suddenly the women began to sing a Ukrainian partisan song: *Rank upon rank the partisans march . . .* and the assault was launched from every direction. Rockets immediately soared into the night sky and from every watchtower machine-gun fire rained on the rebels.

The butchery took the lives of a hundred men and women. But the prisoners did not give up the fight. On the morning of May 20 they again demanded the withdrawal of the soldiers, who left the camp that day. A new period of negotiations began. It lasted until the night of June 25–26.

Throughout this interval the camp was in the rebels' hands. "The Ukrainian women," a repatriated Hungarian, Dr. Varkuny, wrote, "distributed leaflets, made Molotov cocktails, erected barricades to ward off possible attacks, and tended the wounded. The men manufactured improvised side arms." [24]

The MVD had engineered radio news broadcasts according to which the prisoners had abandoned themselves to violence and murder and represented a danger to the city. But the prisoners too had managed to improvise a broadcasting station, and they began transmissions on June 16. Their broadcasts, it was said, were heard in Alma-Ata and Karaganda (three hundred miles from Kinghir). One of these messages was addressed to the International Red Cross—an appeal for help. This desperate cry could not reach any free country.

Meanwhile the MVD was grouping fresh troops. The camp was under aerial surveillance. On June 24 the public-address system broadcast an announcement by General Bichkov, ordering the insurgents to surrender and abandon the camp. Their reply was brief: "We will not move until a representative of the Central Committee arrives."

Bichkov ordered an attack on the night of June 26–27. At three o'clock in the morning seven tanks and two thousand soldiers stormed into the camp. Once again the rockets soared into the sky, holding the barracks, the fences, and the barricades erected by the rebels in their glaring light. The soldiers moved in behind the tanks, firing continually and finishing off

[24] Cf. *The Ukrainian Bulletin*, March 1–15, 1956, and *Five Hundred Ukrainian Martyred Women.*

the wounded with the bayonet. The insurgents retaliated with Molotov cocktails.

The battle was still raging four hours later. Then five hundred Ukrainian women and girls counterattacked. Arms linked, they marched in compact ranks against the tanks. Undoubtedly they hoped that the drivers would stop. But the MVD's tanks rolled over this human mass and left crushed bodies behind them.

The insurgents' radio operator was in a barracks inside the women's camp. He slashed both his wrists, but he went on broadcasting: "SOS! SOS! Save us! We are being massacred . . . SOS!" His cry was lost in the air. One can imagine him tapping on his key, riveted to his transmitter in order to get the message out, while blood spurted irregularly from his severed arteries.

At nine o'clock in the morning Anatol Zadorozhny ordered the end of all resistance. He and the other members of the international committee were arrested at once. What happened to them is not known. Probably they were shot. Sixteen hundred prisoners were loaded aboard cattle trucks and shipped to Kolyma.

So ended the insurrection of Kinghir.

(24)

FOREIGN ADVENTURES

O N FEBRUARY 18, 1954, a man rang the door-
bell of a certain Georgi Okolovich in Frankfurt am Main. When he had been admitted,
he identified himself and coldly announced
that he had been dispatched by the Soviet secret service to
kill Okolovich.

The Koklov case (the caller was Captain Koklov of the
MVD) created a great sensation. In fact, Koklov betrayed two
of the men who had been sent with him to carry out the mission. He also produced the special weapon that he was supposed to use: A pistol concealed in a cigarette case. At the
same time he explained why he had refused to carry out his
mission. His wife, who was deeply religious, had persuaded
him to go first and warn the victim, regardless of the consequences to her and their two children.

Koklov was also a member of the NTS. Okolovich was one
of the major leaders of that Organization of Russian Solidarity
that we have already mentioned. Furthermore, he was a specialist in clandestine activity within the Soviet Union. In 1938
he was one of a group of six men created in Warsaw for the
purpose of crossing the border. Three of them were killed in

the attempt and the fourth retreated; two succeeded and spent four months in the USSR. Okolovich was one of them.

This was not the first occasion on which the NTS had been the object of special attention since the end of the war. One of its members, Georgi Tregubov, was abducted in East Berlin and spent eight years in Soviet camps, from which he was not released until 1955. Two months after the failure of the plot against Okolovich, on April 13, 1954, Dr. Alexander Trushnovich was abducted. A member of the Council (in other words, the executive committee) of the NTS, Trushnovich was also the director of a refugee-aid committee. In this capacity he was in contact with a certain Gläske, who lived near the German demarcation line. On this April 13 Gläske telephoned and asked Trushnovich to go to his house. It was a trap. At Gläske's house Trushnovich was probably drugged and, when he was unconscious, loaded into a car parked outside the house for transfer to East Berlin.

Two months later, Valerian Tremmel, also a member of the NTS, was abducted in Linz, Austria. Thus the Soviet secret service was making it clear that it ascribed a certain importance to the work of the NTS.

As we have said, the organization was founded in Belgrade in 1930 as the result of a revolt by young Russian emigrants against their elders, a determination to change the methods of operation. These young men started from the principle that Soviet ideology should be opposed by another ideology, Soviet organization by another organization.

The ideology was embodied in the doctrine of "solidarism" that was based, although in rather confused fashion, on Max Scheller, Berdyayev, Emmanuel Mounier, and Léon Bourgeois and that attempted to oppose its own concepts to both collectivism and individualism. On the economic level it would not be possible to say that the NTS, even while defending private property, had rejected certain gains of the Revolution, and it is probable the influence of the NTS had made itself felt to a perceptible degree in the program worked out by Vlassov's movement. Otherwise the NTS refused for the moment to deal with the question of the future form of government, whether republic or monarchy, and its program envisaged a whole set of institutions such as a National Assembly, an Upper House, a Council of the Peoples, a Council of Labor, and so on.

All these plans evolved on foreign soil may seem fanciful. It is more interesting to study the work of the NTS as a combat organization, small in number, perhaps, but thoroughly structured into a hierarchy. Its chief leaders today are Poremsky, Okolovich, Lev Rahr, etc.

Before the war the NTS lacked sufficient time to assert itself in relation to the other emigrant movements. But the conflict with the Soviet Union showed that it constituted a minority already versed in propaganda and infiltration. Taking the opportunities accorded by circumstances, the men of the NTS directed their operations in various directions.

They made every effort to establish sections in the areas under Soviet occupation. They also made their way into the camps housing prisoners of war and forced laborers. Some of their subalterns got into the propaganda agencies set up by the Germans, in particular the training camp in Wustrau, near Berlin, and in Wulherde, a Berlin suburb. Wustrau was under the control of the minister for the East, Wulherde under that of the *Wehrmacht.*

In addition the NTS endeavored to infiltrate Vlassov's army. Though Vlassov himself was not a member, Trukhin, one of his deputies, was. When the question of forming a Russian army of liberation arose, Trukhin headed the school in Daubendorf, near Berlin, with the assistance of NTS members. This school's purpose was to train propagandists who would work with Vlassov's army.

At the same time the NTS was attempting to infiltrate some of its men into Soviet territory and to make contact with guerrilla movements. Such work could not fail to create certain difficulties with the German authorities, and the NTS was suspected of playing a double game. Some of its officers were arrested by the Gestapo. In the period immediately preceding the unsuccessful attempt on Hitler's life sixty members of the Berlin NTS group were arrested, including a number of the leaders, such as Baidalakov and Poremsky. The reserve center that backed up their activity, headed by Okolovich, was destroyed a few months later, and its leaders were placed in concentration camps.

Germany's collapse did not wholly interrupt the work of the NTS. Its leaders say today that many of its members carried on their activities in the Soviet Union, into which they had made their way with the repatriates. Obviously such a statement is impossible of verification. In the West, NTS men were suspect because they were regarded as accomplices of the Germans. Nevertheless the presence of more than two million Soviet citizens interned in displaced persons' camps, a large number of whom had no desire to return to the Soviet Union, created a favorable climate. With great difficulty a group of NTS militants reestablished operations. Settling in Thuringia, they had set up a construction company that served as their cover. Little by little they succeeded in taking over the administration of a number of refugee camps. When the American troops evacuated Thuringia, the group moved its activities to the Minchehof camp near Kassel. It was at this time, in 1945, that *Possev* (*The Seed*), which was to become the mouthpiece of the movement, began to appear in mimeographed form.

The dramas that were enacted in the refugee camps were obviously useful to the NTS. But they also led to the internment of a number of its members. It is conceivable that the NTS enjoyed a certain protection on the part of American officers. At the same time it was quite clear that in general governments tended to be hostile to it. It was not until the beginning of the Cold War that a certain change in course could be observed. In July 1946 the Council of the NTS was finally able to meet for the first time since 1942.

An organization that succeeds in keeping itself alive through all the dramas and crises of war, reviving its broken ties, gives evidence of a certain aptitude for conspiracy and a tactical flexibility that enables it to take new turns. This impression is confirmed when one analyzes the structure of the NTS. Its supreme body, the Council, is composed of fifteen members elected for six years. This Council is chosen not by a congress but by the "circle of leaders," which is made up of "the oldest and most active" militants of the NTS. Who draws up the list of these militants? The Council, on the instance of local groups. This closed circuit is extremely undemocratic. It must be added that the leaders of the NTS have not called a congress since 1934, alleging that the members of the movement who operate in Russia could not be represented in it. In addition they justify their system of coopted leadership by emphasizing that it creates great obstacles to infiltration of the leadership positions by enemy agents. The argument is indeed valid, but it has a converse, too: By becoming, so to speak, the property of the "veterans," the NTS deprives itself of new blood at the top.

The same concern with security has led the leaders of the NTS to abandon any structured clandestine organization inside the Soviet Union, experience having shown that it would run the risk of speedy destruction by the Soviet police.

The NTS has replaced illegal hierarchic structures with the so-called "molecule" system. A "molecule" operating within the Soviet Union is composed of one, two, or if necessary three individuals in a given town. The "molecule" does not attempt to enlist other followers there; its object is to prove the existence of the movement, for example by painting the trident, the symbol of the NTS, on walls and stuffing mailboxes with leaflets imported from abroad or confected on the spot with whatever means may be at hand. The leaflets may call on other Soviet citizens to form their own "molecules" based on the same model. But these microscopic islands of agitators never attempt to make contact with one another or to expand, for this would expose them to the actions of *provocateurs* and to counterattacks by the forces of repression. Thus the "molecule" is difficult to pin down. Nor does its discovery make it possible for the police to carry out a chain reaction of arrests.

In addition, members of "molecules" are urged to find responsible positions in the apparatus of the state in order to be in a position to play decisive parts in the event of a crisis in the system.

But how can the leadership assure the management and control of these tiny units scattered across Soviet territory? Through the broadcasts of the radio station of the NTS, the dispatch of instructions camouflaged as ordinary letters or in parcels of merchandise, and through personal contact by liaison agents who have been able to make their way into the Soviet Union and whose task it is to keep the foreign center informed of the local activities of the "molecules."

The leaders of the NTS believe that, if the "molecules" multiply, it will be possible to mobilize them by radio on the day appointed for internal insurrection and to weld them quickly into an organization that will then be structured. I shall have something to say later of my views on the efficacy and the scope of such a system.

The radio plays an important part in the various activities of the NTS. The station called "Free Russia" began its broadcasts from Germany in December 1950. At that time its power did not exceed thirty-eight watts, and it was mounted on a small truck that shifted position constantly in the woods. (For lack of a permanent mast, the antenna had to be strung from a tree.) In 1951 these daily broadcasts led to a protest by the Soviet authorities. In 1953 a more powerful permanent transmitter was set up near Frankfurt-am-Main, broadcasting on two wave-lengths: 26.7 and 46 meters. This led to an unending battle with the Soviet jamming experts. There were also to be times when the NTS would find itself embroiled with the Western authorities because of its broadcasts.

According to the leaders of the NTS, the importance of the broadcasts is based on the fact that many young Russians are enthusiastic radio amateurs and have short-wave receivers and transmitters, thus facilitating the dissemination and heightening the impact of NTS propaganda. (See Chapter 25).

Other technical means have also been employed to enable propaganda to reach behind the iron curtain. Balloons fifty feet in diameter, carrying more than two hundred pounds of leaflets, are released into the air stream. An automatic mechanism is timed to release the leaflets after a fixed interval, and they are then strewn by the wind above the area desired. This method has the disadvantage of entailing substantial waste.

The changes in internal conditions in the Soviet Union after Stalin's death and especially after Khrushchev's report, the manifestations of an unmistakable discontent in the population, and the relaxation of police surveillance opened the way to other possibilities. In particular, the policy of peaceful coexistence has brought about some lowering of the barriers between East and West. Cultural and scientific exchanges, trade negotiations, and travel both for business and for pleasure have increased in both directions. The volume of correspondence has risen substantially. Emerging from its political and economic isolation, the Soviet Union finds many advantages in this. But at the same time control of enemy infiltrations is made more difficult.

Groups of Soviet citizens touring foreign capitals began to appear in Europe in 1956. These groups, which sometimes included several hundred persons, were certainly well guarded. But in every city of Europe NTS men endeavored to establish contact with these travelers, exchange ideas and impressions with them, and form connections with certain of them. Occasionally this led to encounters with the Soviet "gorillas."

Journeys by Soviet intellectuals and scholars taking part in congresses and seminars abroad, as well as the travels of the various trade missions, also made it easier to establish contacts. Regardless what precautions were taken, it was impossible to watch everyone, and the end of the Stalinist terror stimulated initiatives that would have been unthinkable a few years earlier.

After the Twenty-first Congress, the Soviet Union's serious economic difficulties compelled the government to import foreign credits and goods from Western countries. Hence these exchanges acquired a further importance and afforded new opportunities for contacts. In addition the number of foreigners in the Soviet Union has increased considerably.

The NTS claims too that it has been able to establish a network among the seamen of the merchant fleet, thus imitating the old methods employed by the Komintern.

The rise in exchanges with the West has led to a gain in the volume of correspondence, which was to reach a monthly volume of two million units with the United States alone. Such a flood becomes impossible to control. Relying on information received from the Vatican, the leaders of the NTS assume that one mail bag in every twelve is subjected to examination. But the Soviet authorities have perfected devices that make it possible to detect the presence of printed matter inside an envelope.

The Soviet authorities have long maintained silence on the various activities of the NTS. Beginning in 1954, however, the press attacked it along the classic lines: "White Guards, traitors to their country," etc. The NTS men were also accused of being among the tools of the Central Intelligence Agency.

Then silence fell again, but it was spectacularly broken in 1956, perhaps on the instance of Shelepin, then minister of the interior, by the trial of Gerald Brooke and his confederates. Brooke, a young British intellectual, had agreed to make contacts with members of the young Soviet intelligentsia on behalf of the NTS. The publicity given to this trial and Brooke's sentence were evidence of the need to make an example and to show that such adventures were doomed to speedy failure.

Precisely what is the influence of the NTS? This is a matter of bitter controversy in emigrant circles, where its enterprises and its methods are much debated. Sometimes the NTS is denounced for accepting subsidies from the American Intelligence Service, sometimes it is accused of lying about its efficacy and its influence. There are those who deny the slightest worth or importance to the much touted "molecule" system. Others attack the NTS for the positions that it adopted during the war. It is extremely difficult to separate truth from lie in the statements made by the NTS, and this is equally true of the criticisms of which it is the target.

The security reasons that the leaders of the NTS invoke in order to assure secrecy for their operations are perfectly plausible, but they make any verification impossible (and this does not apply to the NTS alone). By way of illustration, the NTS refuses to disclose the number of its "molecules." But in any case any claim embodying a specific figure would be hardly more informative.

The most that can be said is that the reaction occasionally produced in the Soviet press by the NTS shows that the movement is regarded as capable of constituting one of many dangers for the system. Press reports seem to prove that units of the "molecular" type exist or have existed (see Chapter 25) on Soviet territory, that they can contribute to a certain agitation, and that the appearance of the famous trident on a wall should logically excite the interest and comments of a population greedy for anything that is different from official propaganda and should hence help to create a "legend."

On the other hand, the "operational" possibilities of the "molecule" system would appear to be limited. While it is true that the "molecule" provides the best insurance against discovery by the police, its autonomy represents a considerable obstacle to any coordinated activity. Neither instructions broadcast by radio (on the assumption that they are received) nor letters, and not even intermittent contacts with special emissaries, can remedy this major disadvantage.

Even in a structured clandestine organization that includes permanent communications facilities it is extremely difficult to assure unity of action of the whole, to prevent deviations

and unfortunate local initiatives, to correct faults, to resolve a
host of concrete problems that are constantly arising. The confidence that on counterrevolution's D-Day hundreds of puta-
tive "molecules" can be coordinated by a central leadership,
springing up by some miracle, and that they will accept its
authority and form ranks in terms of a given strategy seems
fairly utopian. Moreover, for my own part, I have no knowledge that at the time of the uprisings and the strikes in the
concentration camps the NTS was in any position to assume
their leadership and provide their staffs.

In October 1964, during a meeting sponsored by the weekly,
Possev, one Tretyakov submitted a report on "the experience
and the operational problems of clandestine revolutionary activity." On the basis of the disorders in Novocherkassk and
the Donetz Basin, the outbursts of illegal strikes, and the
weapons traffic reported in the Soviet press, Tretyakov concluded that it was necessary to establish clandestine newspapers, to strengthen anti-Communist positions in the army,
and to create bases of support in the electrical power stations,
the railways, the arsenals, and the broadcasting facilities.

An ambitious and unquestionably precocious program. It
would appear that since then the leaders of the NTS have
turned the major part of their effort on another sector: the
young Russian intelligentsia. It is unchallengeable that sustained contacts have been established in this quarter, that
there have been exchanges of experiences, and that the NTS
has succeeded in bringing out of Russia a number of secretly
written works that have been published in its literary organ,
Grani. And too the clever agitational device on the part of the
intelligentsia that consists in demanding the strict enforcement of the Soviet Constitution seems to dovetail closely with
the views of the NTS, whether this move was conceived by
the command post in Frankfurt-am-Main or initiated by the
Soviet oppositionists.

This may be looked on as a modest result. In reality, given
the difficulties of the undertaking, as well as the lack of sup-

port from the West—and, occasionally, even the poorly concealed hostility of some nations toward such initiatives—it required great skill and courage to succeed in establishing a bridgehead in intellectual circles within the Soviet Union. And that is an important achievement. For in the final analysis it is the new generation that constitutes an essential stake in the struggle, and there can be no cohesive revolutionary action without the collaboration of intellectual leaders.

I have deliberately left aside one major point in the program of the NTS because it constitutes a permanent subject of dissension among the opposition. In sum the NTS professes to be a patriotic *Russian* organization, and it is in Russia itself that it seeks to make its chief effort. But the terminology chosen for the formula, "the peoples of Russia," in itself grants the preponderant part to the large nation. In this connection it is appropriate to quote from one of the movement's pamphlets:

It is no accident that the NTS invokes "the peoples of Russia." Russia is a multi-national state, and the movement's program takes this fact largely into account. *In this respect it emphasizes the right of self-determination that is enjoyed by peoples in a democratic system; in other words, it recognizes for all the peoples that are integral parts of Russia the right to become independent when this desire is expressed in a consultation of the people in conformity with democratic principles.* Nevertheless, in the view of the NTS, dismemberment is desirable neither for the state as a whole nor for the component parts taken separately. Therefore it appeals for the preservation of the unity of the great family of the peoples of Russia and it proposes a federated national state.[1]

If this passage is compared with the corresponding passage in the Vlassov movement's manifesto, it will be found that they are virtually identical. Vlassov had already used the formula of "the peoples of Russia." Moreover, the right of peoples to free disposition of their own destiny is not denied, but it

[1] NTS, *Revolutionary Organization of Russian Resistance* (1961). (Italics in the original.)

is postponed until a time subsequent to the downfall of the Soviet system. Finally, there can be no doubt that the NTS takes an unfavorable view of any possible separatism.

At once we observe the resurgence of the problems that had deeply divided Vlassov's supporters and the representatives of the national minorities during the war. The minorities did not want the question of independence deferred to some future period when circumstances would (or, as they said, would not) permit the democratic consultation of the people's will. They intended this independence to be proclaimed at once as an unchallengeable principle.

This deeply rooted division, which continues to haunt anti-Soviet emigrant circles and which occasionally erupts into polemics of the utmost violence, consists in more than the mere contrast between principles difficult of reconciliation. It has immediate consequences on actions. Naturally it prevents the formation of a united front, which the Germans were unable to achieve in spite of all their pressures. But, above all, this extremely important opposition calls for different strategies. It is obvious that the NTS will not attempt to nourish the centers of dissidence that may arise within Soviet territory. Conversely, the national minorities base their strategy on the exploitation and amplification of the conflicts between the peoples and the central power, and they ascribe major importance to the struggle against Russianization.

The Ukrainians are the spearhead of this movement. They have the advantage over the other emigrant peoples (with the exception of the Russians) of sizable representations in the Western countries, particularly in the United States, Canada, Australia, and England, which are very closely linked (in spite of the inevitable internal quarrels) and which constitute an important base of support. In addition, the combat carried on before the war by Ukrainian nationalists and the battles of the UPA during and after the war have made it possible for them to strike deep roots into the population, at least in the area of the western Ukraine.

If Frankfurt-am-Main is the seat of the NTS, Munich is the general headquarters of the ABN—the Anti-Bolshevik Bloc of Nations—which represents sixteen eastern and central European nationalities: Ukrainians, Georgians, Balts, Croatians, Hungarians, Macedonians, Azerbaidzhanis, Turkestanis, etc. The Ukrainians of the OUN, under the leadership of Stetsko, who in June 1941 was the premier of the Lvov government that was speedily dissolved by the Germans, constitute the dominant element in this federation of subjugated nationalities. Thus the ABN is the extension of that clandestine committee of the peoples that was brought together in the Ukrainian underground by the UPA in 1943.

The ABN maintains quite close contacts with another organization, the anti-Communist League of the Peoples of Asia. When this league held its Eleventh Conference in November 1964, the resolution that it adopted on the satellite countries very accurately reflected the concepts of the ABN, which indeed may have suggested its text:

The conference declares itself in favor of the dissolution of what is called the Union of Soviet Socialist Republics into independent democratic national states of the peoples who are oppressed within it, on the basis of ethnographic frontiers; in favor of the restoration of the sovereignty of the peoples of the so-called satellite countries, and in favor of the dissolution of states artifically created by force, such as Czechoslovakia and Yugoslavia.

This alone shows that the ABN's field of action extends beyond the Soviet Union to the people's democracies, with the notion that the struggle by the nationalities in the satellite countries can have reprecussions inside the Soviet Union. In its monthly bulletin, *ABN Correspondence,* the ABN establishes an ethnic basis for its activity and concedes an important place to the defense of national traditions, cultures, and religions.[2] This theme is developed in the same sense by var-

[2] Notably to the persecutions directed against the Ukrainian Catholic Church and its leader, Monsignor Slypy, recently released by the Russians.

ious Ukrainian publications (*Ukrainian Review* and *l'Est européen*). It seems too that the ABN finds some support in Vatican circles, from Chiang Kai-shek, in Spain, and among certain sectors of the Republican party in the United States.

As a result the hostility that the ABN displays toward the Soviet government is always accompanied by violent denunciation of Russian imperialism and colonialism. One might say even that anti-Russian feeling often seems to get the better of anti-Communism; in any event it imbues it with a very strong coloration and feeds it constantly. It follows that the strategy of this movement tends to array the peoples of the Soviet Union against the various forms of oppression of which they are the object by exploiting not only the grounds for discontent connected with economic demands (wages, food, etc.) or internal policy (the defense of civil liberties) but also whatever damages or wounds the essence of a people: the suppression of its culture, the persecution of a national religion, *de facto* privileges granted to Russian citizens, etc. In the final analysis this attitude is directed toward the dislocation of a huge empire of which Russia appears to be the mortar.

This attitude, too, is totally incompatible with the positions taken by the NTS. To the extent to which the NTS concerns itself with national minorities and finds it impossible to approve such actions as the deportations of Latvians and Lithuanians, it endeavors in its propaganda to urge the populations not to confuse Russians with Soviet citizens in their enmity and not to ascribe to a people the deeds of the Bolshevik system.

The difference in the attitude of the NTS toward the army is no less characteristic. The NTS believes that it is necessary to penetrate into the interior of the Soviet army and to proceed to create cells inside it. But, from a long-range point of view, the Soviet army can be only the instrument destined to liberate the Russian fatherland from the Soviet yoke. In contrast, a man like Stetsko believes that the work of demoralization within the army should be based above all on the national-minority elements conscripted into it, so that the motley coalition dominated by the Russians can be smashed. Thus, the sabotage, agitation, desertion, etc., that might occur in the event of a major crisis would be the work of men who refused to consider the Soviet army their country's army.

The leaders of the ABN base their hopes on the continuation of armed combat in the Ukraine or the Baltic countries by strike and revolt action in the camps, where in fact it was the Ukrainian, Lithuanian, and Latvian nationalist groups, already tempered by long and bitter fighting, who represented the moving forces.

What is the situation today? The leaders of the ABN believe that the center of gravity of the struggle, which was situated at first in the western Ukraine with the UPA and which was later shifted to Siberia and the camps or among the more or less slave laborers working on the reclamation of virgin soil, is now established in the Donetz Basin, in Dniepropetrovsk, Notocherkassk, and Odessa. The movement is also advancing among the young Ukrainian intelligentsia.

The Ukrainians in the ABN insists that they maintain close contacts with these movements, but they refuse to say anything further on the matter. Like the leaders of the NTS, it appears, they attach great importance to radio broadcasts and think that these can largely take the place of human contacts. For example, a broad proliferation of the Novocherkassk movement of revolt could constitute an excellent lesson in revolutionary action and incite other risings elsewhere. As for the Ukrainians, they have three broadcasting facilities: one in the Vatican, devoted to religious programs; one in Spain; and the third on Formosa. A clandestine transmitter also operated for a short time in the Belgian Ardennes, but it was shut down as the result of a Soviet protest. The Slovakian and Hungarian representatives also have their own facilities in Spain.

In addition, journeys by tourists in both directions also afford numerous opportunities for meetings.

I have already said what I thought of the possibilities of conducting a clandestine movement with these methods. Besides, we lack sufficient information on the possible connections with other national minorities inside the Soviet Union.

If one consults the Soviet press, it appears that it continues to be especially concerned by the menace of internal Ukrainian nationalism. On September 30, 1961, the Twenty-second Congress of the Ukrainian Communist party adopted this resolution: "The chief subject of concern for the party's organisms ought to be . . . the total elimination of the vestiges of bourgeois ideology, and especially of Ukrainian bourgeois nationalism, from the population." The same view appeared in a speech by Podgorny on February 20, 1962, during a conference of party functionaries in Kiev: "The most important problem facing our ideological activity is the intensification of the struggle against bourgeois ideology, particularly against the ideology of Ukrainian bourgeois nationalism."

As for the emigrants, they were consistently accused of "being in the pay of the imperialists and their intelligence services" (*Radyanska Ukrayina,* Kiev, February 28, 1957). But, regardless of the scorn in which Soviet propaganda professed to hold Ukrainian nationalism, its leaders did not escape the vigilant attentions of Moscow's secret service.

On October 15, 1959, Stepan Bandera, the major leader of the OUN and the incarnation of the struggle for independence as Petlyura [3] was in another time, was taken to a hospital, where he soon died of poison. He had been found unconscious in the stairway of his house in Munich, where he was living under a false name. The most mysterious rumors on his decease began to circulate—some spoke of suicide, some of rivalries among the Ukrainians, some of a murder by the West

[3] The glorification of the Petlyura brothers as patriotic nationalists is a recent phenomenon initiated by certain West German circles mentioned in an earlier footnote; for the preceding thirty or forty years these men had been recognized as nothing but the leaders of marauding brigand bands and instigators of pogroms. Bandera was a collaborator with the Germans during the war.—Translator.

German intelligence forces under Gehlen, who held an important position in the Federal Republic. The case would never have been cleared up if a certain Stashinsky had not been arrested in 1961 in West Germany. A Soviet citizen and an agent of the KGB, he confessed to having murdered Bandera and, earlier, another leader of the OUN, Lev Rebet.

Stashinsky was tried in Karlsruhe and sentenced to eight years in prison. He testified that he had killed Bandera on the stairs, using a special pistol that sent a poison spray into the victim's eyes, and that he had used the same weapon against Rebet. Stashinsky stated also that he had acted under orders from Shelepnin, then minister of state security and one of the most prominent "young men" in the Soviet ruling group. For this dual achievement he had received the Order of the Red Flag. Another murder was being prepared: The intended victim was Stetsko.

The trial produced certain clarifications of the way in which such operations were decided on. During Stalin's time the orders came directly from Beria's staff. But, after the Twentieth Congress in 1956, in order to restrict the initiatives of such bodies, it was decided, the testimony alleged, that such orders could be issued only by a committee composed of several members of the government. "This information," the official record of the trial observed, "is based on the precise and consistent statements made by the accused as to the manner in which he received his orders, and at no time did he contradict himself on this matter."

If his testimony was truthful, it showed that the Soviet government attached a certain importance to such "precise" operations. For that matter, Soviet policy with respect to emigrant organizations had followed an immutable course since the beginning of Soviet power: liquidate their leaders by murder or abduction. The "wrecks of the White Guards" were insignificant in Moscow's eyes, perhaps, but Moscow was not altogether negligent in dealing with such trivialities.

(25)

FROM ACTIVISM
TO MASS ACTION

ROM THE time of the October Revolution, when Insky was eighteen years old, his parents had always been hostile to the Soviet system. Every evening at the table their conversation always summed itself up in the same question: "Will they be able to stay in power long?" Insky's parents convinced themselves that it would not last. But then they died, perhaps in deportation. Insky was left alone. He was fortunate enough to be able to finish his studies and become an engineer in the Scientific Research Institute in Leningrad.

Before they died (or were arrested), his parents had given him the address of "good friends" who lived abroad. Many years later, after the Second World War, the friends wrote a letter, inviting Insky to the city of M——, where at a specific place a man would be waiting for him.

Although he had become a government technician, Insky did not hesitate. He kept the appointment. The man who met him suggested that he find "unstable people" (the Soviet vocabulary's designation for those who had deviated from the party line). Before he and Insky parted, the stranger turned over a suitcase "containing base slanders against the Soviet Union."

This story was printed in *Leningradskaya Pravda* on July 13, 1958. It added that further secret meetings took place in M—— and then in Leningrad, where Insky met another agent in the Pushkin Theater on the Nevsky Prospekt. Shortly afterward he was arrested.

Pravda did not say whether the other members of the ring had been captured. It gave no details on their activities. Since the agents who had come from abroad were Russians, it is legitimate to suppose that they might have been members of the NTS. We do not know how many "unstable people" Insky was able to enlist. *Pravda's* story was obviously designed to persuade the reader that Insky's was an exceptional case and that this was an isolated instance, hardly more than a minor news item. But the mere fact that the Soviet press reported such cases instead of hushing them up shows that the authorities believed that matters had reached a stage at which public opinion should be warned against such action.

On August 6, 1958, the same paper reported new activities. In the beginning it was a question of a printer, Bagretzov, who was described as embittered because he had been unable to make his dream come true: "to acquire fifty acres of land of his own and have dozens of cows and pigs." The account continued:

Bagretzov began to write many slanderous letters in which he flung mud at our Socialist society. Late at night, furtively looking in every direction and selecting deserted streets and unlighted entrances, Bagretzov stuffed these base letters by the packet, with their hateful fabrications, into mailboxes.

Then came the leaflets composed by Gordyenko, a medical student—"filthy forgeries on our system and our people." All these cases were reported as individual instances, though one might well wonder whether the individuals in question were not members of a clandestine group. But in other instances the press did come to recognize the existence of organized groups, particularly among the students; witness *Komsomolskaya Pravda* for December 23, 1955:

Recently the group of students of the University of Vilnius who had signed frivolous, decadent poems has published a manuscript paper called *The Fig Leaf.* Instead of publicly pillorying these demagogues and vulgar minds, the *Komsomol* committee made every effort to hush up the case with great precautions.

On January 4, 1956, the same paper reported a similar occurrence, this one in Leningrad:

What explanation can there be, apart from the unpardonably low level of cultural work among the students, for the appearance of a manuscript publication called *The Blue Button* at the university, containing wretched stories and vulgar little slobbering verses?

In the December 16, 1956 issue it was reported that a group of students in the Railway Engineers' School of Leningrad was publishing a periodical called *New Voices* that "in a nihilist fashion denigrates the achievements of our Socialist culture." A similar publication, *Heresy,* emanated from the Krupskaya Institute in Leningrad (*Komsomoslkaya Pravda,* December 28, 1956).

From that period on, the opposition did not restrict its manifestations to clandestine publications. It also expressed itself in conferences and official meetings. Again I quote from *Komsomolskaya Pravda* of December 16, 1956:

Our people and our party have never been tolerant of dabblers in fine words, undisciplined chatterboxes, and demagogues who pride themselves on knowing and passing judgment on everything. But such individuals exist among the students. Their voices have made themselves heard at times in the annual conferences and meetings.

Clandestine action assumed other forms that utilized the facilities of modern technology. Soviet youth had evinced a keen interest in radio, and many young Russians had built short-wave transmitters, in most cases for perfectly legal purposes.

But some of them used these transmitters to disseminate statements opposed to the system. The press attacked them on a number of occasions, denouncing "the radio gang" and the "hooligans of the air waves." *Trud* said on October 3, 1963, that "the radio represents a powerful ideological weapon, and consequently the contamination of the air should no longer be tolerated." Nevertheless the "aerial pirates" continued to function in Dniepropetrovsk, Kiev, and Kazakhstan, continually shifting their bases of operations in order to avoid detection. They made tape recordings of foreign programs and rebroadcast them. Jehovah's Witnesses also used this method for religious programs. It would appear that initially the Soviets lacked sufficient trained personnel to track down these broadcasts, given the large number of owners of short-wave radios. But it is probable that the government was compelled to make substantial improvements in both personnel and technical equipment.

On the basis merely of information gleaned from the Soviet press, it also appears that some groups had begun to arm themselves. On August 3, 1963, *Vechernya Moskva* reported that students from the University of Moscow had hidden rifles in an office of the DOSAF Committee, a para-military organization. On September 14 *Literaturnaya Gazeta* told of students in the Aeronautical Academy who had stolen rifles from the school's arsenal and turned them over to girls to be hidden in their bedrooms.

At first glance all these actions together seem hardly threatening to a government whose immediate power was so vast. But in a totalitarian country this is how armed action begins: with more or less trivial incidents and the employment of microscopic means. That students in a city like Moscow were beginning to arm themselves by stealing rifles or obtaining revolvers was a far from negligible indication of the transformation that had taken place in attitudes.

Quite often the newspapers make much of a resurgence of banditry and point out the necessity of putting a stop to it. There can be no doubt that many of these offenses are committed by ordinary criminals who, having profited by an amnesty, have returned to their former careers, which are of course barren of any political coloration. But the authorities obviously have every reason to make banditry the ostensible source of the attacks on party "activists," kolkhoz managers, militiamen, and *druzhniki* (police auxiliaries usually recruited among members of the *Komsomol*). And an "expropriation" perpetrated by a group of guerrillas in order to replenish its treasury can all the more easily be classified under the head of robbery since the government has defined all its political enemies *a priori* as common criminals.

When the attorney general of the Tadzhikistan Republic spoke of criminal acts committed by recently amnestied offenders (*Kommunist Tadzhikistana*, January 5, 1956), there was some uncertainty as to the exact nature of these offenders: Were they former politicals or former criminals? The prosecutor rebuked the republic's militia and other institutions for their passivity. Is this to be interpreted as sympathy for compatriots who engaged in guerrilla activities? The same question arose when *Babinsky Rabochy* of Baku reported robberies in trains and burglaries of railway stations on April 12 and July 16 and 17, 1956.

And was it not a political trial in the northern Caucasus that was reported in *Krasnaya Zvyezda*, the army's newspaper? The story mentioned the names of only two of the accused. But, strangely, the trial lasted eighteen days, a time that seems rather protracted for establishing the facts about the activities of two persons. Even more strangely, a group of men attempted to rescue the defendants during the trial. Was this an attack by a guerrilla group?

Emigrant organizations insist that such guerrilla units are operating today in the Soviet Union and that they have never completely halted their work in the peripheral areas of the country, especially those covered by immense forests. The ABN's publication for April 1965, for example, reported that groups of armed young men had hidden themselves in the forest in the vicinity of the fortified city of Kamenyetz-Podolsky, and that the people called them "the sons of the forest." Supposedly they engaged in assassination attempts against overzealous local functionaries and in holdups of trucks carrying wheat and other grain, which they allegedly gave away to the population.

Similar units were reported to be operating in the forests of White Russia. In October 1963, it was said, a KGB unit ran a fine-tooth comb through the forest in the Orsha region after such groups had looted food reserves in the town. In the district of Brest-Litovsk, according to rumor, these guerrillas even ventured into the town at night in order to paste up posters reading: "Down with Communism!" and "Death to the tyrants in the Kremlin!"

How closely do such stories correspond to reality? All that can be said on the matter is that often the Soviet press yields indirect confirmations of them, with the reservation that it always presents each one as an isolated instance. On October 18, 1964, for instance, *Hudok*, the railway newspaper, contained an account of the arrest of one Mashkin, who had killed a secretary of the Communist party of the Drabin district, near Cherkassy. Mashkin was arrested but managed to escape; then he was seized a second time by railway police near a station when he was returning from the forest.

Was he an ordinary criminal or a man belonging to an organized group? The Soviet version and the emigrants' version are diametrically opposed in every such instance. And it is impossible to know which is accurate.

There would appear to be far greater significance to the report in *Prykarpatska Pravda* describing a trial of a group of

Ukrainian nationalists that began on February 28, 1964.[1] The principal defendant, Dmytro Lutanyuk, also known as Madyar, was a member of a combat group led by one "Martyn" after he joined the UPA forces in 1944. In 1947 he took refuge in a clandestine shelter beneath the house of the Kozherchuka sisters in the village of Strymba. He remained in communication with his commander, "Martyn," and for six years he carried on his activities, in particular assassinating a kolkhoz chairman and a *Komsomol* leader. In 1953 the OUN, the Ukrainians' political organization, transferred Lutanyuk to another village, where he was introduced to a Ukrainian priest, Ignat Soltys.

He was listened to with attention [the newspaper said]. He received a blessing and he was advised to disguise himself as a monk. Then he was sent to Pereginsko to stay with a fanatic named Yustyna Melnykovna; a year later he was shifted to Gvzid, sheltered there by Katerina Kepeshchuka, and from there he was moved to Krasne, to the house of Anna Kharyshaka. He was very carefully hidden. . . . Even in 1963 not one of the residents of the village of Krasne knew that for eight years an armed man had been living in their midst.

The story disclosed also that the same woman harbored another terrorist, Synyak, and two women who served as liaison agents. One of these women, who was taking night courses in the workers' youth school in Kolomya, was also hiding a guerrilla in her house, helping him to get out into the woods, and arranging meetings between Lutanyuk and Synyak. The other defendants were charged with having concealed weapons.

It is a remarkable story because it reveals the existence of a network of fanatically dedicated supporters. Thanks to this network, men who had fought in the ranks of the UPA since 1944 had been able to carry on their work until 1964—*for twenty years*. To hold out under such conditions and carry on the armed struggle is no ordinary accomplishment.

[1] Cf. *l'Est européen*, August 1964.

Further corroboration of these illegal activities was afforded by the disclosures of a Ukrainian Jew, Alexander Rathaus, a former professor at the University of Kharkov and a former member of the Communist party. Rathaus, who was able to leave the Ukraine in 1962, confirmed the existence of underground cells.[2] According to Rathaus, cultural resistance began while Stalin was still alive; in particular, students refused to sit for examinations in Russian. Approximately eight hundred of them were deported, expelled from the university, or included on blacklists. Thirty-three of their leaders were shot after a secret trial.

This occurred in 1951. Ten years later the number 33 was painted in black on the walls of the Universities of Kiev and Lvov. This was the emblem of an organization that was based on the men shot in 1951. Rathaus wrote:

When I was in Kiev on May 23, 1961, I wanted to visit the rector of the university and several professors. I found police vehicles at the gates of the university. Inside, plainclothesmen and security officials were checking a long line of students who stood along the wall, their hands outstretched, palms up. I tried to leave, but two policemen blocked my way. So I started toward the rector's office.

A group of several high police officials and two policemen in colonels' uniforms were already there. Then I listened to one of the discussions of the appearance of the symbol, 33, painted in black that same day, on the walls, ceilings, and floors of seven of the university's buildings. At least a hundred students must have taken part in that operation. The policemen were making every effort to find at least one of them by examining their hands for signs of paint. I left the university without knowing whether any of them had been arrested.

Rathaus then catalogued a whole list of actions carried out by guerrillas: sabotage of the grain harvest in the region of

[2] In *The Ukrainian Review* (Vol. XVIII, No. 3, 1962), an article reprinted by the *Revue militaire générale* under the title "La Résistance actuelle en URSS," December 1963.

Rovno in the western Ukraine, executions of high party officials in the districts of Tarnopol, Stanislavov, and Uzhorod. He said that these men's tactics were different from those of their predecessors in the UPA. The UPA's forces lived in camps in the forests and worked cooperatively. Their successors lived at home, worked as farmers, tractor drivers, building laborers, teachers, accountants, or mechanics. They attended the meetings organized by the Communists, and they paid their taxes. On certain nights, in obedience to a prearranged signal, the five or nine freedom fighters of the "activist cell" would meet in the forest, follow their leader to the place where their weapons were concealed, select the required arms and explosives, and set out to perform the mission that had been assigned to them. They returned before dawn, cleaned their weapons, and hid them in a different place. They washed, changed their clothes, and went to their jobs, and, when party agitators called a meeting to protest "the crimes perpetrated by the mercenaries of American espionage and the murderous lackeys of Wall Street," they too voiced their indignation. The Russians, Rathaus added, "never acknowledge the existence of the Ukrainian nationalist guerrilla forces, which operate with impunity and success in at least nine of the twenty-two administrative districts of the Ukraine."

Rathaus also mentioned another form of spontaneous opposition, the sabotage that was practiced, for example, in the port of Odessa. According to him, the tractors shipped by the Soviet Union to Ghana and Guinea were unusable because of such deliberate damage. Nevertheless he believed that cultural resistance and the various forms of passive resistance were more effective than armed actions.

Whatever the actual size of the activist groups and the extent of their operations, their chances of success were of the sparsest without some major domestic or foreign crisis that would unsettle the government. Their function in the present phase is that of keeping the forces of repression on edge and sustaining hope in the population.

Other forms of opposition have developed. For a long time the working class was passive. During the great period of industrialization in the 1930s, the labor force was made up in the main of people snatched away from their land and speedily proletarianized. Without any tradition of labor struggle, uprooted from their natural environment, living under the worst of material conditions, they could concentrate on nothing but survival. Their opposition never went beyond the stage of passive resistance, absenteeism, refusals to fulfill the production standards imposed on them. The aggressive elements in the working class and the politically educated (the Workers' Opposition, the Trotskyists, the anarchists, the Mensheviks, the Revolutionary Socialists) had for the most part been purged. Hence the working class was deprived of staffs to direct its struggle. The Great Purge and then the war had not contributed to concerted activity.

It required Stalin's death to bring about mass movements on a large scale. These ranged from the slowdown to the full-fledged strike and sometimes to street fighting and rebellion.

On October 3 and 5, 1959, the campaign for the reclamation of virgin land led to a rising in the little town of Tamir-Tau, near Karaganda in Kazakhstan. Fifteen hundred young people, weary of the deplorable material conditions imposed on them, stood up to the militia and then to the soldiers sent to reinforce it. Finally, on October 5, KGB troops brought from Alma-Ata smashed the last resistance in street combat.

It might be noted that the local party secretary, Belayev, was relieved of his duties shortly afterward, on January 20, 1960, and that his successor, Kunayev, told the Tenth Congress of the Communist party of Kazakhstan: "We should draw the necessary conclusions from the interruptions that occurred last year in the construction of metallurgical installations."

It is believed that armed units operated in Kazakhstan in 1960, pillaging food warehouses and liquidating KGB men.

In 1962 there were demonstrations in Minsk in consequence of the poor management of the food supply. Let us point out too that it was at this time that there was a rumor of an attempt to assassinate Khrushchev. In the same year agitation spread in the Donetz Basin. The most important mass phenomenon was reported from Novocherkassk in June.

The discontent arose from the rise in the prices of basic living necessities, which were being exported in large quantities to Cuba, India, and Egypt. Students and young workers were reported to be in the leadership of the protests, shouting: "Down with Khrushchev! Down with the government and the colonialist system!" In the face of the swift spread of the disorders, the militia and the army refused to act. The KGB and the *druzhniki* were less hobbled by scruple. They opened fire and killed a number of persons.

The rising in Novocherkassk has often been cited by diverse quarters. It would appear to be certain that the region was placed under a state of siege as of June 1 and that this isolation continued for several months. According to one source, more than five thousand persons were killed.

It was reported also that during these riotous days an officer who was ordered to open fire refused and shot himself in the head. But the identical story came also from another place in the Donetz Basin.[3] Hence it must be credited only with reservations. The act recalls that of a colonel who did the same thing in February 1917. If it could be confirmed that an officer chose death over obedience, such a decision would have a significance far greater than that of an isolated action. For every commander of a unit who preferred to kill himself rather than execute an order for repression, how many others are there who obey only with revulsion?

In June 1963 there were also clashes in Krivoi Rog, an iron-mining center in the southern Ukraine.

All these events bear witness to an absolutely new spirit of

[3] Y. Stetsko, *Khrushchev's Unchanged Stalinist Policy Toward Nationalities and New Revolutionary Liberation Strategy.*

attack. Here opposition came out into the open with much violence. It took its stand on illegality, since strikes are forbidden in the Soviet Union, and it went into the streets. That in addition the KGB was detailed to put down these revolts indicated a reversion to the conditions that prevailed in 1929 during the battle of collectivization.

In the present state of affairs such revolts are circumscribed. They are doomed to more or less speedy destruction. But they assume a place in the vast process of struggle against the tyranny of the system. Much discussed, perhaps exaggerated by rumors that are transformed into legends, they set dangerous precedents and they condition minds for new confrontations.

Other strikes were organized too, in more peaceable fashion. It was reported, for example, that the workers of Leningrad and Moscow often resorted to the slowdown. This subtle pressure action had no other goals than rises in wages or reductions in production norms or improvements in working conditions. But the recurrence of such actions has a double significance: Working discipline is weakened just when the ruling class is endeavoring by various means to increase productivity, and these limited-objective movements contribute to the education of the working class and its awakening to its own interests and strength.

In terms of activism, peasant resistance seemed to have been shattered after collectivization. It was resumed in certain regions during the war to the extent to which hostility to the kolkhoz could be harmonized with national feelings.

The peasants believed that the end of the war would mean the abolition of the kolkhoz. Not only did nothing of the sort come to pass; until Stalin's death the condition of agriculture was such that millions of kolkhoz workers lived in misery. In 1953, according to the avowal that Khrushchev was to make ten years later, the peasants were dying of hunger. This was the very year in which certain soothsayers in France were proclaiming without a tremor that in a short time the Soviet Union was going to outstrip the capitalist countries and distribute bread for nothing.

The peasants offered only a sorry passive resistance to the kolkhoz system, reducing their productive efforts to the barest minimum. After Stalin's death, essentially under pressure from Khrushchev (although during the dictator's lifetime he had pushed for the supercollectivization of the agrovilles), many attempts were made to hoist Soviet agriculture out of its morass and improve the yield of the kolkhoz. In the spring of 1954 Khrushchev launched the campaign for the reclamation of the fallow lands in Siberia and Kazakhstan. In March of 1955 he decided to make agricultural planning more flexible. In 1958 another stage was reached: The machinery and tractor stations were abolished. Thus the kolkhoz was emancipated from the tutelage of the state, but only to be brought under the even stricter control of the party, a control made the more effective by the decrease in the number of kolkhozi.[4] In the same year, the elimination of the mandatory deliveries to which the kolkhoz workers had been subjected made it possible to improve market supplies.

While the land-reclamation campaign culminated in disaster, the "liberal" steps taken by Khrushchev succeeded so well in raising production that, when he launched the Seven-Year Plan in January 1959 he felt justified in predicting that the output of the major farm products, both overall and per capita, would exceed that of the United States in 1965. This boastful challenge came to nothing. In complete contrast, the farm situation began to deteriorate again in the ensuing years, as much because of a poor harvest in 1959 as because of a tremendous rise in military expenditures that curbed investments. Production was beginning to stagnate again, and this led to a reinforcement of the bureaucracy. In September 1963

[4] The Communist party's roots in the kolkhoz had always been very weak. Hence a diminution in the number of kolkhozi made it possible to entrust important positions to reliable men.

Russia had to resign herself to importing wheat from capitalist countries.

Based on duress, the kolkhoz system clashed with the enduring hostility of the peasants. The Soviet press continued to mourn over waste, lack of initiative and care, and looting "of Socialist property." In vain. If the state's death-grip was relaxed somewhat, production rose to a degree. But the leaders could not move far in this direction because they feared the entrenchment of a class fundamentally hostile to their rule and the reappearance of the specter of the kulak.

Consequently, although peasant opposition is not currently a threat to the government in terms of an organized force, it remains a permanent open wound and the proof of a major defeat. Nothing could illustrate this better than a comparison between the productivity of individual parcels of land, although they amount to only an infinitesimal proportion of the total area under cultivation (3 per cent) with that of the collectivized sector. In 1962 these parcels furnished the market with 67.4 per cent of its fruits, 63.4 per cent of its vegetables, 33.2 per cent of its meat, 32.8 per cent of its milk, etc. The statistics need no commentary. The *izba* and its little private fenced-in patch, this little island of private property, represents the bastion of the indomitable peasant hostility to collectivization.

Fifty years after the October Revolution the government had made no greater progress in solving the problem of the national minorities. In spite of optimistic assurances and proclamations, nationalist opposition was still firmly rooted.

The brutal revelation of acute nationalism was provided in a paradoxical form by the riots in Tiflis in March 1956. Let us emphasize the date: immediately after Khrushchev's secret report. As described in an interview with Kupradze, the rector of the University of Tiflis, the course of events was this:

On March 5, the anniversary of Stalin's death, the populace gathered at the monument to Stalin in Tiflis. In the ensuing days these meetings assumed a mass character. Poems and speeches in praise of Stalin were read from the official platform. The meetings of March 9 were completely legal, authorized by the government, and organized by the party in consequence of the pro-Stalin attitude of the population during the preceding days.

That the Communist party of Georgia had taken the initiative in the demonstrations was confirmed by *Zarya Vostoka* on March 9: "Meetings were organized today in public squares and in halls throughout the republic to commemorate the third anniversary of Stalin's death."

Certainly Stalin had spared neither the people nor the Communists of Georgia. Why did they feel the need to pay him solemn tribute a few weeks after Khrushchev had revealed his crimes? Why was the Communist party of Georgia—assuredly with the authorization of the rulers in Moscow—the instigator? Perhaps because, after the deaths of Stalin and Beria, their Georgian collaborators had been eliminated and to national pride this had the aspect of persecution. Suddenly the dead tyrant was once more *Sosso*, the native son, whose memory was being outraged by the Russians.

But things are more complex. The organized, channeled demonstrations soon turned into a riot. According to Kupradze, "hooligans stopped all traffic in the city's streets. They overturned the trams and, seizing private cars, they raced through the streets sowing panic and causing accidents." It must be believed that the demonstrations were extremely violent, for at another point the rector asserted "that it is clear that the military forces learned a hard lesson during the pro-Stalin demonstrations of March 9 and that they will have the wisdom to profit by it."

It would appear that the homage paid to Stalin was merely a pretext for inciting to riot, or at the very least a detonator to explode Georgian national feeling. The rector's statements, in fact, make it plain that

provocateurs and disorderly elements *that do not like* Stalin aroused
the students' national sentiment and exploited it for their own
ends. . . . During the disorders the demonstrators shouted illegal
and prohibited nationalist slogans. . . . The *provocateurs* had specific goals and awakened Georgian national feeling. These trouble-
making elements must have been loafers, declassed men, such as
former kulaks, and perhaps members of parties that were long ago
liquidated. *Many of them are former deportees and it is possible
that some of them are malcontents.* (Italics added.)

Behind these confused, embarrassed statements one feels
that one can descry evidence that adversaries of the Soviet system had exploited the pretext of destalinization to revive Georgian national feeling and channel it into a great anti-Moscow
demonstration. Stalin's name was the unanticipated spark that
ignited the flame of Georgian patriotism.

This is indirectly corroborated by a statement in *Zarya Vostoka* on March 11: "There is a great difference between creative Soviet patriotism, patriotism in action, and the nationalism
or chauvinism evidenced in Tiflis on March 9." [5]

In the existing state of affairs, however, neither the activities
of the guerrillas in the Ukraine or White Russia (which we
have discussed earlier) nor riots like that in Tiflis represent
the most important phenomenon. The major struggle is being
waged in less spectacular fashion on the cultural front.

Until about the 1930s the rulers had attempted to win over
the national minorities by granting them a certain cultural
autonomy. Stalin put an end to this period of toleration by encouraging all forms of Russianization. After the grievous
breaches created by the war it was essential to resume this
policy in order to root out every form of the dissidence and
separatism that had been aroused by the German occupation.

That was why a systematic offensive was waged against
"bourgeois nationalism." At the same time the struggle of the
national minorities against tsarism was henceforth to be presented as an unprogressive phenomenon.

[5] For these quotations cf. G. Sharashidze, *Est et Ouest,* June 1, 1956.

After Stalin's death there was a brief period of thaw. Some observers believed indeed that Beria, isolated in the midst of the other members of the Politburo, was seeking support among the national minorities. In any event it was possible to confirm a certain reduction in Russian elements in the party and government apparatus in the Baltic states.

But this very limited pause did not last. On the contrary, after the Twenty-first Congress in 1959, a systematic drive for Russianization developed. There was in fact a whole series of measures all tending in this direction. In 1959 and 1960 there was a number of changes in the personnel of both the party and the government, notably in Latvia, Azerbaidzhan (where Semichastny, the future minister of the interior, replaced Mustafeyev as first secretary), Kirghizia, and Kazakhstan (where only one of the five secretaries of the Central Committee was a local man and the four others were Russians).

In addition, a resolution of the Central Committee of the Communist party of the Soviet Union in January 1960 proclaimed a "struggle without concessions against nationalism, against tendencies toward the idealization of the [national] past and the distortion of the true history of any nation, and against manifestations of national bigotry."

Similar measures and resolutions followed the introduction of the party's new program in October 1961. It stipulated that "general Communist construction signifies a new stage in national relations within the Soviet Union, characterized by a new reconciliation among nations and the realization of complete unity."

How was this complete unity to be accomplished in a multinational state like the Soviet Union? The new program gave the answer, for it envisaged "the disappearance of national and especially linguistic differences." Such a disappearance, it was obvious, could redound only to the advantage of the Russian culture and language.

This was a colossal undertaking that the rulers were confident of carrying out in the ensuing decades. It collided, however, with obstinate resistance. On the language level alone, if one compares the data gathered by the censuses of 1926 and 1959, one observes that in 1926 the Russians constituted 54 per cent of the population of the Soviet Union and that the Russian language was spoken by 58.5 per cent of the population (in other words, by 4.5 per cent of the non-Russians). In 1959 the census showed 54.5 per cent of Russians and 59.3 per cent of the population giving Russian as their native language. Hence only 4.8 per cent had been Russianized. In thirty-three years, then, the gain amounted to only 3 per cent, or approximately six hundred thousand persons.

If on the other hand one looks at the various national minorities, one finds that 87 per cent of the Ukrainians considered that language their mother tongue in 1959, against 87.1 per cent in 1926: a meaningless decline. The decline in the native language was also very negligible among the Kazakhs, the Kirghizi, and the Baltic peoples. It was somewhat larger among the Tartars (92 per cent against 98.9 per cent), the Chuvashi (90 per cent against 97.7 per cent), and especially the Mordvinians (78 per cent against 94 per cent). In contrast, 84.2 per cent of the White Russians claimed their mother tongue in 1959 against 71.9 per cent in 1926. The Georgian figures were 98.6 per cent against 96 per cent.

Could these facts be changed in the next twenty or thirty years? Certainly the Soviet Union has tremendous means available to it. The eight million Ukrainians who live outside their traditional territory, a large number of them beyond the Urals, are deprived of schools, institutions, books, and newspapers, all necessary to the preservation of their language. On Ukrainian territory itself the number of mixed marriages is rising, thus fostering assimilation. Russia's colonial expansion has taken a great number of Russian citizens into the virgin lands of Siberia, the Baltic countries, and the Ukraine. The persecutions that are directed against the national religions (Roman Catholicism in Lithuania and the Ukraine, the Independent church in the Ukraine, Islam in the eastern regions of the Soviet Union, Judaism, etc.) also contribute to the subversion of one of the foundations of national sentiment to the extent to which religion is part of the traditional heritage. And finally it is beyond question that the road to social, political, and professional success necessarily includes the learning of Russian, the assimilation of a system of education that exalts the dominant part played by the "elder sister," and at least the ostensible adoption of Soviet values.

At the same time, the very question of training national elites entails consequences that are not favorable to the system of assimilation and Russianization. Whatever the nature of the teachings imparted, whatever the falsifications of the historical past, the education given to a foreign people awakens it to an awareness of its national entity, to efforts to understand and possess its national past, that cannot be totally stifled by any disguise, however skillful. In other words, education given to an increasingly larger mass of citizens, regardless of its content, contributes to the maintenance of national feeling. This is a phenomenon that has been exceptionally brought out by Richard Pipes:

The instruction of the masses also fosters national differences: Language, history, literature, and other local factors become veritable institutions. This is equally true of the intelligentsia, the emergence of which is everywhere a concomitant of the collapse of the old class structures. Whence those pulls that the process of modernization exerts on nationalism.[6]

Even inside the party—in other words, within an apparatus in which indoctrination is carried to its maximum level—tensions are inevitable. The central power, held by Russians in the majority, cannot allow all the control switches in any given area to fall into the hands of local Communists. That is why very often the actual authority (in general the post of second secretary of the party, which controls all the functionaries) is held by a Russian. Thus the national-minority members of the

[6] Pipes, *Op. cit.*

ruling council are effectively reminded almost daily that their authority is only formal or in any event subsidiary. How in the long run can they avoid feeling bitter resentment? This is the reason for the frequent changes in personnel.

A typical instance in this domain is that of the Moslem intelligentsia. At the very outset the Soviet leadership had to eliminate the traditional intelligentsia with its essentially religious culture. In the past fifty years this class has been completely overlaid or annihilated, and it is true that the elite of the new generation has been shaped in the Soviet mold, in the crucible of Russian culture, in accordance with a process that is universal in all the various republics.

This new elite is atheist, Russianized to a certain degree, and converted to the victories of the Revolution. On first sight it seems closer to the Soviet west than the Moslem populations outside the USSR. The fact remains, however, that this intelligentsia is still kept out of certain technical command positions (a fact that can be justified on the ground of lack of sufficient training and experience) and also out of certain political posts. And it can be observed that it in no way mingles with the Soviet European populations (Russian, Ukrainian, Latvian, etc.) in the country. Mixed marriages are extremely rare. Although the religion of Islam has lost ground, the women still wear veils. Europeans and Moslems live side by side but in different worlds separated by an invisible barrier.

In 1952, at the height of the Soviet offensive against bourgeois nationalism, the Soviet authorities decided to discredit the heroic national epics of the Turkish peoples. The reaction of the indigenous intelligentsia was immediate, "especially in Kirghizia, where the condemnation of the national epic, *Manas*, created a deep division in university circles and the local Communist party. Kirghiz Communists were heard denouncing the 'imperialist chauvinism' of their Russian comrades, who retorted with the accusation of 'bourgeois nationalism.'" [7]

[7] A. Bennigsen, "L'intelligentsia musulmane en URSS," in *Le contrat social*, July 1950.

Are the Jewish problem in the Soviet Union and the anti-Semitic reactions that it has aroused to be viewed as a national or a religious problem? The question is decidedly complex. The Soviet government has carried on a vigorous offensive against the Jewish religion, an offensive that in principle is indistinguishable from the attacks on the other religions but that took on a special intensity before Stalin's death, whereas the Orthodox religion, for example, was still enjoying a relative tolerance for political reasons. (See also Chapter 26.)

But it is more logical to classify the Jewish question in the Soviet Union under the category of national minorities. In fact the remote origins of the conflict between the Soviet authorities and the Jews go back to a time considerably anterior to the seizure of power by the Bolsheviks, and they have to do with the national-minority problem, for it was on the score of this problem that Lenin launched into his first controversies with the Jewish *Bund* at the beginning of this century.

The Jewish *Bund* was a Social Democratic organization established by followers of Otto Bauer, an Austrian Socialist. The *Bund* did not demand the right for the Jews to set up an independent state within the framework of the future proletarian state, but it did insist that they be granted a large measure of cultural autonomy. In other words, the Jews, it held, ought to have their own schools, theaters, press, and religious institutions, and select their own administrators without any intervention or regulation by the state. Within the Social Democratic party the Jews, like all the other national groups, ought to enjoy the same autonomy.

On the party level Lenin's centralist tendency and his authoritarianism could not tolerate this federalism. On the state level, by virtue of the dispersion of the Jews, he was no more inclined to recognize them as a distinct national unit with the same status as the Poles, the Georgians, or the Ukrainians, each of which nationalities was established within a given area and united by its language.

In Lenin's eyes the Jewish problem ought to be resolved

through assimilation, which, he believed, had already begun among the more advanced Jews. To him the idea of a distinct Jewish nation was ludicrous. After the Revolution it appeared that assimilation within the framework of the new state was not so simple.

Undoubtedly many Jews who had had to suffer from the discrimination and the pogroms of the tsarist government were favorably disposed toward the Revolution. It gave them the opportunity of establishing themselves wherever they chose, whereas under the tsars they had been confined for the most part to the fringes of the empire (Poland, the Baltic countries, the Ukraine), and barred from certain occupations. (For instance, they were forbidden to till the soil.[8])

At the same time, the occupational structure of the Jewish community itself contained the seeds of conflict. In fact, in 1913 the majority of the Jews was engaged in either artisan trades or commerce (27 per cent and 29 per cent respectively).[9] As long as the NEP was in effect, they could continue in these activities. The end of the NEP led to the absorption of many of the Jews into the apparatus of the state.

An article in *Correspondance internationale* (No. 15, 1931), described the situation of these Jews:

Men who had formerly been self-employed saved themselves by enlisting in time in the apparatus of the state, the offices of economic institutions, the innumerable accounting offices and banks of the cooperatives, and the administrative staffs of factories, thus be-

[8] This statement would appear to be debatable: A relatively substantial number of Jews in the old Russian Empire owned farms of varying acreage and some of them employed *muzhik* labor. Under the tsars, on the other hand, it was extremely difficult for Jews to enter the universities and still more difficult for them to become members of the liberal professions.—Translator.

[9] The others were distributed as follows:

Office workers, minor functionaries, etc.	7%
Liberal professions	3%
Urban labor	20%
Farm labor	2%
Miscellaneous	12%

coming employes. Most of the time these employes represented the ostensible pretext for anti-Semitism, which was fought in the most rigorous fashion, both ideologically and juridically.

In fact, the vocational distribution of Jews in 1934 was as follows:

Employes, functionaries, etc.	33.0%
Liberal professions	7.8%
Workers	23.6%
Agriculture	8.7%
Artisans	16.6%
Independent small business	2.5%
Miscellaneous	7.1%

Thus artisanry had declined, small business had collapsed under the weight of industrialization, and the results of the government's attempts to establish Jewish farm colonies were minor.

At the same time there had been no diminution in the anti-Semitic feelings prevailing among the peasant masses, especially in the Ukraine. Under the tsars the Jews had been reproached for not tilling the soil. After the Revolution, those Jews who had become peasants were denounced for having taken over the land.[10] The Jews who gave up their artisan

[10] The occupation of land in White Russia and the Ukraine by Jewish colonists was indeed effected by force at the start, assisted by the civil war. This "wildcat" colonization, according to *Correspondance internationale* (No. 17, February 28, 1931), involved 12,477 Jewish families and about 19,000 acres of land in 1925. In 1924 the government created a "Committee for the Colonization of Jewish Workers," which assumed the task of systematic colonization by distributing land from the government's colonization reserve to Jews. "The financing," *Correspondance internationale* asserted, "was accomplished partly with budget funds, partly with credits from Soviet banks, but above all through foreign organizations, among which must be cited the Agro-Joint (Distribution Committee), an American organization with a capital of $20 million." [A challengeable figure for the capital of an ostensibly nonprofit relief organization dependent wholly on voluntary contributions.—Translator.] The

shops and their small businesses in order to go to work for the apparatus of the state may have done so only against their wills. But at once they were accused of being in the service of an oppressor state. And, inasmuch as a certain number of Jews held important posts in the *Cheka,* hatred for the police tended to merge with anti-Semitism. But, if on the other hand the Jews practiced their religion, they incurred the same persecutions by the authorities as the rest of the believers. And too Zionism,[11] the establishment of a so-called Jewish national home in Palestine, held a strong attraction for Soviet Jews and thus incited the wrath of the government against this form of bourgeois nationalism.

The attempt, begun in 1926, to establish an autonomous Jewish republic in Biro-Bidzhan amounted in essence to granting the Jews what, according to Lenin, was lacking to make them a nationality: that is, a territory. This artificial effort ended in definitive failure. In actuality the Jews felt no attraction toward the area, which they had no reason to regard as their own.

During the 1920s Jewish cultural institutions had been able to enjoy free development. But the growth of the combat against Trotskyist and Zinovievist opposition, which included a number of Jews, led to a definite anti-Jewish reaction encouraged by Stalin, of whose dislike of Jews there can be little doubt. Many Jews, especially in intellectual circles, were victims of the Great Purge.

Stalin, though hostile to the Jews, was at the same time sufficiently realistic to recognize that he could make use of them when the Soviet Union was invaded by the Germans. That was why he authorized the formation of a Jewish Anti-Fascist

periodical added that by the end of 1929 the amount of land thus distributed had risen to almost one and one-half million acres and the number of persons had mounted to two hundred thousand. In all probability it was the policy of collectivization that put an end to this effort.

[11] Condemned by the Communist International in its Second Congress in 1920.

Committee headed by Mikhoels and placed under Beria's control. This Committee was for external consumption. Its objective was to recruit, principally in the United States, the help required for the battle against Hitlerism.

The end of the war led to a new change in course. The Jews were the major targets of the accusations of the crime of "cosmopolitanism" lodged against Soviet citizens. Suddenly the bonds that some of the Jews had been able to forge in the West in the interests of the Soviet Union became suspect because the imperialist powers were once more becoming the enemy. The establishment of the State of Israel, at first approved by the Soviet Union in the United Nations, further intensified Stalin's distrust. The undeniable attraction that Israel exercised on Soviet Jews became a crime in his eyes. The persecutions were resumed. After 1949 not a line in Yiddish was printed, whereas in 1932 (the high point) there had been 668 Yiddish publications and in the 1959 census 472,000 of the 2.268 million admitted Jews had listed Yiddish as their mother tongue. The persecutions against the religion were heightened. Deportations began. There seems to be little doubt that the trial of Rudolf Slansky in Czechoslovakia, the atmosphere of which was clearly anti-Semitic; the trials of "economic criminals" in the Soviet Union, in which the Jewish identity of the defendants was systematically labored, and above all the famous "doctors' plot" were omens of a broad purge of the Jews that was aborted by Stalin's death.

If that purge had not been launched earlier, it was undoubtedly because of the large proportion of Jews employed in the scientific sector. Their mass elimination would have entailed the risk of destroying this essential domain.

The attitude of Stalin's heirs, although it has rejected any solution resembling genocide, is nevertheless deeply hostile to the Jews on the cultural and religious planes. In the whole of the Soviet Union there is only one Yiddish magazine, published in Biro-Bidzhan, where there must not be more than fifteen thousand Jews left. The practice of the Jewish religion is subjected to the same harassments as that of the other faiths. There are barely a hundred synagogues, in contrast to five hundred at the end of the war. The "economic" trials, in which the part played by Jews was emphasized, have not really ceased. Jews are the targets of a discrimination that is denied by the authorities but that is beyond dispute in certain areas of employment (diplomacy and the army, for instance). And Khrushchev hardly concealed his own anti-Semitic feelings.[12] His successors are better versed in dissimulation, but they have made no changes in a policy that is founded on profound distrust.

Yet the Jewish population has been neither crushed nor assimilated. Although every means has been employed to cut off the Jewish youth on both the cultural and the religious planes from anything that might remind it of the history of Israel, a powerful underground current survives beneath the appearance of submission, the resignation, and the fear. In *Les Juifs du silence* (*The Jews of Silence*), Élie Wiesel has described the annual explosion of joy that has marked the feast of Simkhat Torah (the Rejoicing of the Law) every year since 1964 at the Moscow synagogue. Within the jammed synagogue and outside in Arkhipova Street, tens of thousands of young Jews dance, shout their enthusiasm, and proclaim their Jewishness at the top of their lungs. The celebration lasts all night. Far from all the celebrants are practicing Jews. Some are virtually ignorant of Jewish history. And most profess deep attachment to the State of Israel.

Therefore a relaxation of the tension will be enough to bring back into the open the Jewish problem that the authorities profess to have resolved. It is a problem that the Soviet leaders cannot resolve. For the authorization of free expression for the Jewish culture and religion would add new vigor to the Jewish separatism the durability of which is made manifest by demonstrations such as those in Arkhipova Street. It would also impair the extremely vigorous offensive that the govern-

12 Cf. Serge Groussard's interview with him in *Le Figaro*.

ment is waging against all forms of religious belief if a privilege were granted to one of them. To authorize the Jews to emigrate would court the danger of the choice of Israel as the fatherland of a large proportion of them. Not only would such an exodus be incompatible with the Kremlin's consistent policy toward the Arab countries; it would also represent a spectacular repudiation of the system, the symbol of a failure, a powerful encouragement to secession for the national minorities that have their own territories within the Soviet Union.

Thus the problem of the Jewish community, which has its own characteristics and its deep-rooted individuality, cannot be resolved by the granting of autonomy without grave repercussions on the two levels of the other minorities and the other religions.

(26)

THE ROAD TO THE

CATACOMBS

I N THE midst of the war, on September 4, 1943, Stalin granted an audience to the three highest dignitaries of the Orthodox Church: Metropolitans Sergey, Nikolai, and Alexey. The next day *Izvestia* announced that the government had authorized the convocation of a council for the election of a patriarch, a post in which Metropolitan Sergey was solemnly enthroned.

The leaders of the Orthodox Church had maintained a position of unflagging support of the government from the start of the hostilities. On the day when the German attack was announced Metropolitan Sergey issued a message denouncing the invasion. Metropolitan Alexey remained at his post in besieged Leningrad and the collections raised among the faithful in the city produced three billion rubles.

Stalin needed all the traditional forces of Russia in order to win. And undoubtedly he reckoned that, when the victory had been gained, this church that he so rigorously controlled and that discouraged all political opposition could be extremely useful to his expansionist aims.

Therefore he decided during the first year of the war to dissolve the League of the Godless. There were other fronts besides the anti-religious front to be defended. Besides, the gesture made a good impression on foreign opinion.

After the end of the war the Orthodox Church continued to enjoy a certain toleration because of its leaders' unqualified loyalty to the government. On the thirtieth anniversary of the October Revolution Alexey spoke of "the most wise leader whom Divine Providence has chosen." And he did not hesitate to denounce the use of bacteriological warfare by the Americans in Korea—in other words, to add his endorsement to one of the most laughable fabrications of Soviet propaganda.[1]

As long as Stalin lived, even if some of its members were deported, the Orthodox Church enjoyed a privileged position in comparison with the merciless persecutions before the war. It was able to open a number of seminaries (there were eight in 1954), to enlarge the ranks of its priesthood, and to carry on its religious activities without too much harassment. Its influence was still substantial. Almost all babies had been baptized until 1928, so that in 1954 there were some ninety million baptized persons and twenty-two thousand functioning churches in the Soviet Union.

It is estimated that on the average each church was visited every Sunday by two thousand persons—in other words, approximately forty million persons were communicants. True, this army of the faithful was very unevenly distributed, both geographically and sociologically. Thus the Ukraine was a fortress of faith, inasmuch as its population had eighty-five hundred of the churches, three of the eight seminaries, forty of the fifty-seven monasteries. In Moscow, on the other hand, there were only thirty-eight churches for five million residents. Religion was more firmly rooted in rural areas than in the large industrial cities, each of which had only two or three churches at most. And the congregations were made up predominantly of women and old persons.

The tolerance that Stalin had displayed toward religion, an

---

[1] Whether the charge was based on fabrication or fact has not yet been definitively resolved.—Translator.

atoll of paradox in a system ruled by terror, survived his death by only a few years. In 1958 the leaders in the Kremlin began a fierce and systematic offensive against every form of religious belief. Apart from brief intervals of respite, that offensive has been virtually unceasing.

In general, however, the persecution has not assumed either the savage or the vulgar forms that were adopted during the civil war and then during the terrible years of collectivization. It has employed a large variety of methods, both openly hostile and insidiously oblique: the closing of churches and monasteries on a variety of pretexts, pressures on families, a multitude of harassments of clergymen, the resurgence of atheist propaganda.

It is possible that this resumption of persecution is a direct consequence of the effects of destalinization. After Stalin's death and Beria's downfall, the police power was weakened. Bishops and priests returned from deportation. Larger congregations turned out for services. New churches were built. In 1954 seventy-two churches were undergoing restoration in the diocese of Chernovotzy alone. Many former religious edifices were turned back to their original use.[2]

To the leaders in the Kremlin this was one of the vexatious consequences of the thaw. Their doctrine assured them that the construction of Socialism would entail the progressive atrophy of religion. Reality was proving the opposite. At the end of 1957 or the beginning of 1958 the leaders in the Kremlin decided to undertake a vast liquidation of religion.

The assault was launched with massive closings of churches. In the western regions of the Soviet Union the German occupation had allowed a large number of churches to be reopened, especially in the Ukraine and White Russia. This decision had been nullified by a decree adopted fifteen years earlier but never enforced by Stalin, undoubtedly because he feared that its application would fuel a new separatist ardor in those areas.

[2] On this subject cf. Nikolai Struve, *Les Chrétiens en URSS*.

His successors suddenly revived the decree: Hundreds of churches were closed.

Many other closings were ordered on other pretexts. For example, commissions established that a church was in urgent need of restoration and required the immediate inception of costly major repairs. If the parish could not supply the necessary funds, the church was closed. Some other church would be declared a "historical monument"; therefore it belonged to the citizenry as a whole and not to the faithful alone, who were forbidden to hold their services there. In another instance it was discovered that the cathedral in Perm was attracting so large a crowd that it had become an obstruction to traffic.

Once a decision was made, it was thoroughly executed. Crews arrived at night to dynamite the buildings. Then bulldozers went into action to level the rubble. Yesterday a church, tomorrow a vacant lot.

The envelopment maneuver of the timely decree and the frontal attack by means of dynamite and the bulldozer made it possible to score spectacular successes on the anti-religious front: 1500 churches were closed during 1961, according to a Reuter dispatch of February 23, 1962; in the region of Grodno 40 Orthodox and twenty Catholic churches had been closed since 1958 (*Komsomolskaya Pravda*, August 7, 1962); in the Odessa region 75 churches were converted into clubs and libraries in 1961; 68 cultural groups were dissolved (Radio Kiev, February 5, 1962); in the Volhynia region, 180 places of worship were closed in a few years (*Komsomolskaya Pravda*, June 14, 1962); 40 churches were closed in the Cherkassy region in 1959–1960 (Radio Cherkassy, October 18, 1960), and so on. In Kiev only eight of twenty-five churches were left in 1963; in Odessa, nine of twenty-three; in Rostov on the Don, four of twelve. In addition the cathedrals of Orel, Bryansk, Riga, and Kaunas had been closed to the faithful. Early in 1962 an anti-religious pamphlet by a Bolshevik named Yudin stated that, of the 22,000 Orthodox churches operating in 1959, only 11,500 remained. In 1961 only forty of the sixty-nine monasteries listed in 1958 were in being, and five of the eight seminaries.[3]

It is obviously impossible to believe that in three years almost half the Orthodox churches were closed on the wishes of the faithful because their number had declined so steeply that it was no longer necessary to keep the churches in operation. This fact alone is proof of persecution.

After the churches came the clergy. In this area all that was necessary, as a rule, was to enforce to the letter the civil-war legislation that had been enacted for the collectivization campaign but that had been allowed to fall into desuetude. The priests were receiving regular wages. It was decided to apply the law that classified them as artisans and to tax them as such. (It should be pointed out that in such cases the tax amounted to the modest figure of 83 per cent of income). In addition, a priest was forbidden to serve more than one parish; and, where there was no longer an officiant, there was no further reason to keep the churches open. The profits on the sale of candles, which provided a large income to the church, were declared illegal; henceforth they would be sold at cost.

Here again, in this battle for the annihilation of the clergy, the government scored major successes. Whereas Father Wenger had been able to state in an article in *La Croix* (*The Cross*) on November 28, 1956, that many young men were candidates for the priesthood, whereas the patriarchate of the Orthodox Church announced that in 1955 there were 35,000 priests, as against 5165 priests and deacons in 1943, Yudin's pamphlet declared that only 14,500 priests were still working in 1962.

The continuing assault on the clergy and the steps intended to make it difficult, if not impossible, to hold religious services were accompanied by pressures on the believers, primarily on that basic unit that has maintained a secretive but stubborn resistance against the government throughout the existence of

[3] The seminaries have now been reduced to two.

the Soviet Union: the family. In theory, it was the duty of the Soviet school teacher not only "to be an unbeliever but also to serve as an active propagandist for atheism, as a messenger of the idea of militant proletarian atheism." No doubt this principle had fallen into a certain disuse, for in February 1959 the minister of national education, E. Afanassiev, issued a bulletin calling school superintendents' attention to the importance of anti-religious education.

The family still retained the right to give its children religious instruction if it wished to do so. This right had become insufferable to the leaders in the Kremlin. On November 25, 1963, Leonid Ilyichev told the ideological commission of the Central Committee:

> Give a moment's thought to the situation of the child who finds himself caught between the school and his devout mother and grandmother. The school inculcates scientific conceptions, the mother and grandmother inculcate belief in God and take him to prayer meetings. Such a split in the child's conscience is an extremely harmful thing against which we ought to take a stand in the most categorical fashion and mobilize all our ideological instruments. Think . . . how important it is that ignorant, illiterate persons should feel that their efforts to inculcate religious ideas in children, adolescents, and even adults encounter universal reproof. . . . *We cannot allow blind and ignorant persons to bring up their children in their own image and deform them.* (Italics added.)

Beginning with the school, the attack was continued in the Young Pioneers and the *Komsomol;* in 1954 eighteen million children between the ages of nine and fourteen were members of the Pioneers and nine million adolescents were enrolled in the *Komsomol.* The *Komsomol's* regulations, moreover, implied war on religious superstition, since it was the organization's task to "combat drunkenness, profligacy, the vestiges of religious superstitions, and the lack of comradeliness in relations with women." These juxtapositions left religion somewhere between alcoholism and depravity.

A special effort was directed toward the conversion of adults. In 1947 the dissolved League of the Godless was replaced by the Society for the Dissemination of Political and Scientific Knowledge, but for a number of years the new organization's anti-religious activity was very limited. All that was changed by Stalin's successors. The Society awoke from its torpor: It produced pamphlets, conferences, radio programs, television broadcasts, films, plays, neglecting nothing in its battle to counter the effects of the "opiate of the people."

The Society distributed a whole set of publications: magazines such as *Nauka i Religia* (*Science and Religion*), which had a press run of 161,000 copies in the beginning of 1964, and books such as reprints of Yaroslavsky's two works, *The Bible for Believers and Unbelievers* and *Fundamentals of Scientific Atheism,* each published in an edition of more than 100,000 copies. This series was reinforced with translations of such works as Charles Hainchelin's *Origines de la Religion* and the collective volume by A. Denis, R. Garaudy, G. Gogniot, and C. Besse, *Des marxistes répondent à leurs critiques* (*Marxists Answer Their Critics*). Thus Garaudy, who in France is the spokesman of "fraternal" dialogue with Christians, plays quite another part in the Soviet Union. In 1962 the number of books and pamphlets published in this field totaled 5.422 million copies of 355 titles, a figure more than double that of 1930, when the anti-religious campaign was at its previous high point.

In their effort to destroy religious belief the Soviet leaders attributed extreme importance to systematic propaganda based on scientific reasoning. Religious ideology and the fanciful explanation of the world, they believed, ought to be combated by scientific truth. A prominent place in this program was given to the conquests of space: In their orbits round the earth the cosmonauts had encountered neither "the kingdom of heaven" nor flying angels. That was one of the first remarks made by Gagarin, and obviously it had been dictated to him

by propagandists. In the speech quoted earlier Ilyichev gave
particular attention to this aspect:

> The conflict between science and religion has entered on a new
> phase, the phase of an offensive by science along the whole front.
> . . . Scientific successes have definitively undermined the founda-
> tions of the traditional religious image of the world. Modern sci-
> ence has boldly invaded the secrets of the universe. . . . The tre-
> mendous successes scored by the Soviet people in the discovery of
> the cosmos have had a major atheist influence.

But it was apparent that, if this anti-religious battle was to
be waged on a scientific basis, the government would have to
train adequately armed leaders. So on October 7, 1963, *Pravda*
reported that since the Twenty-second Congress the party in
Volhynia had been devoting much more attention to the atheist education of the workers: "Every year the Regional Committee of the Ukrainian Communist party organizes month-
long courses to train lecturers and propagandists dealing with
questions of atheism."

Peripatetic clubs were also established in rural areas, inasmuch as the peasants did not willingly inconvenience themselves to travel to lecture halls. One of these clubs was
equipped not only with the usual lecturers but also with an
arsenal of musicians, scientific atheist films, an atheist exhibi-
tion, and an album of newspaper and magazine clippings on
the subject. The club traveled to kolkhozi, villages, and farms
with this material.

The party demanded of its own faithful, furthermore, that
they dedicate themselves to unremitting word-of-mouth propaganda in order to convert all those who were still bound by
religious superstitions.

How did religious believers react to this concerted offensive? In different ways, depending on their adherence to the
official Orthodox Church, the clandestine churches, or the ex-
ceedingly numerous sects.

There was no doubt that the Orthodox clergy was placed in a very delicate situation. Closely watched, its ranks infiltrated by men who were certainly police informers, it could hardly voice any protest without incurring the risk of bringing on greater persecution. Since there were only two seminaries, the number of calls to the cloth dwindled. Since many churches had been closed and priests were no longer permitted to serve more than one parish each, great masses of the faithful were deprived of officiants.

Nonetheless the peasant world remained firmly bound to its religious customs, and this is evidenced by a study of religious behavior in a kolkhoz in White Russia, published in the June 1957 issue of *Soviet Ethnography* (No. 2). According to the writer, the war years were the incitement to a general religious revival in the Soviet Union, and this continued into the postwar years. In addition, deported laborers had popularized certain religious practices when they returned.

Church attendance, it was true, had declined: how could it have been otherwise when the believer found that the nearest church was some twenty miles from the kolkhoz, whereas in other times the distance from one church to another had never been more than four miles? But religious holidays on the whole were still observed: on such days the kolkhoz did no work.[4] The article continued:

On religious holidays the cathedral of Minsk and many churches are packed to the doors. Baptism is still widely practiced. Since the priest visits each village twice or three times a year, the parents take the opportunity to have their children baptized. Every *izba* has its ikon, set in a part of the room covered with curtains like a place that has always been respected.

[4] Much vexed by this "absenteeism," the Soviet leaders have never been able to eliminate it. That is why they have now arrived at a new tactic. On religious holidays they make great efforts to organize secular celebrations, in which songs, dances, and athletic events are interspersed with anti-religious skits.

Travelers in other areas observed identical phenomena. Chombart de Lauwe, for example, found ikons in *izbas* in the Moscow region.

Unquestionably the survival of the Othodox religion in the cities is much weaker. But the communicants' faith, a minority phenomenon, seems more deeply rooted and more individualized. Moreover it is often to be observed among people of culture. "The hysterical bigots," Ilyichev asserted indignantly, ". . . cite 'intellectuals' of this character as examples: 'Look, there is an educated man, but he believes in God.'"

In spite of the surveillance and the pressures of which they are the victims, many believers are not afraid to attend anti-religious conferences and, since they cannot formally interpose contradictions, which would not be permitted, to ask embarrassing questions. An article in *Molodoy Kommunist* in August 1963 complained bitterly that anti-religious conferences were "sabotaged" by believers who asked: "How is it that there are still believers, especially among the young, when everyone has been brought up as an atheist?" or: "Why should we fight religion when the church contributed to victory during the war?" [5]

Ossipov, a former professor of theology who had broken with the church and who was often utilized by Moscow for radio programs, received letters that were filled with insults and threats: "How many pieces of silver did you collect?" "When you are devoured by cancer, you traitor, don't pray to heaven!" "All the Godless are swine!" "We are believers and we will remain believers." [6] Some of the sentiments are not those of Christian charity, but they can be understood in the light of the resentment among persecuted people fighting without support against the mass of a gigantic machine.

Occasionally the Soviet press reports "illegal" acts perpetrated by believers. The writers' publication, *Literaturnaya i*

[5] *Sovyetskaya Byelorossiya,* June 15, 1963.
[6] *Ibid.*

Zhizn, told of the case of a twenty-four-year-old electrician, Sergey Kazeyev, who was arrested because, in collaboration with a number of employes of a publishing house, he arranged for the clandestine issuance of prayer books. Vadim Shavrov, a thirty-five-year-old former naval officer and a graduate of the Odessa theological seminary, succeeded in converting a number of girls who were members of the *Komsomol*, and in addition he recruited schoolboys to serve at mass.

His "crime" was all the more serious because the Soviet press often laments the fact that *Komsomol* members take part in religious ceremonies.

In certain *Komsomol* organizations, the behavior of party and *Komsomol* members who observe this or that religious ritual is not even discussed. It is accepted with resignation, under the impression that being a member of the Communist party or the Union of Young Communists can be compatible with the observance of religious rites.[7]

In addition there are many secret Christians who have severed every visible connection with the religious community in order to be able to pursue their careers without harassment. Ilyichev denounced such men, who "pass themselves off as atheists in their places of employment and in their homes observe religious rites, attend church, have their children baptized, and have their marriages celebrated by priests."

Tendryakov, a Soviet author,[8] reported the "exceptional case" of one such man, a teacher of mathematics, whose secret practices were unmasked by one of his students during a surprise visit to the teacher's home:

He tried to block the way to his bedroom, *but I went in regardless*. On his desk I saw his pupils' work . . . and the whole wall was covered with ikons. . . . He never went to church; he did all his praying at home. In order to avoid trouble, he never had guests. (Italics added.)

[7] Quoted by *Oktyabr*, October 1963.
[8] Quoted by Struve in *Les chrétiens en URSS*, p. 185.

The sequel of this episode is no less revealing, and the author recounted it as if it were the most natural thing in the world. The next day the head of the school went to visit his colleague (obviously the pupil had turned stool pigeon):

"Yes," the professor said, his back to the wall, "I am a believer. . . . But this is a strictly private matter. One might say it was the private property of my soul. I do not allow anyone to come near it and I have no intention of doing so. What blood-curdling oath could I swear to make you believe that I have never let slip one word of religion in my classes?"

"God on one side," the principal replied, "and work with persons who deny him on the other. Such duplicity is beyond all understanding."

"What else was there for me to do? I am a teacher of mathematics, I have no other profession: Should I abandon my livelihood? be a Don Quixote? I am not capable of that. While I have said nothing on God's behalf in class, I have said nothing against Him. I live and I keep my mouth shut, satisfied to be let alone and not have people come burrowing into my soul."

It was this basic tolerance that the system would not suffer. The poor devil's soul was no more his private property than his bedroom. The teaching of mathematics was deemed to be incompatible with that cranny in his conscience in which in secret he intended to pray to his God. What is remarkable about the whole episode is the fact that a Soviet author could relate it in such a way as to make its victim someone abnormal while portraying the pupil who invaded his privacy and the head of the school as models of civic spirit when the pupil was obviously a little stool pigeon and the principal was nothing more or less than a policeman.

Such a story helps us to appreciate more fully the courage demonstrated by some believers who make no secret of their faith in spite of all the perils. On December 16, 1964, Monsignor Anton, the Russian Orthodox bishop of Geneva, submitted to U Thant, secretary general of the United Nations, three petitions that had come to him from parishioners and pilgrims to the monastery of Pochayev in the Ukraine. In these petitions, which they had *signed,* the faithful listed the harassments and persecutions that were practiced against them. In particular, the militia forbade the young to enter the churches (two hundred of which were closed in the beginning of 1967). The petitioners added:

> If the members of the Nicodemus and Pimenos synods deny the facts, they are guilty of lying. Most of our true pastors have been refused residence permits because they defended the apostolic traditions and the ecumenical councils. They have been placed under the ban of the church and they lead wandering lives.

Another petition accused a militia major named Belik of hunting down the pilgrims who journeyed to the monastery and imposing fines on peasants who offered them hospitality. When there were arrests, a psychiatric hospital was utilized as a screening office. A hundred Christians were locked up in three of its wards.

On December 1, 1964, the militia broke into the monastery, removing five monks who had already been expelled in 1960–1961 and who therefore, the militia charged, had no official residence permits. But these monks had taken vows to remain in the monastery for the rest of their lives. Between their oaths and "Socialist legality" they opted for the former.

The petition emphasized that Metropolitan Pimenos and Archimandrite Augustine had not spoken: "Perhaps they are blind, but perhaps too they are traitors." Twenty-three signatures followed.

More recently, two Orthodox priests in Moscow, Fathers Echlimann and Yakunin, sent a letter to Patriarch Alexey in which they attacked the tremendous persecution directed against religion. In addition to new closings of churches and monasteries, the priests reported that parents who wanted to have their children baptized were required to identify themselves to a representative of the parish council. Identical regulations—completely illegal under the Soviet Constitution—were applied to the celebration of weddings, extreme unction, religious funerals, communion at home, etc.

"Thus," the priests wrote, "unqualified obedience to the established illegal order turns the *pastor* into an *informer* with respect to those who place their confidence in the protection of the church our mother." In an extremely stern tone they accused the staff of the Patriarchate of Moscow of full knowledge of the fact that "the records of all these religious matters are then systematically examined by the local authorities, and only recently they were again utilized by the anti-religious propaganda teams in a merciless persecution of those who had had their children baptized or their marriages performed religiously."

In effect these two priests were drawing up a veritable indictment of the upper hierarchy of the Orthodox Church. "It has not fulfilled its obligations to Christ and the church," they wrote, "and it has succumbed to the life of the world, thus violating the apostolic precepts." It passively obeyed the oral instructions of the Council for Orthodox Church Affairs, a governmental body: "Orders issued by telephone, oral directives, agreements never officially recorded: this is the mystery-ridden, unhealthy atmosphere that hangs like a dense fog over the relations between the Patriarchate of Moscow and the Council. . . . It is all the more revolting to see the work of the Patriarchate directed in secret fashion by *atheist* officials." [9]

It would also appear, according to the two priests' testimony, that these officials practiced an arbitrary selection of candidates for the seminaries in order to further the infiltration of morally dubious persons into the ranks of the clergy.

Fathers Echlimann and Yakunin concluded that this systematized interference had no other aim than the ultimate

[9] All these quotations are taken from *Un cri de désespoir des prêtres de Moscou,* a pamphlet published by Orthodox Action and the Orthodox Information Center. Cf. also Bernard Féron in *Le Monde,* April 7, 1966.

destruction of the church. In certain of its aspects this exceptionally disturbing picture of the state of the Orthodox Church is reminiscent of the Trust, the strings of which were manipulated by the *Cheka*.

This open letter addressed to the Patriarchate of Moscow in November of 1965 called for the convocation of a council. The Patriarchate's only response was a letter dated December 24, 1965, that accused Fathers Echlimann and Yakunin of "offending against the peace of the church and sowing scandal in it," but there was not a word to confute the priests' charges against the hierarchy. In 1966 they were barred from all ecclesiastical activity.

On the periphery of the official church there still existed the dissident movement that in 1927 had refused to pledge obedience to Metropolitan Sergey. For some time this branch enjoyed a semi-official status. Its major center was in Leningrad, where it still had several churches until 1936, when they were closed. The "true Orthodox Church" then went underground, and it has not yet emerged. In 1938 and 1939 *Besbozhnik* (*The Godless*) and *Antireligiosnik* (*The Enemy of Religion*) carried several reports of discoveries of "Josephists" (followers of Archbishop Joseph) and their subterranean chapels beneath *izbas*.

There was no news of the "true Orthodox Church" until the Second World War, during which some of its faithful, as prisoners of war or deported laborers, were able to make contact with the West. Thus it was learned that one bishop of this clandestine church was a locomotive driver, another was a shoemaker, and its priests held specialists' positions in industry and agriculture, while others lived vagabond lives.[10] Margolin was acquainted with a number of deported priests of this church.

In this church that had no houses of worship, prayer meetings were held in secret in private apartments or in the woods.

[10] On this matter cf. Trubnikov in *Est et Ouest*, July 16, 1963.

Confession was usually handled in writing, being taken to the priest by a messenger. Since they were still loyal to the monarchy, the "true Orthodox" lived on the periphery of society, refusing to join a trade union or a kolkhoz.

Born of a schism, this church itself gave birth in turn to another: the True Orthodox Christians, whose existence has often been reported in the region of Tambov. Its members must break with all the institutions of the government and resign from the kolkhoz, the trade union, or the factory. Their children must be taken out of school at the end of the fourth year. All official documents must be destroyed. When members are arrested and asked their names, they reply: "God knows my name."

The Soviet press had long denied the existence of these catacomb churches. In 1958 it began to mention their activities. Actually the persecution directed against the Orthodox Church, coupled with the passivity of the hierarchy, contributed to the growth of all kinds of clandestine worship. The leader of one such cult, a monk named Vatlaan, who was recently identified (Pervyshin), had established clandestine religious schools in Alma-Ata and Tyulkulas. In 1964 the leaders of local groups were sentenced in a trial in Alma-Ata.[11]

Side by side with these dissident churches there was a multiplicity of sects, which have always been numerous in Russia. Some were extensions of the Russian tradition, such as the Old Believers, the Priestless, the *Khlysty* or Men of God, the *Dukhobors*, etc. Others came into being after the Revolution. Such for example was the case of the *Fyodorovtzy*, who identified Communism with Antichrist, or the *Bozhy Deti* (Children of God), whose major stronghold was in Kazakhstan.

A third group was composed of those born of Western influences, some of which resulted from the Second World War. The Baptists, who were introduced into aristocratic circles at the end of the nineteenth century, had merged with the Evan-

[11] Cf. *Bulletin of the Institute for the Study of the USSR*, Vol. XII (1965), No. 4.

gelists in 1944. Enjoying official recognition, they had five hundred forty thousand adherents in 1960. Their growth has been especially great in the Ukraine, the Baltic countries, and the Far East. It is said that they enroll fifteen thousand new believers every year, particularly among the young. The Baptists respect Soviet institutions, but in recent years persecution has led to dissidence among them. Under the pressures and harassments of every kind, anything of a religious character that enjoys official recognition gives birth sooner or later to underground movements.

In contrast to the Baptists, Jehovah's Witnesses collided with categorical opposition by Stalin, who refused in 1949 to recognize the sect. Most of the members of its Moscow Regional Committee were arrested or deported in 1952 when a new purge was threatening. Seven thousand Witnesses, supposedly, were deported at that time. Opposed to all forms of violence, they refused to serve in the military.

The Seventh-Day Adventists, who were very few before the Revolution, have increased rapidly under Soviet rule. They seem to be especially strongly established in the Ukraine.

Some of these sects have only a few thousand followers, yet their activities arouse apprehension among the Soviet leaders. Let us quote again from Ilyichev:

It is these sects of Western origin—the Baptists, the Adventists, the Pentecostals, Jehovah's Witnesses (especially active and able propagandists of religious ideology)—that have intensified their activities during the postwar years. Rejecting the ceremonials and the conventional nature of the Orthodox Church, they have practiced the maximum adaptation of Biblical texts to modern conditions. . . . The activity of religious organizations such as Jehovah's Witnesses, the True Orthodox Christians, the Uniates, and others is forbidden by law. Nevertheless, under the cloak of religious dogmas, they disseminate anonymous anti-Soviet literature, spread alarmist rumors, and criminally infringe the rights guaranteed to Soviet citizens by the Constitution, imperiling their health and even their lives.

The leaders of certain sects require that their disciples refuse to recognize Soviet laws or work in Soviet enterprises or institutions; they do not permit their children to attend the secondary schools, the technical schools, or the institutions of higher learning, or to join the Pioneers or the *Komsomol*. Their religious beliefs are frequently exploited to incite nationalist tendencies.

While it is probable that these sects would exist regardless of the Soviet system, it is the pressure exerted by that system that fosters their growth. The sects offer a place of refuge to all those who are not satisfied with life as it is lived in the Soviet Union or with the preachments of an official church that meticulously avoids any possibility of conflict with the authorities. They also attract those men and women who are violently opposed to the existing institutions and who are determined to evidence a radical break with them. They appeal to an individualism in revolt against a uniform way of thinking, against a carefully conditioned public opinion (it is no accident that sects of Protestant origin find a fertile soil in the Soviet Union). Finally, they form small, profoundly fraternal groups that demand specific tasks and commitments of each of their members and that inspire a tremendous devotion. Those who join them find in them a climate of zeal that is no longer provided by the clumsy, sclerotic groups of the *Komsomol*, a system of routine for some and of careerism for others.

By multiplying the pressures on listed Christians, kept in line by a clergy constrained to submission and caution, the Soviet authorities themselves construct and maintain all the underground channels through which religion continues to be propagated beneath the seemingly unbroken surface of a monolith.[12] From time to time a cursory news item tells of the

[12] Persecution, obviously, is not restricted to the Orthodox Church alone. The Roman Catholic Church, whose influence was weak in Russia properly so-called, embraced on the other hand some twelve million adherents in the Baltic countries, the Polish territories annexed by the Soviet Union, and the sub-Carpathian Ukraine. It was attacked without quarter. In the former Polish territories most of the churches have been

discovery of a group of worshipers in a woods, or a secret monastery, or an underground chapel beneath an *izba*. These are little dramas, episodes in the long war to which the churches of silence, with their infinitesimal means, have committed themselves against the gigantic power of a state that has set itself the goal not only of shattering organizations but also of triumphing over consciences.

It is a terribly unequal combat. But one day, after the closings of the churches and the victories of the lectures, in spite of the tons of paper dedicated to the establishment of scientific truth, in spite of Gagarin's insistence that he was unable to find God in the sky, the world heard a strange revelation: The daughter of the old boss, brought up on the best principles of Marxist "science," had become a convert.

---

closed. In Lithuania, where the overwhelming majority of the population is Catholic, the clergy was reduced by half. Many priests and bishops, such as Msgr. Matulionis and Ramanauskas, have suffered the cruelties of deportation. Nonetheless the population remains profoundly Catholic.

In addition, the Uniate churches in Galicia and the sub-Carpathian Ukraine, although they preserved the Byzantine rite, were linked with Rome. They suffered the same repression. Monsignor Slypy, the metropolitan of Lvov, spent eighteen years in deportation before he was released in 1963 (he had been arrested on April 18, 1945, with all the other Uniate bishops). After these deportations a few priests engineered the alliance of the Uniate churches with the Orthodox Church in the interests of Moscow.

The objective of the persecution of these churches was not so much to extirpate religious feeling as it was to destroy an influence exerted by the Vatican. It is probable that in addition at least some of the clergy of these churches constituted the spiritual backbone of guerrilla movements in the struggle against Soviet occupation.

(27)

ATTACKS AND
COUNTERATTACKS ON
THE LITERARY FRONT

T HE INTELLECTUALS had endured particular hardships in the Great Purge. Many of them were sent to camps in which they vanished. The party had other matters on its mind during the war. Certain writers and artists, however, were utilized for propaganda purposes in various missions that brought them into contact with the West. It was absolutely essential to bring them back to the treadmill of strict orthodoxy and prevent them from contaminating others. On Stalin's orders, this was Zhdanov's job. Philosophy, the theater, poetry, history, music, and painting were brought into line. Any sign of bourgeois ideology or cosmopolitanism was denounced and repressed. Science was not exempt from these dictates. Physicists were reprimanded, biologists were rebuked for following the bourgeois theories of Weissman or Morgan. Lysenko's theses were put forward as the only ones conforming to the true spirit of the party. The peak of absurdity was reached when proletarian science was set up in opposition to bourgeois science.

Stalin himself took a hand in the battle. One day the linguistic school of Mar, which had thus far enjoyed the government's good graces, was denounced as heretical. The school had no choice but to bow.

Khrushchev's speech to the Twentieth Congress in 1956, the denunciation of the cult of personality, and the shock that these revelations caused acted as a leaven on the intellectuals and encouraged them to express themselves with greater freedom, to reject the guidelines that were imposed on artistic and literary creativity. But, in all honesty, some of them had not waited for this signal before they began to fight.

After Stalin's death the magazine called *Novy Mir,* the major organ of liberal tendencies, had already emerged as a hotbed of heresy. It was in *Novy Mir* (No. 12, 1953), for example, that Pomerantzev championed the concept of *sincerity* in literary expression, a concept that he opposed to everything that was conventional and stereotyped.

Behind his prudent choice of words it is not difficult to see that Pomerantzev was championing the rights of the artistic creator and the judgment of the individual against the dogmatic spirit of the party. The dogmatists had no illusions on the matter. *Literaturnaya Gazeta* retorted on March 20, 1954, that Pomerantzev was expressing "his incomprehension of the part played by the party spirit in artistic creation."

From this time forward new currents began to stir in the world of letters and to spill over into the university. In its July 1954 issue, *Oktyabr,* the major organ of the conservatives, discussed the agitation that prevailed among the students of the Faculty of Literature of the University of Moscow as a result of the attacks on Pomerantzev. The crisis must already have been regarded as quite serious, because in the Second Congress of Soviet Writers on December 15, 1956, Konstantin Simonov said, as soon as discussions began:

. . . It must be emphasized once more that the principle of loyalty to the party in matters of literature, as well as that of literature's active and total participation in the struggle for Communism, is open to no discussion from our point of view. All the points of view expressed openly or by innuendo that tend to divert literature from the active struggle on behalf of Communism represent to us not points of view that are open to discussion but, quite to the contrary, points of view that are fundamentally hostile to the very spirit of Soviet literature.

In Stalin's time such a statement would have had the force of law. But the tyrant was dead; the camps had begun to open. Fear was no longer so obsessive. The liberal clan, though it could not strike its chains, was already endeavoring to undermine the dogmas with oblique language.[1]

Khrushchev's report, which was ostensibly restricted to party people but which was soon known in intellectual circles, created quite a different climate. It struck a harsh blow at dogmatic positions. For the famous party spirit, that citadel so tenaciously defended, had in fact been for years nothing but the spirit of one man, the author of abominable butcheries. Everything that he had imposed in the name of this dogma was now being challenged.

The thaw was beginning. Between February and December 1956 it reached into every field: literature, cinema, music, drama, painting. Impressionism, that "decadent" art of the middle class, was timidly allowed to enter. It was during this period that a young poet, Yevgeny Yevtushenko, spoke out and became the representative of the new generation and that Vladimir Dudintsev published *Not by Bread Alone,* a novel in which the protagonist is an inventor persecuted by the bureaucracy.

Then came another shock: the Hungarian revolution of October 1956, instigated by intellectuals and followed by Soviet intervention, and coupled with Poland's October, the Polish intellectuals' explosion of liberalism. These events had their repercussions in the Soviet Army in the form of desertions as well as among the young intellectuals of Moscow. A meeting

[1] It was at this time (1955) that the clandestine student publications *The Blue Button* and *Heresy,* which we have already mentioned, began to appear.

there to discuss Dudintsev's novel turned into a riot; militia-men on horseback had to intervene. On December 16 *Pravda* told of stirrings in the Technological Institute of the Leningrad Municipal Council, the Repin Institute of Painting, and the Conservatory. And on January 6, 1957, *Literaturnaya Gazeta* drew quite a gloomy picture:

> The year has begun in an atmosphere of bitter ideological conflict with the forces of world reaction. . . . This has shown itself in the cultural domain in the attacks against the very foundation, against what is most dear to us: the party spirit and Socialist realism.

It would indeed appear that discussions were many and fevered among the students and in literary circles. *Komsomolskaya Pravda* observed on January 10, 1957, that "it is still very often the case that the leaders of the *Komsomol* are in no position to answer students' questions or make the proper responses to the loud-mouths and demagogues who make themselves conspicuous with their speeches." Some persons took the liberty of raising questions that were paid for with expulsion.

Evidence of the fact that the growth of an "unhealthy" state of mind was rapid was afforded by a series of some fifty meetings that were convened in the major intellectual centers of the Soviet Union in order to bring the "rebels" into line. The attacks on "formalism," "nationalism," "cosmopolitanism," and "nihilism" flared up on all sides.

The leaders had every reason to be apprehensive. After all, the Hungarian revolt was part of an intellectual movement. The leaders, and Khrushchev first of all, could not avoid drawing lessons from it.

The reaction was too strong for the liberal group not to restrict itself to the bounds of cautious discretion. When Boris Pasternak offered his famous novel, *Dr. Zhivago*, to *Novy Mir*, the magazine refused it. The novel was published abroad without eliciting any reaction from the government. But, when the Nobel Prize was awarded to Pasternak, there was a scandal. In the face of the storm of slanders and insults Pasternak was compelled to refuse the great honor that had been conferred on him (October 1958).

It is probable that at that moment the Presidium, even though it was divided by so many problems, maintained a common front on everything that bore on artistic expression. Its members were fully aware that the struggle against tsarism had begun in intellectual circles and that challenges to dogmas, even in diluted or oblique guises, sooner or later lead to the gravest revolts. The infection was spreading of necessity to university circles, which were the future functionaries of the government.

Some estimate of the extent of this taint may be gleaned from the May 13, 1958, issue of Komsomolskaya Pravda. The newspaper disclosed that during the previous year forty-three hundred students had been expelled from the higher schools and institutes in Leningrad.

It is valid to say that henceforth.official literature was to be divided into two large camps: one centered on Oktyabr, under the direction of Kochetov; and the other on Novy Mir and its editor in chief, Alexander Tvardovsky. Each camp warily watched the other and waited for a favorable opportunity to resume major operations.

This was presented after the Twenty-second Congress in October, 1961, in which Khrushchev made a violent attack intended to produce a radical condemnation of the anti-party group (Molotov, Malenkov, and Voroshilov). In order to settle things for his rivals, Khrushchev exploited to the full the theme of abuses of the cult of personality. The criticisms of Stalin that had become more or less a memory were resumed with vehemence. In the end his body was removed from the mausoleum in which it lay beside Lenin's.

The new denunciation of the cult of personality acted as a ferment. This was quite clear in April 1962, in the elections for the executive committee of the Moscow branch of the Union of Writers. Kochetov refused to be a candidate. Eight leading figures were defeated, including Albakin, the literary columnist for *Pravda*. On the other hand, such rebels were elected as Yevtushenko, whose poetry had declared his desire (it was to be granted) to visit foreign capitals, and Voznessensky. Shortly afterward Yevtushenko was appointed to the editorial board of the magazine, *Yunost*. The liberal camp had scored real gains.

This sudden advancement of the most popular poet of the young generation could not have taken place without a green light from the authorities. The authorities meant Khrushchev. Confirmation of this came quickly with the publication of Alexander Solzhenitsyn's novel, *One Day in the Life of Ivan Denisovich*, the story of a prisoner's day in a concentration camp. Now this story went quite far. A ruthless depiction of concentration-camp life, it showed that the Great Purge not only had not been an operation limited to members of the party—as Khrushchev had given the Twentieth Congress to understand—but also had been a terrible ordeal for the entire population. The story appeared in *Novy Mir*.

In his remarkable study on *Le Pouvoir en URSS* (*Power in the Soviet Union*), Michel Tatu shows that the new liberal spirit that was asserting itself in literature and the arts was part of Khrushchev's game in his battle against the anti-party group and those of his colleagues in the Presidium who did not wish to carry destalinization too far. Literary activity was a flank on which the secretary general was attempting to wage a political offensive against his opponents. In this connection there is great significance in Yevtushenko's poem "Stalin's Heirs," which was published in *Pravda* on October 21, 1962. It was a direct attack on the current defenders of Stalinism:

Certain inheritors prune their rosebushes in their retreats
And think to themselves that retirement is only temporary.
Others even attack Stalin from the rostrum,
But at night they yearn nostalgically for the time that is gone:

It is no accident that they suffer heart attacks,
They do not like the times.[2]

Undoubtedly it was also no accident that this poem was
written just after the conclusion of the Twenty-second Congress. Yevtushenko recited it frequently at poets' meetings.
Nevertheless it was not to appear in print until October of
1962.

Although it has never been specifically put into words, the
slogan of the liberal camp can be reduced to the simple principle of freedom of expression. Now this watchword not only
led to the undermining of the foundations of party spirit and
Socialist realism but also constituted an implicit rebellion
against the very foundations of political power. When he made
use of this movement for his private ends in his battle against
his rivals, Khrushchev undammed a torrent that went far beyond his own objectives. He was able to establish this for
himself when he visited the Moscow branch of the Artists'
Union on December 1, 1962. There he saw not only pictures
by artists who had been condemned in the 1930s but also "abstract" paintings hung in a separate room. It was too much for
him. He gave way to an access of temper, which was certainly
genuine, and let his gutter vocabulary flow unchecked.

It was necessary to put limits to the abuses. On December
17 Khrushchev arranged a major confrontation of four hundred representatives of literature and the arts in the presence
of the Presidium. The violently contradictory discussions revealed irreconcilable antagonisms. Above all, they ended in
the recognition of a grave situation: There was no longer any
clear distinction between the permissible and the prohibited.

It was during this confrontation that the conservatives
launched their counterattack. It was waged with great tactical
skill on indirect lines, no doubt with the behind-the-scenes in-
stigation of Khrushchev's adversaries, and all the weight of it
fell on a single representative of the liberal camp: Ehrenburg.

[2] Some analysts think that the pruner of rosebushes is Bulganin and
the victim of the heart attack is Kozlov.

A former camp inmate, a woman, denounced him vehemently. The attack was continued in the press with a violent
article by Ermilov in *Izvestia* on January 30, 1963. In his memoirs published in *Novy Mir*, Ehrenburg had in fact written
that he had known the falsity of the charges made during the
Great Purge but that in the face of that tidal wave he had
"gritted his teeth" in silence. This was an incautious avowal,
for it contradicted what Khrushchev had told the Twentieth
Congress: "Stalin had organized everything. The rest of us
knew nothing about it." The conservatives were to use this
contradiction to surprising advantage.

"What!" Ermilov thundered; "Ehrenburg knew, and said
nothing? Enjoying an immeasurable advantage over the vast
majority of 'average citizens,' knowing the horrible truth, he
allowed himself, through his silence, to become an accomplice
in the crimes."

Ehrenburg retorted at once that he had not seen a single
Soviet citizen protest publicly, and this was true. In those days
terror was not just a rhetorical figure. But his statement involved him in a major controversy. Ermilov took the fullest
advantage, protesting that, "in his attempt to give himself a
clean bill of health," Ehrenburg was insulting a whole generation of Russians by portraying them as completely aware
of the crimes committed but muzzled by their fear.

At this point in the quarrel, Ehrenburg should have replied:
"I am not defaming anyone. Ask Comrade Nikita; in fact, he
too had to grit his teeth in silence." Obviously there could be
no question of doing this. But it was nonetheless clear that the
debate had taken a dangerous turn and that to carry it farther
would be to put everyone's responsibilities at issue.

Thus the weapon of the literary thaw that Khrushchev had
used against his rivals threatened to turn against him. The
thaw could not be controlled; there was the danger that it
would turn into a flood that would sweep away all the dams
that it was essential to preserve. Destalinization was raising
the most fearsome questions, threatening to blow to bits the

myth of Stalin's and Yezhov's monopoly of guilt and to un-
mask the brutal truth: Those who were directing destalinization had in their day been Stalin's accomplices.

Khrushchev very soon recognized the danger and made an
about-face. Whereas he had declared in the Twenty-second
Congress that the whole truth about Stalin must be told to the
people, he insisted in a major speech on March 8, 1963, that
there was nothing more to be disclosed. As for the crimes of
Stalin, whose finer qualities he pointed out, he reduced them
to the level of mere excesses, and on the very delicate issue
raised by Ermilov he gave the unqualified lie to Ehrenburg:
"The question that arises is whether the ruling circles of the
party knew of the arrests made during this period: yes, they
did know of them. But did they know that absolutely innocent
persons had been arrested? No, that they did not know. They
believed in Stalin, and they could not even imagine that repressions might be employed against honest men dedicated to
our cause."

Nor could there any longer be any thought of publishing
new works such as Solzhenitsyn's. Here Khrushchev had reason to be frightened: It is said that ten thousand manuscripts
dealing with the camps and repression had been submitted to
the editorial boards of reviews and publishing houses. It was
time to turn off the taps.

The hierarchs could go on with their rivalries for the possession of power. But they had been dramatically shown that
this fierce competition would have to take place in a sealed
chamber, inside the walls of the "apparatus." At the same
time, they were finding that they had a minimum of interests
in common, those of a generation that had come up through
the ranks and got to the top in Stalin's shadow. At a given
moment Khrushchev might have thought that a young poet as
popular as Yevtushenko might be useful for his purposes. But
in the end this exploitation encouraged the young generation
to assert itself, to put forth its opinions, to raise embarrassing
questions with increasing audacity. In its utter freedom from

responsibility for the Great Purge, it could turn to its *fathers,*
like the same generation in Germany, and ask them: "How
were such things possible? What were you doing in those
days? Why did you keep silent?"

The innumerable questions on that terrible period that were
asked of parents were of a nature to trouble the leaders, the
more so because at the same time the press was pointing out
another peril: the political apathy of the young, their lack of
enthusiasm, their thoroughgoing indifference to the victory of
Socialism, combined with an intense interest in the West. The
past was being challenged. The present offered no attrac-
tions. "What is the explanation," *Komsomolskaya Pravda* asked
on April 18, 1959, "for the fact that last year in Moscow more
than a thousand rank-and-file organizations were unable to
bring a single new recruit into the *Komsomol?*" [3]

There were other subjects of concern. Side by side with the
manifestations of the "liberal" camp, which were appearing
in duly authorized publications and therefore passed by the
censors, a whole clandestine literature was beginning to appear. Young men and women met in a room to listen to forbidden poems recorded on tape. Mimeographed magazines
like *Phoenix* or *Syntax* circulated from hand to hand. People
were no longer satisfied to demand a little freedom. They
bluntly criticized the system. They turned their backs on it.
And these heretics grew bolder and flaunted their anger even

[3] There was an echo of this conflict between generations in a novella
published by the magazine, *Molodoya Guardia,* in August 1964. A couple overheard a conversation between their son and some friends whom
he had invited to the house while they were away:

" 'And then what after that? Let's admit that this was not very brave.
But one must take into account the fact that their generation had a hard
life.'

" 'Then it must be admitted frankly: they were scared to death'. . . .

"A feminine voice rose then, rather shrill: 'But they believed in it.'

"Someone shouted back: 'They believed in it? Even when the police
came to arrest their closest friends? What kind of friendship is that?'

"Again Dima spoke: 'Yes, unquestionably, they had no guts.' "

This was quoted by Mickhai Slavinsky in *Le drame des intellectuels
en URSS.*

in the public squares. The literary opposition was no longer confined to "drawing rooms" and secret parleys. It went out into the street.

The first demonstration undoubtedly was held in Mayakovsky Square in Moscow in November 1961. A group of young persons met at the foot of the poet's statue and began to recite verses. This scene created stupefaction and then indignation in one member of the party who described it in the magazine *Dalny Vostok* (*Far East*), No. 2, 1962:

> I noticed a rather large crowd, surrounding the monument. It seemed to me that poetry was being read. "How wonderful!" I said to myself, touched. "Poetry at Mayakovsky's statue: The modern poets consecrate their works to the tribune of the Revolution." I made my way through the crowd. In fact, a young man was standing at the foot of the monument and reciting in a loud voice. . . . I listened carefully. But what was he saying? It was some kind of modernist hash thrown together by an illiterate under a bombastic title *Human Manifesto.* . . . "Bastard!" I shouted, trying to make him come down from where he stood. But some people grabbed me under the arms and brutally hustled me out of the crowd, warning me: "Careful, old goat, or we'll wash your mouth out with soap so you'll know just where the truth is." [4]

Komsomolskaya Pravda of January 10, 1962, and *Molodoy Kommunist* in its January and February issues were to speak with equal horror of this poetic demonstration and to shower contempt on its organizers. They were called "pygmies," "zeroes," and "parasites" steeped in Western ways.

Their trousers were too tight, their other clothes were "motley," and they sported long hair and beards. These "peanut-shaped" young heretics had their "salon" in the lodgings of an old woman out of the "dark ages." There they read their works, which were full of "filthy anti-Soviet slanders," while they drank cocktails that inflamed them to their shabby exploits. And they talked about the terrible injustice of life: " 'Colorless individuals,' shock workers, or 'headliners' win

[4] Quoted by Slavinsky, *op. cit.*

nationwide fame while the real giants of the mind, the authentic spokesmen of the age are relegated to the background and vegetate in mediocrity. Can one resign oneself to this? Certainly not! So they all rush out to the square. . . ."

It seems that these boys, all of whom were quite young, had been expelled from the university, like Nassov, who "spat on the ground in contempt when things that are dear to us were mentioned in his presence," or like Bukovsky, a nineteen-year-old "no-good" who had written a thesis to prove that the *Komsomol* did not exist, or like that Galanskov, the author of the *Human Manifesto* that amounted to an outright call to revolution:

> Do not believe the ministers, the rulers, the newspapers.
> Up, you who are prostrate!
> Look! the marbles of atomic death
> Are rolling through the orbits of the world.
> Up!
> Up!
> Up!
> O scarlet blood of revolt!
> Go, complete the destruction
> Of the worm-eaten prison of the state.
> Go through the fearful groups
> And for those who are hungry steal
> The black bombs like plums on the plates of the cities. . . .

N. Nor wrote: "We are only ordinary people. It does not matter that we are few. It does not matter that we are weak. . . . We can die. Our hour will come."

It was this same attitude of individual revolt, this affirmation of the individual against the structures of the state, that Kharbanov voiced as early as 1957:

> Frightening men,
> Frozen brains.
> I advance alone to encounter
> Their uncountable columns.

Discussing this poem on April 28, 1957, *Komsomolskaya Pravda* could not contain its stupefaction: "How can such a thing happen? And yet they come out of our own schools, they have been brought up in the spirit of the works of Fade-yev, Sholokhov, Ostrovsky. And suddenly there is decadence."

There can be little doubt that some connection was established between these young intellectuals and the emigrants' magazine, *Grani*, published by the NTS in Frankfurt. For several years *Grani* has been printing a whole series of works that circulate secretly in the Soviet Union or have been refused by Soviet publications.[5]

So Mayakovsky Square became the meeting place for the young rebel poets. The statue of the poet who had committed suicide rose on its pedestal like an emblem to which to rally, serving the same symbolic function as Kossuth's statue in Budapest. Young men and women strolled there in little groups, reciting their verses. As soon as the militia came into view, they ostentatiously began declaiming lines of the purest orthodoxy, returning to their forbidden poems when the militia disappeared again. It was a little game that could hardly deceive the police. (What use would there be for stool pigeons?) But these meetings took place at the height of the thaw, after the Twenty-second Congress. (It is probable, however, that Galanskov was arrested during this period.) The adoption of brutal measures would undoubtedly

---

[5] For example:

1956, verses written in a concentration camp and signed with the pseudonyn of A. Ivanov;

1960, *Le Chant inachevé*, an autobiographical novel signed "Nari-mov," the pseudonym of Mikhail Naritza, a professor of sculpture in the School of Fine Arts in Leningrad, who was later interned in a psychiatric hospital (which often takes the place of the concentration camp for the intellectuals), like Tarsis and Ovechkin, in 1962;

1962, the complete contents of the magazine *Phoenix 1961*, and Tar-sis' novel *The Blue Fly;*

1963–1964, Tarsis' *The Beautiful Life* and *Requiem*, by the famous poet Anna Akhmatova;

1965, Tarsis' *Ward Seven* and the magazine *Syntax*, Nos. 1–3.

have compromised what was being tolerated in other quarters—that is, activities like Yevtushenko's. On October 8, 1961, which was Poetry Day in the Soviet Union, Yevtushenko had been carried in triumph on men's shoulders in that same Mayakovsky Square and forced by an enthusiastic youthful crowd to recite his nonconformist poems.

Things unquestionably changed as soon as Khrushchev reversed the engines. In addition, the young rebels' rowdy doings were all the more insufferable because Galanskov and a number of his friends paraded a pacifism that was recommended for capitalist countries but was not for use in the Soviet Union. In January 1962 *Molodoy Kommunist* said:

Not one of the zeroes is willing to serve in the army. Military service, you see, standardizes personality. . . . Like hypocritical rabbits they listen to the serpent hisses directed against our country by The Voice of America. . . . They nose through Moscow in their obsequious way in search of foreign tourists, from some of whom they obtain, in addition to the usual trinkets and dirty postcards, bits of gossip from White emigrants. They stand careful guard in their memories over all these lying mouthings about our people, our party, and Soviet youth.

Khrushchev's downfall on October 14, 1964, led to further action against the liberal and clandestine currents. But this offensive was waged without too much cohesion, a fact that revealed the confusions and contradictions among the *apparachiki;* nor did it succeed in drawing a clear line of demarcation between the permissible and the prohibited. The authorities resorted to rigorous measures, like the internment of Tarsis and some others in psychiatric hospitals. But these measures produced petitions signed by the liberal intellectuals. And, above all, the embarrassing cadaver of the former genius, Stalin, even if every effort was made to mention it as little as possible, was still there. It was still poisoning Soviet society. Some reflection of this taint appeared in an article in

Novy Mir (No. 9, 1964) devoted to Solzhenitsyn's book, *One Day in the Life of Ivan Denisovich:*

> With respect to the crimes described in this book, some say: "That is all that there was"; others say: "This is not the truth." Some speculate sacrilegiously on this tragedy. Others conceal the fact that the cult of personality in fact means a new tragedy. Some rejoice; the others are afraid. *It is obvious that all this does not concern the past alone.* (Italics added.)

The conflict continued almost surreptitiously between the advocates of conservatism and the liberals, between *Oktyabr* and *Novy Mir* or *Yunost.* The government was intent on the utmost minimization of awkward reminders of the past. On August 29, 1965, the first secretary of the *Komsomol,* Pavlov, delivered a judgment on the cult of personality:

> It is undeniable that the denunciation of the cult of personality has had tremendous influence on the education of the younger generation. It is hardly possible, however, to justify a certain unilateralism in the views of certain theoreticians and writers who look at whole stages of the Socialist society's history exclusively through the prism of the negative aspects of the cult of personality. The 1930s, for instance, have often been described only in their darker colors. And yet what was essential in the Soviet society of those years was determined above all by industrialization and the Socialist transformation of agriculture, the working-class enthusiasm of the masses, . . . *and the victory of Socialist realism in art and literature.*

This amounted to a declaration that the crimes of Stalin and Yezhov and the prison camps with their millions of victims were ancillary phenomena, mere "stains" on the grandiose advance to Socialist victory. There were many other signs of a visible desire to halt destalinization. In particular, the tenth anniversary of the opening of the Twentieth Congress was officially ignored on February 14, 1966.

Nevertheless literary extremism did not put aside its weapons. On April 14, 1965, young intellectuals coursed through the streets of Moscow, brandishing placards and demanding freedom of speech and artistic creation. The police had to be called out to disperse them.

Foreign news services described this demonstration. The Soviet press said nothing. Somewhat later, it was learned that the demonstration had been organized by a new group, the SMOG. In July the SMOG began publishing a magazine called *Sphinxes*, the manifesto of which soon reached *Grani*, which reprinted it:

. . . Today we are fighting desperately against everyone: from the *Komsomol* to the small minds, from the police to the lower middle class, from the incompetent to the ignorant, they are all against us. We turn to the free world, which has already expressed itself so often on the subject of Russian art. Help us. Do not let us be crushed beneath the heavy boot.

Remember that in Russia we exist.

We, the SMOG!

There is certainly a good deal of bombast in these lines, but there is also a firm tone that would have been inconceivable ten years earlier, a defiance of the established order for which there was no precedent. These groups, which were created perhaps among the children of the new Soviet middle class, are reminiscent of the clubs of the 1870s under tsarism, those "nihilists," also the sons of the upper classes, who were the forerunners of the great wave of terrorism.

Terrorism in these circles has been limited thus far, it appears, to literary violences like those in Galanskov's *Human Manifesto*: "Go . . . and steal the black bombs . . ." But the Soviet leaders are sufficiently conversant with the history of tsarism to remember how things began. And they must wince when they find that a clandestine publication circulating among students is called *Kolokol* (*The Bell*).[6]

[6] The title of the publication issued by the famous revolutionary Alexander Herzen.

On top of all this the Daniel-Sinyavsky case exploded.

Andrey Sinyavsky, a member of the Union of Soviet Writers, and his friend, Yuli Daniel, who earned his livelihood as a translator, were arrested by the KGB, Sinyavsky on September 5, 1965, and Daniel a few days later. They were accused of having smuggled certain of their works out to the West and arranged for their publication there under pseudonyms. Sinyavsky, under the name of Abram Tertz, was indeed the author of various stories: *Gentlemen, the Court!*, *Lyubimov*, and others, as well as an essay, *What Is Socialist Realism?* Daniel, under the pseudonym of Nikolai Arzhak, had smuggled out *Moscow Calling!*, *Hands*, *Expiation*, *The MINAP Man*, and others. None of these manuscripts, many of which were largely fictional, could ever have appeared in the Soviet Union. They were slashing satires on the Soviet system and society. In *Moscow Calling!*, for instance, Daniel imagined that on August 10, 1961, the Presidium of the Supreme Soviet of the Soviet Union had decreed a "legal murder day." *Glavlit* (the censorship agency) found this a "monstrous pamphlet."

Obviously the government wanted to make an example by bringing these two writers to justice and staging a public trial. Its purpose was not merely to denounce the content of their works but also to castigate the duplicity of the authors. By arranging for publication abroad, the writers had infringed the canons of the system, committed anti-Soviet acts, and given the capitalist press the opportunity to defame their country. The harsh penalties imposed on them would certainly act as a deterrent to others who might be tempted to follow the same course.

The era of impunity was over. The time had come to call a dramatic halt. But the consequences of this sensational trial were far from useful to the government.

The arrests of the two writers aroused a certain emotion abroad and led to a series of protests by intellectuals. The sentences made matters worse. Aragon himself made plain his disavowal in *l'Humanité* on February 16, 1965:

It is indeed to be feared that this kind of procedure may be thought to be inherent in the nature of Communism, the judgment recently handed down being taken as an omen of what justice will be in a country that has abolished man's exploitation of man. It is our duty to proclaim that that is not and could never be the case, at least in France, where the responsibility is ours.[7]

Under conditions that were difficult in other ways, reactions within the Soviet Union occasionally assumed a very active form. On December 5, 1965, there was a public demonstration that was quickly put down by the police and that led to three arrests. The demonstration had been announced previously, with specific instructions, in "A Civic Appeal" distributed at the University of Moscow and signed: "Resistance."

Many Russian intellectuals wrote to protest certain articles that attacked the defendants. Mrs. Sinyavsky and Mrs. Daniel sent letters of protest to Brezhnev, to the director of the KGB, and to the prosecutor. They denounced the interrogations to which they themselves had been subjected, the searches of their homes, and the various pressures exerted on them. They declared their complete solidarity with their husbands. Mrs. Daniel, for example, wrote, among other things:

[7] Aragon went on to assert that, if the Communist party gained power in France, there could be no question of putting people on trial for intellectual offenses. This position committed no one but himself. It was hardly consonant with that taken by the editor in chief of *Pravda*, Zamyakin, in his reply to a letter sent to *Pravda* by seventeen French writers and actors, including Jean-Louis Barrault, Madeleine Renaud, Simone Signoret, Yves Montand, and Armand Lanoux:

> It seems to us that French cultural figures have no reason to feel that they are affected by the case of Sinyavsky and Daniel. We emphasize once more that it is a question not of writers . . . but of persons who have chosen slander as their trade. Now calumny has never been and will never be regarded as a form of criticism. . . . We deeply regret that yourself and your colleagues regard this matter, which involves the *smugglers, common criminals, and slanderers, Sinyavsky and David,* as a serious blow to French-Soviet friendship. (Italics added.)

Zamyakin's letter was printed in *Le Monde* on May 21, 1966. Whether nonconformist writers would be regarded as holding opinions or engaging in smuggling, crime, and calumny under a Communist government in France remains an open question.

The examining magistrate allowed himself to indulge in disguised threats: If I behaved badly . . . I might have problems at my job "when they hear about it there." . . . The investigators have gathered information on my husband's and my private lives. . . . But what is most disgusting is the fact that this information has been transmitted to persons completely unconnected with the case and to people who know my husband and myself.

Alexander Ginzburg, the editor in chief of *Syntax*, addressed a long letter to Kosygin in which he cited the Declaration of Human Rights adopted by the United Nations and ratified by the Soviet Union. His letter also denounced the KGB for smashing the demonstration on December 5.

After the trial, which resulted in prison terms of seven years for Sinyavsky and five years for Daniel, sixty-two Soviet authors wrote to the Presidium of the party. In addition, a hundred Soviet scholars and writers declared that they were "overwhelmed" by the decision to dismiss a professor specializing in Russian literature who had been one of the witnesses.

Thus the reactions both before and after the trial were serious. A large part of the intelligentsia repudiated the very basis of the prosecution and refused to accept its conclusions.

The trial itself was conducted in the presence of an invited audience whose servile laughter was strongly reminiscent of the reactions to the very private wit of Vyshinsky. In the secrecy of the preliminary interrogation Sinyavsky and Daniel had been induced to make a certain number of concessions. Everything changed in the public trial. Daniel, a tall man with thick hair, and Sinyavsky, short, chestnut-haired, and fragile, defended themselves step by step.

They declared at the outset that they did not acknowledge any guilt. They admitted that they had been wrong to send their manuscripts abroad. If, however, they had done so, it was because they knew that these works would never be published in their own country. And every writer wants to see his work published.

They denied that they had invested their work with any anti-Soviet content. Could they be held responsible for the interpretations drawn by foreign critics? Besides, not all the critics had made the same interpretations.

A large part of the proceedings was given over to the interpretation of the "guilty" works. The exchanges were savage, the more so because it was as if the accused were talking to a wall. They pointed out repeatedly that isolated excerpts taken out of context were no basis for an impartial evaluation, and, in addition, the presiding judge and the prosecutor were systematically confusing the views expressed by fictional characters with those held by their creators. Here is a typical passage from the testimony:

Q. (the prosecutor reading from a manuscript): "I hate them so much that I have spasms, I can't breathe, I tremble all over. Oh, if only one could get them all together and destroy the lot at one shot!" Who are these people whom you hate? Who are those whom you want to eliminate?

A. (by Daniel): To whom are you speaking? to me, to my protagonist, or to someone else?

Q.: Which person in your story is the positive hero? Which character presents your point of view?

A.: I have already told you during our preliminary hearing that no one in my story plays the part of the completely positive hero.[8]

Sinyavsky defended himself with a special acerbity. In his final statement, he showed in slashing terms that the court was clinging to absolutely literal interpretations of words that were part of an imaginative work:

In sum, on the legal murder day there were only two executioners, Daniel and Sinyavsky. Here, in a way that is truly most strange and most unexpected, the literary image loses its essence as a convention and is taken so literally by the prosecutor that the trial follows the manuscript as if it were its natural consequence. I was unlucky enough to date the epilogue to *Gentlemen, the Court!* in

[8] *Le livre blanc de l'affaire Sinyavsky-Daniel,* pp. 147–148.

1956. So the author has slandered the year 1956. Ah, there, author, you predicted correctly: now go into a camp in 1966.[9]

His statement scintillating with rapier-like thrusts, he posed a problem that should be examined by all Soviet intellectuals:

A question arises: What is agitation and propaganda and what is literature? The prosecution's position is this: Literature is a form of agitation and propaganda. Agitation can be only Soviet or anti-Soviet. If it is not Soviet, then it is anti-Soviet. I do not agree with this. But, if a writer must be examined and judged by such standards, *then what will be done when it is a question of men who publish proclamations?* They too fall within the jurisdiction of Article LXX. If a work of literature must be judged by imposing the maximum penalty provided under that article, then what will happen when leaflets are in issue? Or is there no difference? From the prosecution's point of view there is none.[10]

The severity of the punishments was certainly intended to give pause to any possible emulators. This was an error in judgment on the part of the rulers. In every way Sinyavsky and Daniel maintained an exemplary attitude. For this was the first instance of defendants in a public trial who refused to confess their guilt. They had defended themselves fiercely throughout the proceedings. They had defended *their own values* against those of the prosecution. What a contrast to the meticulously contrived spectacles of the Great Purge, when terror forced the accused to their knees!

This difference in attitude may have had its roots in the abstention from torture during the preliminary investigation. It was connected also with the change in climate that was affecting the whole of Soviet society. Sinyavsky and Daniel knew that they were not speaking in a vacuum. Many writers and young intellectuals and thousands of Soviet citizens stood with them. And the government itself could not dispense justice under the conditions of *Yezhovchina*. In the context of

[9] *Ibid.*, p. 248.
[10] *Ibid.*, pp. 253–254. The prosecution was grounded on Article LXX.

peaceful coexistence, when even the basis for the prosecution brought down condemnation from certain members of foreign Communist parties, it was essential to give the proceedings an apparently democratic character and to allow the accused their day in court. This entailed the risk of transforming the tribunal of repression into the tribune of opposition. And that was what actually occurred.

With fewer repercussions in the West, the Moscow phenomena had their parallels in the Ukraine. A young poet named Simonenko died of cancer. His poems, in which he voiced his wrath against the bureaucracy and his deep love for his native country, began to circulate from hand to hand and were recopied with fervor.

The repression soon struck other intellectuals. On April 7, 1966, *The New York Times* reported the arrests of two literary critics, Ivan Svitlyshny and Ivan Dzhuba. They were accused of having smuggled Simonenko's manuscripts to the West. Twelve other intellectuals were arrested in Lvov. Svitlyshny's sentence was the same as Sinyavsky's: seven years at hard labor. Dzhuba was released after the trial. A few months later he was to die of an incurable tuberculosis.

But the opposition did not surrender. On January 22, 1967, there was a new demonstration in Pushkin Square in Moscow. A short time later a number of members of the SMOG were arrested: Vadim Delon, Yevgeny Kushev, and Vladimir Bukovsky.[11] Prosecution was initiated against Ginzburg, whose crime consisted in having assembled the material for *The White Book on the Sinyavsky-Daniel Case,* and Galanskov, Dobrovolsky, Vera Lashkova, and P. Rodzeivsky, all of whom were connected with the magazine, *Phoenix 1966.* They were all compelled to undergo examination in the Serbsky Institute of Fo-

[11] After what amounted in effect to a closed trial, Bukovsky was sentenced to three years in prison. Kushev and Delon were released. The trial of Galanskov and Ginzburg will probably be postponed until after the fiftieth anniversary of the October Revolution. [They were sentenced after the publication of the French edition of this book, and their sentences led to fresh protests both in Russia and abroad.—Translator.]

rensic Psychiatry in Kropotkin Alley in Moscow. The government's newest brainstorm was to regard all its opponents as psychotics.

And this occurred on the eve of the fiftieth anniversary of a revolution that had made a record of a few insanities of its own.

CONCLUSION

ON NOVEMBER 4, 1917, a few days after the seizure of power, four People's Commissars —Rykov, Noghin, Milyutin, and Fyodorovitch—submitted to the Central Committee a statement countersigned by seven other Bolsheviks, including Ryazanov, Larin, and Shlyapnikov.

We are of the opinion [they wrote] that it is essential that the Socialist government be formed with the participation of all Soviet parties. . . . *We believe that, apart from this course, there is only one solution: to maintain a purely Bolshevik government by means of political terror.* This is the course that has been adopted by the Soviet of People's Commissars. We cannot and will not follow it. We see that this will lead to the exclusion of the proletarian mass organizations from political life, to the establishment of a government without responsibility, and to the destruction of the Revolution and the country.[1]

The signers of this statement, whose views were virtually the same as those held at that time by Zinoviev and Kamenev, were in error on one point. The Revolution—that is, *de facto,*

[1] Italics added. Cf. the official record of proceedings of the Central Committee of the Bolshevik party.

(511)

the Bolshevik government—was not destroyed. But the country was. It was destroyed by a government that in fact could preserve its power only through the practice of terror and the growing importance acquired by the instrument of that terror, the *Cheka*. The terror liquidated the White Guards and, at almost the same time, the Socialist parties. It shattered the enthusiasms of the workers and peasants. And, after the Tenth Congress, during Lenin's lifetime and on his initiative, it began to impose remarkable limitations on the rights of the opposition within the party. It would be the work of Stalin to destroy it completely, in successive steps, in order to establish himself at the end of the Great Purge as the all-powerful master of the "apparatus."

What was the reason for the defeat of the various political opposition forces during the 1920s? Terror is far from being the only explanation. The White armies were handicapped by their internal dissensions, their total lack of political sense, and their inability to wage the civil war on a basis that could rally the masses. Theirs was a defeat of military technicians who saw only the technical side of operations. But technicians were also serving the enemy, by choice or constraint, and the enemy had a policy for his war. This was beyond the capacities of the Whites.

It was not political intelligence that was lacking to Trotsky, Zinoviev, and, later, Bukharin. But all three were the victims of principles to the establishment of which they had contributed. It is essential to remember what Radek told the Tenth Congress: "I am voting for a document that can be turned against us." This was what in fact happened. Any opposition that attempted to create a "structure" within the party was accused of making itself a faction, opening the way to schism, and thus being disloyal to the spirit of the party and serving the enemy, because it was taken for granted that the party and the working class were the same. The oppositionists were constantly backed out to the end of a limb. Their defense was to argue that the majority was a faked majority, prefabricated by the Secretariat, and this was true. But such protestations were academic from the moment when it became demonstrably impossible, the party's internal democracy having been perverted, to overthrow the bureaucratic majority.

Did not the solution lie in leaving this corrupted party, appealing to public opinion, seeking support outside the party? This meant putting oneself at the same time outside the law, acknowledging oneself to be a White Guard, an enemy of the people. Instead of merely being subject to the prying of the *Cheka* one was inviting its physical attacks and its prisons. And in any case what response could Zinoviev, Kamenev, and Trotsky have aroused in the country? The great mass of the peasants loathed them. Zinoviev's rapid downfall in Leningrad was evidence of the contempt in which he was held by the working class in that city. The Trotskyists enjoyed greater esteem among the young people in the universities, the political commissars in the army, and, perhaps, certain sectors of the working class. But all the same the workers of Russia could not easily forget that Trotsky had wanted to militarize them. Moreover, millions of men at grips with the immediate problems of food and shelter were hardly interested in all the talk in Trotskyist circles about permanent revolution, the future of the International, Thermidor, or the respective parts played by the Bolshevik leaders in October. Therefore one should not be misled into illusions as to the substance of the Trotskyist phenomenon by the man's remarkable personality and the courage of a handful of militants in the Soviet Union. The violent disturbances that Trotsky created within the party produced only feeble stirrings on the surface of the Soviet people. In exile Trotskyism survived only as a sect. It vanished in the Soviet camps and left behind no posterity.

Bukharin and the right seemed to be better armed at the start of collectivization. They were beaten everywhere without a fight, with the exception of one attempt to seize the majority in the Politburo and pitiful palavers with Kamenev that were quickly brought to light.

The right could expect, however, that its policy would enjoy the support of the great mass of the peasants and perhaps a certain complicity on the part of Yagoda. If it attempted nothing forceful, it was undoubtedly because it was afraid of causing its own destruction. Bukharin was keenly aware of the dual danger that menaced his friends and himself: If Stalin succeeded in his policy of collectivization, the right would be liquidated; but, if Stalin lost, if the peasant risings spread through the country, it would be the whole Bolshevik party that would founder, the right included. Even if it were conceded that the right could assume the leadership of the movement, it was more than obvious that it would not be able to control the revolt and that other forces would take over its place.

Under these conditions it was better to keep one's mouth shut, gain time, and wait for a more favorable opportunity. But it was Stalin who was the master at creating and exploiting opportunities.

In the phase of acute struggle created by collectivization and industrialization with their unprecedented massive sufferings, it was quite clear that what kept Stalin in power was not only the *Cheka* but the bureaucratic apparatus of the party. The *apparachiki* trembled at the dreadful crisis created by the boss. But their reflexes were the same as Bukharin's. If Stalin perished they too would be carried off. Pyatakov was quite right when he pointed out to Kamenev that the Central Committee would not overthrow Stalin and that, even if such a thing did occur, power would go not to a Bukharin or a Kamenev but to a Kaganovich, a sub-Stalin—in other words, a hard-fisted man that the party needed in this difficult stage.

There was also a complete break between the lower leadership and the masses, and this made it possible for the Stalinists to gain the victory. The staffs of the democratic parties had been liquidated. Those of the emigration, split by their disputes and undermined by police provocations, were incapable of establishing effective contact with quarters hostile to the Bolsheviks and of breaching the system's police guard. As for the secondary leaders of the various opposition groups within the party, they had no chance of winning against the Stalinist bureaucracy, and the basic opposition in the country was not theirs. It was that of counterrevolution.

This spontaneous counterrevolution was smashed in the beginning of the 1930s. All that remained for Stalin was to liquidate associates who were undoubtedly weary of his tyranny, rid himself of possible rivals, and base his support on a "new class": that of the young *apparachiki* and the young technicians, impatient to rise and all the more tractable because they would owe that rise to Stalin.

Two equally important events were required for the creation of conditions that would give rise to new oppositions: the war and Stalin's death.

The war was a redoubtable destroyer of myths. It created hundreds of thousands of deserters, revealed the unpopularity of the kolkhoz, revived the national minorities' aspirations to independence, rekindled religious feeling, opened a major breach in a world cut off from the West, carried the "invincible" Red Army and the government of the "proletariat" to the edge of disaster, and rallied almost a million Soviet citizens to the armies of the invader, in spite of the Germans' insane, merciless behavior in the occupied territories. But the effects were no less to be felt in the areas that remained under Stalin's control. For what he had to do in order to win was not to invoke the goals of the International and the Revolution but to revive faith in the destiny of the Russian fatherland and draw on the reserves of national feeling. He accepted the support of the Orthodox clergy and agreed to the "obscurantism" of concessions that ended only after his death. He reached into the camps for officers sentenced for "treason" and entrusted them with the fate of his system. He allowed the peasants to believe that the end of the war would also be the end of the kolkhoz system.

The importance of these acts was erased in the eyes of

world opinion by Stalin's final victory. The undeniable courage and in fact heroism that were displayed by the Red Army, after the first disasters, in the defense of Leningrad, Moscow, and Stalingrad were even placed to the credit of the system. But the effects of four years of war that were negative for the government could not be easily erased, and they laid the groundwork for today's opposition movements. The millions of workers and prisoners of war "contaminated" by the West had to be deported to isolation in Siberia, and a savage campaign against bourgeois nationalism had to be resumed. No one dared lay a hand to the churches that the invader had reopened, and the kolkhoz problem became acute. The battles waged by the Ukrainian, Lithuanian, and Latvian guerrillas were continued in other guises in the concentration camps and led to strikes and revolts both before and after Stalin's death. And, whatever one may think of the activities of the NTS, it is symptomatic that this organization allied with the Germans —while at the same time pursuing its own ends—has been able to overcome the disgrace to which its collaboration led and has succeeded in establishing certain contacts inside the Soviet Union.

The second blow fell after the war, when the idol's mask dropped. The denunciation of the cult of personality precipitated a crisis to which the government has not been able to find a solution. No matter how one tries, it is impossible to dissociate the crimes of the man from those of the party, as Stalin's daughter pointed out in one of her press conferences in the United States. Thus it is a whole generation of builders of Socialism that is compromised and compelled to justify itself to the new generation, which tends to turn into a tribunal. The successive amnesties and rehabilitations, although they put an end to crying injustices, at the same time revealed the extent of a plague that had affected the entire population, for there are few families in which one or two members were not victims of tyranny. Everyone knew this. But it was dangerous to talk about it. It was forbidden to say that the deportees were not traitors and criminals but victims. Now everyone talks about it and the whole atmosphere of Soviet society has been infected by these disclosures.

Under such conditions the Soviet leaders opt for the least bad solution: to mention these dangerous matters as little as possible in speeches and the press, to remain silent on the crimes and the murders. But it is impossible to prevent people from digging into these painful questions.

The concussion that the system has suffered is all the greater by reason of the fact that the dispute over Stalin's part is closely bound up with the battle for the succession, which set various interest groups in the ruling class against one another. The conflicts within that class have in general been poorly understood in the West, where the struggle among the heirs has been described as a confrontation between a "liberal left" and a "conservative Stalinist right." To imagine that in the Soviet Union's "apparatus" there exist organized tendencies on the style of Western political parties is to take a simplistic view; the reality is infinitely more complicated. In his battle against Malenkov, for example, Khrushchev began by defending the privileges of the party and the prerogatives of heavy industry against a rival who called for increased production of consumer goods. Then, in a complete reversal, he became the champion of liberalization against those Stalinists, Molotov and Kaganovich. These quick changes of front should be no surprise. The heirs are still behaving in the manner of Stalin, who preached the battle against the kulak after he had opposed the same policy.

There can be no question here of analyzing the conflicts in the ruling class and their many implications. On a schematic basis it might be said that the major confrontation in the post-Stalin period, as Boris Nikolayevsky has so clearly seen, seems to be that between the economic and technical apparatus, which hopes for the relaxation of the party's tight grip, and the *apparachiki* properly so-called (ideologists, propagandists, men responsible for party organization). But this basic rivalry is complicated by the intervention of various pressure groups, managers of heavy industry, *sovkhaarkhozi,* leaders of the army and the KGB, etc. This subterranean battle that leads at times to brutal crises (the ouster of the anti-party group, the fall of Khrushchev) creates major difficulties for the government of the inheritors.

If out of the antagonisms at the summit a man emerged and imposed his absolute power, it would revive the cult of personality and there would be the danger of a return to a situation that the Soviet upper class still holds in horror. Such an attempt was definitively ended with Khrushchev's defeat in 1964. But, if responsibilities are divided among a number of men in small shares, as is the case today with the triumvirate of Brezhnev, Kosygin, and Podgorny, there is an equilibrium, however unstable. Behind the seeming monolith, in the antechambers of the government, there is a fierce conflict that tends to endanger once more the balance that has been established. When problems like the Middle East crisis arise, there are changes in personnel that are symptomatic of the inner tensions. The first secretary of the party in Moscow was dismissed, his colleague in Leningrad was subjected to criticism; Shelepin, the party's hope, was transferred to the leadership of the trade unions, which did not represent a promotion. A short time earlier Semichastny had been replaced at the head of State Security.

All these shifts, the meaning of which is not always too clear, compromise the government and contribute to the creation of disorder and uncertainty in the clumsy apparatus of the bureaucracy. The functionaries of state and party are not too certain who is in command or whether the man who gives orders today will still be there tomorrow. In Stalin's time one at least knew where one stood. Some bureaucrats have begun to be sorry that they are no longer under orders.

Thus the government is trapped between the desire to turn backward, with all the consequences that might ensue, and the fear of accentuating a liberalism that entails the danger of opening the floodgates of new demands. These uncertainties and contradictions concern only the ruling class, and they exist in a relatively closed circle. But on the one hand they are to a certain extent a reflection of the population's demands and aspirations. (The ruling class, for example, cannot be unaware that an increase in military expenditures or foreign aid may incur the risk that internal consumption will suffer.) On the other hand, the antagonisms within the ruling class make it easier for opposition movements to appraise the situation and tend to make them tougher and bolder.

At the present time in the Soviet Union there are many centers of opposition, each of which is growing autonomously and has its own concerns. In the case of the intelligentsia, it is unquestionable that it is still far from presenting a united front. It is probable that there are many differences between groups like those of *Novy Mir* or *Yunost* and the "Young Turks" of the SMOG, and that the young Ukrainian intelligentsia is fighting on its own ground for the defense of its language and its culture. But all these men have at least the common bond of a desire to fight for greater freedom of expression and for its defense when it is seriously threatened. It is significant in this connection that the defense of Daniel and Sinyavsky was undertaken by Ehrenburg as well as by Galanskov and Ginzburg.

Elsewhere there is scattered activity: Believers fight for their religions, little groups of activists distribute leaflets or try to obtain weapons, guerrillas attempt a few attacks from the forests of the Ukraine and White Russia or the mountains of the northern Caucasus. Mass movements erupt unheralded and with particular violence in industrial centers. It is probable, too, that certain released deportees take part in underground operations.

It seems, however, that it has been impossible to coordinate these activities; this is prevented today by the police system, which is as vigilant as ever even if it does not practice the same massive repression. Repression similarly makes the task

of emigrant groups extremely difficult. As a result the organization of the opposition bears no relation to its real strength,
and this gap, which is inevitable in the light of the circumstances, substantially curbs the growth of the movement.

Notice should be taken, however, of the emergence of a
most effective slogan: the enforcement of the Soviet Constitution. It has been exploited by the intelligentsia of Leningrad
and Moscow as well as by that of Kiev and Lvov. It appears
in the letter of Fathers Echlimann and Yakunin. By demanding the strict application of the Constitution the opposition un-
masks the lies of the government. The logical development of
this political battle would in the end be all power to the Soviets (and not to the party): in other words, the revival of
the Kronstadt program.

Undoubtedly these demands do not yet mean much to the
great masses of workers and peasants, whose essential concerns are increases in wages, decreases in the work week, better food, etc. It is these concrete problems that were at the
root of the great revolts in the Donetz Basin. Participation in
the struggle by the great working masses of Leningrad and
Moscow would constitute a huge step forward and perhaps
make it possible to effect a junction between the working
class, an important element in the opposition's battle, and the
intelligentsia and the universities.

The attitude of the West is hardly helpful to the growth of
the struggle against the system. The West stood by unmoving
when the Budapest Commune was crushed, when East Berlin
and Poznan revolted, when the Berlin wall went up, and Western passivity mocked the hopes that had been born in the
people's democracies and even in the Soviet Union. The
United States is unwilling to do anything today that would
further impair a peaceful coexistence already gravely compromised by its war in Vietnam. Western Germany has enough
friction with the Soviet Union to avoid aggravating relations
that are already difficult. It is pointless to speak of the French
government, which overlooks nothing that will win it the good

graces of the Kremlin. But it is extremely difficult for subversive movements to build organizations if they have no solid bases abroad. In this respect the international situation appears to be definitely unfavorable to the enemies of the system.

But other factors come into play at the same time. Not only has the conflict between the Soviet Union and China led to a major rivalry for the leadership of the Communist International; at the same time it raises the problem of the pressures that China can exert along an immense frontier. The chief danger consists not in the initiation of armed conflict, or even in border raids, but in the encouragement provided by Mao's partisans to national minorities and in the preparation of possible subversive actions. Suddenly the leaders of the Soviet Union have become aware of the fragility of a multi-national empire. It is true that the danger is limited by the existence of minorities in Mao's empire and by the fact that the Soviet Union is not without means of reprisal.

What seems more important is the evolution of the satellite countries in central Europe. The governments of these countries have sought in varying degrees to keep their distance from the Kremlin, and what happens in these countries cannot fail to have repercussions in the Soviet Union. This was the case earlier with the Hungarian revolt and the Polish October.

Today, when the Czechoslovak intellectuals are engaging in conflict with the Communist party, how can it be thought that the Soviet intelligentsia is insensible to the fact? When satellite countries little by little retreat from collectivization, how can there be any doubt that Soviet peasants will begin to say to themselves: "Why not here too?" When the problems of the Croatian and Macedonian minorities are dramatically raised in Yugoslavia, the national minorities' demands in the Soviet Union cannot help being fortified.

Our time, furthermore, is dominated by the question of national liberation, encouraged, sometimes in an absurd fashion, by the UN. The African populations have been released from colonialism. Most of them constitute independent countries today. But what is the Congo, for example? A conglomeration of tribes incapable of reaching agreement among themselves, a "nation" whose borders were arbitrarily drawn by whites, a country without a past or national traditions or unity of language. How on the one hand is it possible to justify the existence of a Congolese nation, a veritable monster, and at the same time to refuse independence to old countries bound to deep historical memories like the Ukraine, Georgia, and Armenia?

Emigrant circles are divided on this question of independence, and thus it obviously contributes to the enfeeblement of the forces of resistance to the Soviet government. But the struggle for national independence is a reality that has manifested itself all through the history of the twentieth century. The separatist forces appeared when tsarism fell and again during the civil war. At that time they were successfully exploited by the Bolsheviks, who were compelled in consequence to make tremendous efforts in order to subdue them. They reappeared during the Second World War and gave birth to fearless fighters. They provided a basis of organization in the deportation camps. To reject their collaboration, to neglect or minimize their claims, is to ignore one of the essential causes of the tensions in the Soviet Union.

To what extent can the forces of opposition that exist at present in the Soviet Union hope either to change the system in an unmistakably more democratic sense or to overthrow it? At this time it is impossible to offer any very clear reply to the question. Such changes cannot occur unless the system itself experiences major internal or external crises. As long as the ruling class retains the character of an apparent monolith, the opposition, which has to confront a gigantic police apparatus, faces remarkably restricted prospects. All that it can hope to do is to maintain sufficient pressure to intensify the conflicts in the ruling "apparatus." It is only in direct proportion to the acuteness of the conflict that can be created in that "apparatus" that revolutionary prospects can be enlarged. Nonetheless it is certain that serious crises that could not be kept secret from world opinion, such as a massive strike in Moscow or Leningrad, or a general uprising by a national minority, would contribute to the intensification of the tensions in the ruling class.

Can the army play a decisive part in this process? Thus far there is nothing to indicate as much. Still subject to close surveillance, it is totally dependent on the political apparatus that has always been adept in playing on the rivalries among its leaders and liquidating or removing those whose popularity might make them dangerous. Ever since it came to power the government has lived in dread of a Russian Bonaparte, but it has always been able to protect itself extremely skillfully against the danger. While Zhukov helped Khrushchev in his attack on the anti-party group and perhaps contributed to the liquidation of Beria, Khrushchev had no difficulty later in getting rid of him. There is no indication that the situation has changed in this respect. Undoubtedly the high officer caste feels a certain bitterness over its subjection to the suspicious surveillance of the police system, but on the other hand it stands among the ranks of the privileged. It would therefore appear that a *Putsch* cannot be anticipated in the present state of affairs—in other words, as long as the ruling apparatus of the party enjoys sufficient cohesion.

It is not certain, however, that the army would be a reliable instrument for the execution of a massive repression. Any work that can be done within it at the levels of the enlisted men, the noncommissioned officers, and the junior officers with a view to eroding its cohesion would of course be a major achievement. But it would encounter formidable obstacles.

The government was preparing, when this book was written, to celebrate the fiftieth anniversary of the October Revolution, and this was to be the occasion for an ostentatious catalogue of the gains of Socialism. Gains they may have been, but at what price?

This entire half-century of Socialism in power is riddled with bloody combats, unprecedented ordeals, all of them required in order to shatter inestimable resistance. Let us attempt that catalogue, on which Bolshevik propaganda will certainly be more reticent:

A civil war without quarter and with innumerable atrocities, the cause for millions of deaths, for hundreds of thousands of orphans left to their own resources, and followed immediately by the mutiny of Kronstadt; the annexation of Georgia by armed force in 1921 and the smashing of a revolt there in 1924; the suppression of revolts and guerrilla warfare in Turkestan, Tadzhikistan, and Bashkiria; the long war against the kulak (preceded by many acts of terrorism against members of the party) that also claimed millions of victims, was accompanied by tremendous religious persecution, and created an appalling famine; the purges of the party, the army, the national minorities, the nonparty members, which undoubtedly affected further millions of citizens; the defections in the Second World War that gave birth to Vlassov's army, the savage combats of the Ukrainian, Lithuanian, Latvian, and Estonian guerrillas; the deportations of whole populations—the Chechens, the Ingushi, the Kabardians, the Volga Germans, etc.; the new purges that were imminent when Stalin died.

All this engendered and sustained the monstrous concentration-camp system that in fifty years was able to engulf twenty to thirty million prisoners. And yet, in this sorely tried empire in which the government waged unending battles of extermination, Stalin had barely died when new opposition came into being.

So the history of these fifty years is the history of a fierce struggle, unremittingly renewed, in spite of a dreaded police system. This system has been able to destroy the organizations of the most varied kinds of opposition and even, through its efficient surveillance, to prevent them from coming into existence. But in fifty years it has encountered three major lines of resistance that thus far it has not yet been able wholly to break: language, land, and religion.

Language: it constitutes the basic essence of a people, expresses its individual genius, that irreplaceable sign of recognition that establishes immediate contact in a camp or a prison. Land: the wretched *izba*, the meager inheritance bequeathed by generations, the refuge of a stubborn resistance to every effort at collectivism. Religion: persecuted, hunted, but still burning beneath the ashes, in spite of the closed churches, the anti-religious museums, and the sputniks hurled up to conquer the sky.

In fifty years the government has been unable to gain total victory on any of these fronts. On the contrary, however slightly it slackens its grip, the "dark forces of the past" surge up again. But this government itself has lost some of its faith and some of its dynamism. It has been profoundly shaken in its prestige both on the domestic and on the international level. It would be risky to predict to what extent, at what time, and in what guise the forces of opposition in the Soviet Union will gain the victory. It is much less risky to predict that the Soviet leaders will not succeed in creating that Communist society of which Lenin dreamed and that the Stalinist terror was unable to impose.

APPENDIX:
SVETLANA ALLILUYEVA
AND STALIN'S DEATH

SVETLANA ALLILUYEVA's account of her father's death is remarkable for more than the deep emotion that it reveals. It focuses attention once again on the strange circumstances of that death, as dramatic as it was mysterious.

When Svetlana arrived at Stalin's *dacha* in Kuntsevo on March 2, the atmosphere round the patient was one of feverish agitation. It is true that Svetlana wrote that "everyone did his job without slacking in the struggle to save a life that no one any longer could save." But surprise is not out of place at the fact that the only treatment that she identified was the placing of leeches on her father's neck and throat. Quite an archaic technique for a medical science that likes to boast that it is the best in the world.

There is more reason for surprise. "An artificial respiration machine," Svetlana wrote, "had been brought from one of the medical-research centers. Some young internes had also been fetched, because they were the only ones who knew how to operate it. *The intrusive machine was there, unused, and the young doctors, like fish out of water, kept looking anxiously round.*" (Italics added.)

Later, describing her father's final agony, Svetlana wrote that "during the last twelve hours he suffered from an acute lack of oxygen." Was this in spite of the machine, which it was finally decided to use? Or was the dying man simply left to suffocate? On this subject Svetlana offered nothing precise.

These pages suggest more than they explain. They leave the reader with an uncomfortable impression of disorder, agitation, and also deliberate neglect. One may wonder whether the care lavished on Stalin—perhaps he was beyond all hope— were not a mere make-believe: whether, in short, he was not simply left to die.

Svetlana's testimony is of great interest, too, with regard to the circumstances in which Stalin suffered his cerebral congestion, because on a major point it contradicts the account that Khrushchev gave to Harriman. Khrushchev, it will be remembered, said that it was Stalin's habit to shut himself away every night in a room to which access was barred by armored doors that he alone could open from within. It was because he had shown no sign of life for several hours that the commander of his bodyguard had summoned the members of the Presidium by telephone at night. When they arrived, they ordered that the doors be smashed, and then they found Stalin lying on a carpet in his bedroom.

But Svetlana said: "He was found at three o'clock in the morning in this same room, lying on a carpet near the couch. *He was carried into the next room so that he could be placed on the divan on which he usually slept.*" (Italics added.) According to Svetlana, then, Stalin did not suffer his stroke in the fortified room in which, according to Khrushchev, it was his habit to sleep: He was carried into it.

Svetlana's story had all the *indicia* of authenticity, with this one reservation, that perhaps she did not tell everything that she knew. Why then did Khrushchev find it necessary to tell Harriman a story that was not true? Would it not have been his purpose to convince Harriman that, sealed inside his hermetically closed chamber, Stalin could not have been the victim of an assassin because no one could have come close to him?

Nor, for that matter, was this the only oddity in his version. It is surprising, for example, that he, like his colleagues of the Presidium, should have been summoned by the commander of Stalin's bodyguard. Now to whom would this officer normally have had to report when he found that there was no sign of life from the dictator? To Poskrebyshev, the head of the private secretariat, and it would be up to him to decide what was to be done next. Another element of surprise is the absence of Poskrebyshev—whose final fate is unknown—from Khrushchev's story.

On the other hand, Svetlana's story too shows Beria as a loathsome figure. She described him bending over Stalin's bed, anxiously studying the dying man's face for any slightest reaction. Stalin was barely dead when Beria ran into the corridor. "The silence that reigned round the dead man's bed," Svetlana wrote, "was shattered by his loud voice, clumsily trying to keep down a note of triumph as he shouted: 'Krustalev, my car!'" In Svetlana's words, the other members of the Presidium were as if "petrified" in his presence: "They knew that, from the very instant of my father's death, no one in Russia had greater power."

Threatened by the purge that Stalin had launched, did Beria enjoy this power—for a brief interval—as the result of a wholly natural death? Whence this joy of a man set free of fear. Or, on the other hand, had he been able to bring on the cerebral congestion that felled the tyrant, perhaps with the help of a medical confederate who had prescribed some counter-indicated medicine? While no answer is possible, the fact remains that, of all the members of the Presidium, Beria was in the best position to act.

Thus Stalin's end is still cloaked in mystery. The various versions of the circumstances of that death, with all their contradictions, leave a feeling of unease. The whole climate is such as to make it appear that the inheritors had deliberately circulated the different versions in order to mislead public opinion and conceal something that was unspeakable. Equal suspicion attaches to the haste with which, a day later, Beria sent the servants to different places and ordered the officers of the bodyguard reassigned to various provincial towns, except for two, whom he ordered shot.[1]

In the final second of his life, Stalin opened his eyes. In a flash his glance encompassed all those anxious faces bent over him. Svetlana wrote:

> It was a terrible, a demented look, or perhaps furious, filled with dread in the face of death and of those unknown faces of the doctors who were bending over him. . . . Then something frightful and incomprehensible happened, which I shall never forget and which I do not yet understand. Suddenly he raised his left hand, apparently pointing to something above him, and brought it down as if he were invoking a curse on all of us. This gesture charged with menace was inexplicable, and no one can say for whom or for what it was intended.

Was it the motion of a madman in the grip of his obsessions to the very end? Or was it that of a man reliving some dramatic circumstance that preceded the moment when he fell, forever immobilized, to the floor? A blind fury, or one provoked by some episode still unknown to us? Perhaps the answer will never be known. His destiny ended with this final impulse of impotent rage that remains for us and so many others an enigma.

[1] It was an old police custom to liquidate men who knew too much; in this regard cf. the Kirov case.

BIBLIOGRAPHY

Arshinov, P., *L'histoire du mouvement makhnoviste (1918–1921).* 1928.

Arzhak (pseudonym of Yuli Daniel), *Ici Moscou.* 1966.

d'Astier, Emmanuel, *Sur Staline.* 1963.

Bailey, Geoffrey, *The War of the Soviet Secret Services.* 1962.

Barbusse, Henri, *Staline. Un monde nouveau à travers un homme.* 1935.

Barmin, Alexander, *Vingt ans au service de l'URSS.* 1959.

Barton, Paul, *L'institution concentrationnaire en Russie (1930–1957).* 1959.

———, *Prague à l'heure de Moscou.* 1954.

Bazhanov, *Avec Staline dans le Kremlin.* 1930.

Bennigsen, "L'intelligentsia musulmane en URSS," in *Le contrat social,* July 1959.

Benoist-Méchin, *Histoire de l'Armée allemande,* IV, *L'expansion,* 1964; V, *Les épreuves de force.* 1965.

Béraud, Henri, *Ce que j'ai vu à Moscou.* 1925.

Berdyayev, Nikolai, *Les sources et le sens du communisme russe.* 1951.

Cabell, Paul, *Operation Barbarossa.* 1964.

Chabanier, Colonel Jean, *Les États baltiques depuis 1940.* Stockholm, 1965.

Chessin, Serge de, *Au pays de la démence rouge (1917–1918)*. 1919.

Ciliga, Anton, *Au pays du mensonge déconcertant*. 1950.

Clark, Alan, *The War in the East*. 1966.

Dabernat, René, *Les nouveaux bolcheviks*. 1966.

Dallin, David, *La vraie Russie des soviets*. 1948.

——, and Boris Nikolayevsky, *Le travail forcé en URSS*. 1949.

Dan, Lydia, *Boukharine*, "Dan et Staline," in *Le contrat social*, July–August 1964.

Dankevych, *Future Potentialities of Siberia*. Washington, 1965.

Dedijer, Vladimir, *Tito parle*. 1953.

Delimars, "La Tchéka à l'oeuvre" and "La Tchéka et son Trust," in *Le contrat social*, March–April and May–June 1966.

Denikin, General, *Les événements mondiaux et le problème russe*. 1939.

Deryabin, G., and F. Gibney, *Policier de Staline*. 1966.

Deutscher, Isaac, *Stalin*. 1953.

——, *Trotsky*, I, II, III. 1965.

Dzhilas, Milovan, *Memoirs*. 1959.

Dubnaitis, Evalda, *Der Kampf gegen Religion und Gesittlichkeit in den sowjetisierten baltischen Ländern Estland, Lettland und Litauen*. N.d.

Eastman, Max, *After Lenin's Death*. 1925.

El Campesino, *La vie et la mort en URSS (1939–1949)*. 1950.

Fainsod, Merle, *How the USSR Is Governed*. 1957.

——, *Smolensk in Stalin's Time*. 1967.

Fervacque, *Le chef de l'Armée rouge Toukhatchevsky*. 1927.

Fischer, George, "Soviet Opposition to Stalin," a case study in *World War II*. Cambridge, Mass., Harvard University Press, 1952.

Fischer, Louis, *Lenin*. 1967.

——, *Life and Death of Stalin*. 1953.

Fontaine, André, *Histoire de la guerre froide*, I and II. 1966, 1967.

Fuller, Major General J. F. C., *Russia Is Not Invincible*. 1951.

Garder, Michel, *Histoire de l'Armée soviétique*. 1959.

——, *L'agonie du régime en Russie soviétique*. 1965.

Gaulle, General Charles de, *Memoires de guerre: L'unité, Le Salut*. 1956; 1959.

Bibliography (533)

Goebbels, Dr. Josef, *Diary*. 1949.

Goul, Roman, *Les maîtres de la Tchéka*. 1938.

Granick, David, *Le chef d'entreprise soviétique*. 1963.

Grenard, *La révolution russe*. 1933.

Ginzburg, Alexander, *Le livre blanc de l'affaire Sinyavsky-Daniel*. 1967.

Hagen, Walter, *The Secret Front*. 1952.

Halyshyna, Stephanya, *Five Hundred Ukrainian Martyred Women*. New York, 1956.

Hayit, Dr. Baymirza, *Some Problems of Modern Turkestan History*. Düsseldorf, 1963.

Hernandez, Jesús, *La grande trahison*. 1953.

Hitler, Adolf, stenographic transcripts of daily reports from the headquarters of the *Führer*, 1942–1945. Preface by Benoist-Méchin. 1964.

Honcharuk, O., *If War Comes Tomorrow*. Toronto, 1958.

Inkeles, Alex, *L'opinion publique en Russie soviétique. Une étude sur la persuasion des masses*. 1956.

Istrati, Panait, *Vers l'autre flamme: I, Après seize mois dans l'URSS; II, Soviets; III, La Russie nue*. 1929, 1930.

Kerensky, Alexander, *The Russian Revolution*. 1928.

Kern, Erich, *Les Cosaques de Hitler*. 1964.

Kleist, Peter, *Entre Hitler et Staline (1939–1945)*. 1953.

Kolarz, Walter, *La Russie et ses colonies*. 1953.

——, *Les colonies russes d'Extrême-Orient*. 1955.

Kosyk, W., *Camps de concentration en URSS*. 1960.

——, *L'Ukraïne sous le joug colonial russe*. 1963.

Krakowiecki, A., *Kolyma, le bagne d'or*. 1952.

Krivitzky, Walter, *J'étais un agent de Staline*. 1940.

Kütt, Alexander, and Leonhard Vahter, *Estonia*. New York, 1964.

Laurat, Lucien, *Bilan de vingt-cinq ans de plans quinquennaux (1929–55)*. 1955.

——, *L'économie soviétique*. 1931.

Lazitch, Branko, "Le martyrologie du Comintern," in *Le contrat social*, November–December 1965.

Leneman, Léon, *La tragédie des Juifs en URSS*. 1959.

Leonhard, Wolfgang, *L'Union soviétique, apparences et réalités*. 1953.

Lipper, Elinor, *Onze ans dans les bagnes soviétiques*. 1950.

Liron, Yona, "J'étais un expert soviétique de contre-insurrection," in *l'Est européen,* October 1964.

MacLean, Fitzroy, *Diplomate et franc-tireur.* 1952.

Martinez Codo, Enrique, "La guérilla en Ukraïne," in *Revue militaire générale,* May 1962.

Martovych, Oleg, *Ukrainian Liberation Movement in Modern Times.* N.d.

Mett, Ida, *La commune de Cronstadt.* 1950.

Moore, Barrington, Jr., *Terror and Progress in the USSR: Variations and Stability of the Soviet Dictatorship.* 1955.

Nikulin, Lev, *La vérité sur le maréchal Toukhatchevsky.* 1964.

Oldenburg, S., *Le coup d'état bolcheviste.* 1929.

Peis, Günther, *Naujocks, l'homme qui déclencha la guerre.* 1961.

Penkovsky, Oleg, *Carnets d'un agent secret.* 1966.

Piccard, Eulalie, *Lettres de Moscou (1928–1933).* Neuchâtel, n.d.

Pipes, Richard, "Les forces du nationalisme en URSS," in *Le contrat social,* March–April 1964.

Prokopovitch, Sergey N., *Histoire économique de l'URSS.* 1952.

Raschofer, Hermann, *Political Assassination.* Tübingen, 1964.

Rathaus, A., "La résistance actuelle en URSS," in *Revue militaire générale,* December 1963.

Reale, Eugenio, *Avec Duclos au banc des accusés à la réunion constitutive du Kominform.* Szklarska Poreba, 1958.

Robien, Louis de, *Journal d'un diplomate en Russie (1917–1918).* N.d.

Rosmer, A., *Moscou sous Lénine.* 1953. See also articles in *La Révolution prolétarienne.*

Rossi, A., *Autopsie du stalinisme, avec le texte intégral du rapport Khroushtchev.* Paris, 1952.

Rutych, Nikolai, *Le parti communiste au pouvoir.* 1961.

Rywkin, Mikhail, "Le prix de la soviétisation en Asie centrale," in *Le contrat social,* March–April 1964.

Saint-Loup, *Les hérétiques.* 1964.

Sanchez Salazar, General, *Ainsi fut assassiné Trotsky.* 1948.

Schapiro, Léonard, *De Lénine à Staline.* 1967.

———, *Les bolcheviks et l'opposition. Origines de l'absolutisme communisted. Premier stage: 1917–22.* 1958.

Schatov, *Materiali i Dokumenti ODNR, V Godi 2-oi Mirovoi Votni.*

Schellenberg, Walter, *Le chef du contre-espionnage nazi parle.* 1966.

Schlabrendorff, Fabian von, *Officiers contre Hitler*. 1948.

Scholmer, Joseph, *La grève de Vorkouta*. 1954.

Sedov, Lev, *Livre rouge sur les procès de Moscou*. 1936.

Serge, Victor, "De Lénine a Staline," special issue of *The Mortar*, 1937.

——, *Destin d'une révolution*. 1937.

——, *L'affaire Toulaev*. 1948.

——, *L'an I de la révolution russe*. 1930.

——, *Le tournant obscur*. 1951.

——, *Mémoires d'un révolutionnaire*. 1951.

——, *Portrait de Staline*. 1940.

——, *Seize fusillés*, preface by M. Paz, in *Spartacus*, October 1936.

——, *Vie des révolutionnaires*. N.d.

——, *Vie et mort de Trotski*. 1951.

Serge, Victor, Wullens, and Rosmer, *L'assassinat politique en URSS*. 1938.

Sholokhov, Mikhail, *Terres défrichées*. 1937.

Shub, David, *Lénine*. 1952.

Slavinsky, Mikhail, *Le drame des intellectuels en URSS*. N.d.

Solzhenitzin, Alexander, *One Day in the Life of Ivan Denisovich*. 1963.

Suvarin, Boris, *Aveux à Moscou*. 1938. See also articles in *Le contrat social* and *La révolution prolétarienne*.

——, *Cauchemar en URSS*. 1937.

——, *Staline aperçu historique du bolchevisme*. 1940.

Sukhanov, Nikolai, *La révolution russe, 1917*. 1965.

Stalin, Josef, *The Collectivization of the Village*. 1930.

——, *Doctrine of USRR*. 1938.

——, *Last Writings (1950–1953)*. 1953.

——, *Problems of Leninism*. 1938.

——, *Speech on the Five-Year Plan: Political Report to the Central Committee of the Tenth Congress of the Russian Communist Party on 28 May 1930*. 1930.

——, *Works, Volume V (1921–1923)*. 1955.

Steinberg, J., *Souvenirs d'un commissaire du peuple*. 1930.

Stetsko, Yaroslav, *Khrushchev's Unchanged Stalinist Policy Toward Nationalities* and *New Revolutionary Liberation Strategy*. 1963.

——, *The Kremlin on A Volcano*. New York, 1930.

——, *The Principles of Ukrainian Foreign Policy*. London, n.d.

Struve, Nikolai, *Les chrétiens en URSS*. 1963.

Tatu, Michel, *Le pouvoir en URSS*. 1967.

Tauras, K. V., *Guerrilla Warfare on the Amber Coast*. New York, 1962.

Tertz, Abram, (pseudonym of Andrey Sinyavsky), *Le verglas*. 1963.

Thorwald, Jürgen, *Vlassov Against Stalin*. 1953.

Trakiskis, *The Situation of the Church and Religious Practices in Occupied Lithuania*. New York, 1944.

Trotsky, Lev, *Cours nouveau*. 1924.

——, *Journal d'exil*. 1960.

——, *La bureaucratie stalinienne et l'assassinat de Kirov*. 1935.

——, *La défense de l'URSS et l'opposition*. 1930.

——, *La révolution défigurée*. 1929.

——, *La révolution trahie, II: Les Crimes de Staline*. 1937.

——, *Ma vie*. 1930.

——, *Stalin*. 1948.

——, *Terrorisme et communisme*. 1963. See also articles in *Le bulletin de l'opposition*.

Uralov, Alexander (pseudonym of Avtorkhanov), *Staline au pouvoir*. 1951.

Vaitiekunas, Vytautas, *Lithuania*. New York, 1965.

Valentinov, Nikolai, *Mes rencontres avec Lénine*. 1964. See also articles in *Le contrat social*.

Vardys, V. Stanley, *Lithuania Under the Soviet: Portrait of a Nation, 1940–1955*. New York, 1965.

Volin (pseudonym of Eichenbaum), *La révolution inconnue*. 1947.

Walter, Gérard, *Lénine*. 1950.

Weissberg-Cybulski, Alexander, *L'accusé*. 1953.

Wiesel, Élie, *Les Juifs du silence*. 1966.

Wolfe, Bertram D., *Lénine et Trotsky*. N.d.

——, *Lenin, Trotsky, Stalin*. 1951.

Wrangel, Baron, *Memoirs*. 1930.

Yasny, Naum, "L'agriculture Soviétique," in *Le contrat social*, May 1958.

Young, Gordon, *The House of Secrets*. 1959.

Anonymous and Collective Works

Assassinated by Moscow: Petlyura, Konovaletz, Bandera. Munich, Ukrainian Publishers, 1962.

Les bolcheviks et la révolution d'Octobre. Transcript of proceedings of the Central Committee of the Bolshevik party, August 1917– February 1918.

Bildarchiv über die Ukraine. Munich, 1964.

The Catholic Church of Latvia Under the Bolshevik Torture. Stockholm, Elta Press, 1950.

En notre âme et conscience. La vérité sur Simon Petlyura. 1938.

Les États baltes. League for the Rights of Peoples, 1948.

Murder International, Inc. Washington, D.C., Committee on the Judiciary, United States Senate, 89th Congress, March, 1965.

NTS. Organisation révolutionnaire de la résistance russe. 1961.

Procès des industriels. 1930.

Procès du Centre antisoviétique trotskiste. Stenographic transcript, Moscow, 1937.

Procès du Bloc des droitiers et des trotskistes antisoviétiques. Stenographic transcript, Moscow, 1938.

Pro Baltica. Stockholm, 1965.

Russian Oppression in the Ukraine. Reports and documents. London, Ukrainian Publishers, 1962.

L'Ukraïne indépendante. A collection of articles, bilingual edition, 1946.

Un cri de désespoir des prêtres de Moscou. Orthodox Action and Orthodox Information Center, n.d.

The Struggle of the Ukraine for Freedom; Its Importance for A Free World. Scottish League for European Freedom, 1952.

The Ukrainian Insurgent Army in the Fight for Freedom. New York, United Committee of the Ukrainian American Organizations of New York, 1965.

Periodicals

Bulletin communiste, Les Cahiers du Communism, Le contrat social, Contre le courant, La correspondance internationale, l'Est européen (formerly *Problèmes actuels de l'est européen*), *Est et Ouest, Exil et Liberté, Le Figaro, l'Humanité, les Lettres fran-*

çaises, le Libertaire, Le Matin, le Monde, La nouvelle critique, Le Nouvel Observateur, l'Observateur européen, Preuves, Quatrième Internationale, La Révolution prolétarienne, Revue militaire générale, Le Temps, La Vérité.

ABN Correspondence, The American Legion, The Baltic Review, The Bell, East-West Digest, Elta Press, Grani, Lituanus, The Ukrainian Review, Bulleten Oppozitzy, Izvestia, Komsomolskaya Pravda, Literaturnaya Gazeta, Pravda.

INDEX